IN THE DARK.

images and text by Mike Figgis

Booth-Clibborn Editions

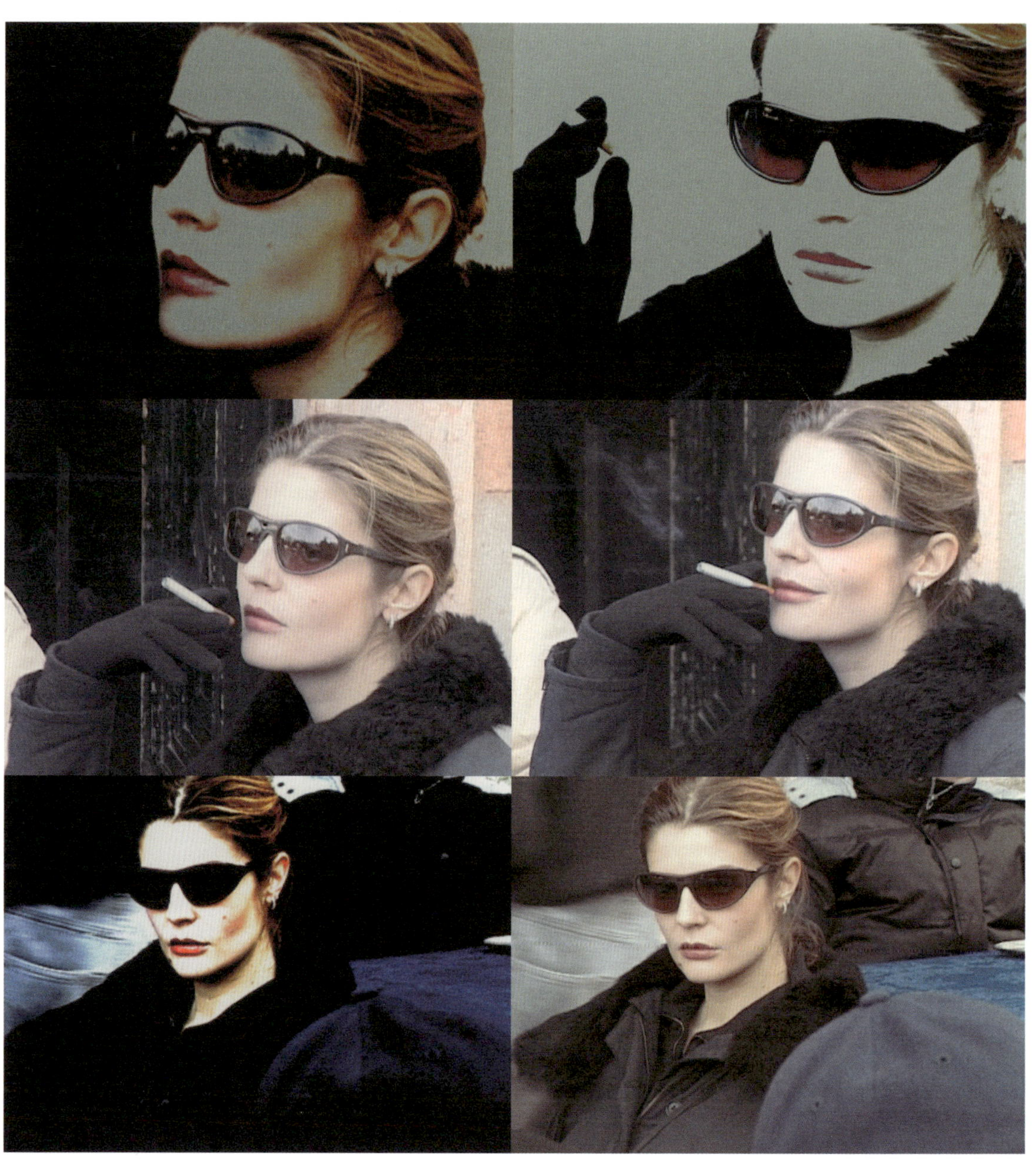

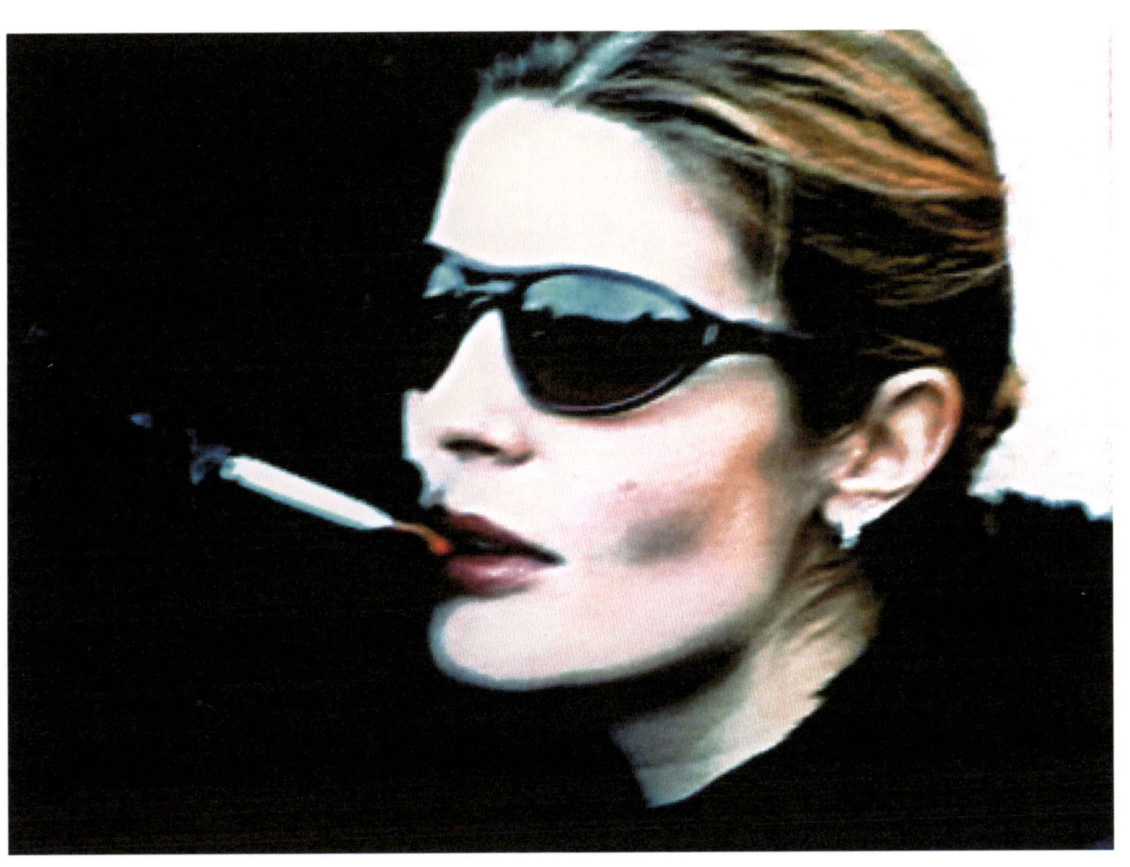

Why in the dark?

A large 35-mm camera is something you would never own. You rent it from a facility and it comes with its own brain surgery team. The film is processed by a factory, printed by that factory, and then mixed by another factory. In that way you come up with an image. By definition a homogenisation of the subject takes place. Jean-Luc Godard said that directors should own their own cameras so they understand their camera and everything that it does. A miner using equipment checks it himself because, if there is a mistake, he could die or be injured. Photographers know every foible of their cameras. Each one becomes different as the springs function to the strength of the thumb, and so on. Knowing your own equipment and having a proprietary interest in it is very important.

Ever since the advent of the amateur movie in the 1930s and 1940s, there have been cameras owned by amateur film-makers – the 16-mm Bolex, the Super-8 camera, the video camera that everybody now takes on holiday, and finally the digital camera. There is a quality to the film taken by these cameras which is entirely different. That is why people are fascinated with home movies and erotic home movies or whatever – because they make us feel: I see, that's real.... Our fascination with reality is to do with these cameras. I've always owned cameras. Nikons, Leicas, Hasselblads. I made my first films on a Canon Super-8 camera which I still have somewhere. I have 2 16-mm cameras – one is a post-war Arriflex ST, which I had converted to Super 16-mm, and the other is an Aaton, a superb camera. Video cameras didn't really impress me until Hi-8 came along, about 13 years ago. I bought an expensive professional version which allowed me to switch systems on the same camera, so I could shoot either Hi-8 or Beta SP. Later I modified the system to allow me to shoot DVCAM system.

TIMECODE was the first film I made with entirely digital technology. It was a "real-time" film, quite theatrical, with 4 films shot at the same time shown on a split screen. The choice of camera for the film was therefore a singular one. Film magazines in a conventional 35-mm camera run for 10 minutes before you have to change them. In the case of MISS JULIE, a film I made in 1999, I was able to use an innovation in terms of their design, which was a 20 minute cassette of 16-mm film. That is the absolute time limit of celluloid. Hitchcock tried to do a fake "real-time" film called ROPE. Every time the film magazine was about to run out he would pan across a very dark piece of shadow and then start his new take by panning across the same piece of shadow – the 2 would be cut together in darkness to give the illusion that the film kept going. To make a "real-time" film with no faking I needed a

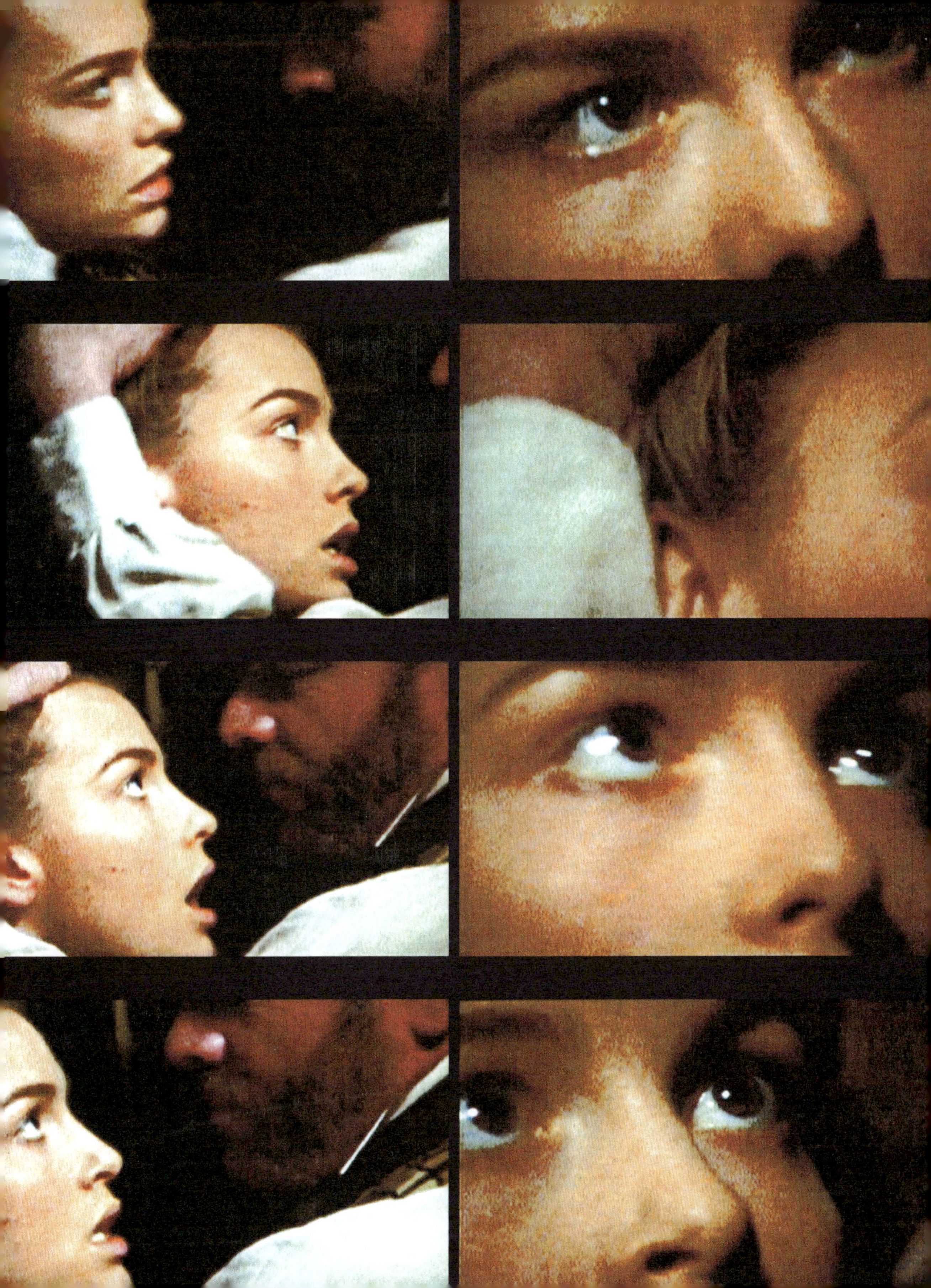

93-minute run. In 1997 digital technology produced the first camera that could support a long cassette tape and produce a high resolution image – the Sony DVCAM, which would run a cassette of 2 hours. It was the only camera in the world that would give me enough time.

TIMECODE was perceived in some ways as being very experimental, but it fell within my own mainstream. The first film I made, when I was working in experimental theatre, was a 14 minute 16-mm film designed to be part of a live theatrical event, although it could also function as a film in itself. I have always seen film as having a very strong parallel with theatre, almost as a theatrical event. My first proper film was THE HOUSE, a 1 hour film shot for television in 16-mm, which was also very experimental in terms of narrative, multi-imaging and layering of sound. Then I made STORMY MONDAY, a feature film, which was a success in America and so I spent a number of years working within the studio system. It was a very difficult time for me, which resulted in me wanting to go back to some kind of way of working that I was more familiar with – ironically, experimental work. I made a completely independent film, LEAVING LAS VEGAS, financed by the French, shot on Super-16 and blown up to 35-mm. I made a conscious decision, pre-Dogme, in fact, not to use a lot of light, not to carry a lot of film equipment, not to use cranes or dollies or steadycam or anything like that, and to shoot it hand-held in believeable situations with available light, using very fast film-stocks that gave the film a gritty, realistic look. I happened to love that grainy look, particularly in a neon-soaked place like Las Vegas. This film was the biggest hit of my career although the original idea could not have been further from commercial or economic success. I made 1 last big film, ONE NIGHT STAND, before deciding to leave the studio system and make a series of experimental films.

The first of these was THE LOSS OF SEXUAL INNOCENCE, in which I used reversal film stock techniques, which are quite dangerous because you do not have a lot of control and you get some quite freaky results. Then came MISS JULIE, which was shot on Super-16, on my Aaton camera, in about 14 days. The cameras ran all the time and the takes were long. After each take we had to review the footage. I suggested that we crudely synchronized the 2 playback machines and run the 2 takes simultaneously to save time. The amount of information that came from the splitscreen fascinated me and I decided to use the technique in 1 section of the finished film – the seduction scene. This is what led me to TIMECODE.

When I was making TIMECODE I bought a very little, much cheaper camera made by Sony, the PD100. I was amazed by what it could do with little or no light at all. I made the decision to buy and use these smaller, cheaper cameras, to design equipment myself to support the cameras, to stabilize them, and to really push the look they produced. I realised they had huge potential and could give aesthetically very beautiful results. In the period when I was discovering the PD100, I found certain settings that I thought were staggeringly beautiful. I discovered, for example, that as the light level drops, blue and red and primary colours are read more intensely by digital cameras whereas celluloid starts to get milky. Digital technology seems to seek out a blue or red, and really start to glow as if those colours have an inner light. Digital reads things as if they have their own light source inside them while celluloid needs the object to reflect light. When you get onto night vision cameras there's another whole different aesthetic relationship between light and objects.

All the years that I've been working in theatre and film, I've been interested in a graphic approach which uses elements of photo-realism. When I was a student I discovered Andy Warhol in his film HAT – and Richard Hamilton and Hockney – and what they did with montage and collage; and Kurt Schwitters, and the great photo-montage artist, John Heartfield. So I have always been fascinated by little pieces of film. I would copy them and blow them up until they started to get very grainy – and I always felt, in truth, they became more beautiful in the process. That all goes into a closet when you work in film because of its almost religious obsession with perfection and clinical reproduction techniques. The history of film technique is one of developing brighter lighting systems, sharper lenses, and so on – no-one ever thought of using less light. Digital film-making opened up a chance to explore the alternatives.

All films need stills as part of the publicity process. Years ago I had been impressed by a quote from Stanley Kubrick, who never used a still photographer, arguing that if the stills person was getting great shots, then the cinematographer was obviously in the wrong position. With this in mind I felt sure that I could find the best images for HOTEL from the digital master-tapes. I started trawling through the footage, downloading clips on to my Mac and selecting frames. The chosen frames were then imported into PhotoShop and worked on. Much later, at the grading stage of the film, I took my Mac into the grading suite and used the stills I had created as the example for each of the scenes. By now I had learned quite a lot about how the colour and contrast works in digital video and for the first time in my career I felt that I had some kind of control in this stage of the film. I used the same system to create all of the images for this book, although the material for MISS JULIE and TIMECODE did not come from purely digital sources.

TIMECODE, Los Angeles, 1999

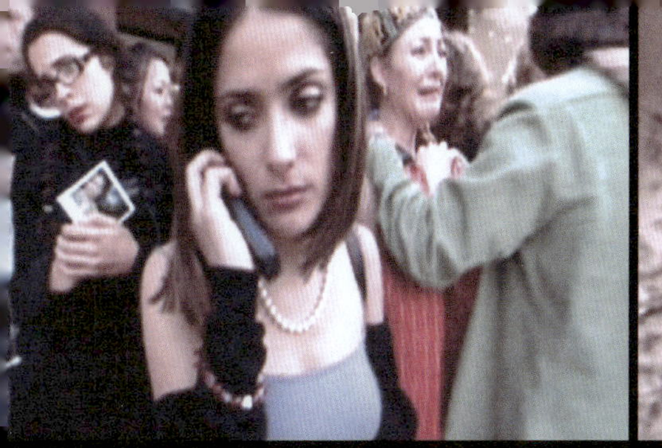

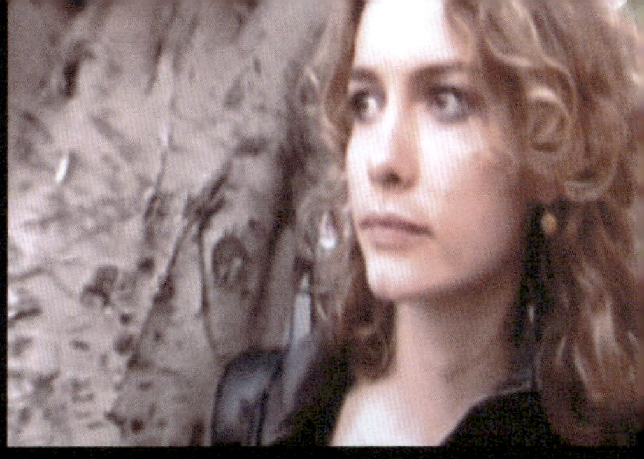

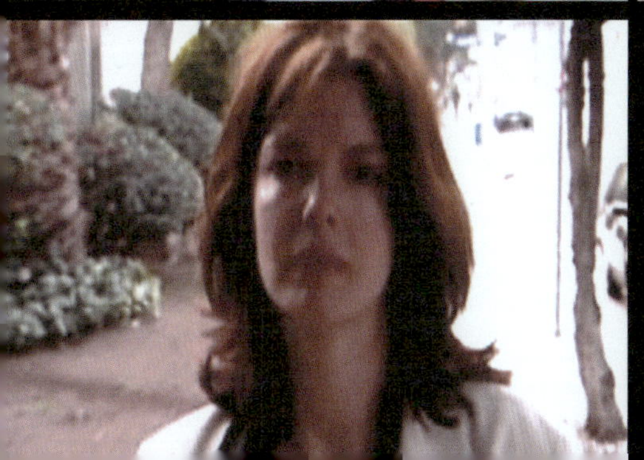

TIME CODE was filmed in
4 continuous takes beginning
at 3:00 pm on friday,
november 19th, 1999.
all of the cast improvised
around a predetermined
structure.

How TIMECODE came about

I'd originally planned to do TIMECODE as a film-performance event in London. I was going to take an ad in TIME OUT and announce the commencement of photography for a feature on a certain date, and then have the première the same evening in a gallery space with live music.

At this time, after the success of LEAVING LAS VEGAS I had an office and some kind of development deal at Sony studios in LA. John Calley, the head of the studio is an ex-jazz musician and we had become friendly. Over lunch I told him my idea and he asked if I would consider doing the film in LA as a studio film. The tie-in with the technical division of Sony was obvious and also there was (and still is) much debate about the inevitable transition from analogue to digital. John felt that this would be a good experiment for the studio (and also a cheap one). He told me that I could make the film with a small budget, something like $4,000,000. This is about a tenth of the average budget in LA. Some time later John rang to ask me if I would mind coming in to make a pitch to the top executives at the studio. He assured me that the film was going to happen anyway and that this was just a formality. I agreed to come in.

The execs were gathered in one of those typical studio rooms, with a large oak table and chairs. Pencils and pads on the table. Between 15 and 20 people were waiting to hear the pitch. After a brief, enthusiastic introduction from John I launched into an attempt to tell 4 stories in parallel. After about 10 minutes of this narrative juggling I looked up and saw the faces. At the back someone was chuckling, another face was shaking slowly from side to side in disbelief, others looked intent. I finished and the questions began. I got the sense that some of them were pissed off to be dealing with a film that just would not fit in with the generic product of the studio. I would say that this attitude never really went away.

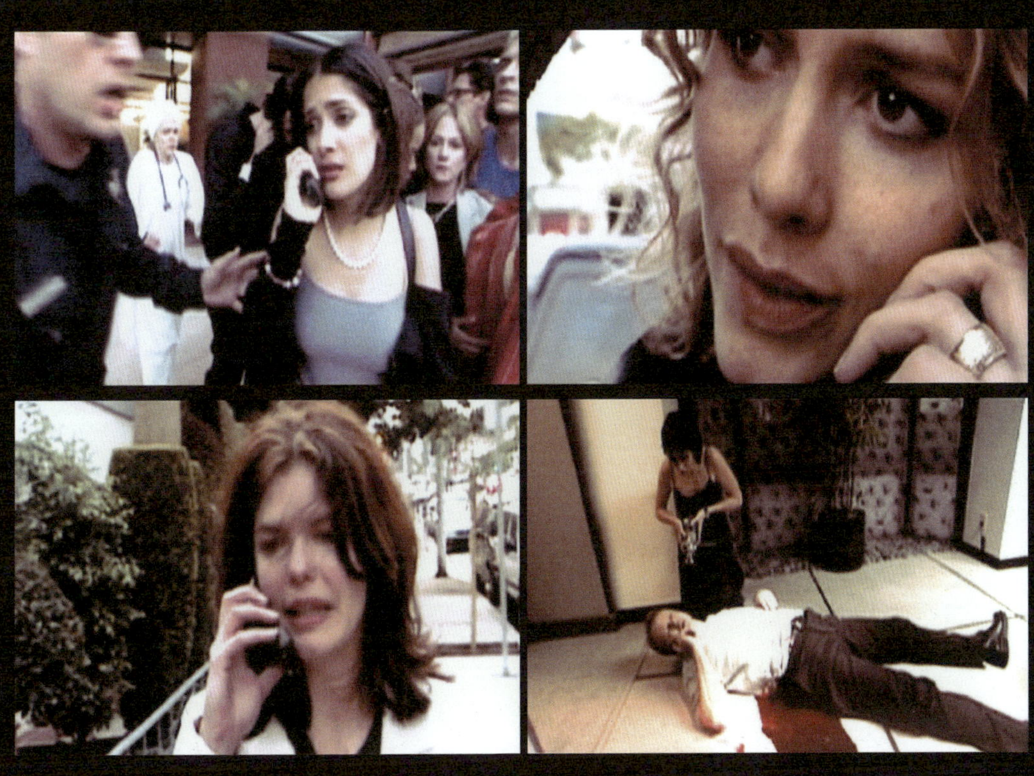

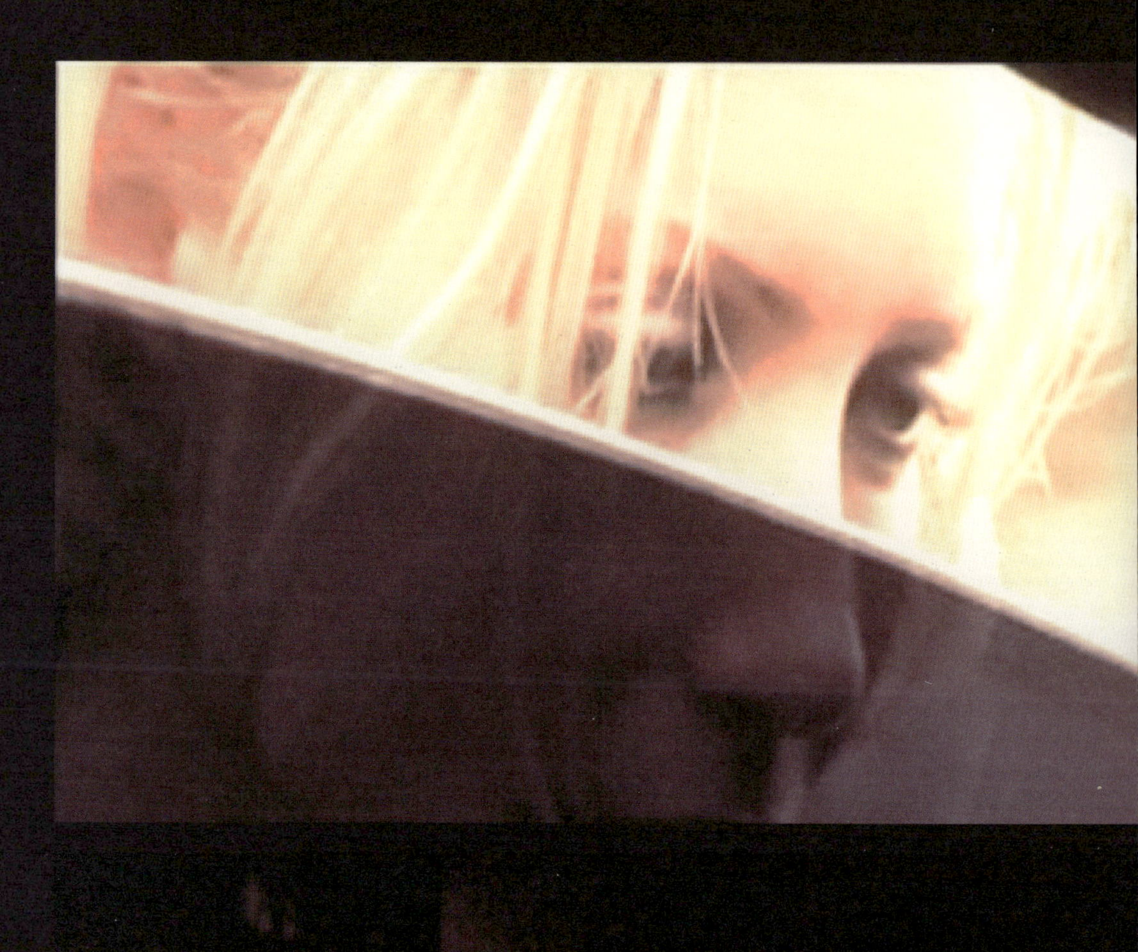

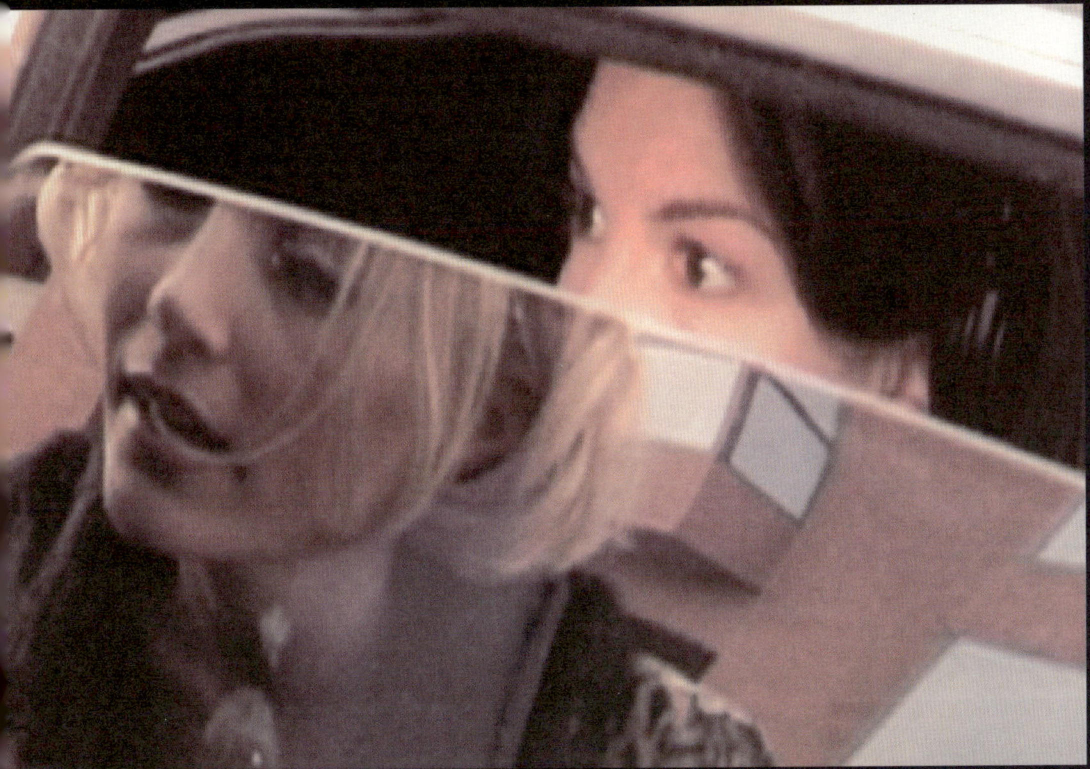

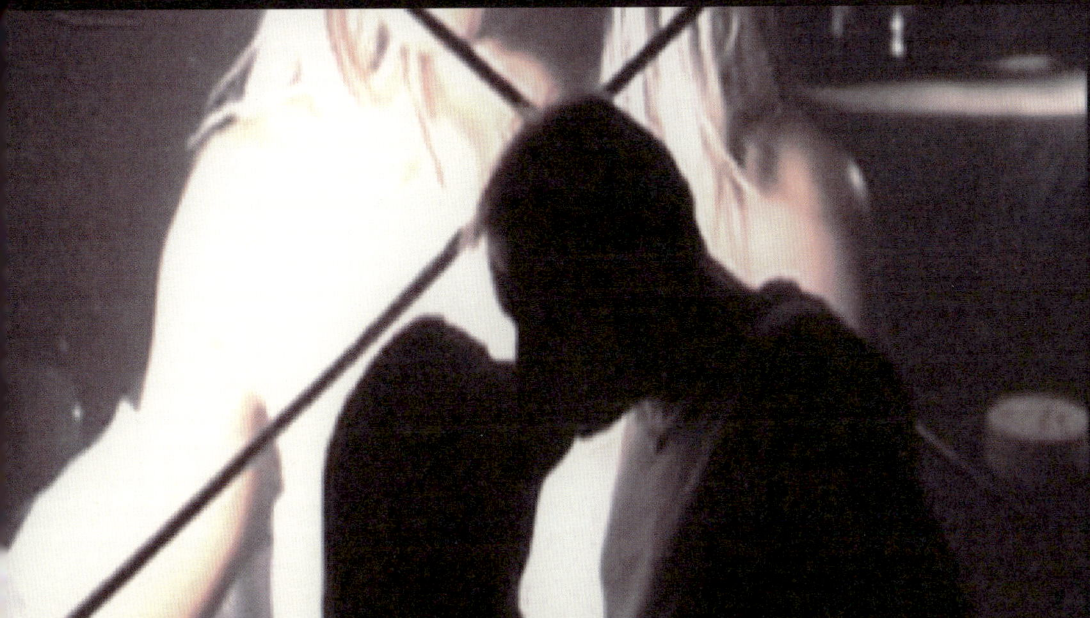

OUTLINE FOR SONY PROJECT.

Because of the secret nature of this film the following information is somewhat unspecific in places. But I will attempt to give a complete picture of what the results will be.

CHARACTERS

There are 4 main characters, 2 men and 2 women. They are 2 couples but all of them are being unfaithful. Although they may suspect each other of infidelity no-one has any proof...yet.

COUPLE No 1

Mr BLUE and Ms RED. I'd like them to be foreign.

Mr BLUE is frightening. He could be RUSSIAN or COLUMBIAN. If he was staring at you you'd become fascinated in a newspaper or the view out of the window, you'd never stare back because you'd know instinctively that **Mr BLUE** had killed several people with his bare hands.

He's 30ish and in great shape. Stocky rather than trendy. He's the alpha male. His English is OK and it is the language he and **Ms RED** communicate in. He is moody and seems depressed at all times, like a volcano waiting to erupt.

Which makes him very sexually attractive to a certain type of woman. **Ms RED**, for example...

Ms RED is FRENCH. She is very sexy in an obvious style. Young, but perhaps not quite as young as she says she is. She could be 35 pretending to be 26. She dresses really well, casual but very thought out. Small breasts, no bra. Shirt unbuttoned that extra button. She just cannot help flirting and sleeping around. **RED** and **BLUE** have been together for 18 months and he knows that she is up to something with someone. She is in her own "JEAN-LUC-GODOT" movie and is leading **BLUE** by the dick. She works within the Hollywood film industry doing what is loosely described as "development", which means she has the licence to meet lots of people all day and gossip and flirt. She is having an affair with...**Mr GREEN**...who is the man in....

COUPLE No 2

Mr GREEN is American and he works as an executive in a small, but successful INDIE film company. He is credited with discovering the latest hot director, a 16-year-old drop-out from Arizona who has made a silent film on Super-8, which is currently topping all the critics' lists.

Mr GREEN is very, very fit and plays power sports at weekends. Over 6 foot and very blonde and tanned. He may go into politics later on if the movie business doesn't work out. **GREEN** lives with **Ms PINK.** They've been together for 3 years and are trying for children.

GREEN drives a big black BMW. He and **Ms PINK** live in a smart house in a smart area, near his office on SUNSET PLAZA.

Ms PINK does not work. She has a busy day though. She and **GREEN** both do sport together and so she goes to the gym every day and also does power yoga with a personal trainer. **GREEN** and **PINK** met when she was still trying to be an actress, but now she has given up that career, which was going nowhere, also he didn't want to be with someone who was also in the business. As we will discover in the course of the film, **Ms PINK** is also having a "thing" with someone but I won't give that away just yet.

THE TECHNIQUE

This has to be treated as confidential information. The idea is very easy to steal and therefore I would like to restrict the number of people who see this.

1) The film is to be shot on four digital video cameras. Each character has his or her own camera at all times.

2) The film is shot in real time (93 minutes) and the result is a wide screen (cinemascope) image consisting of the four video images side by side.

3) At any given time the important image will be on one or more of the screens and these screens will be brighter than the other screens.

4) There is very little post-production in terms of picture editing but some quite complex sound editing.

(cont'd)

5)The intention is to shoot the film in one 90-minute period. This would be repeated 3 times over the course of a week so that by the third pass, technical problems will have been solved.

6)Post-production will take 4 weeks and the film will be ready for the screen immediately. This has to be a major publicity angle.

7)The 4 cameras will be tightly choreographed so that their movements will all match when put together. This is a huge technical challenge and will require very skilled technicians and the participation of the Sony technical experts.

8)The intention is that the entire film is shot on Sony equipment (cameras and sound).

The 4 week pre-production will be an intense time when actors, cameramen and assistants will work together to create this complex scenario and arrive at the definitive schedule so that all of the 4 units are in synch with each other.

I am convinced that this will be a ground-breaking film which will appeal to audiences across the board. But I also feel that it would be a smart thing to open a website immediately to start putting a spin on things and to build up a sense of event. The BLAIR WITCH PROJECT has taught us this.

Remember that each character will, at all times be on a single camera and that characters will cross from 1 camera to another or be seen on 1, 2 or 3 cameras at the same time. All cameras are in synch (in real time). So...with that in mind...picture this. Also it is important to remember that this is a comedy of synchronicitous errors.

THE STORY

CAMERA A starts first.
Mr BLUE and **Ms RED** are in a big expensive car (JAGUAR) driving across LA. He is quizzing her, convinced that she is having an affair. She denies everything. **BLUE'S** mobile phone rings and he answers in Spanish (or Russian), doing some dark, illegal deal. Suddenly he pulls the steering wheel left and right, frightening **RED.**

RED
What are you doing? Are you crazy?

BLUE
I think there's something wrong with the back tire...

And he pulls over to the side of the road, still talking on his mobile.

BLUE (cont'd)
...get out! Go see if the wheel is alright.

She gets out and he slips a tiny sound bug into her handbag.

RED gets back into the car and **BLUE** pulls away fast, causing a car to swerve. A horn blares angrily.

*Meanwhile **CAMERA B** has started up (1 minute after A) and now there are 2 images on the screen.*

CAMERA B
Ms PINK is coming out of a shop and crosses the street. She is almost hit by a big black car. She gives the finger as it drives off.

*We see her out of the window of the JAGUAR from **CAMERA A** and realise that we are in real time.*

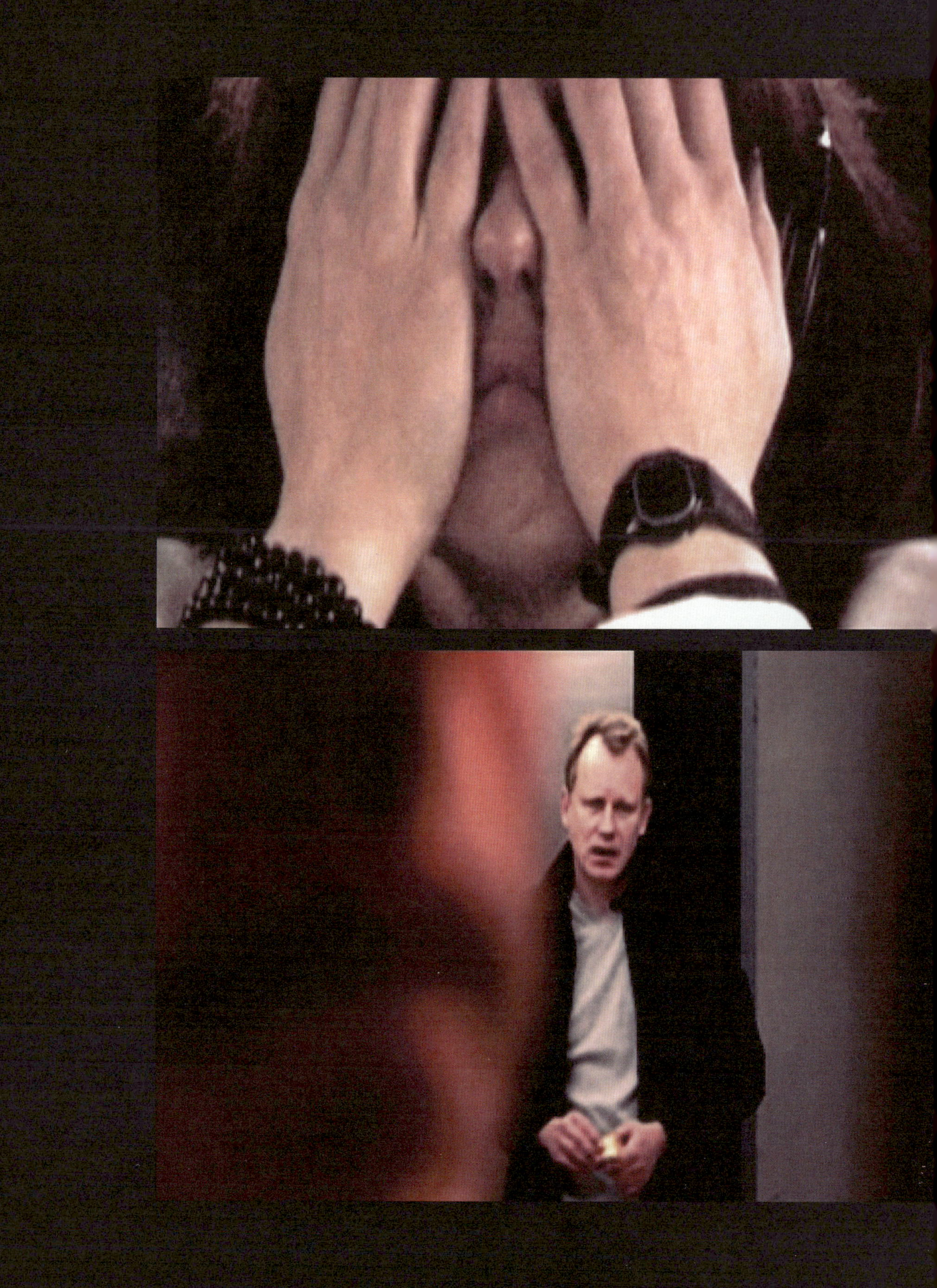

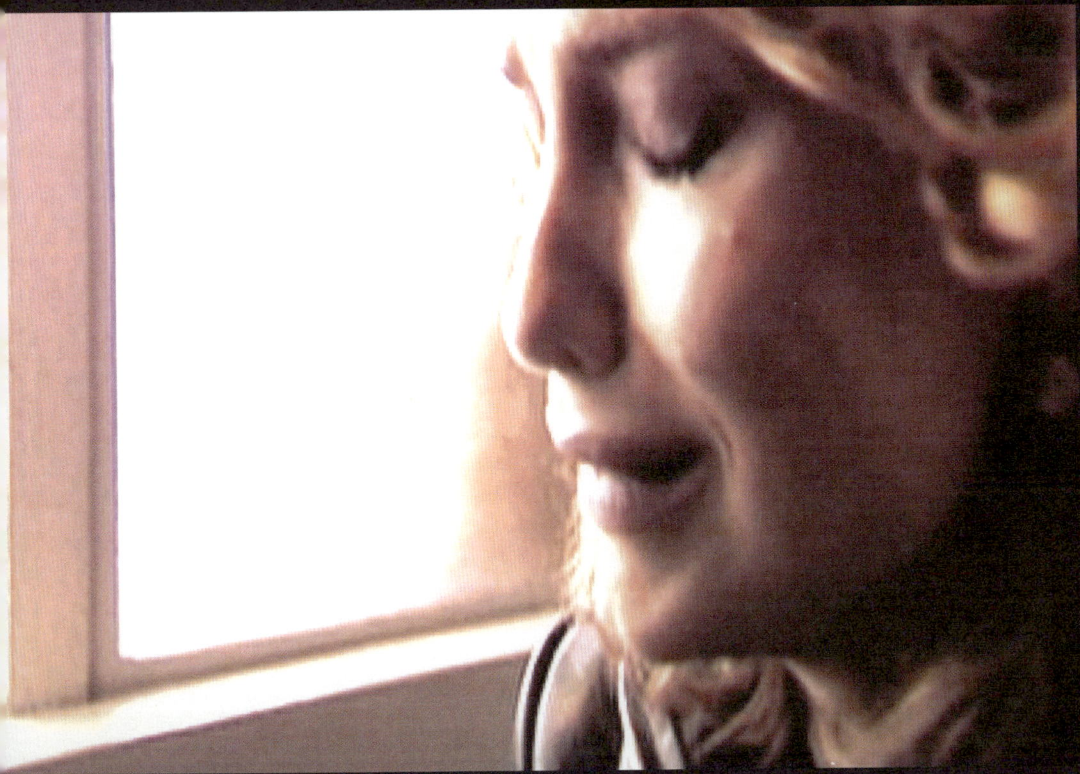

Where the music paper idea came from

I was struggling with how to write 4 stories at the same time, what kind of notation to use. I tried folding a piece of A4 paper into 4 columns but it seemed too fussy and the columns themselves were too small to write more than the basic moves. Then the light bulb clicked on – music paper. Music writing is the perfect system for many stories written in parallel with a very clear definition of what the time is at any given moment.

Suddenly it was very clear. I would write a 93-bar script – each bar line representing exactly 1 minute of screen time. Each stave would represent a different camera, a different story. An interesting bonus from using this system was that I found it very creative as a way of inventing narrative. I would concentrate on 1 story for, say 10 minutes, and then fill in the other stories as a counterpoint – exactly the same system as writing music. It was fairly easy to teach the actors and the crew how to “read” the script, and that gave them a clear idea of the context in which they were to improvise.

9th JUNE 1999..

Some thoughts on split screen

Having tried it in Miss Julie – to good effect – I'm intrigued to experiment with it on two future projects a) A short erotic film b) Fate-synchronicity. What I loved about Miss Julie was that it really was in synch. I'm thinking of lots of different possibilities. Using 2 Aatons and the long magazines with up to 20 mts. Erotic possibilities are just in the split voyeurism and the extra dimension that two viewpoints would bring to the scenario. For example one camera as porn cam and the other as poet cam. Here is a possible script.

A CAM	B CAM
Man waiting in an office. Looks at his watch. Makes an excuse, leaves the space and then gets into a lift. Makes his way to the basement – a vast area of files and corridoors, dimly lit. Some people around, dangerous feeling. Someone passes. He pretends to look for something. Person continues to talk, invites him for a coffee... will not go away – finally gets rid of him. He waits. He hears high heels. He sees her	Women and men in car. Married couple. Bourgoise conversation about shops, holidays, new car, whatever. She has to drop off package. He will wait for her in the car. She gets out. Camera gets out with her. She goes into the office block and down the stairs to a basement. Passes the annoying man from A CAM and is now pretending to look for something. She hasn't seen him yet.

FATE.

TIME CODE

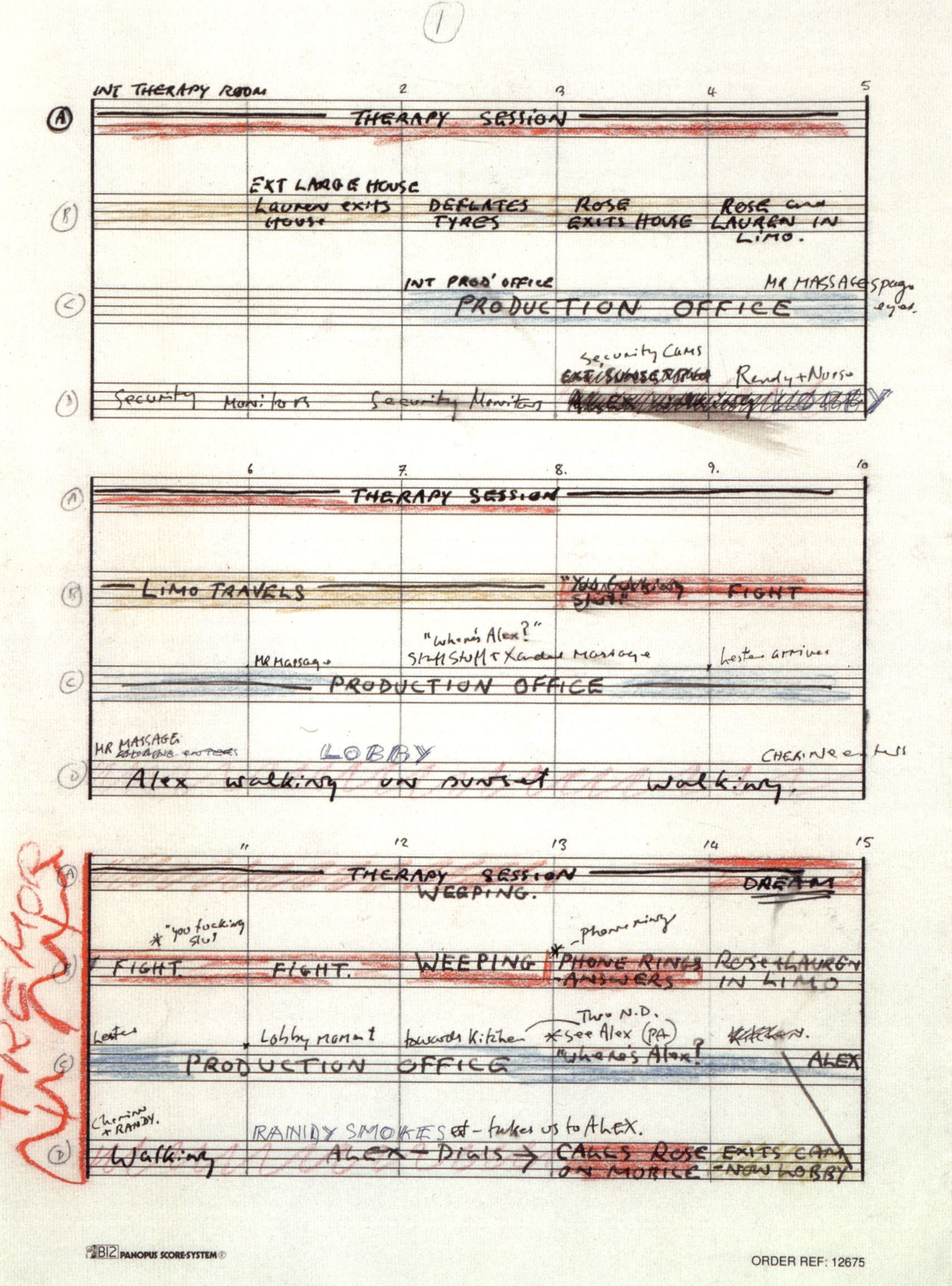

1
INT THERAPY ROOM
THERAPY SESSION
EXT LARGE HOUSE
LAUREN EXITS HOUSE
DEFLATES TYRES
ROSE EXITS HOUSE
ROSE and LAUREN IN LIMO.
INT PROD' OFFICE
PRODUCTION OFFICE
MR MASSAGE
Security Cams
Randy + Nurse
LOBBY
Security Monitors
Security Monitors
THERAPY SESSION
LIMO TRAVELS
FIGHT
"Where's Alex?"
MR Massage
Lester arrives
PRODUCTION OFFICE
MR MASSAGE
LOBBY
Alex walking on sunset
walking.
THERAPY SESSION
WEEPING.
DREAM
"you fucking slut"
Phone rings
FIGHT.
FIGHT.
WEEPING
PHONE RINGS ANSWERS
Rose + LAUREN IN LIMO
Lester
Lobby moment
towards Kitchen
Two N.D.
See Alex (PA)
"where's Alex?"
PRODUCTION OFFICE
ALEX
RANDY SMOKES
takes us to ALEX.
Walking
ALEX - DIALS →
CALLS ROSE ON MOBILE
EXITS CAR - NEW LOBBY
TREMOR
BI2 PANOPUS SCORE-SYSTEM®
ORDER REF: 12675

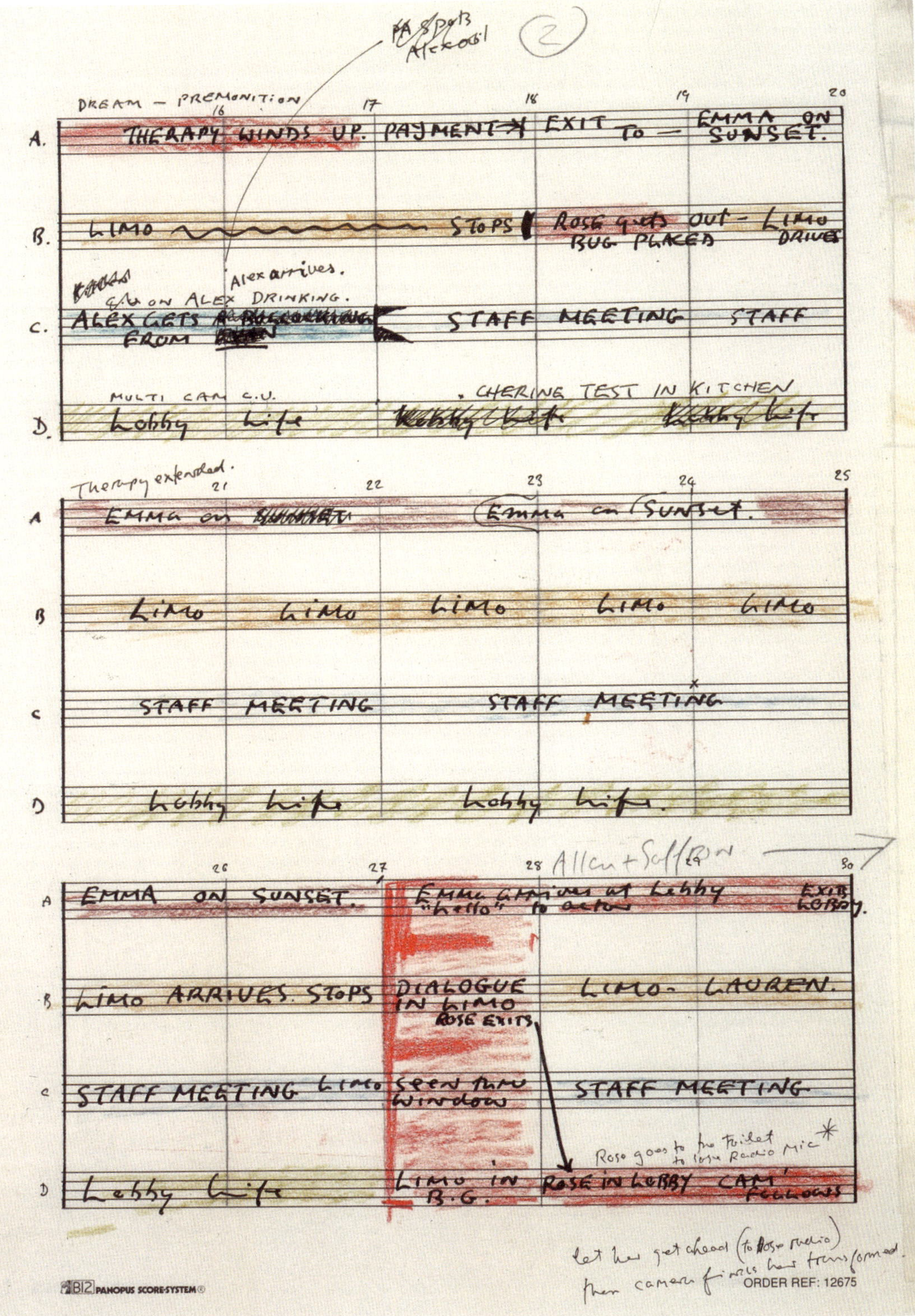

DREAM – PREMONITION
THERAPY WINDS UP. PAYMENT EXIT TO – EMMA ON SUNSET.
LIMO STOPS ROSE gets out – LIMO DRIVES
BUG PLACED
Alex arrives.
C.U. ON ALEX DRINKING.
ALEX GETS FROM
STAFF MEETING STAFF
MULTI CAM C.U.
CHERING TEST IN KITCHEN
Lobby life
Therapy extended.
EMMA on
Emma on Sunset.
Limo Limo Limo Limo Limo
STAFF MEETING STAFF MEETING
Lobby life Lobby life.
EMMA ON SUNSET.
LIMO ARRIVES. STOPS DIALOGUE IN LIMO
ROSE EXITS
LIMO – LAUREN.
STAFF MEETING
STAFF MEETING
Rose goes to the Toilet to lose Radio Mic
Lobby life
LIMO IN B.G.
ROSE IN LOBBY CAM FOLLOWS
PANOPUS SCORE-SYSTEM
ORDER REF: 12675

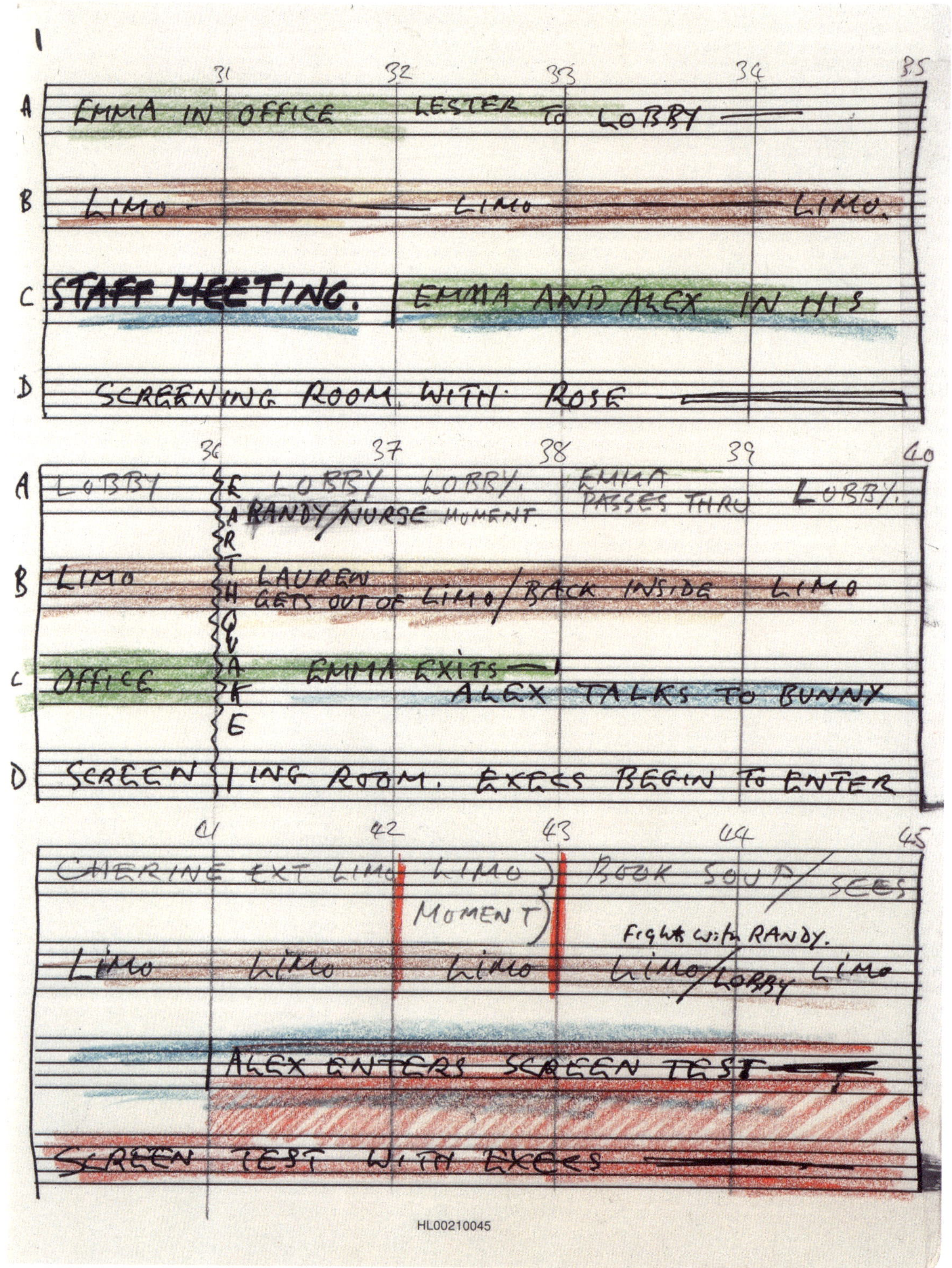

1
31
32
33
34
35
A
EMMA IN OFFICE
LESTER TO LOBBY
B
LIMO
LIMO
LIMO.
C
STAFF MEETING.
EMMA AND ALEX IN HIS
D
SCREENING ROOM WITH ROSE
36
37
38
39
40
A
LOBBY
LOBBY
LOBBY.
EMMA PASSES THRU
LOBBY.
RANDY/NURSE MOMENT
EARTHQUAKE
B
LIMO
LAUREN GETS OUT OF LIMO/BACK INSIDE
LIMO
C
OFFICE
EMMA EXITS
ALEX TALKS TO BUNNY
D
SCREEN
ING ROOM. EXECS BEGIN TO ENTER
41
42
43
44
45
LIMO
MOMENT
BOOK SOUP/
SEES
Fight with RANDY.
LIMO
LIMO
LIMO
LIMO/LOBBY
LIMO
ALEX ENTERS SCREEN TEST
SCREEN TEST WITH EXECS
HL00210045

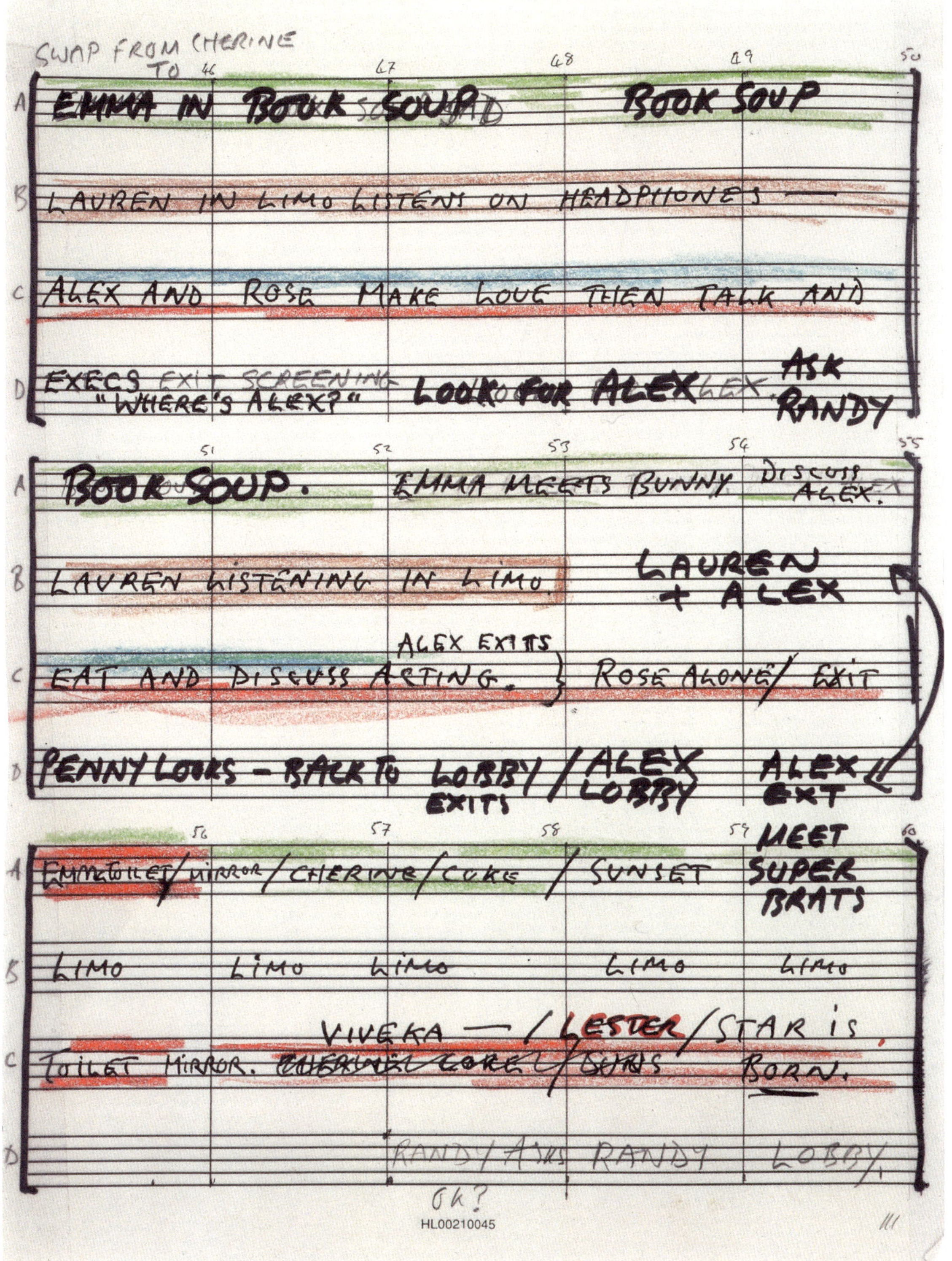
SWAP FROM CHERINE TO
EMMA IN BOOK SOUP
BOOK SOUP
LAUREN IN LIMO LISTENS ON HEADPHONES
ALEX AND ROSE MAKE LOVE THEN TALK AND
EXECS EXIT SCREENING
"WHERE'S ALEX?"
LOOK FOR ALEX
ASK RANDY
BOOK SOUP.
EMMA MEETS BUNNY
DISCUSS ALEX.
LAUREN LISTENING IN LIMO.
LAUREN + ALEX
ALEX EXITS
EAT AND DISCUSS ACTING.
ROSE ALONE/ EXIT
PENNY LOOKS – BACK TO LOBBY
EXITS
ALEX LOBBY
ALEX EXIT
MEET SUPER BRATS
SUNSET
LIMO
LIMO
LIMO
LIMO
LIMO
VIVEKA
LESTER
STAR IS BORN.
TOILET MIRROR.
RANDY
RANDY
LOBBY.
OK?
HL00210045

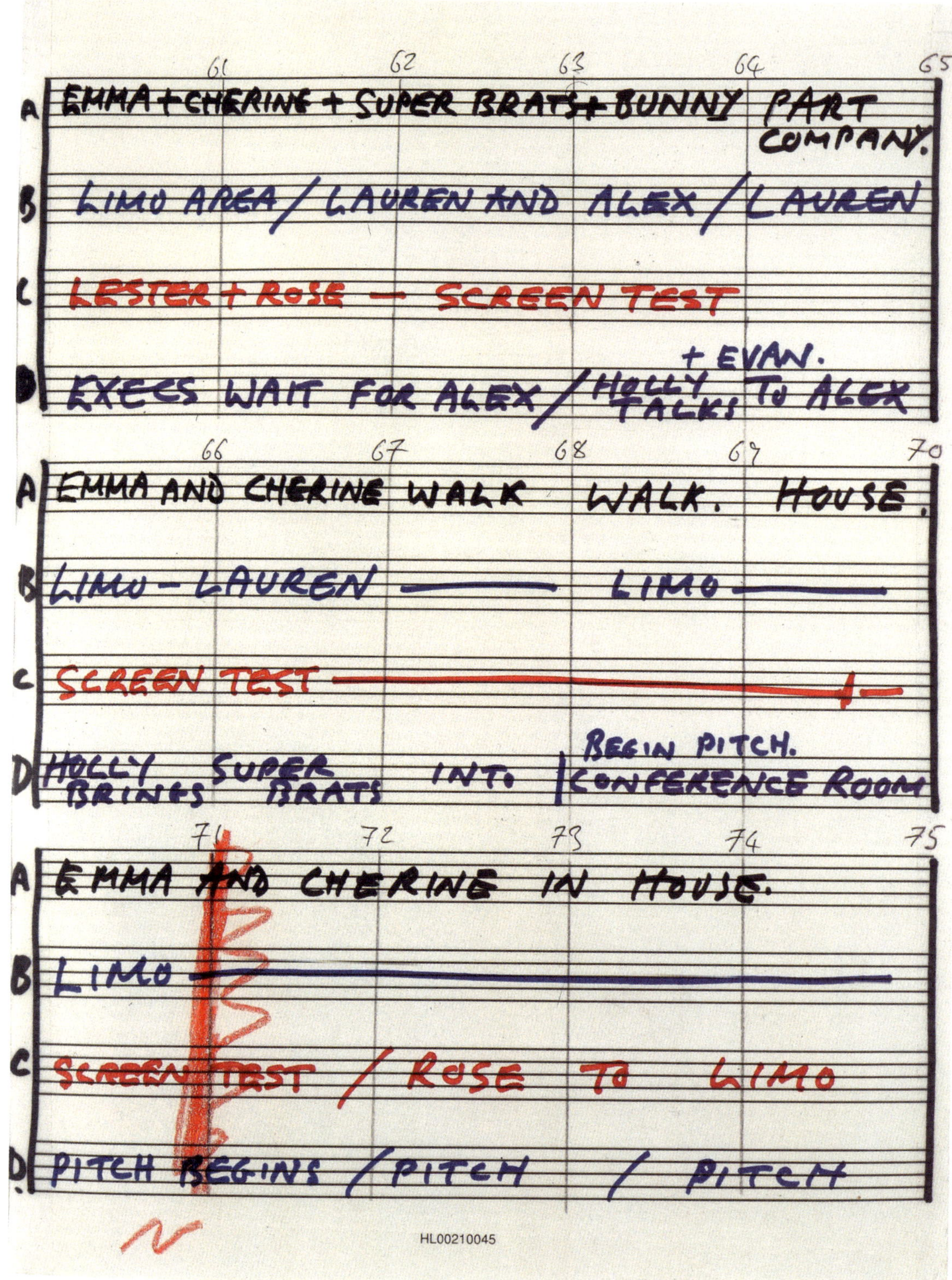
61 62 63 64 65
A EMMA + CHERINE + SUPER BRATS + BUNNY PART COMPANY.
B LIMO AREA / LAUREN AND ALEX / LAUREN
C LESTER + ROSE — SCREEN TEST
D EXECS WAIT FOR ALEX / HOLLY + EVAN. TALKS TO ALEX
66 67 68 69 70
A EMMA AND CHERINE WALK WALK. HOUSE.
B LIMO – LAUREN LIMO
C SCREEN TEST
D HOLLY BRINGS SUPER BRATS INTO | BEGIN PITCH. CONFERENCE ROOM
71 72 73 74 75
A EMMA AND CHERINE IN HOUSE.
B LIMO
C SCREEN TEST / ROSE TO LIMO
D PITCH BEGINS / PITCH / PITCH
HL00210045

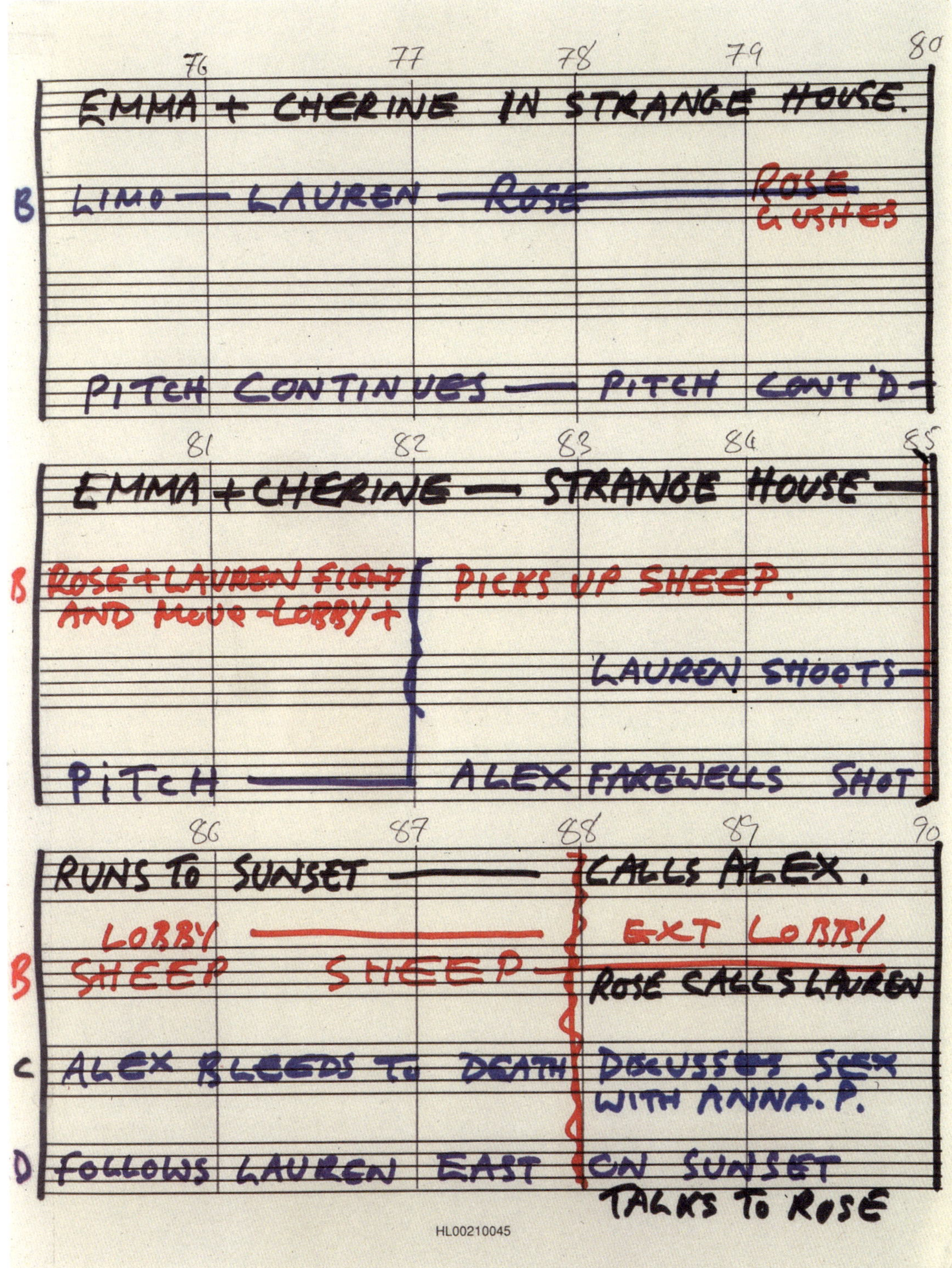

76
77
78
79
80
EMMA + CHERINE IN STRANGE HOUSE.
B
LIMO — LAUREN — ROSE
ROSE GUSHES
PITCH CONTINUES — PITCH CONT'D —
81
82
83
84
85
EMMA + CHERINE — STRANGE HOUSE —
B
ROSE + LAUREN FIGHT AND MOVE - LOBBY +
PICKS UP SHEEP.
LAUREN SHOOTS —
PITCH —
ALEX FAREWELLS SHOT
86
87
88
89
90
RUNS TO SUNSET —
CALLS ALEX.
LOBBY —
EXT LOBBY
B
SHEEP
SHEEP —
ROSE CALLS LAUREN
C
ALEX BLEEDS TO DEATH
DISCUSSES SEX WITH ANNA. P.
D
FOLLOWS LAUREN EAST
ON SUNSET
TALKS TO ROSE
HL00210045

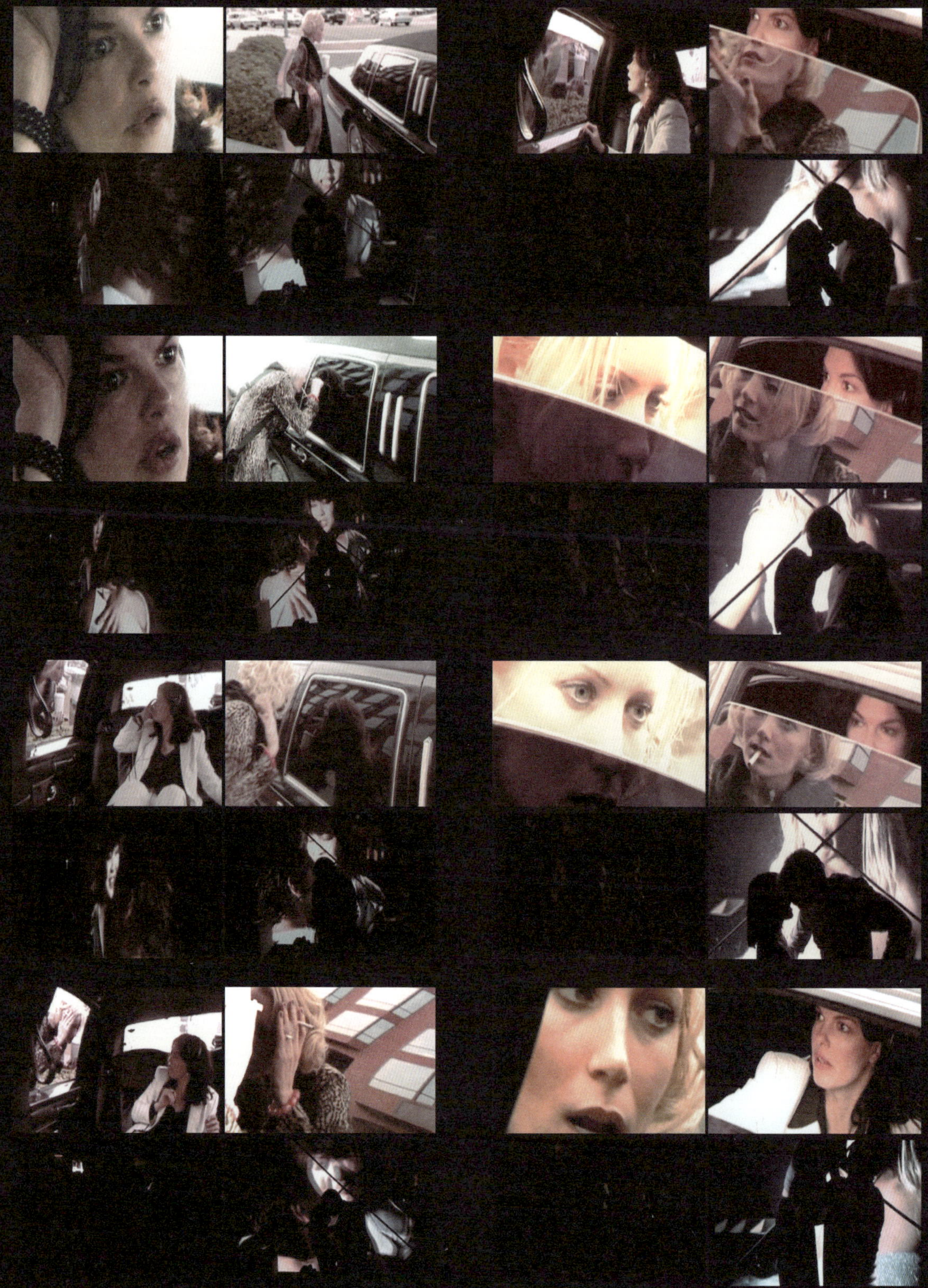

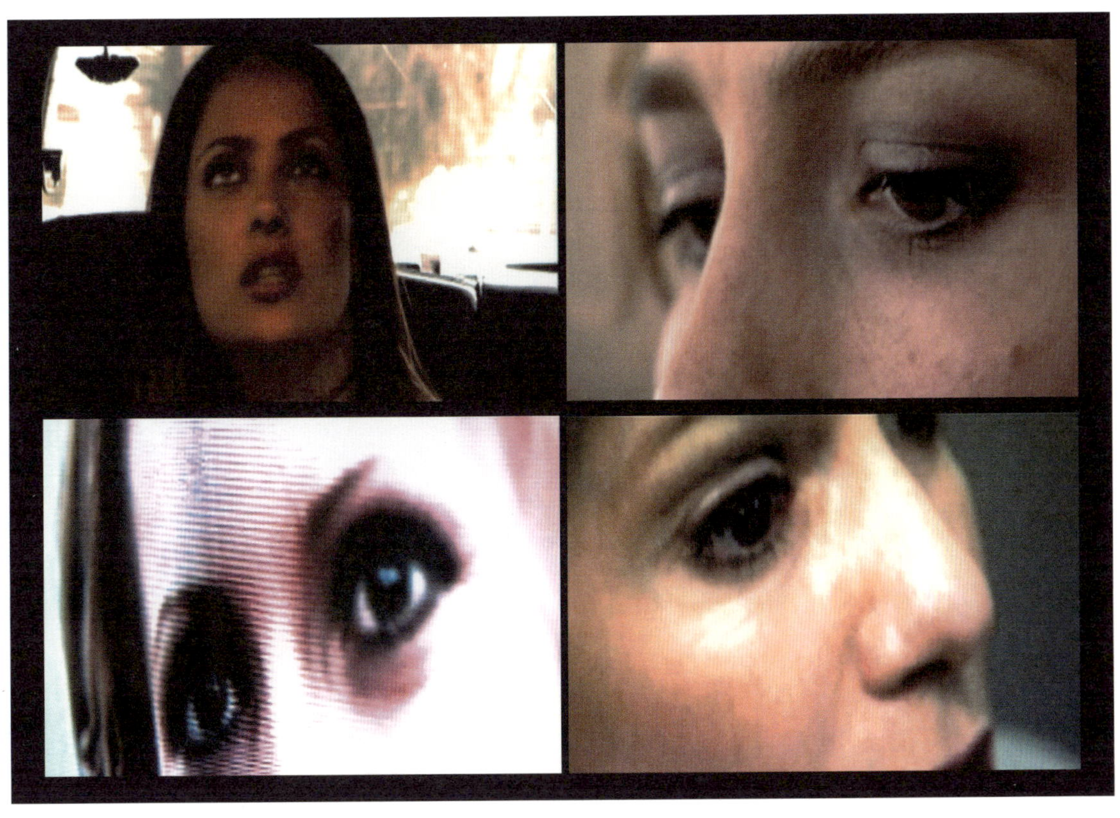

At minute 17 all four cameras were instructed to begin a slow zoom – ending in an extreme close-up of eyes. Three of the cameras made it on time, the fourth was distracted by a technical problem and missed the cue. But I liked the result as it was.

HOW TO PITCH A DIGITAL MOVIE

ANNA PAULS, (an 18-year-old independent film-maker with a big hit on her hands) is addressing the executives of RED MULLET, a successful "indie" company. ANNA speaks with the confidence of an 18-year-old film student from Latin America who has made one film. She is describing what she wants to do next.

ANNA

"My film has the necessity, the urge to go beyond the paradigm of collage. Montage has created a fake reality but now technology has arrived – digital video has arrived and is demanding new expressions, new sensations. As Gropius said in the first Bauhaus exhibition, 'Art, technology, a new unity'. It is now 1999 and it is time to say again 'Art, technology, a new, new unity'...

ALEX GREEN, the founder of the company is a little worse for wear. During ANNA'S speech he snorts some cocaine and giggles quietly to himself.

ANNA (cont'd)

...Eisenstein and Werthe, being influenced by the Russian Formalism, with its theory of the isolation of a word within a poem, of course we are talking about cinema so it would be the isolation of an image or the isolation of a take...

ALEX is finding it difficult to control his laughter now. The other executives are giving him nervous looks because it is very important that this super-brat brings her business to RED MULLET.

(cont'd)

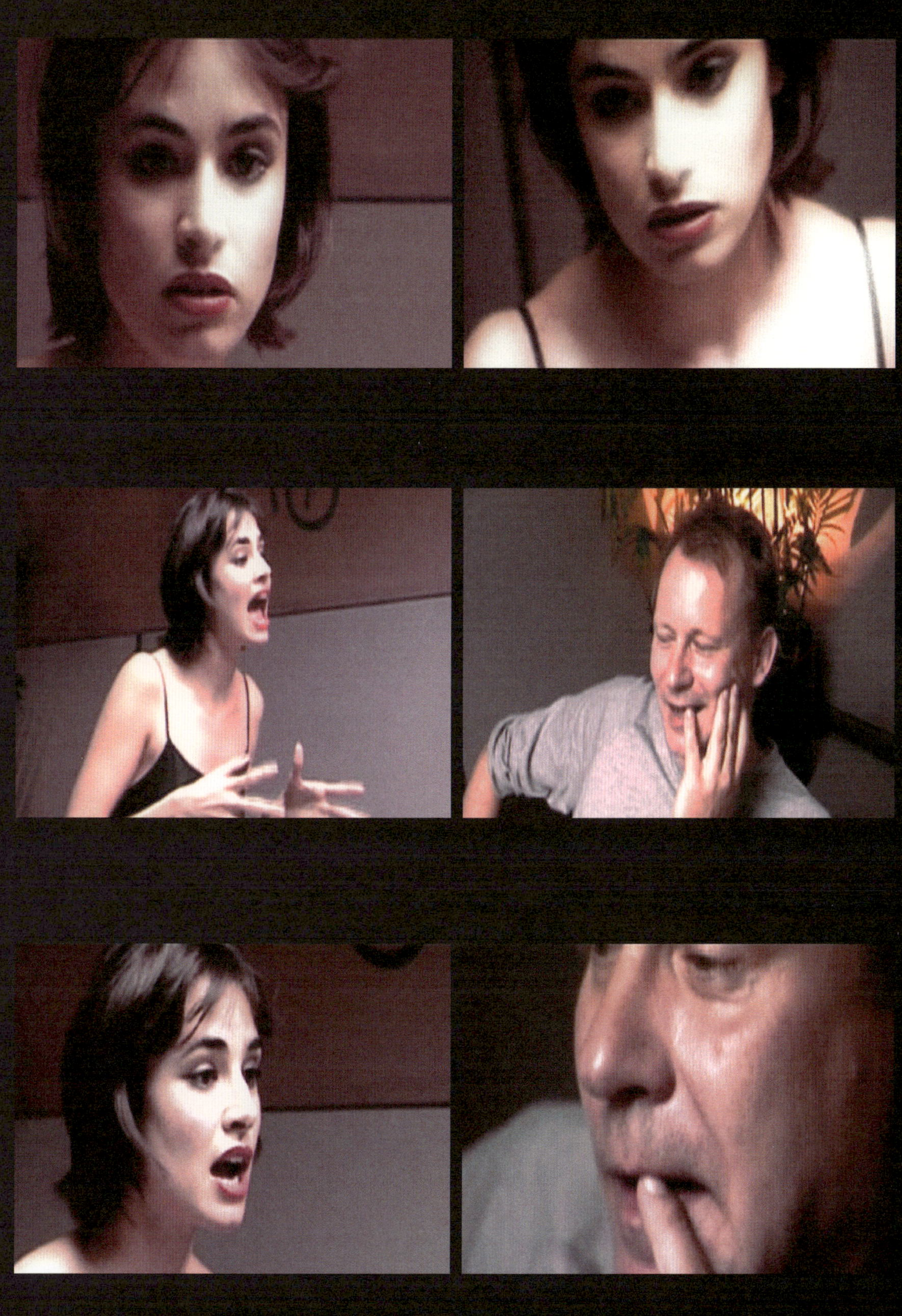

ANNA (cont'd)
...they created the so-called Soviet Montage. The discontinuity in editing - at that time that was the vanguard. It's not the vanguard anymore. The Capitalistic system that we are living in has absorbed all of the innovations, all of the vanguards. It's time to move forward, to move beyond.

ALEX can contain himself no longer. He giggles loudly.
ANNA stops and stares at him as if he was a rare species in a zoo.

ALEX
That is the most pretentious crap I ever heard in my life. Do you think anybody around this table has a clue what you are talking about?

ANNA
Then it's time for them to learn.

ALEX
They think it's crap, but we will do your piece of crap and then you will do ours, and that will be the deal.

Minutes later ALEX is shot by the jealous lesbian lover of <u>his</u> lover. As he bleeds to death on the floor he takes 1 last phone call from his wife. ANNA PAULS films his death on the SONY PD-100 digital camera.

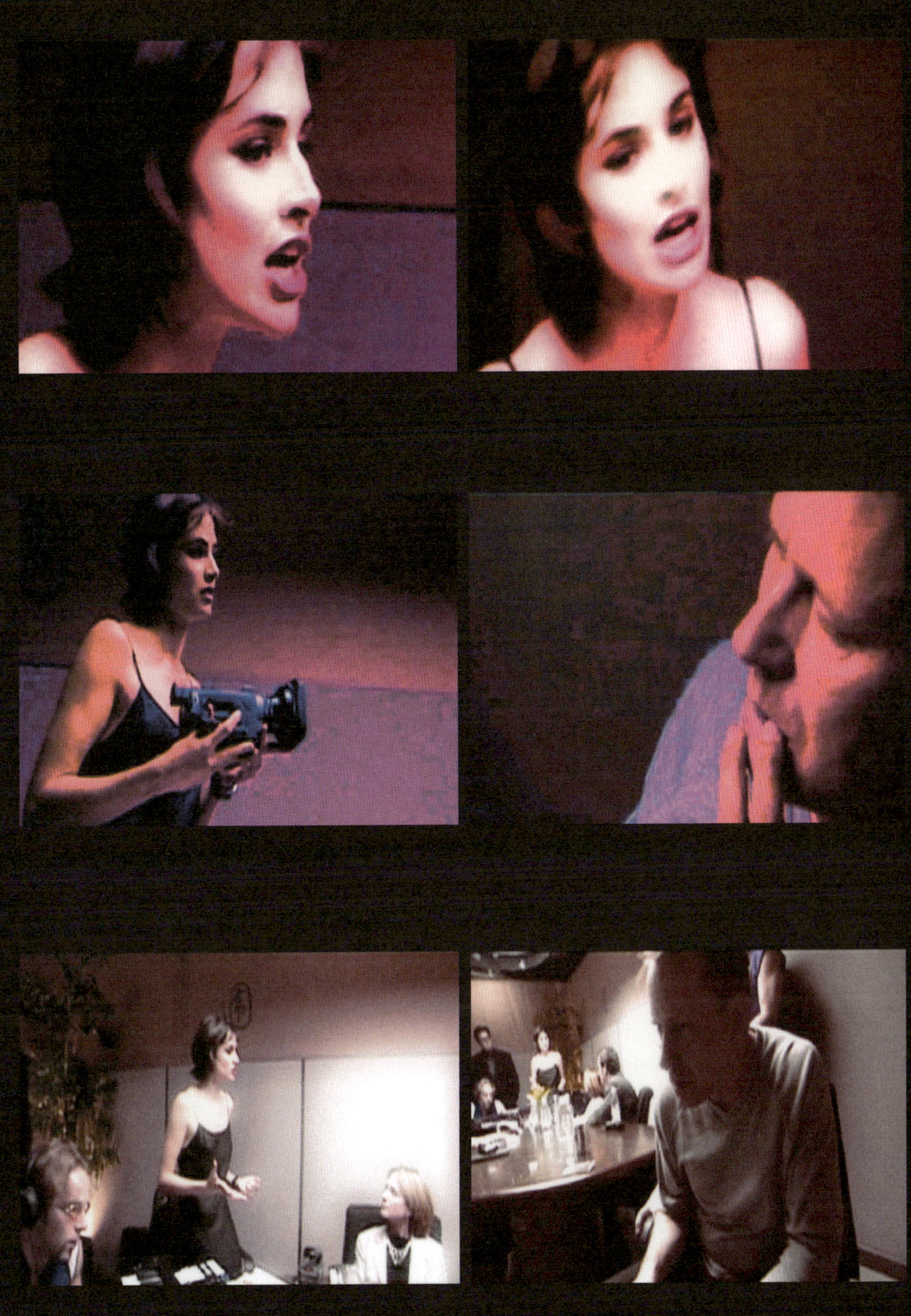

Continuing the experiment

As soon as I had finished shooting TIMECODE over a 2 week period – making an entire feature film every single day with a beginning, a middle and an end, and a lot going on in the middle – I began a new notebook of ideas and techniques exposed by the shoot. I looked at playback in post-production and was reminded of some of the amazing possibilities. I also worked to discover the little Sony PD100 camera that I'd bought during the shoot. I started a separate notebook for it and went through the manual or menu and fiddled and tried different combinations. When I saw something I liked I asterisked it. I worked like that until I knew the camera very well. The same happened with designing the equipment that went on to the camera. So I developed a little system that was entirely personal to me.

I made the decision to use the PD100s for my next films – but with a huge difference from the way most people were shooting with digital cameras. I decided not to play around with the image in post-production. I wanted to set the camera in a certain way so I could not change my mind afterwards. If you look at everything as a post-production technique the jazz or essence of experimentation with the actors is gone. But if you impose a theatrical rule on something that is normally far more controllable; which is to say, we're going to do this together and if it doesn't work, we're fucked, then you create a quite different level of excitement.

Before TIMECODE I had always dealt with the conventional structure of film, in other words storyline and script, which only supports 1 element of the story at a time. Your tools are image – cut to image – cut to image. Here is an example: a shot of a man running down the street – he looks agitated – cut to a blood-splattered figure on the pavement – cut to a police car tearing through traffic. The result is almost colouring-book story-telling.

When I started dealing with the streaming of double images in "real-time" for TIMECODE, I found I had to come up with a complete new technique for structuring the story. When you write 4 parallel narratives the brain functions in a completely different manner, exactly as for a piece of music. When I was 8, my father taught me to judge music as a subtle system of ensemble playing. In a piece for a string quartet, for example, the cello does not lay out while the second violin finishes a phrase; it has to do something interesting. Everyone is working all the time, but sometimes in a supporting role, sometimes in a dominant role; or all 4 may support each other. You never get that in a conventional film script. In TIMECODE the understanding of storyline and rhythm took on a new musical sensibility.

> -----Original Message-----
> From: Anne-Claire Cieutat [mailto:]
> Sent: 29 April, 2002 4:42 PM
> To: Mike Figgis
> Subject: Re: TIMECODE

> Dear Sir,

> My name is Anne-Claire Cieutat, I am a French film critic from the magazine
> "Repérages", from Paris. Our magazine deals with cinema, images, sound and
> audio visual technics in general. We saw and greatly appreciated "TIMECODE"
> and would like to publish an interview with you about this film in our next issue.
> I hope we are not too "greedy" though...
> Thanks so much in advance,
> Best regards,
> Anne-Claire Cieutat

> How did this idea come to mind?

The film I did before TIMECODE was Miss Julie and I shot it on Super-16 using an Aaton camera with very long magazines (20mts). I was shooting very long takes on 2 cameras at the same time and then reviewing the footage side by side on 2 video assist units. I became intrigued by the possibilities of shooting an entire film using this technique and this inspired TIMECODE.

> How did you proceed technically? (In terms of organisation, shooting,
> crews, etc)

I shot 1 camera and the 3 other operators came from a video-film background. I needed camera people who could hand hold for 90 mts and pull their own focus and react quickly to whatever might happen. Every day we shot a complete film. We would do this in the morning. Over lunch I would have the 4 films synchronized and then I did a live mix of the sound for the cast and crew. Afterwards we would discuss the results and make changes for the next version. We shot the film more than 20 times and in the last days we shot twice a day.

> Did you have a script or storyboard?

No script as such, just this funny music paper system with all of the timings written out for phone calls and entrances and exits and so on. These timing were refined each day. All of the actors were responsible for their own timekeeping and also their own make-up, costume and transport.

> What cameras did you use? How many?

Sony DVCAM. The European equivelant would be the DSR 500. We shot NTSC, full-screen and then cropped later for a 1:85 ratio. We used 4 cameras and each operator had a PD100 DVCAM as a back-up.

> What indications did you give to your technicians?

It was a steep learning curve for everyone. After each screening I would give camera notes and sound notes. The biggest challenge was getting everyone to move fast enough to cover all of the action. Cameramen have a tendency to always try and do the aesthetic move rather than the functional one. I was also trying to get them to get in tight and interact with the actors. We had no sound boom operators because of the 4 cameras so all of the sound was either off the camera or from radio mics all going to a central stack of 3 DA 88 digital recorders. Both the DA 88s and the cameras were all running off the same TIMECODE, hence the title.The cameras are very badly designed for sound; it is 1 of the issues I keep raising with Sony, but it is quite an uphill battle.

> How did you direct your actors and when?

After each shoot, during the screening I would give notes and, back up the notes with practical observations about the film. This was a new experience for everyone, myself included and takes the matter out of the abstract and into the practical. I was also adding score each day so the actors also got a sense of how they were going to be mixed - Mahler? Hendrix? Charles Ives? All different interpretations of the same scene.

> How did your actors respect the timing?

Very well. They quickly learned that if they did not respect the timings they would look foolish in front of their peers. Another interesting observation is that when actors have to deal with complicated and precise timings the verbal improvising becomes less of an obstacle for them.

> How many versions of the four actions did you shoot?

21 versions, I think. Each version was joined together and no editing of one take to the other was ever done, though I was tempted.

> What did you change day after day?

The same kind of things that you would on any film. The story got clearer and the timings got better. The camera work became more integrated into the story and the coincidences became more apparent.

> What about editing? How did you decide to organise the 4 images and
> soundtracks together?

There was no editing. The 4 takes were genuinely shot at the same time and just synchronized together and then a very complex sound mix was done. In that sense the editing was entirely sound.

> Your film demands a great concentration and participation from the viewer.
> Weren't you afraid of getting him/her confused or lost?

I was concerned that the film might just be too hard to follow. But I also wanted to make a film that would ask the viewer to work far harder than normal in a cinema. I am very tired of the over simplicity of most films, the banality of most scripts.

> What are, according to you, the main advantages of digital video?

Obviously the long takes - then the cheapness of the medium and the accessibility of cheap editing software. It is the medium of the people.

> How would you define your own film?

A new way of looking at the art of storytelling.

I hope this answers your questions well enough. Good luck with the article.
Warmest regards, Mike Figgis

ABOUT TIME–2, London, 2000

ABOUT TIME - 2

ABOUT TIME - 2

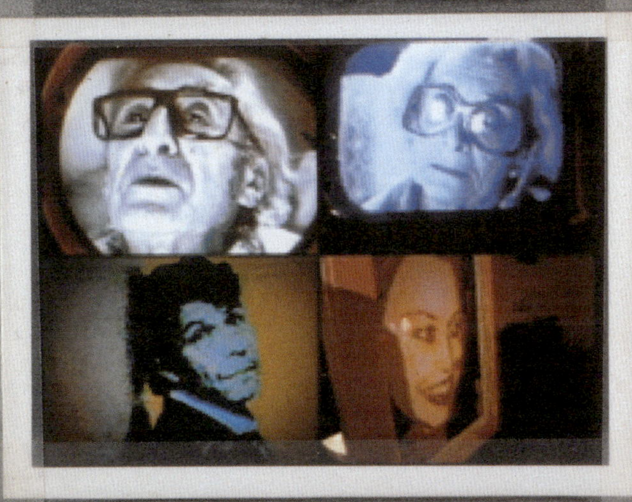

Towards the end of 2000

I was asked to take part in a project called TEN MINUTES OLDER. A group of directors from around the world were all asked to make a 10-minute film that dealt with a personal view of time. The collected short films would be put together into 2 feature length films. It seemed a perfect opportunity for me to continue the experimentation with "real-time" film making. The film, ABOUT TIME-2, was shot over a 2-day period in an abandoned hospital in Hackney, London. The film was shot in its entirety over 20 times. This was the first outing for the newly designed camera rigs that Ben Wilson and I had been working on. The cameras were the Sony PD100s. The central idea of the film is this: a man (Mark Long) is trying to write a paragraph of his autobiography. He walks through a ramshackle house and revisits himself as a young boy, an impotent lover and as a old person in a retirement home.

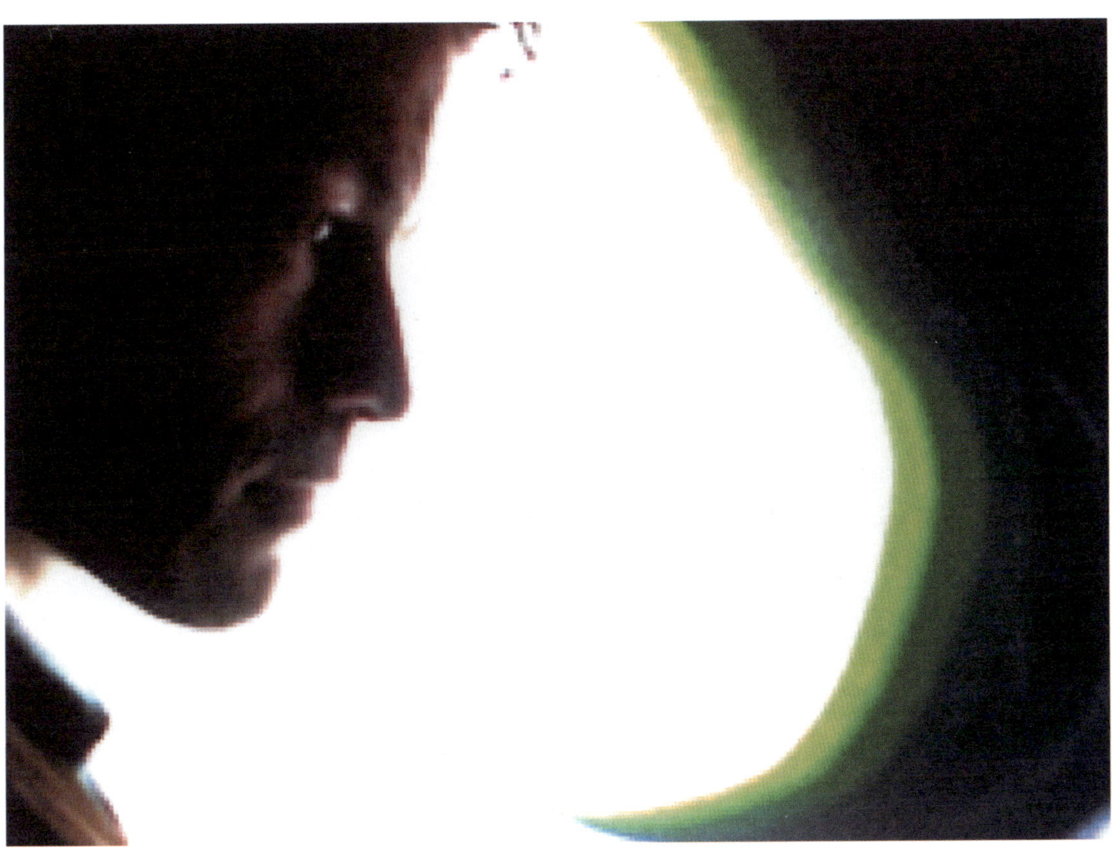

CAMERA + MONITOR LIST.

6 x ON-SCREEN MONITORS – 3 big
4 x large off-screen MONITORS – 3 small

4 Main cameras

1 x 500 (A)

2 x VX1000 (D)

4 x VCR decks
(B) + (C) + (D)

(A)

(C)

W.C.

COMPU

'live' C.U footage
of the 2 x lovers

live Montage
of jumbled imagery
and text that Mark
is writing (live)

BETA S.P.

VCR

VCR

VCR

(B)

V. MIX

(C)

(D)

(A)

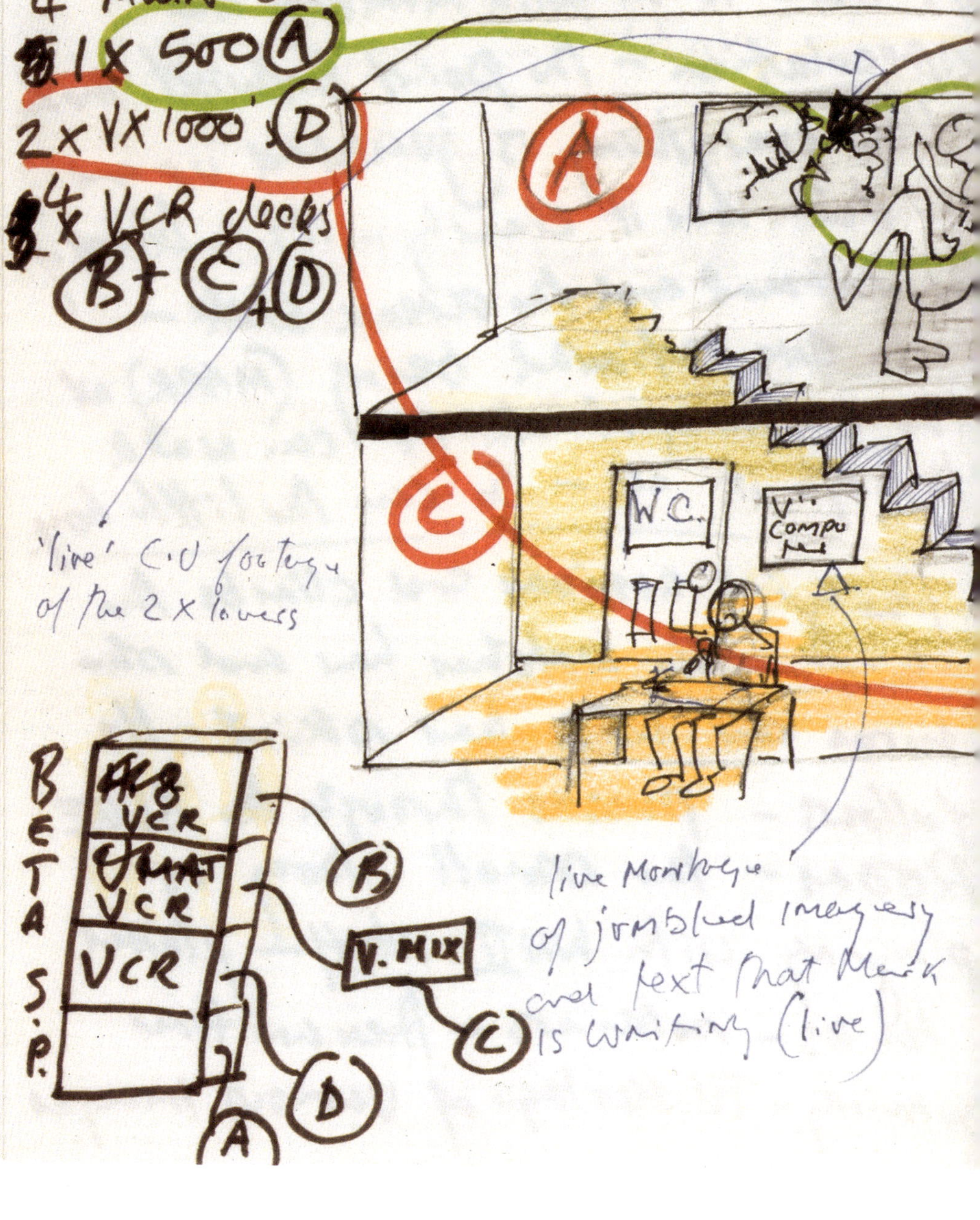

lasma type
ype

WWII Footage
old girlie mags
period
stag films
Auschwitz.

Refinement Home
Florida.

NEW ORLEANS
VISTA.
Never Changing.

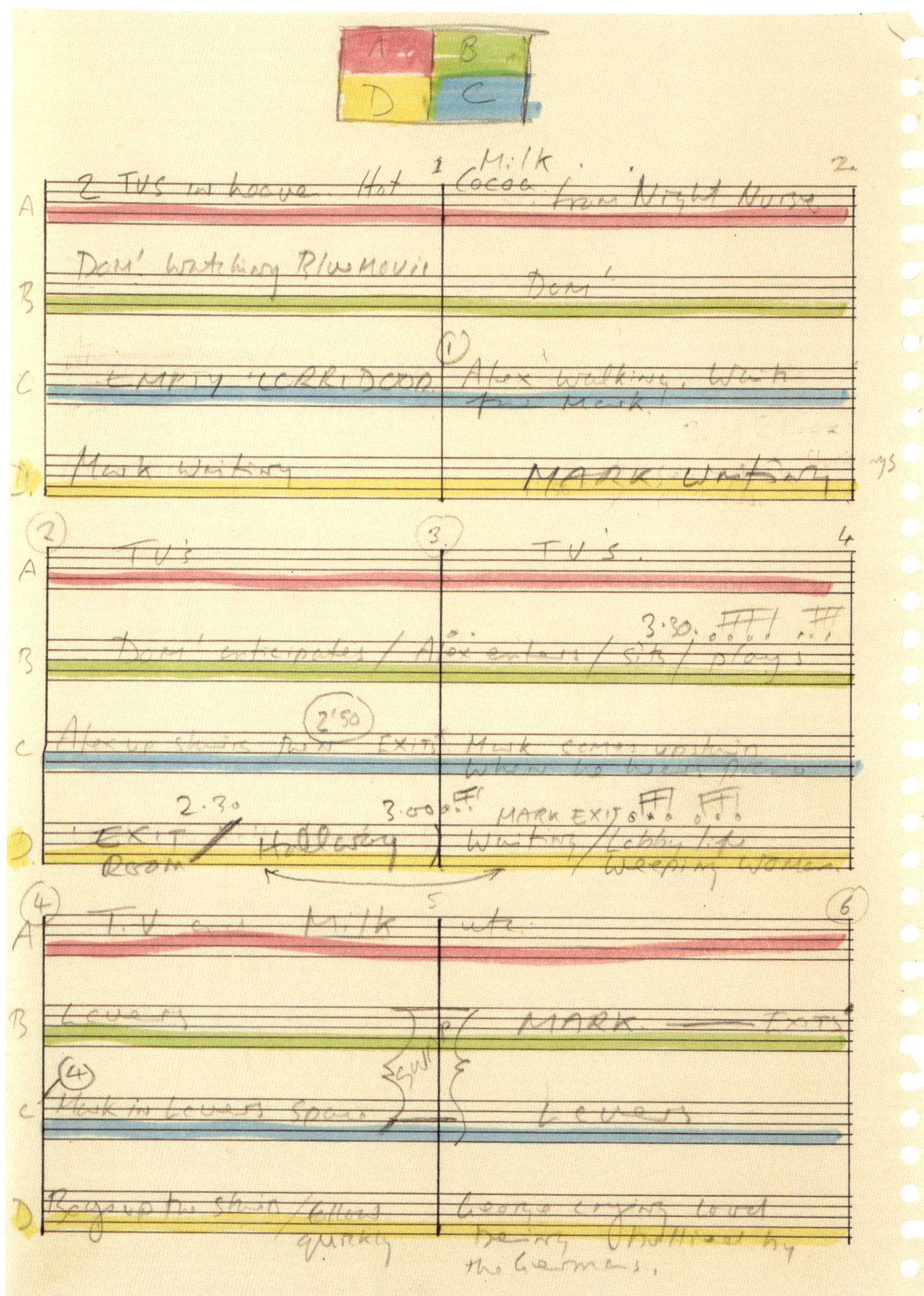

A
B
D
C
A
2 TVs in house. Hot
Milk
Cocoa from Night Nurse
B
Dom' watching Blue Movie
Dom'
C
EMPTY CORRIDOOR
Alex walking. Wait for Mark
D
Mark waiting
MARK waiting
A
TV's
TV's.
B
3.30.
Dom' anticipates / Alex enters / sits / plays
C
2'50
EXITS
D
2.30
3.00
MARK EXITS
EXIT ROOM
Hallway
Waiting / Lobby life
Weeping Women
A
T.V and Milk
etc.
B
Lovers
MARK — EXITS
C
Mark in Lovers Space
Lovers
D
Boy up the stairs / follows quickly
George crying loud being bullied by the Germans.

	7	8
A	T.V. frame up left.	W.S left
B	Mark has moment with Boy	— Heaven TV W.S. Right.
C	Lovers —	Lovers — Dominic Slow zoom in on Both.
D	Boy has moment with Mark	— Boy

	9	10
A	T.V Mark exits.	T.V Slow zoom in on both
B	T.V. Mark exits	T V
C	Lovers.	Piano music (II)
D.	Boy / pick up Mark	MARK on the Stairs with double.

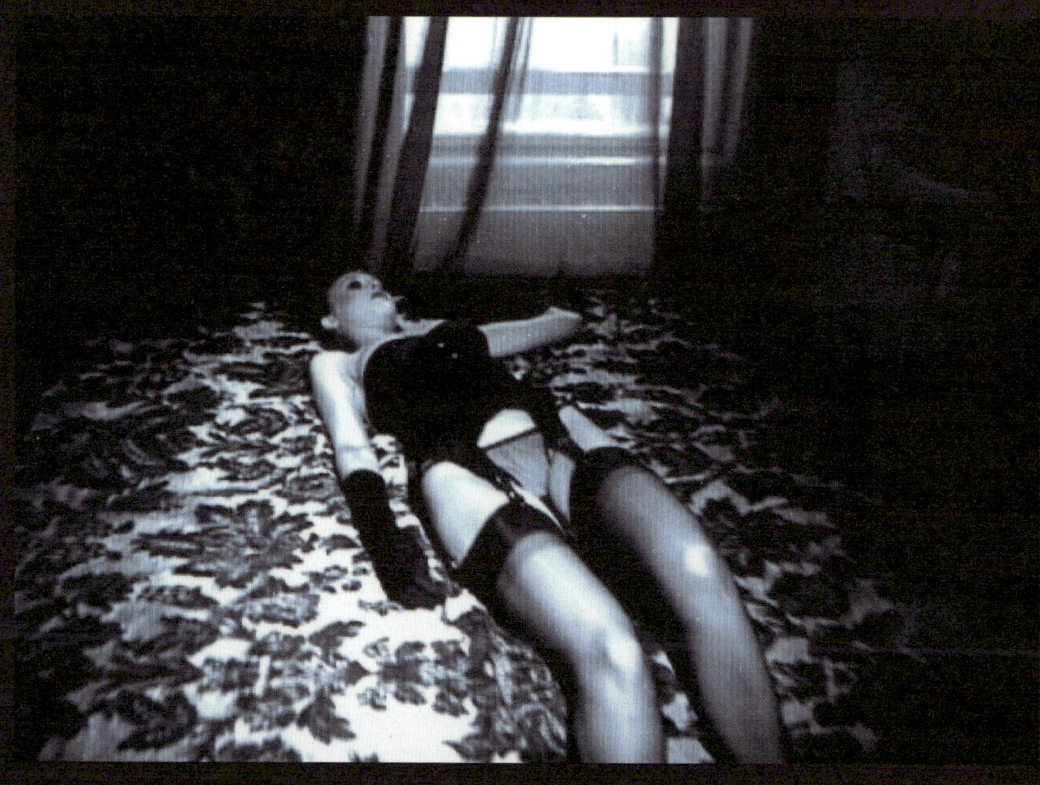

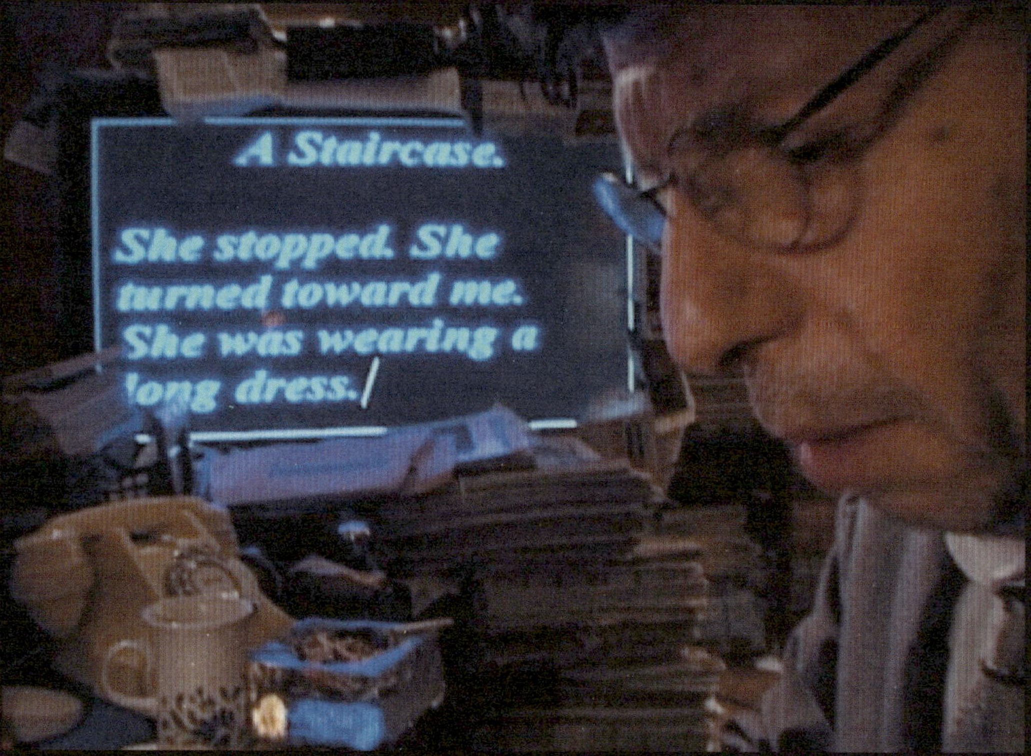

A Staircase.
She stopped. She turned toward me. She was wearing a long dress.

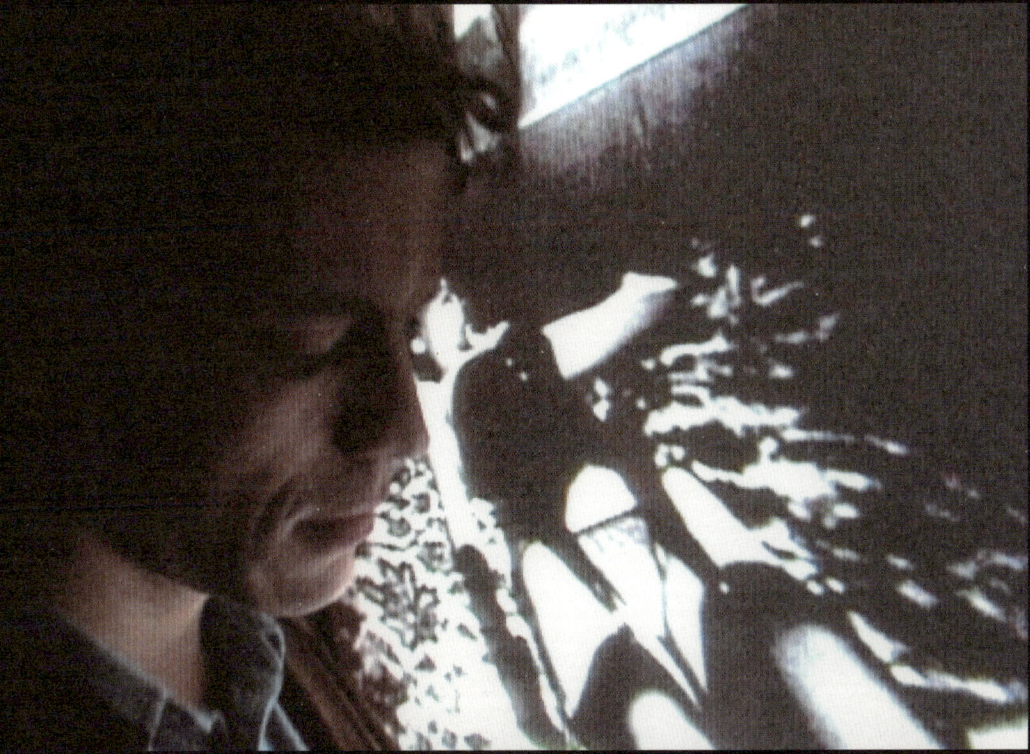

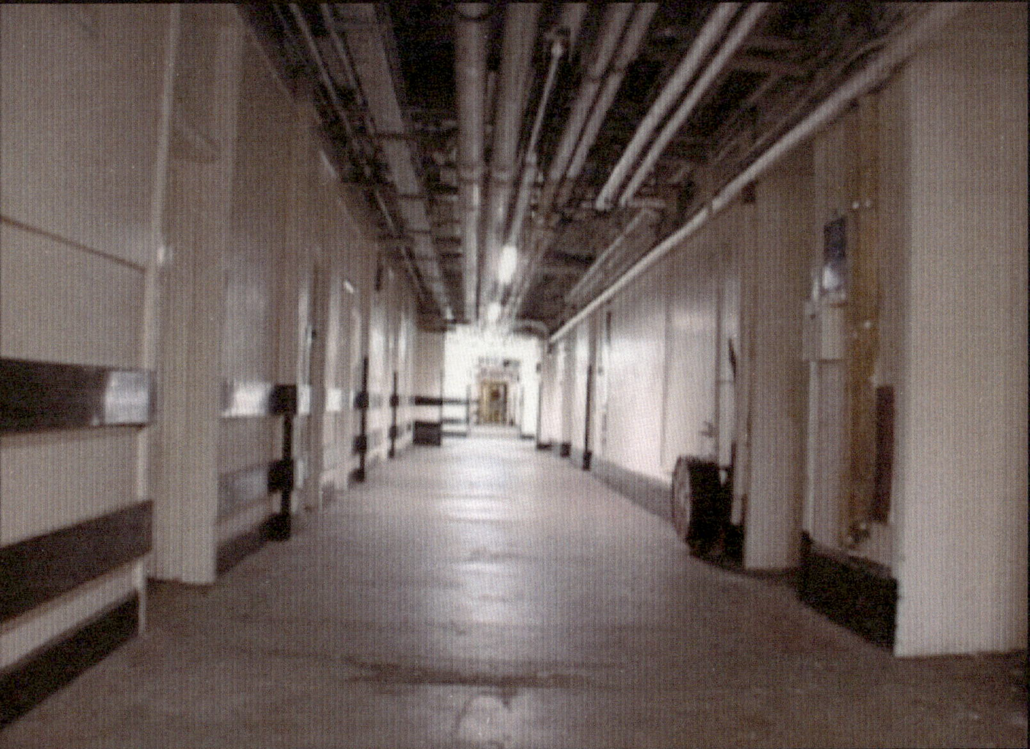

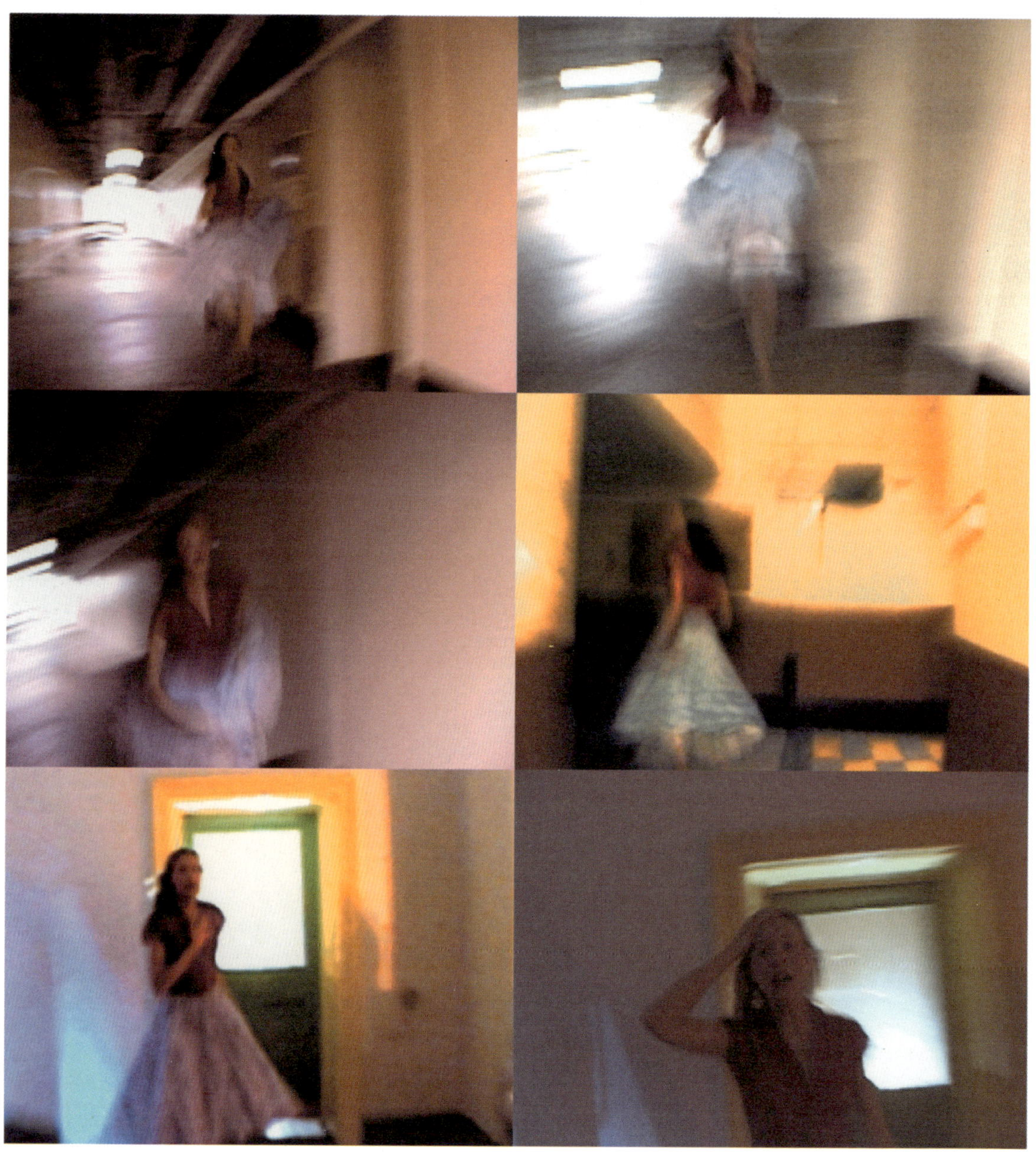

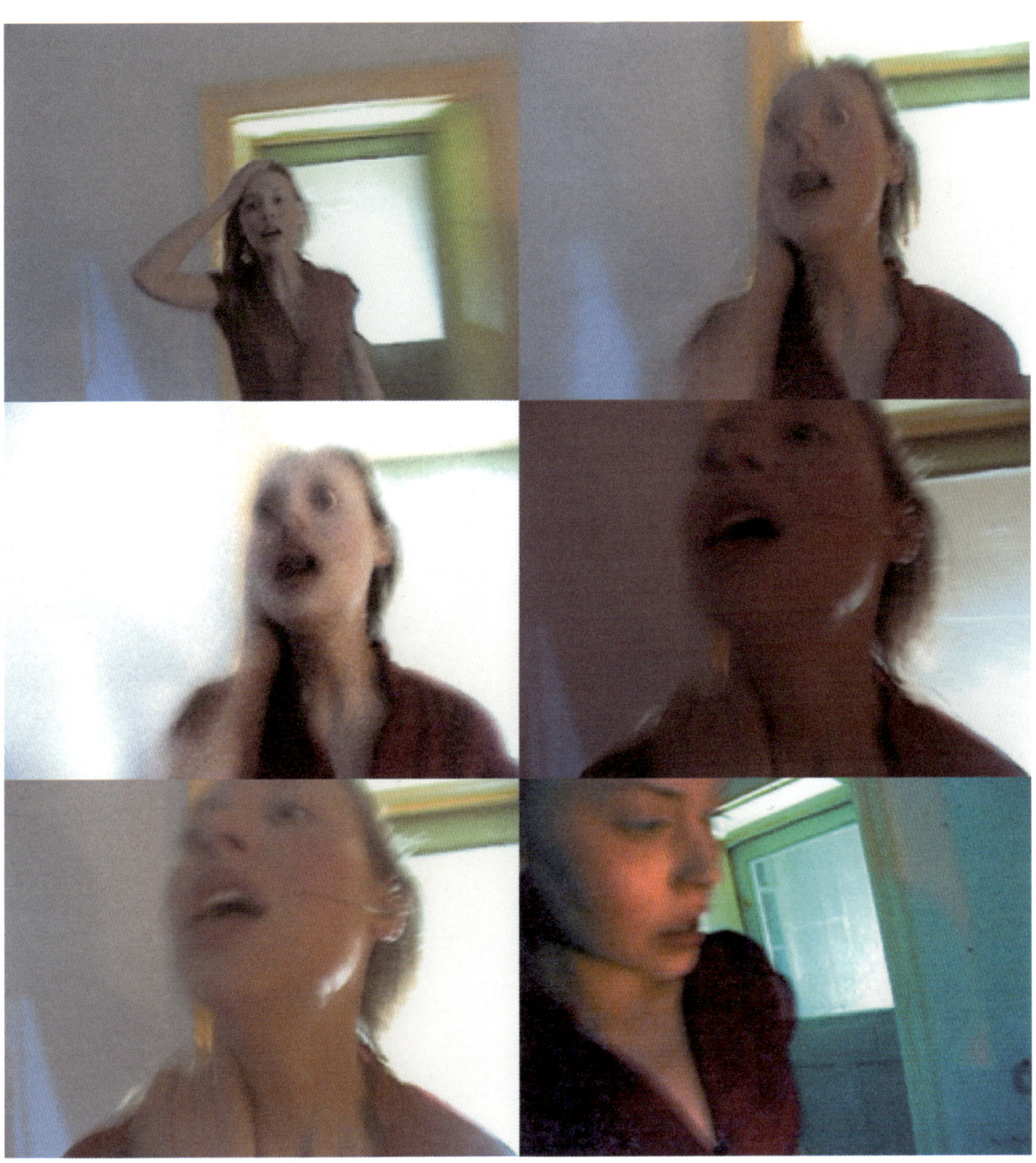

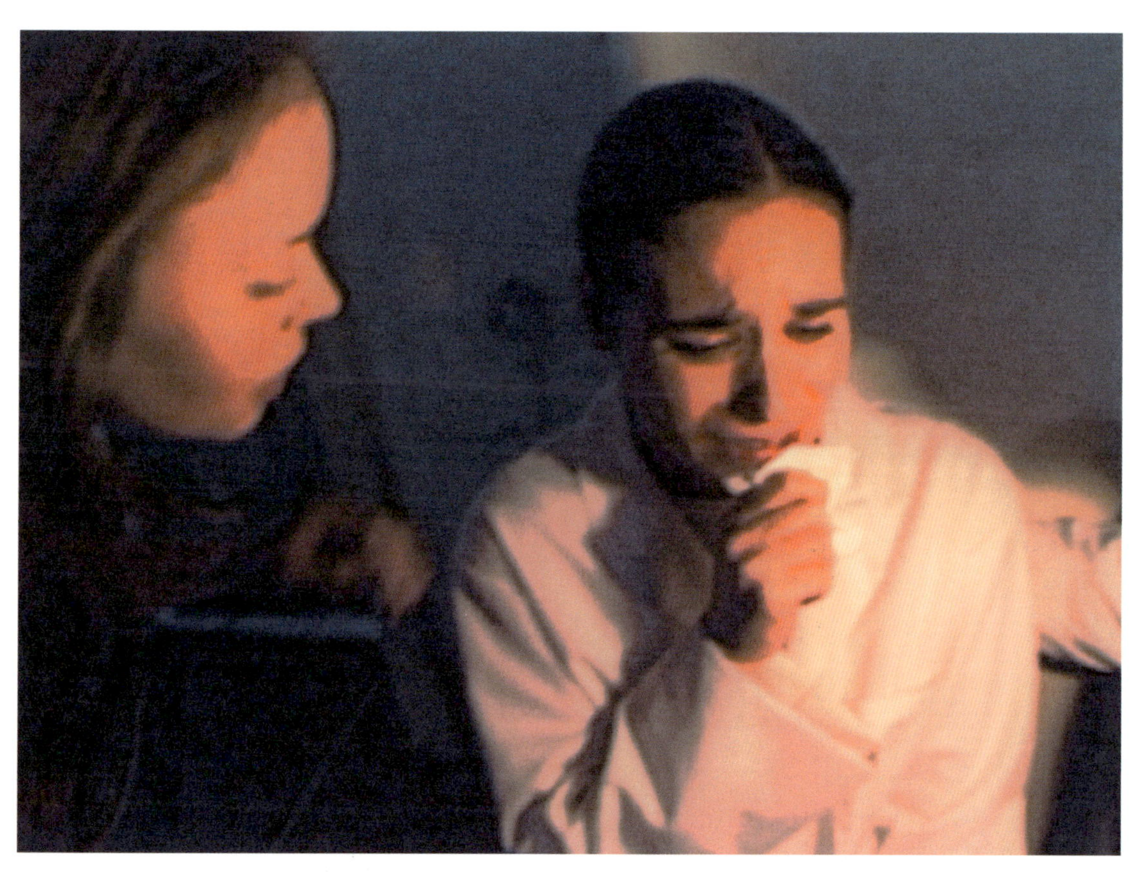

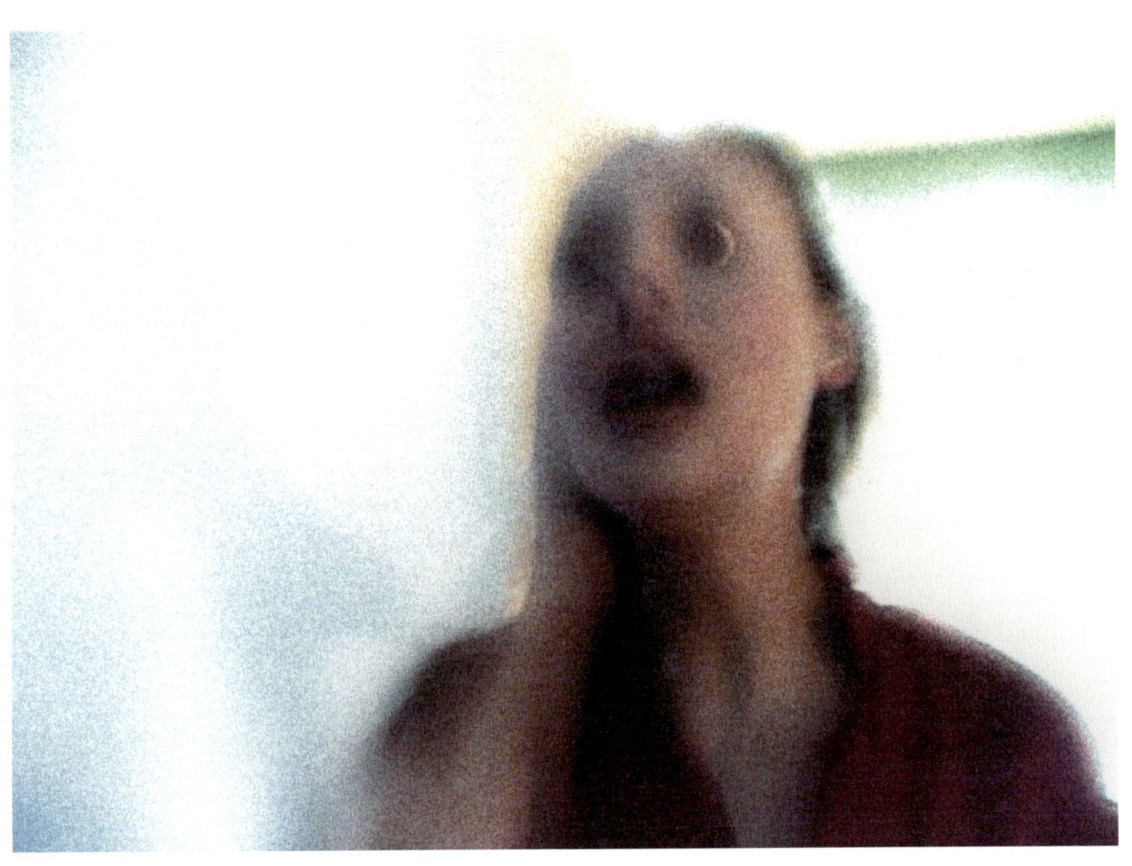

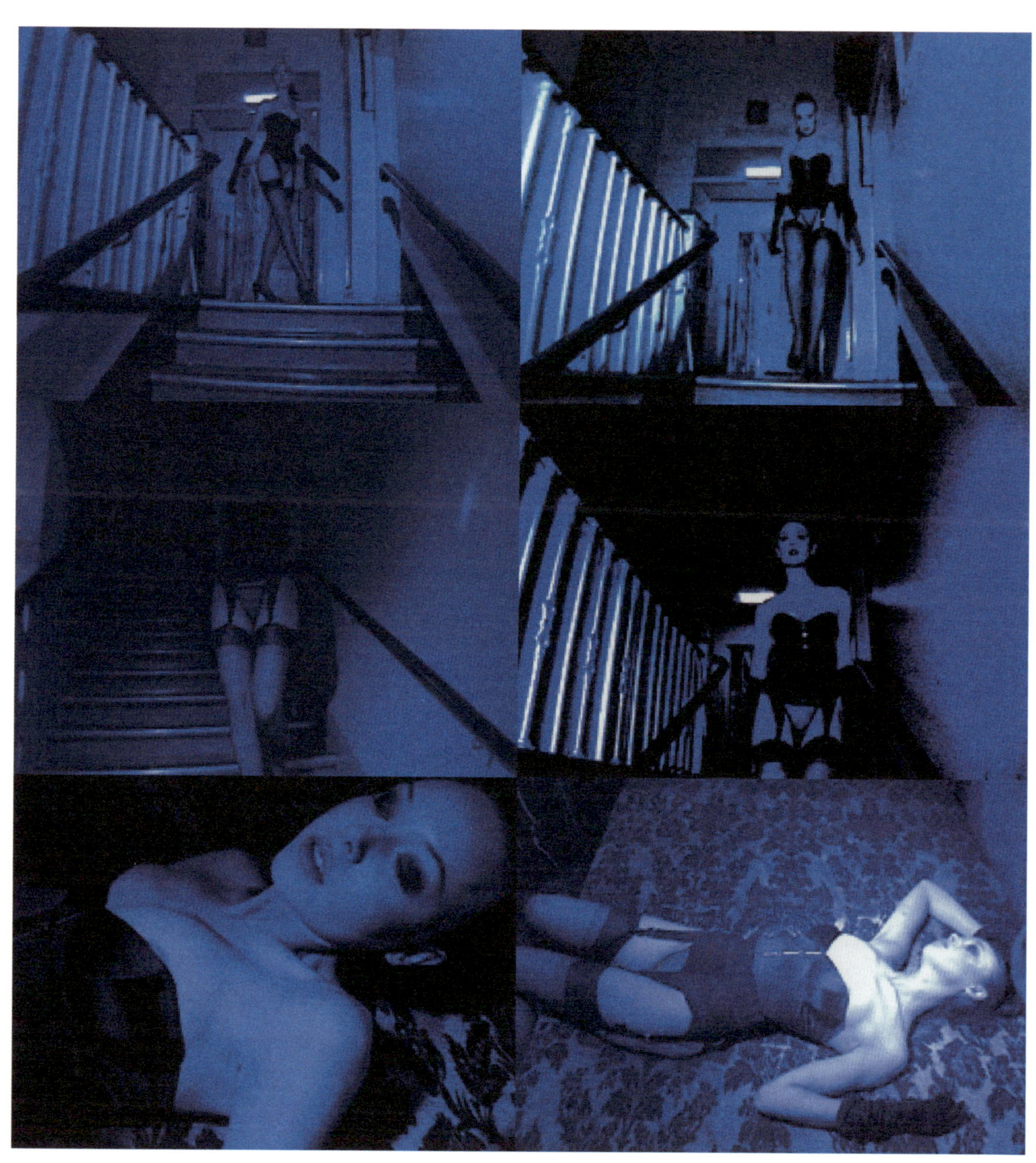

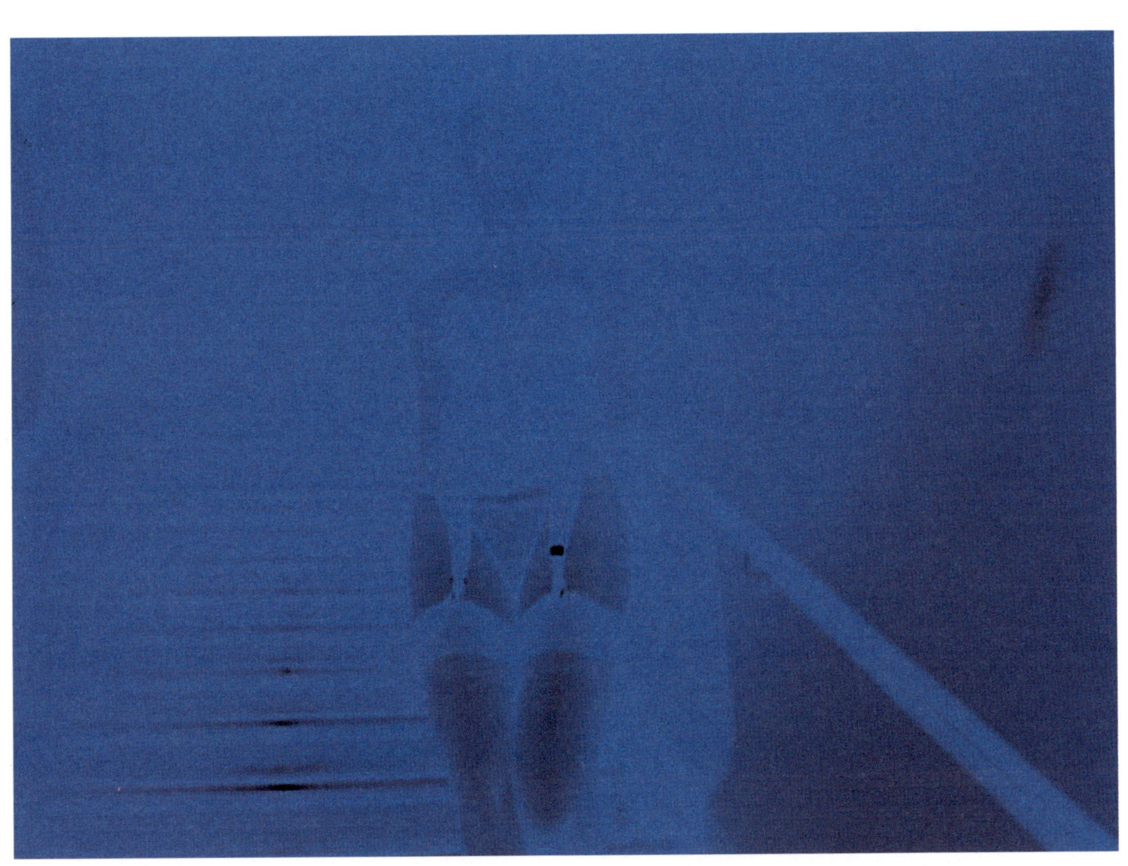

'Blue Movie'

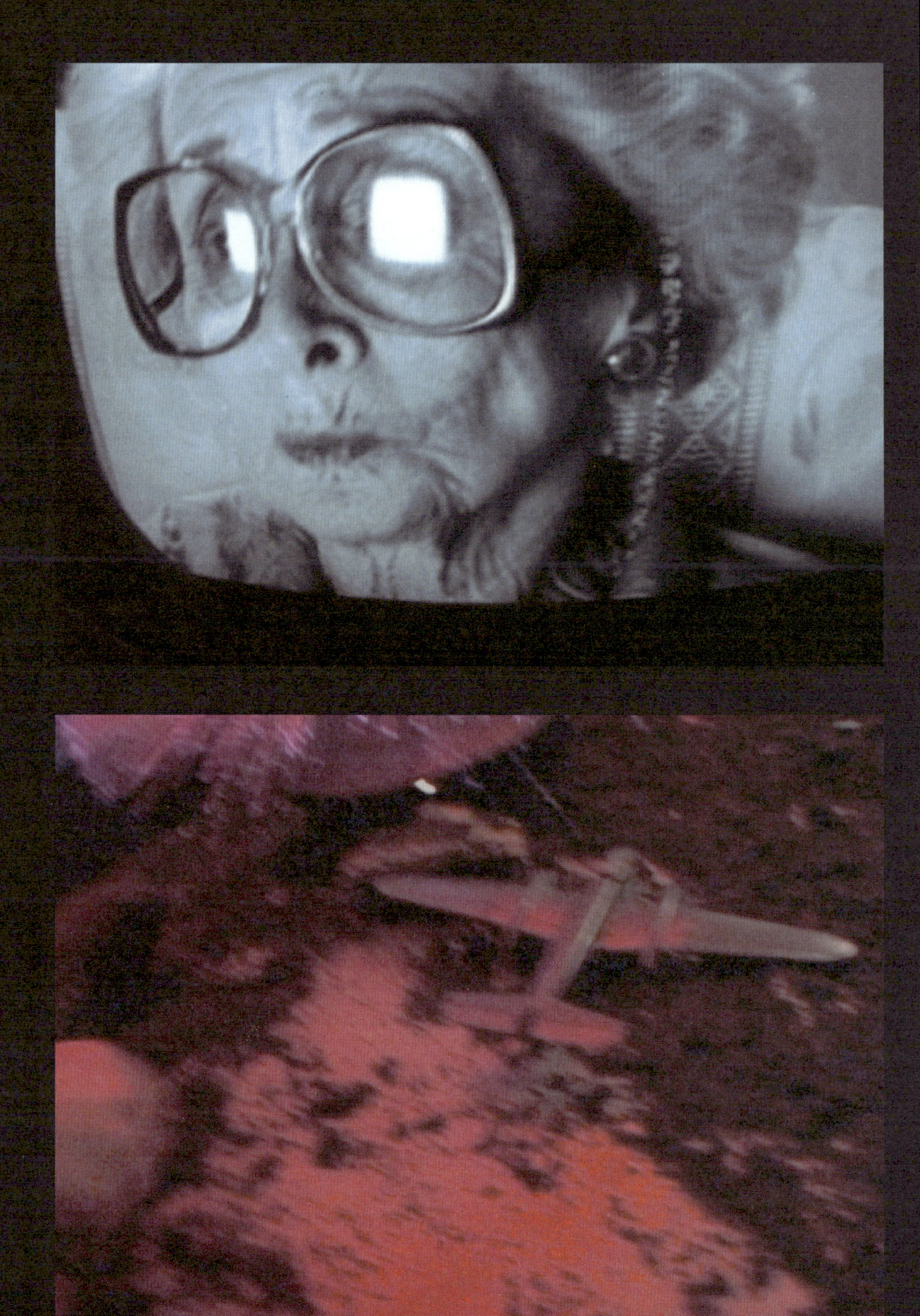

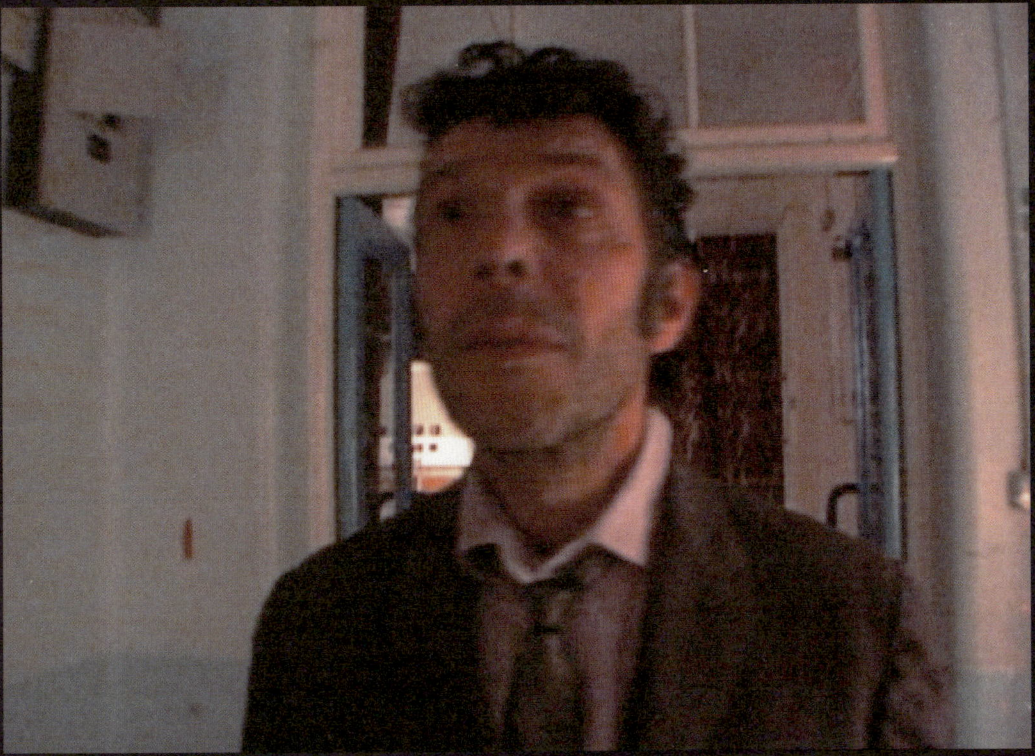

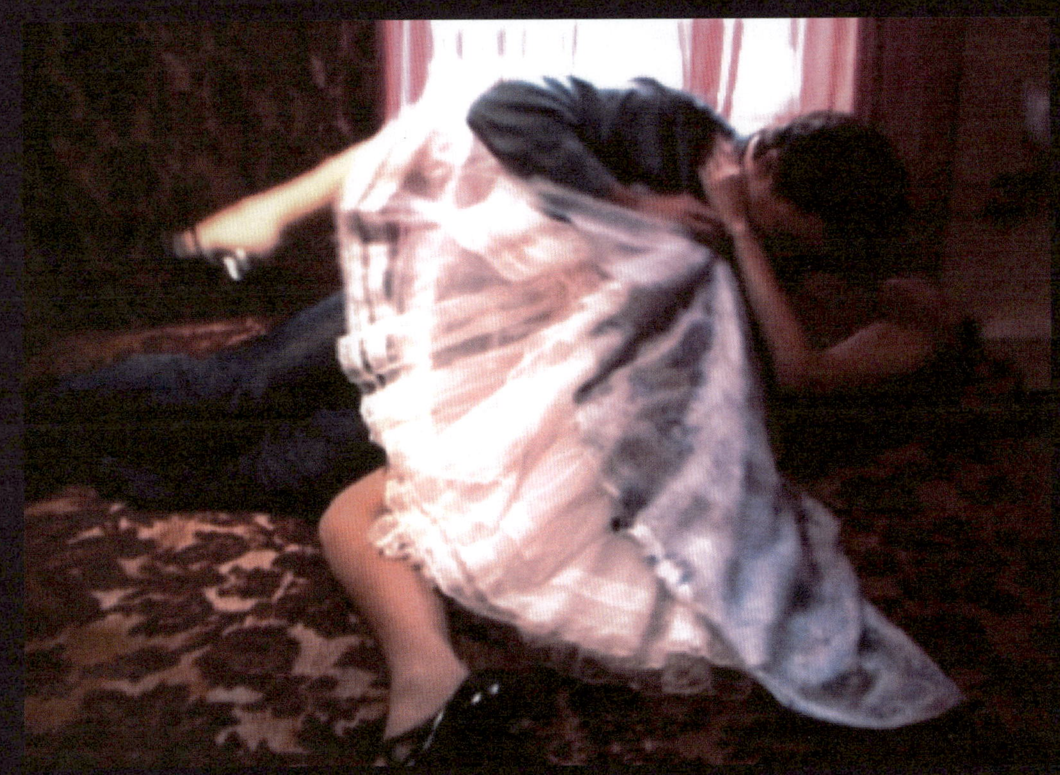

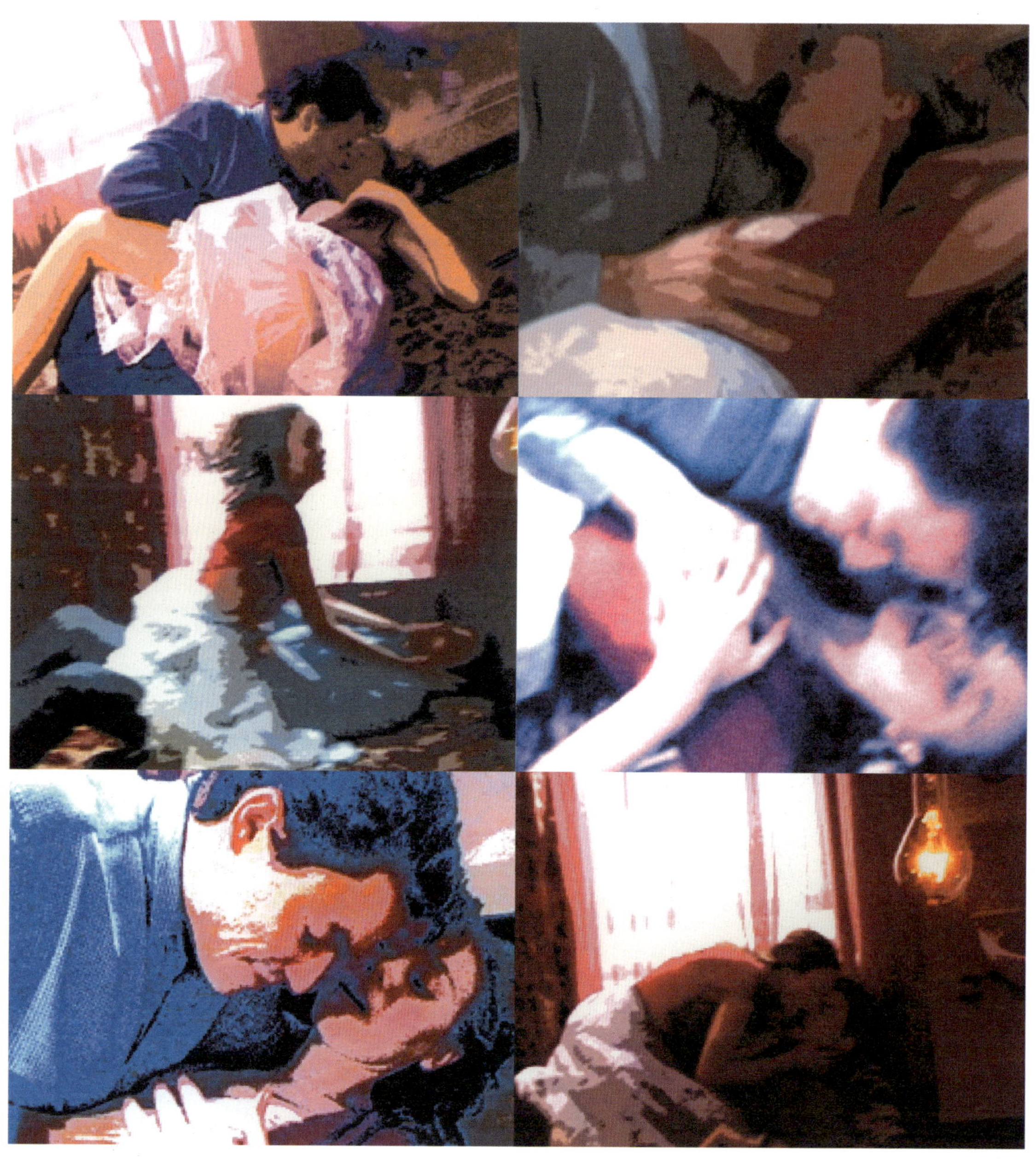

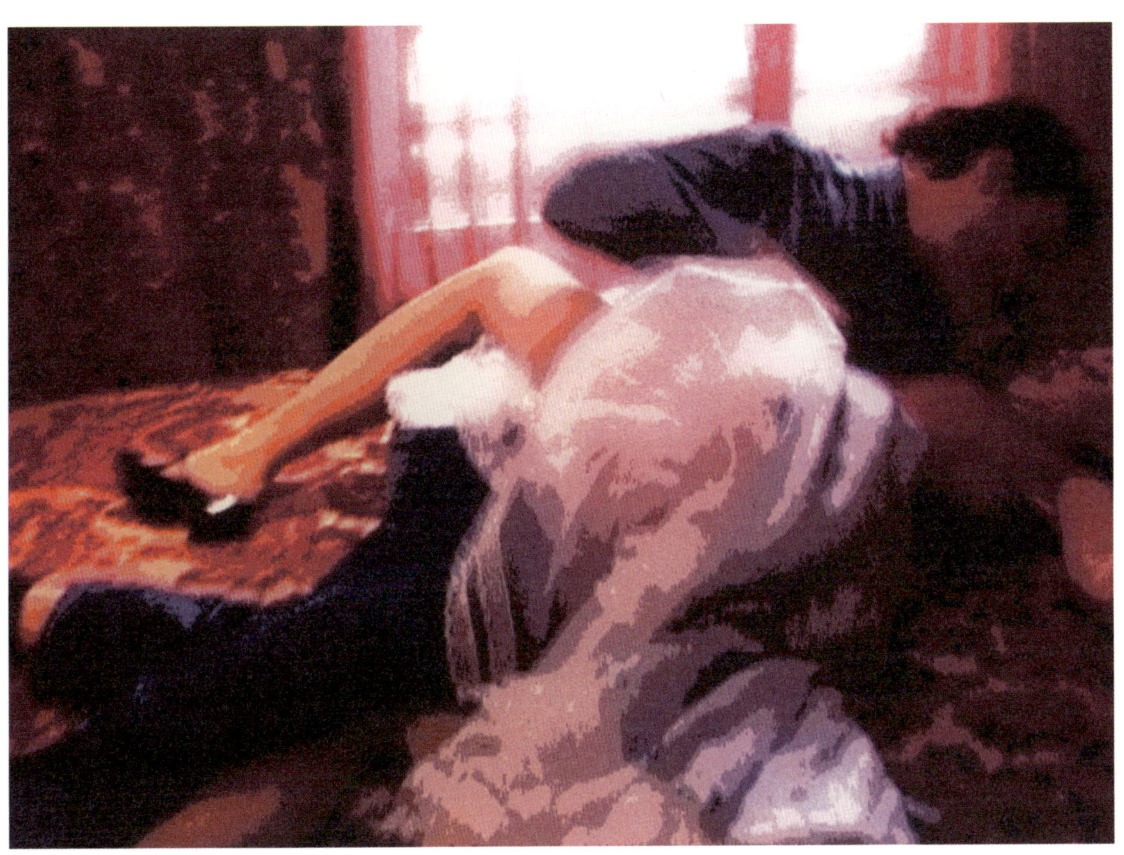

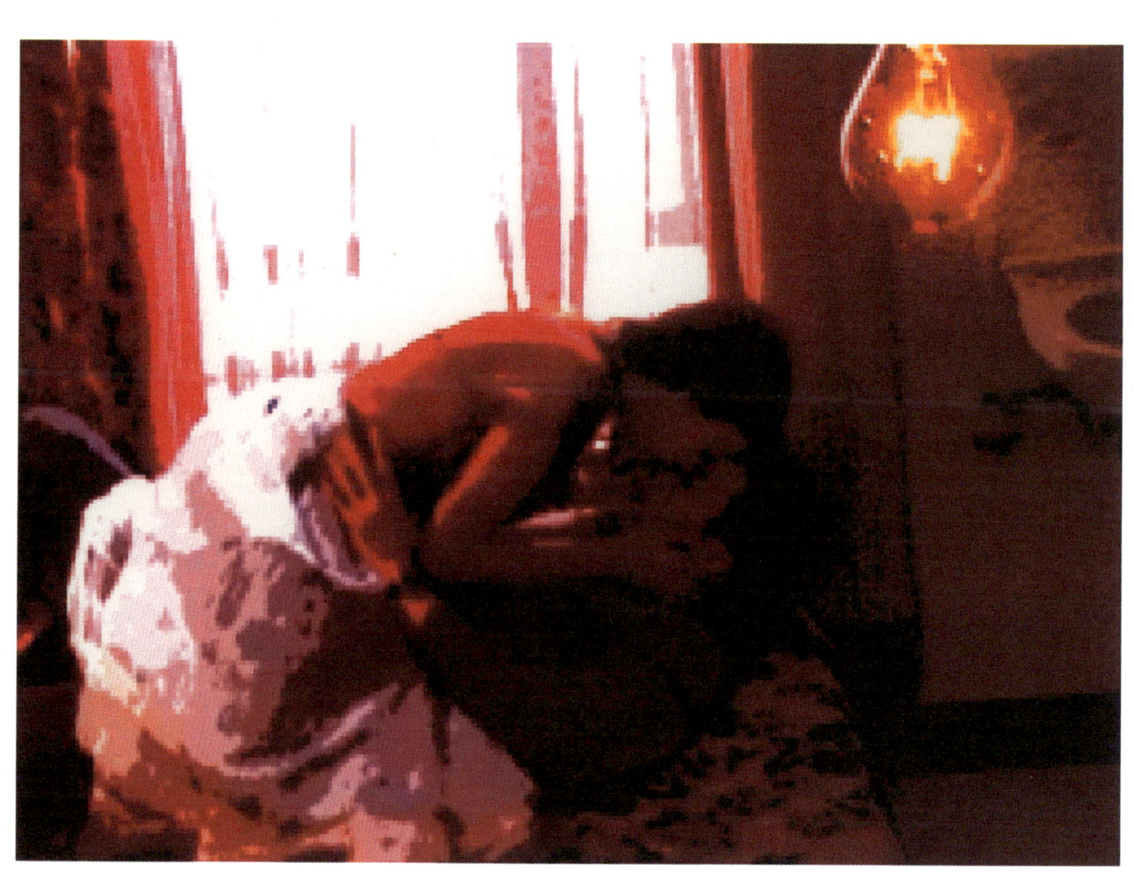

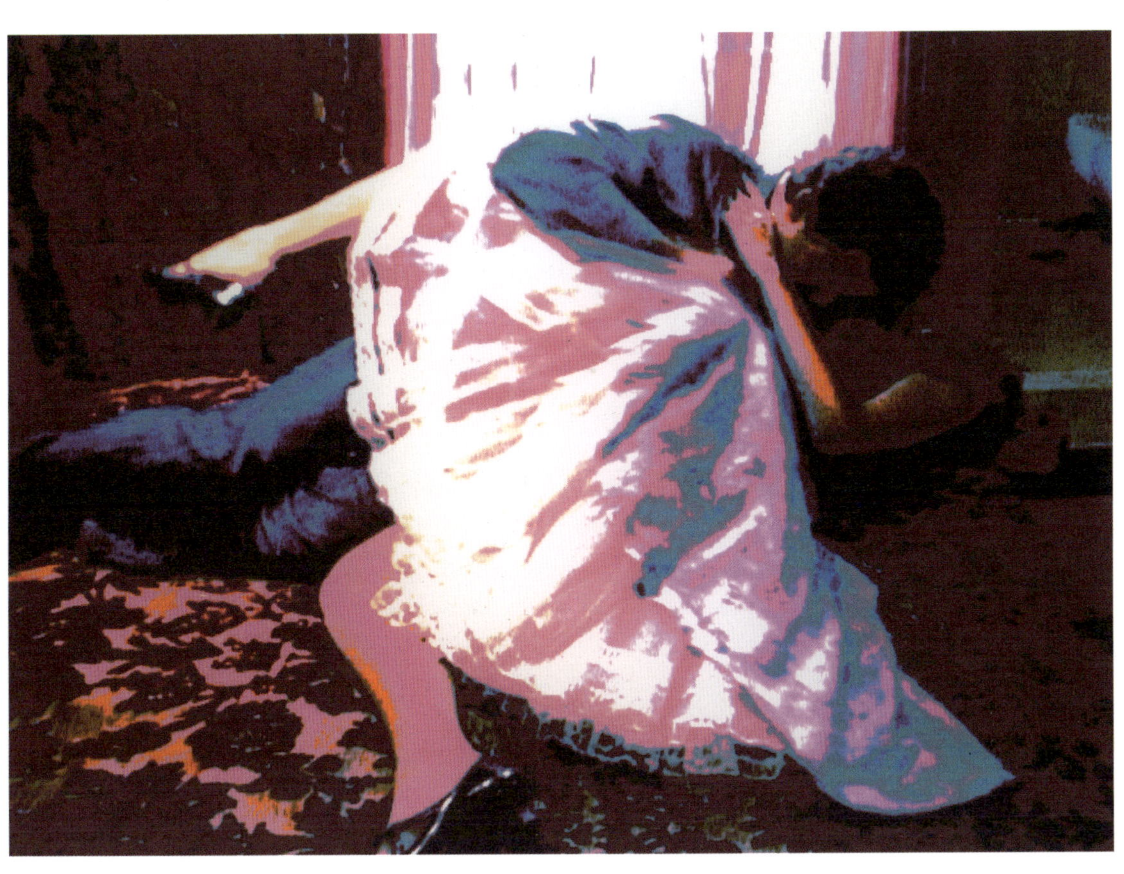

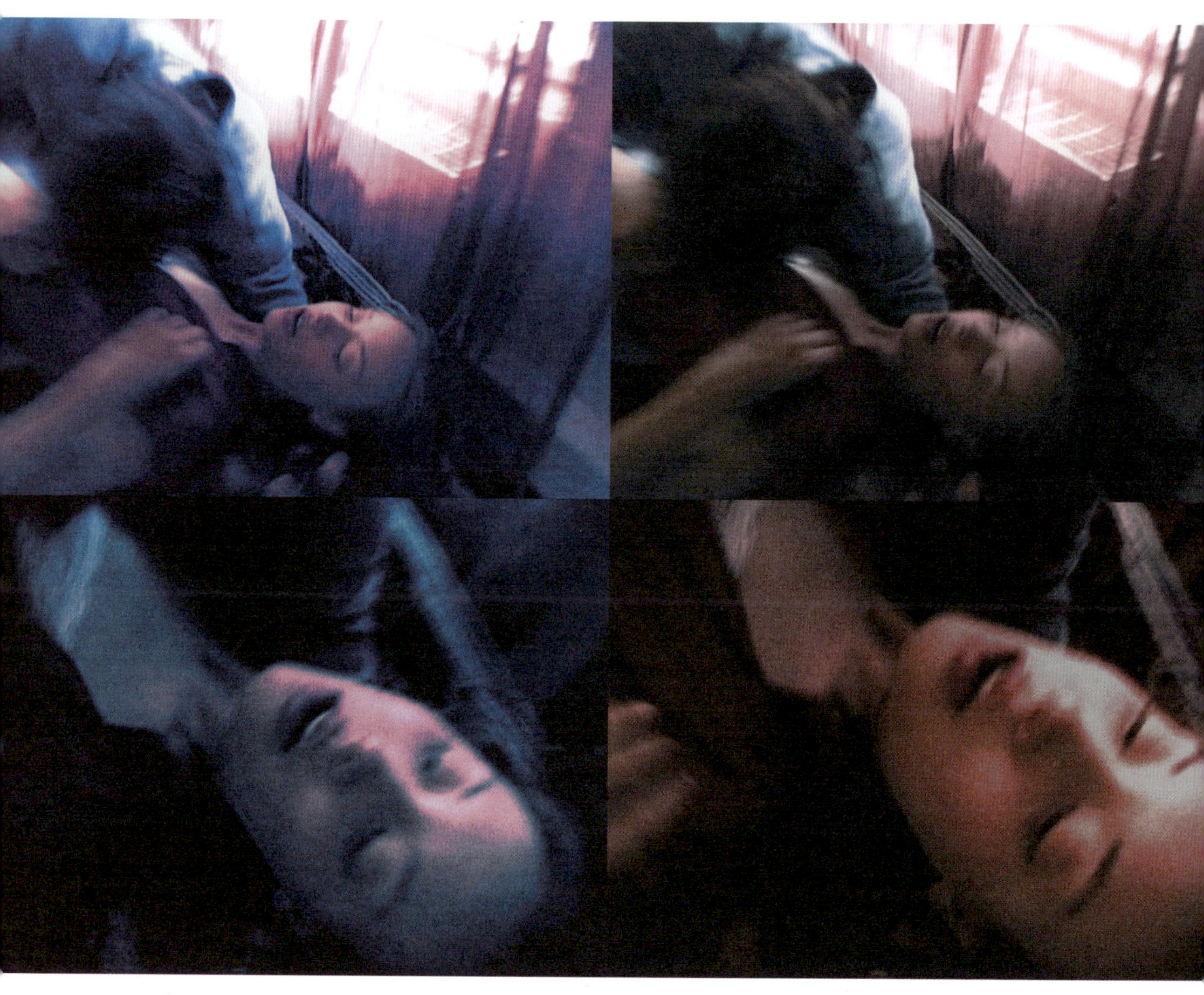

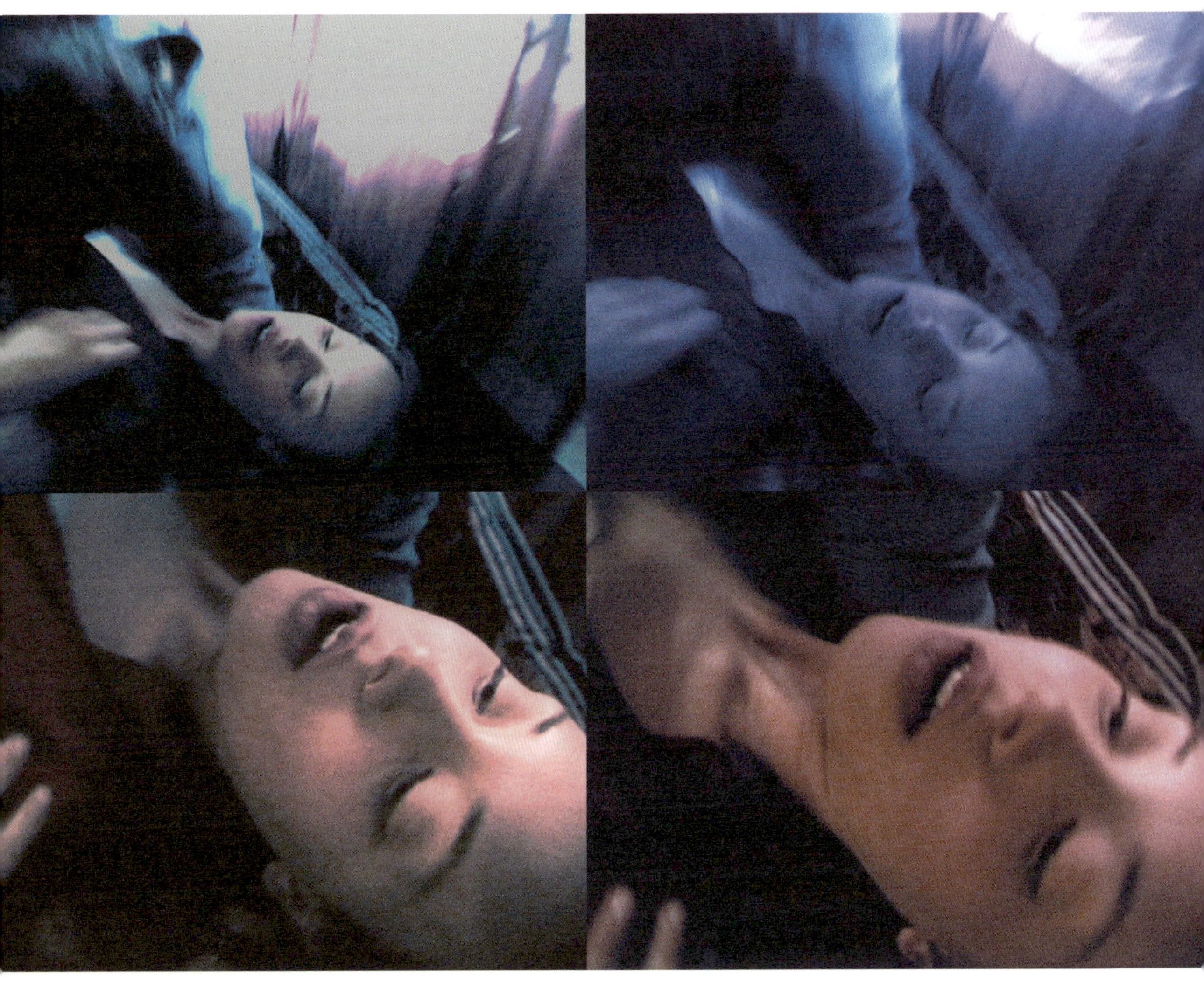

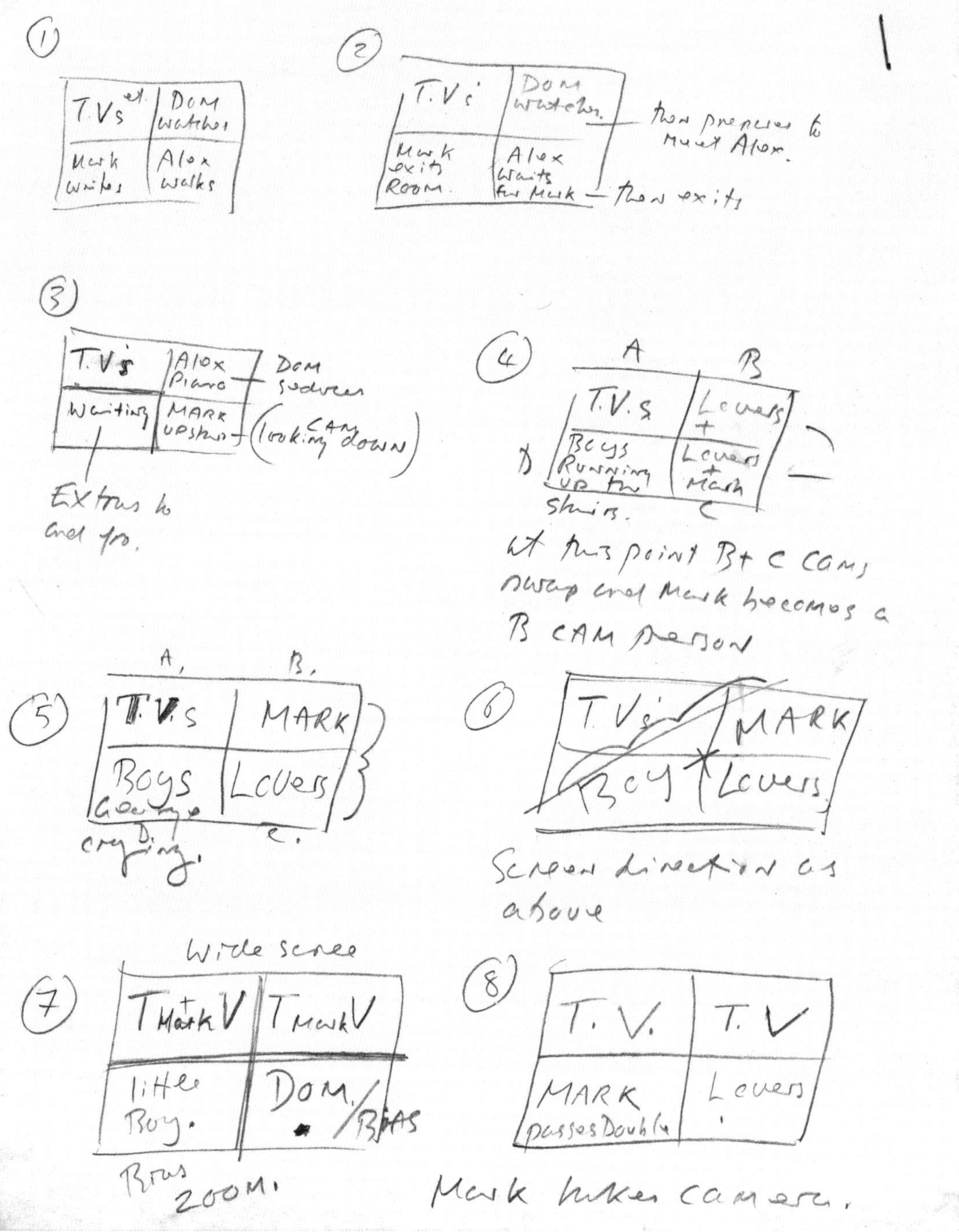

1
T.V's
DOM watches
Mark writes
Alex walks
2
T.V's
DOM watches
then prepares to meet Alex.
Mark exits ROOM.
Alex waits for Mark
then exits
3
T.V's
Alex Piano
DOM seduces
Waiting
MARK upstairs
CAM (looking DOWN)
Extras to end pro.
4
A
B
T.V.s
Lovers + Lovers
Boys Running up the Stairs.
Lovers + Mark
C
at this point B + C CAMS swap and Mark becomes a B CAM person
5
A,
B.
T.V.s
MARK
Boys Going crying.
Lovers
6
T.V's
MARK
BOY
Lovers.
Screen direction as above
Wide scree
7
T Mark V
T Mark V
little Boy.
DOM. / BIAS
Bias ZOOM.
8
T.V.
T.V
MARK passes Double
Lovers
Mark takes camera.

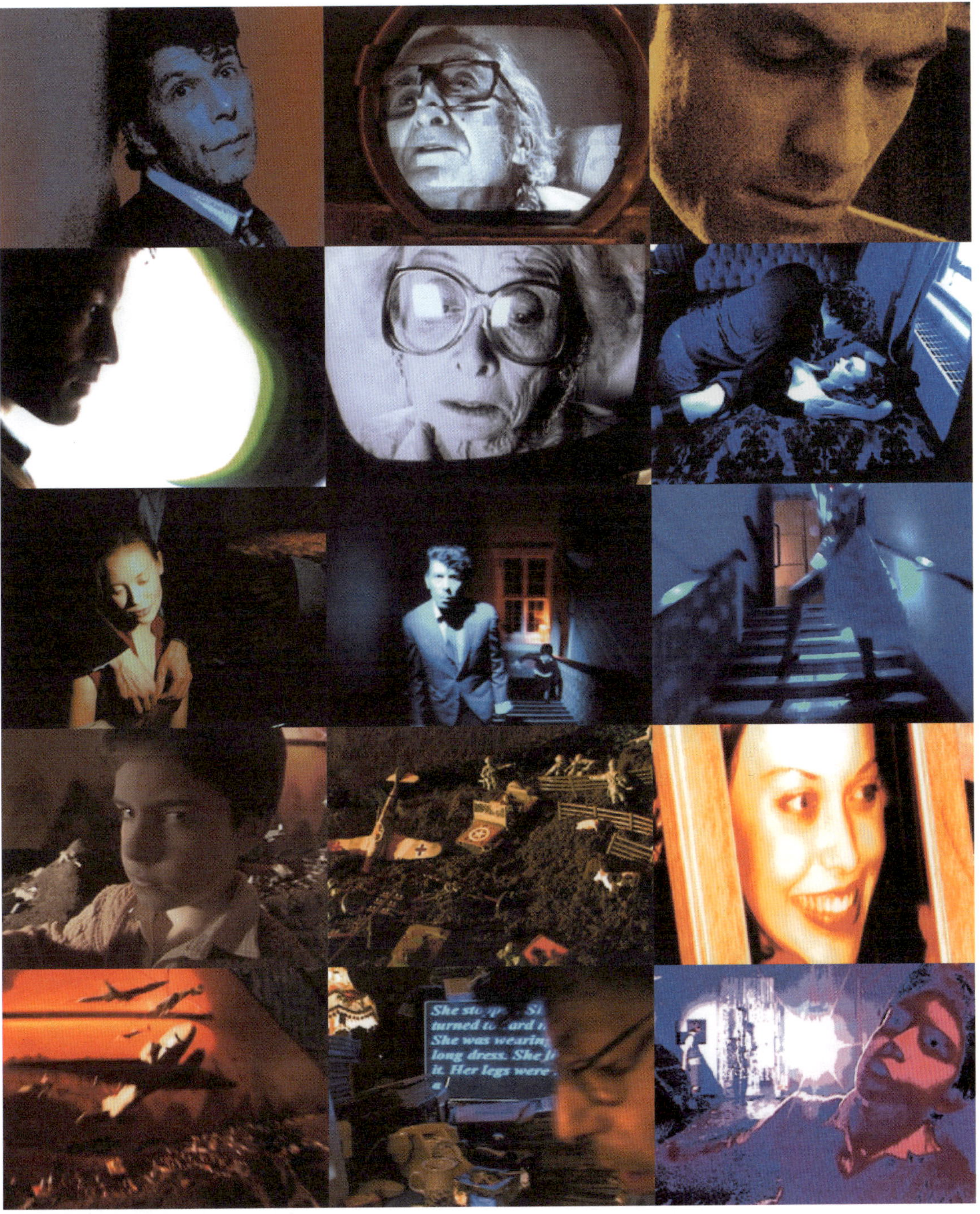
She
turned
She was
long dress. She
it. Her legs were

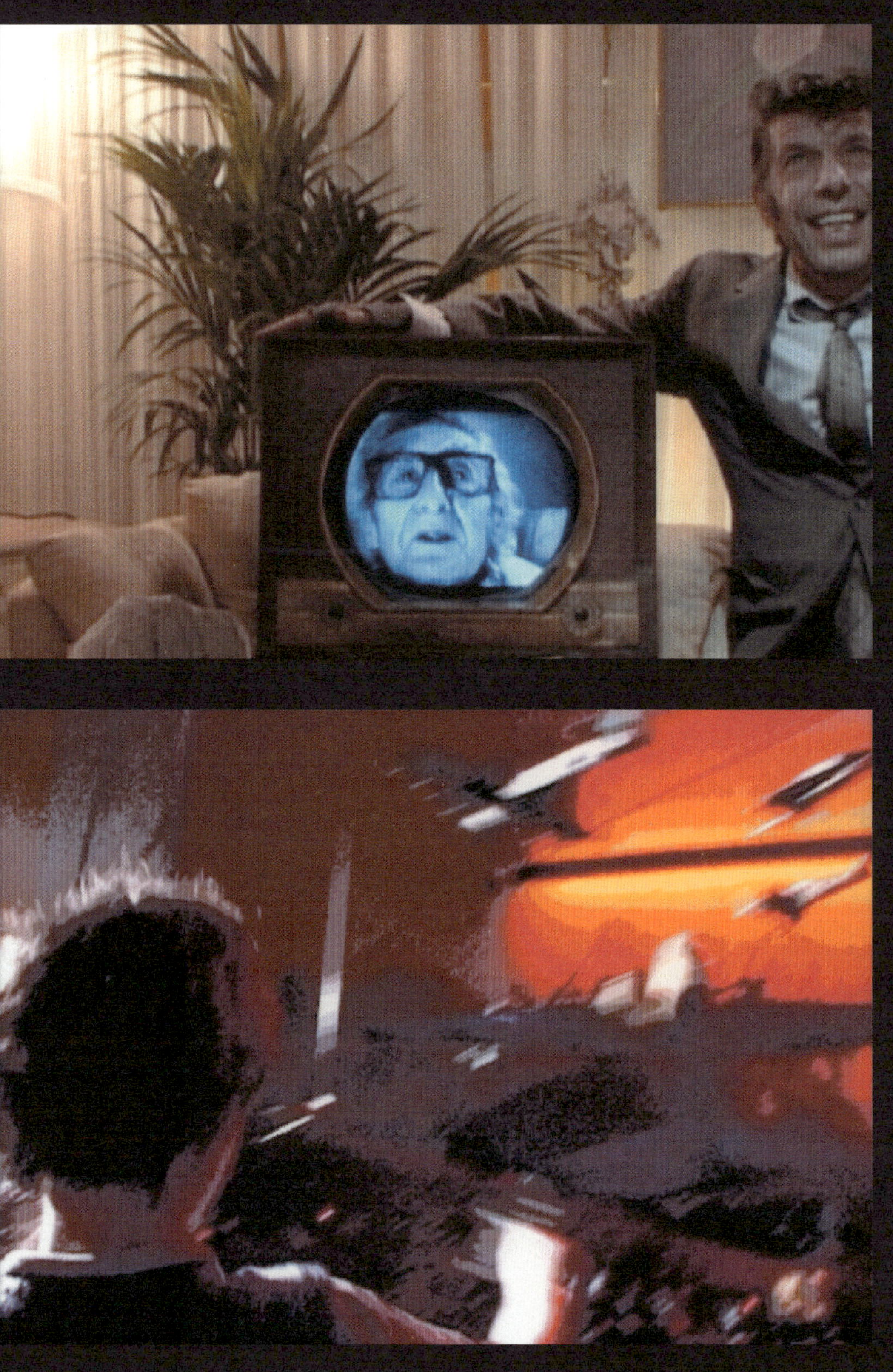

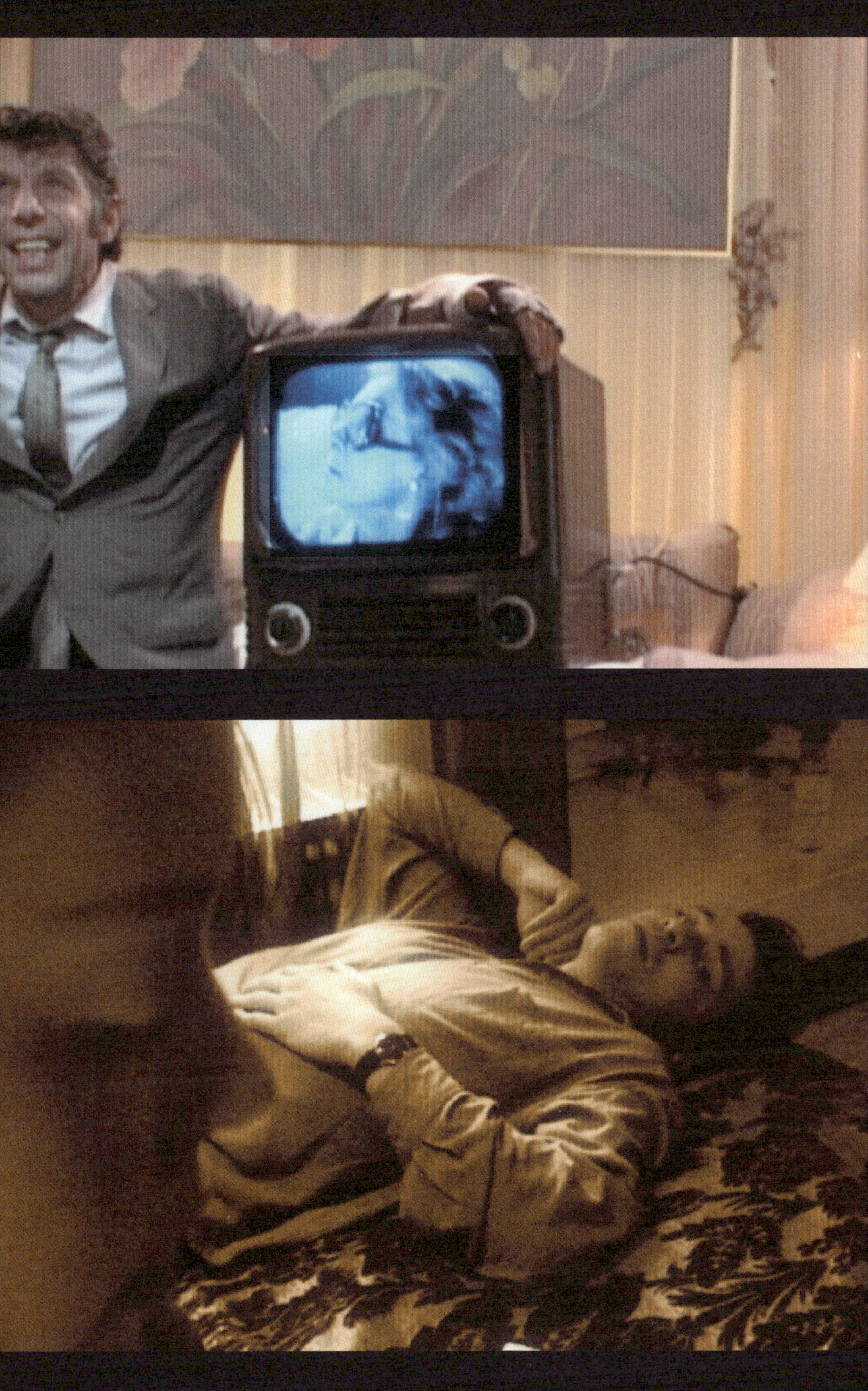

HOTEL, Venice, 2001

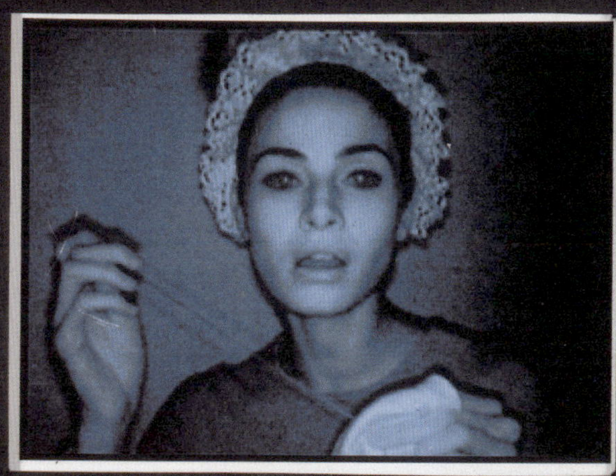

Hotel.

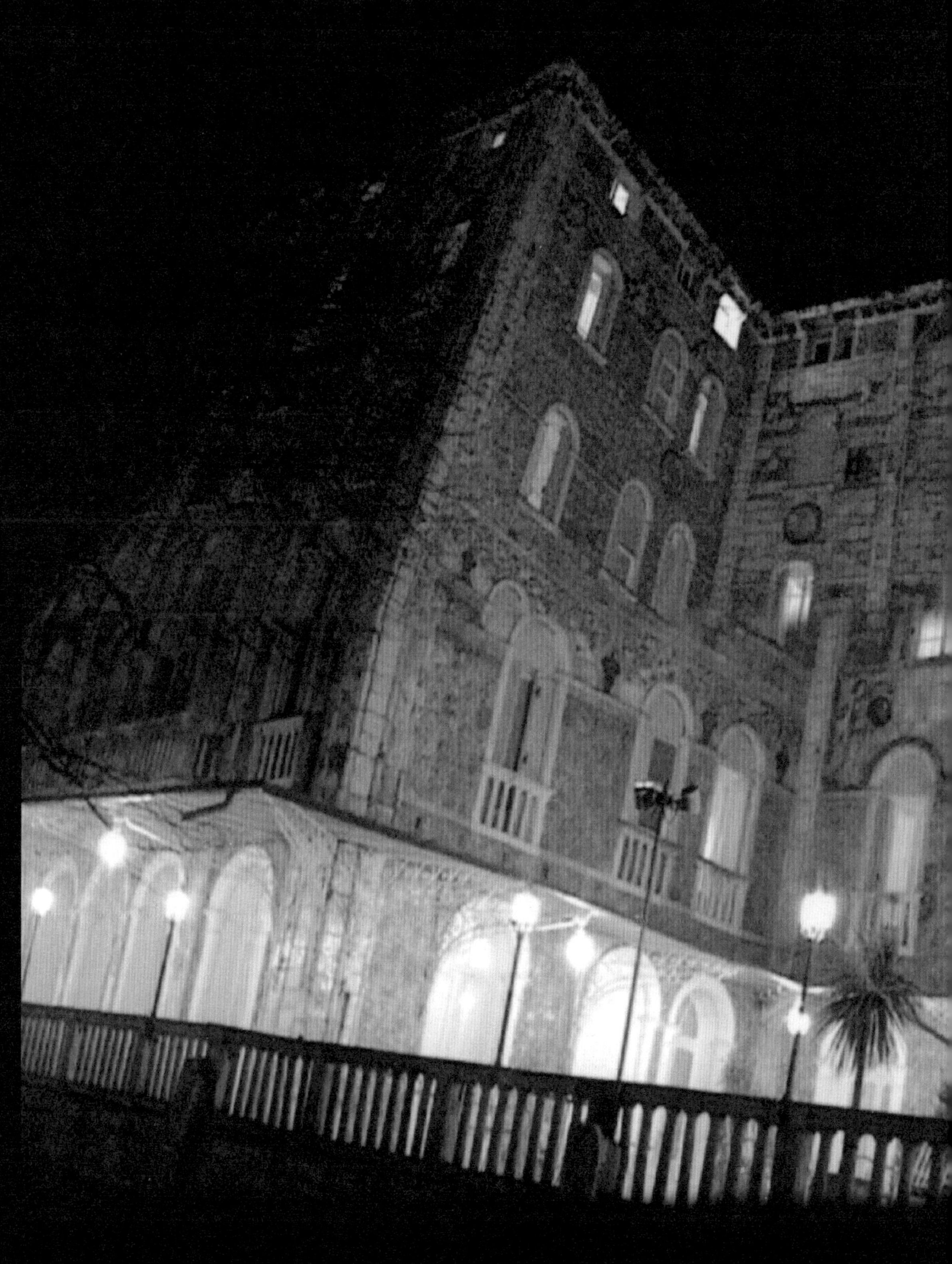

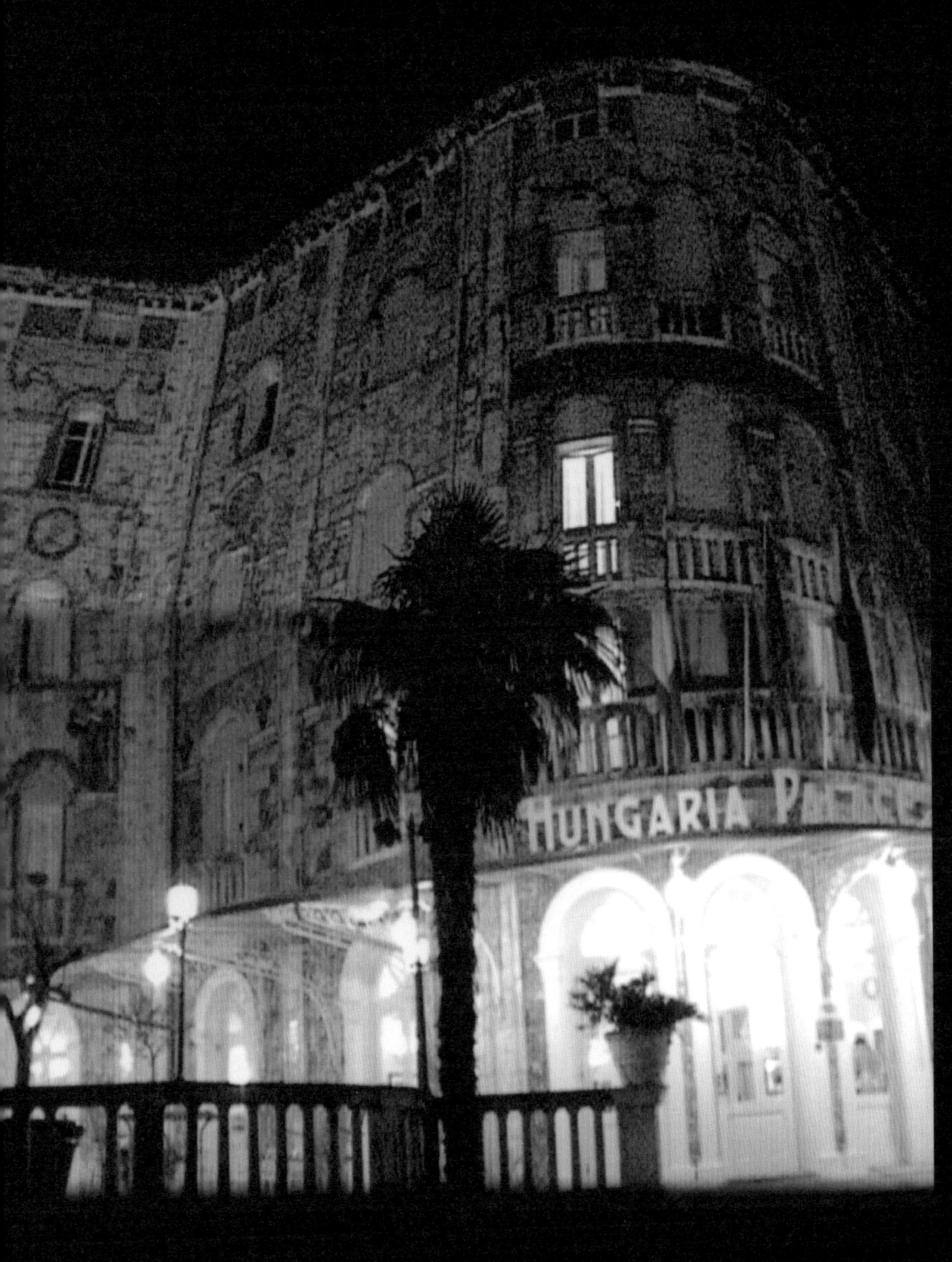
HUNGARIA

About voyeurism

I have always had a problem with cinema's essentially singular, voyeuristic eye, which loves looking through keyholes. If it is a thriller, that is acceptable, but there are elements of the porno-eye in pretty much all film-making and we love it because we are sitting in a gang of people facing in the same direction looking at a big, bright screen with this singular eye at our beck and call. As an artist you are suddenly in an area of perversity. Interestingly, Diane Arbus talked about this in terms of the action of taking a photograph. She said, I love the perversity of the moment. But until recently I always found that perversity uncomfortable.

If you ever film or photograph a nude, for example, it feels perverse, uncomfortable. But then something I realised when I was doing HOTEL was that as an artist, you have to find the courage to deal with the perversity of the moment and, if you can, then you can be more honest about what you are doing; you can have a dialogue with your actors – and not just discuss focus and lighting.

Life is perverse and I am attracted to extremes of behaviour between 1 human being and another – I see Goya as a mentor here – and I want to ask why people do extreme things, whether sexual or violent or physical or whatever – and speculate on the tragic in a certain and specific way.

The reason people are fascinated by sex is that it is fundamental to our lives, but in terms of our religious upbringing we feel there is something post-Adam and Eve about it, dirty and hidden. I suddenly discovered that when you use 4 screens and you deal, for example, with something erotic, it somehow diffuses the perversity because you are not 1 person looking through a keyhole any more. You are 1 of 4, in the case of a quadrant, so you are able to look more analytically. Anything which technically allows you to look at any subject – life, death, sex, tragedy, whatever – with 4 different angles at the same time can help to open it up.

Really great novelists have done that. Film has to work on a different level because it is not so intellectual – but nonetheless, I think that looking through 4 cameras can help us see in much more satisfying and adult ways. And it was lovely to discover that, almost accidentally.

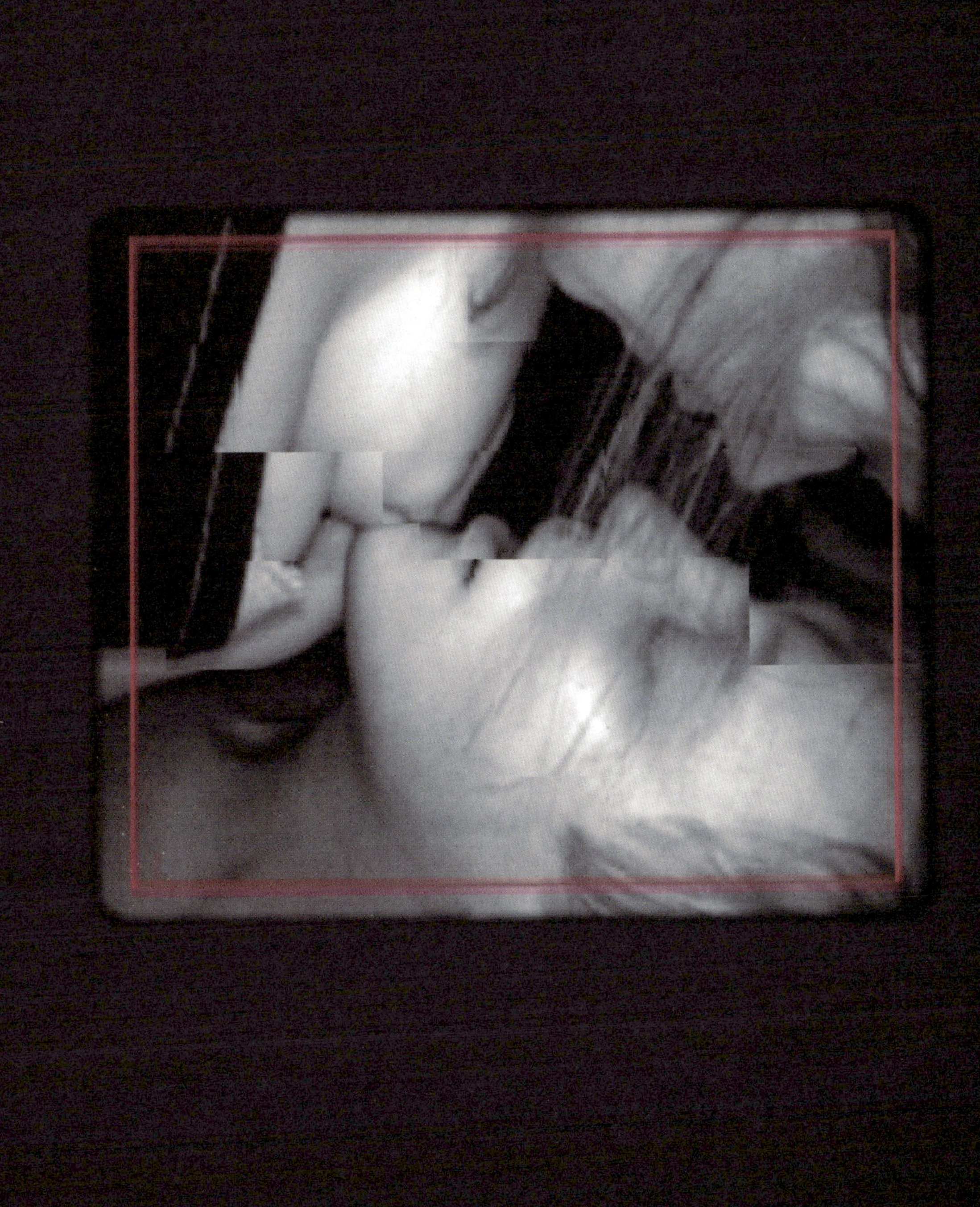

THE PREMISE

Imagine if you will, a rather magnificent HOTEL on the Lido, Venice. Built at the turn of the 20th century with an Art Deco façade and beautiful wooden floors in every bedroom.

It is the kind of HOTEL that gives one a sense of security, a sense of a time when the world was a kinder place.

But dig a little deeper and you will begin to see that this hotel is not quite what it seems.

The 4 cameras of the film take us into every nook and cranny of the HOTEL. To the 4th floor which is out of bounds to the guests and through the basement kitchen to a series of cellars (but where the Secret Police seem to have a torture room); we begin to see an entirely different world.

As the film progresses we enter a world of dark sexual intrigue where no one is quite what they seem and the staff are more in control than the guests.

WHO ARE THE GUESTS?

1. An **American film director**, his **producer**, his **actress** (also his current girlfriend). The film they are shooting is a **DOGME-style period film** set in the ancient city of Venice. (Written specially for HOTEL in the style of Shakespeare). The production is in trouble, they are behind schedule and budget and the studio is threatening to close them down. The producer is trying to talk some sense into the director but he is stubborn and refusing to compromise his "artistic vision". The Americans hate being away from the US and refuse to speak the language and hate the food. They are not happy.
2. **BORIS and GRETA**, an **eastern European couple** who are here to do shady business deals. He is some kind of sleazy politician and she is his trophy wife. He' s a pig and she' s on the make. He uses her to seduce other politicians.
3. A killer called **MAGIC** who is addicted to strangeness and has to have sex just after he' s bumped someone off. **TONY** may well be bumping off characters throughout the film.
4. **SOPHIE**, a **very expensive call girl** who has her own business suite in the HOTEL. Perhaps she is Russian?

OTHER CHARACTERS

5. The **MAID**, there are many maids, but this one is very important. At first she seems ordinary, timid even. But as the film progresses we see how important she is. She has the master key to every room in the hotel and the camera follows her everywhere. She becomes more exotic, strange, sexual as the film progresses. No one seems to notice her as she takes the order of croissant and coffee to the torture room, or Madame Sophie' s suite.
6. **QUINTUS**, the **tour guide**. A failed English actor who now conducts guided tours of the ancient city of Venice. His dialogue is an odd mix of truth and lies,and he leads a double life, his other job being as chief torturer for the police in the darkness of the cellars.

1. MAX BEESLEY is ANTONIO in the DUCHESS OF MALFI
2. FABRIZIO BENTIVOGLIO plays a FAMOUS DOCTOR
3. BRIAN BOVELL is one of the Malfi actors, THE CARDINAL
4. SAFFRON BURROWS plays NAOMI, the leading actress in the Dogme film. She is the DUCHESS.
5. ELISABETTA CAVALLOTTI plays a HOTEL GUEST and she is abducted by the hotel staff.
6. VALENTINA CERVI plays the MAID, a strange woman who works in the hotel and becomes involved with TRENT once he has been shot and is in a coma.
7. GEORGE DICENZO is BORIS, a film producer with a taste for sex and dairy produce.
8. ANDREA Di STEFANO plays a KILLER, a death figure.
9. NICOLA FARRON is a LOVER in the hotel.
10. CHRISTOPHER FULFORD plays the BUSINESSMAN who gets involved in the red dress scenario.
11. VALERIA GOLINO is an ACTRESS in the Dogme film. She becomes involved with the hotel vampires.
12. JEREMY HARDY plays BURT REYNOLDS' s ASSISTANT.
13. SALMA HAYEK plays CHARLEE BOUX, the video jock who is making an MTV style documentary about the Dogme Malfi.
14. DANNY HUSTON plays the HOTEL MANAGER. All of the hotel staff are vampires.
15. RHYS IFANS plays TRENT, the director of the Dogme film.
16. JASON ISAACS plays an Australian actor called GAVIN, who leaves the film to work with Ridley Scott.
17. PACO JARANA is a FLAMENCO GUITARIST, husband of EVA, THE DANCER.
18. LUCY LIU plays KAWIKA, an ambitious video jock who visits the film and takes over from CHARLEE.
19. MARK LONG is a strange HOTEL WORKER.
20. MIA MAESTRO plays the Duchess of Malfi' s maid, CARIOLA, in the Dogme film that is being shot in Venice.
21. JOHN MALKOVICH is hotel guest OMAR JONSSON.
22. CHIARA MASTROIANNI plays a woman who lives in the hotel. She could be described as a gay vampire. She becomes the NIGHT NURSE of the character TRENT.
23. LAURA MORANTE plays GRETA, the wife of BORIS. She is unhappy but ends up with the KILLER.
24. ORNELLA MUTI appears briefly in the film as a member of a Flamenco troupe.
25. BURT REYNOLDS plays the MANAGER of a Flamenco troupe.
26. STEFANIA ROCCA is SOPHIE, a prostitute in a red dress. She is also SOPHIE' S TWIN BROTHER, who works, briefly as a WAITER in the hotel.
27. JULIAN SANDS plays QUINTAS, a right-wing tour guide who lives in the hotel and is also a vampire.
28. DANNY SAPANI plays AJ, CHARLEE' S producer.
29. DAVID SCHWIMMER plays JONATHAN, the producer of the film that is being shot in the hotel. He takes over from TRENT after his "accident".
30. ALEXANDRA STADEN plays a PA on the film.
31. MARK STRONG is FERDINAND, in the Dogme Malfi.
32. HEATHCOTE WILLIAMS plays BOSOLA in the Dogme Malfi.
33. EVA LA YERBABUENA plays herself, Flamenco dancer extrordinaire.

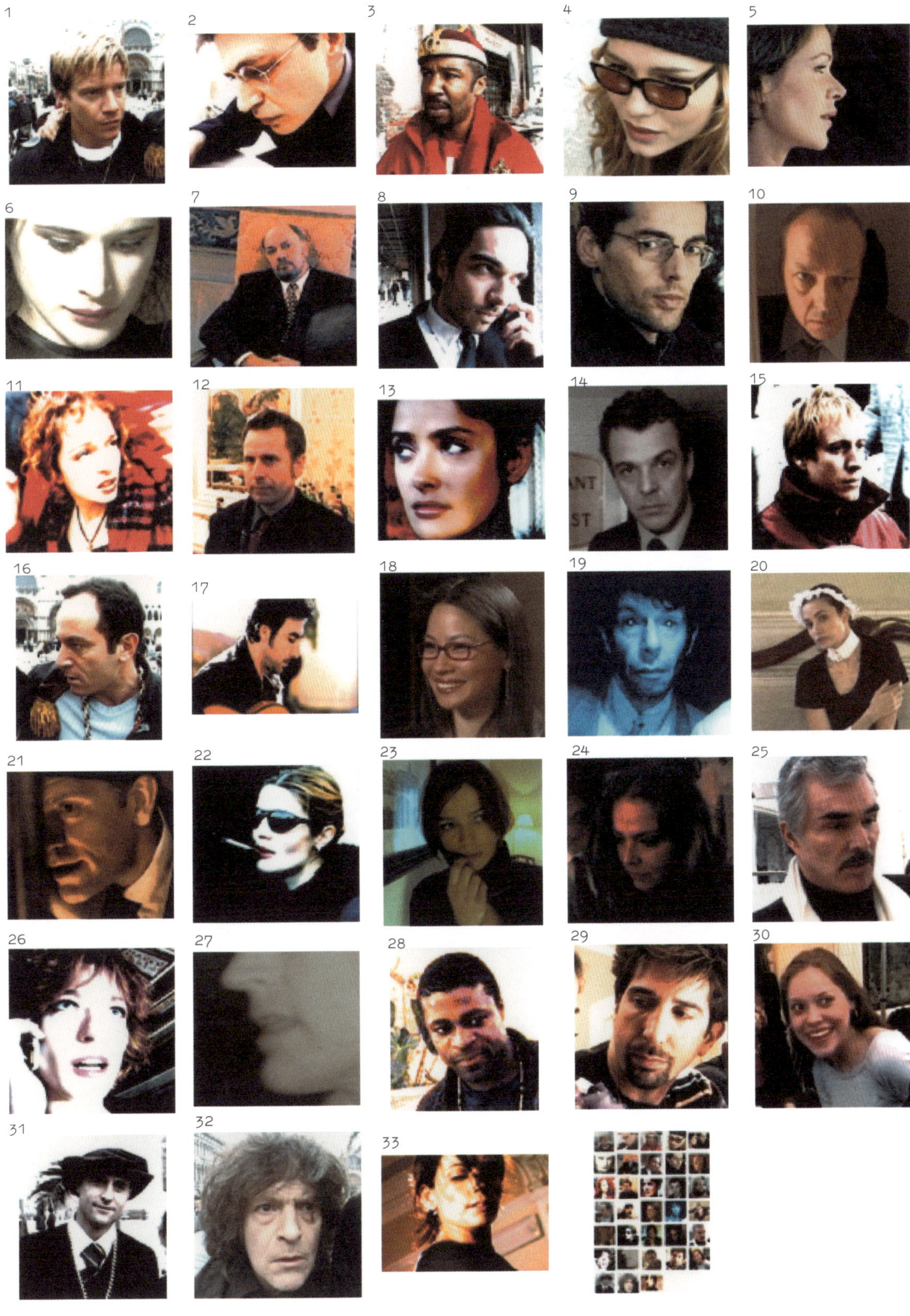
1
2
3
4
5
6
7
8
9
10
11
12
13
14
15
16
17
18
19
20
21
22
23
24
25
26
27
28
29
30
31
32
33

Letter e-mailed to all of the actors before the shoot began.

3/12/2001

I'm putting together an ensemble of actors and film people to make a digital movie in Venice. Last year I did TIMECODE in LA and it was a very interesting three week event. I think everyone got something out of it and it was one of the best working experiences I've had in the film business.

Venice is a magical environment to work in. Just walking around the town gave me so much inspiration. We will be shooting for about five weeks. The main location is an hotel on the Lido, the rest will be out and about in Venice itself. I thought it would be useful to lay down some thoughts about the system that I wish to use. I'd hate to have this come as a surprise later on.

1. I like the actors to wear their own clothes. This is not a hard and fast rule. Clothes can always be found and we do have a wardrobe mistress, so cleaning the clothes is done by that department. I ask the actors to bring a selection of their own clothes. Because of the way I shoot it is possible to wear different clothes on different days. Continuity is not an issue.
2. There is no hair or make-up department. Actors are responsible for their own appearance. Working with digital cameras and available light means that make-up is not as crucial anyway.
3. There is no transport system (Venice is car-free) and actors turn up under their own steam for meetings.
4. We are working on a favoured nations system. All the actors get the same money. The money is not great. Sorry about that. I'm working out a points system so that if the film ever makes any money some of it will make its way back to the ensemble.
5. There is no script. Much of the film is improvised but that is not as scary as it sounds. We shoot a scene and then watch it soon after and then there is discussion and then we shoot again until the scene begins to work. I am entirely there for the actors and the process of developing a scene in this way is very enjoyable and very much an ensemble experience.
6. It's very difficult to accurately plan how the time is going to be scheduled. I will be working everyone quite hard for periods of time and then there will be periods where the pace slacks of while I work out what to do next. Therefore it will not be an orthodox week as in conventional shooting schedules. I never take anyone past the point of exhaustion though.

These are the ground rules and they may all modify or change as we proceed, I hope they do. If there is anything specific anyone needs to know call me on [illegible]

Mike Figgis

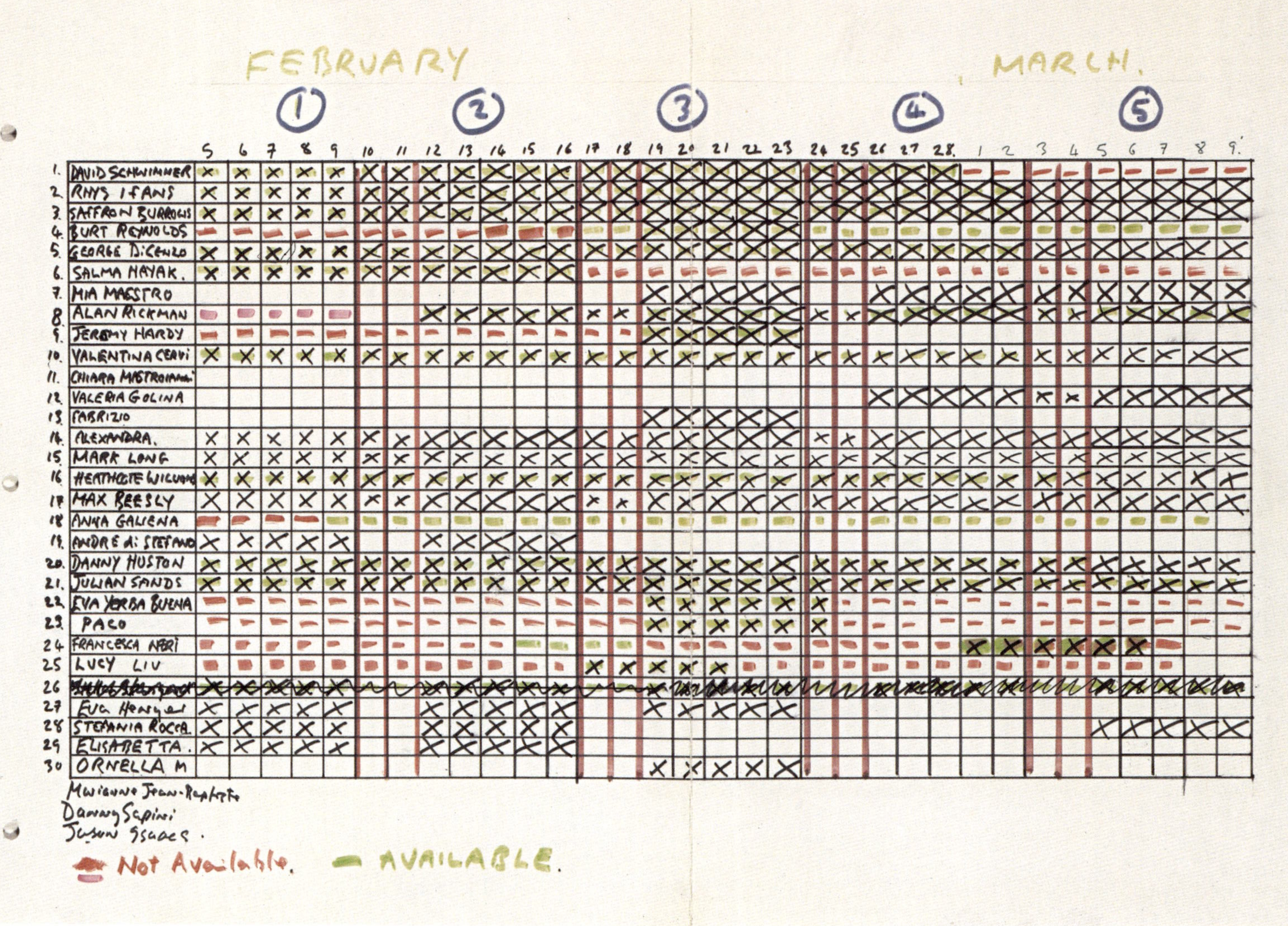

This became a vital document – a schedule

Night vision

I'd heard about this camera which is used for shooting animals at night and wanted to try it out. It was a bit tricky at first because it's not really designed to be used for drama. We constructed a rig, not unlike a food tray with everything gaffered onto it. It was so effective that it wasn't necessary to use any light at all. We had to practice operating in the dark. I had to sometimes point the camera at the floor to see where I was going. The actors could not see each other at all. Sometimes it was just me and the actors. It felt very perverse but film making is very perverse and it's not unhealthy to have to admit it from time to time. I can say that it was unique for me. I have never ever come near to this feeling before. I think the actors found it very stimulating as well.

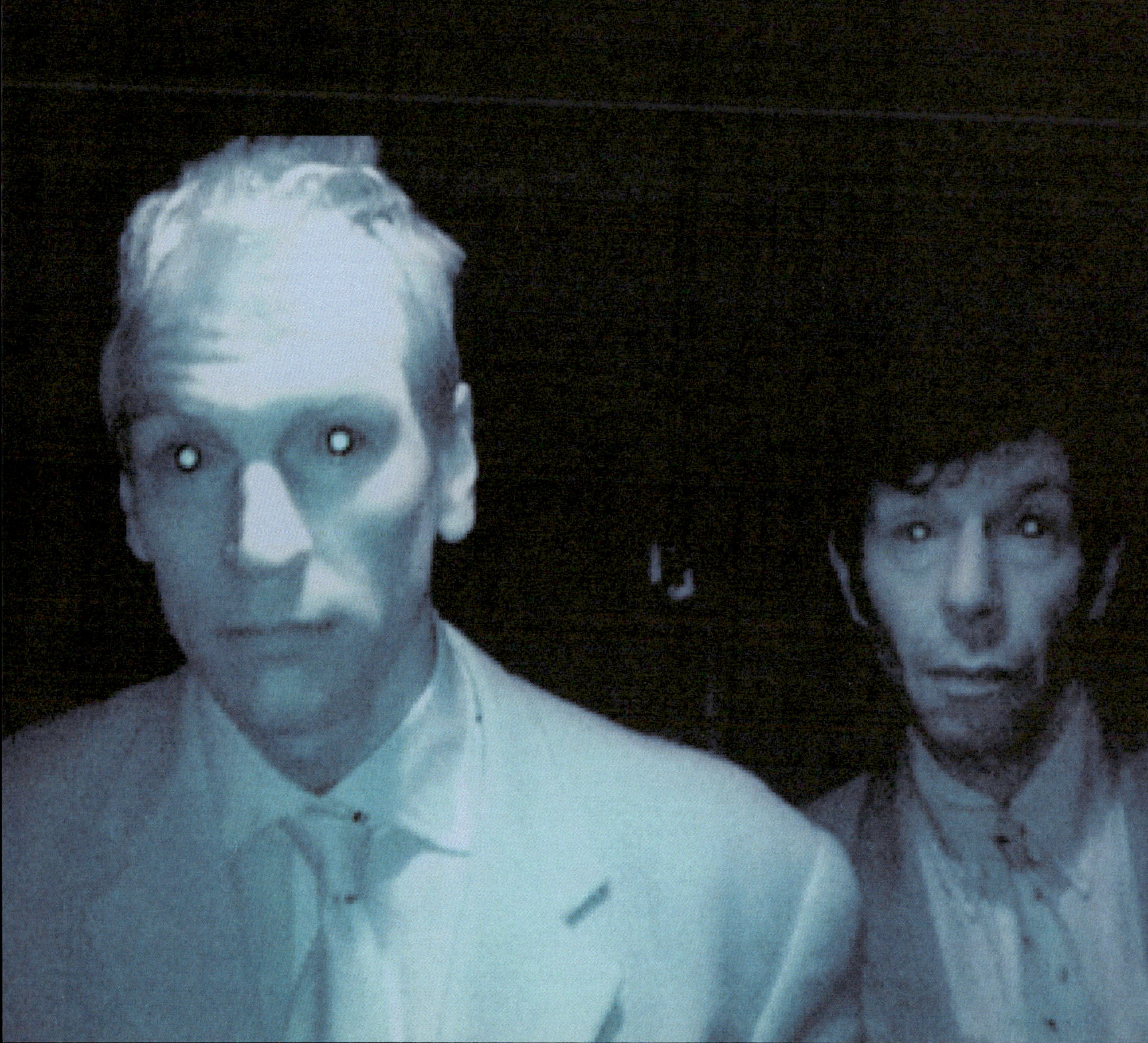

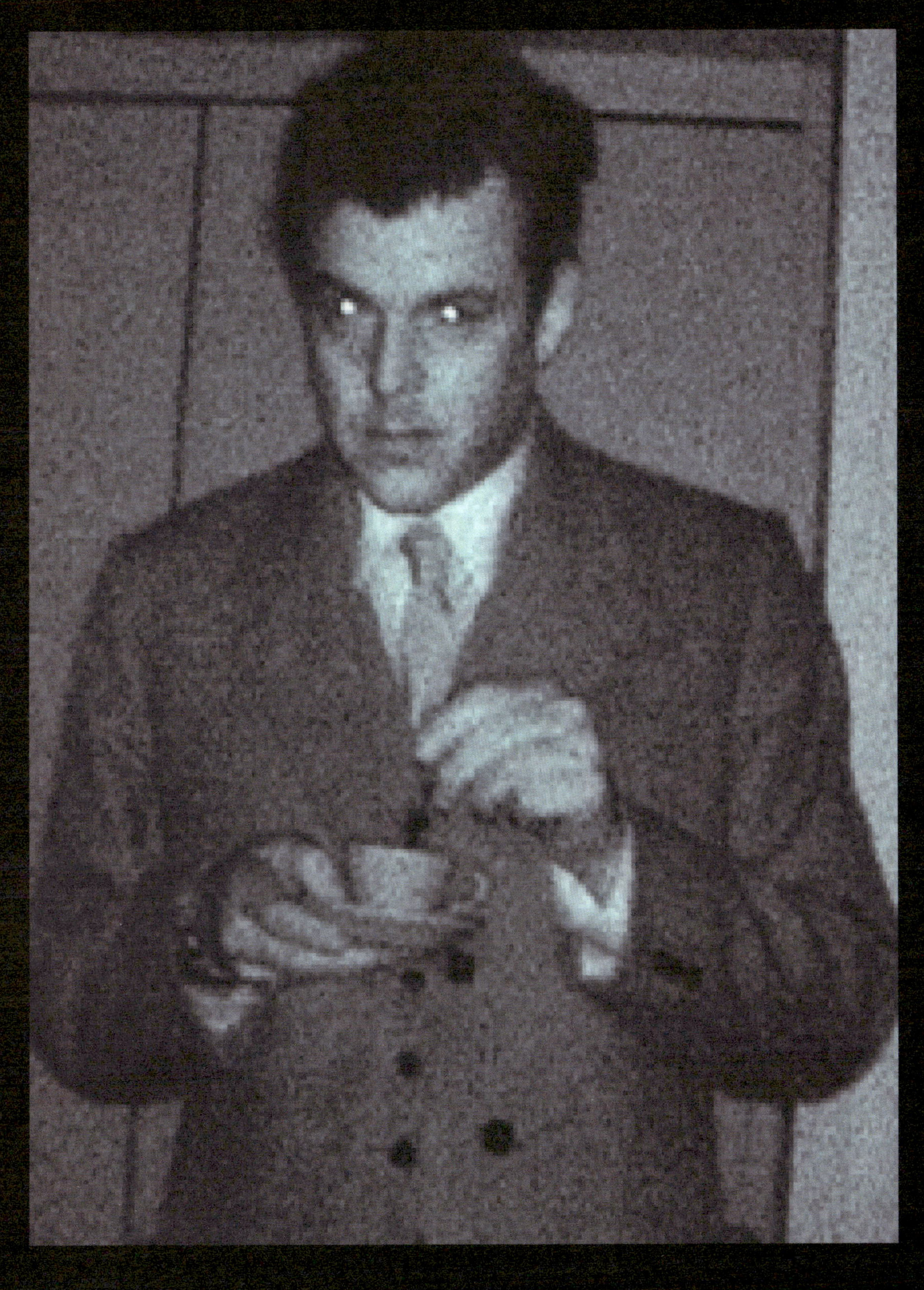

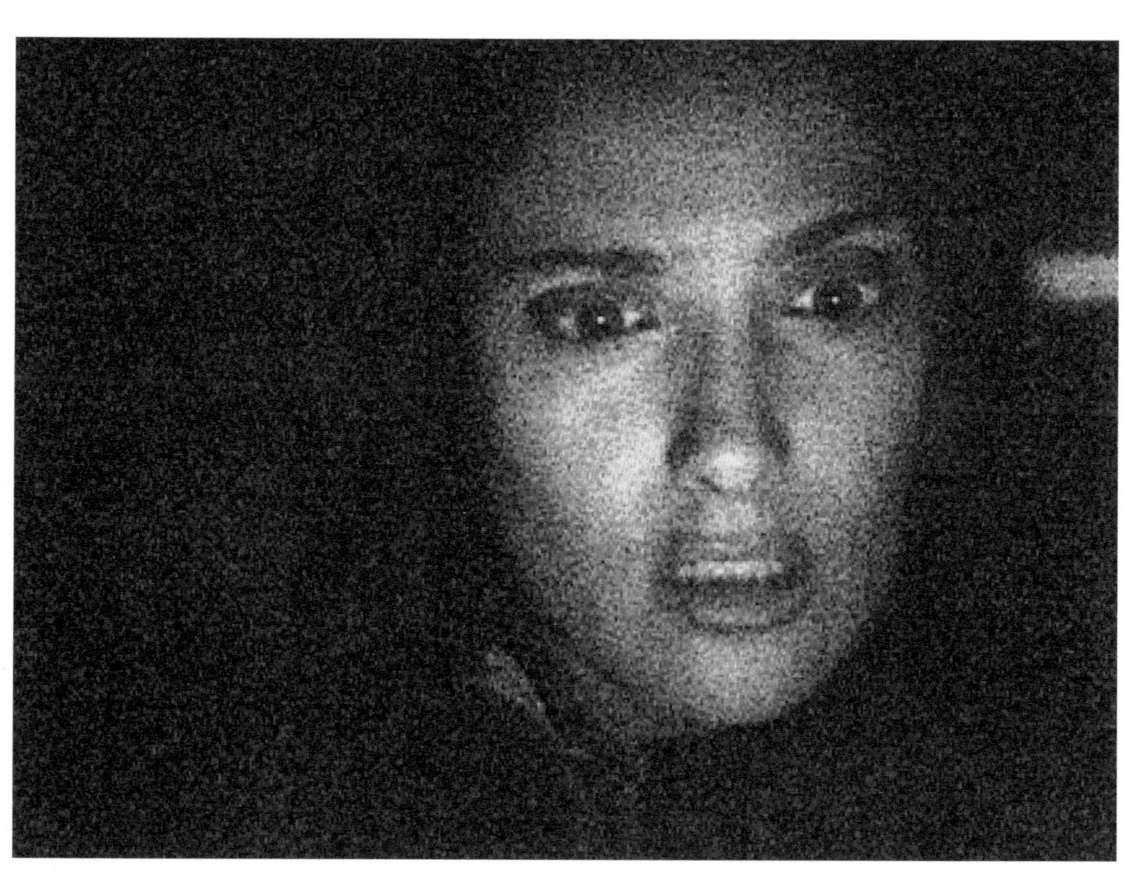

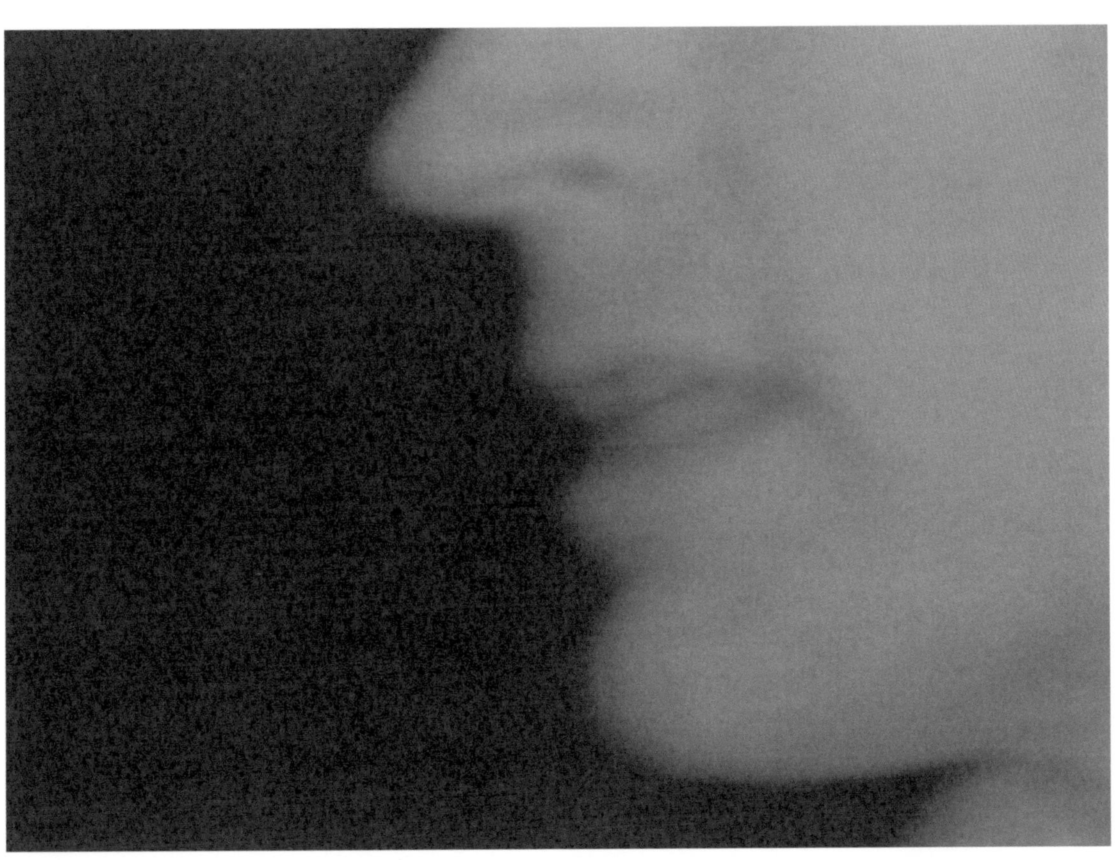

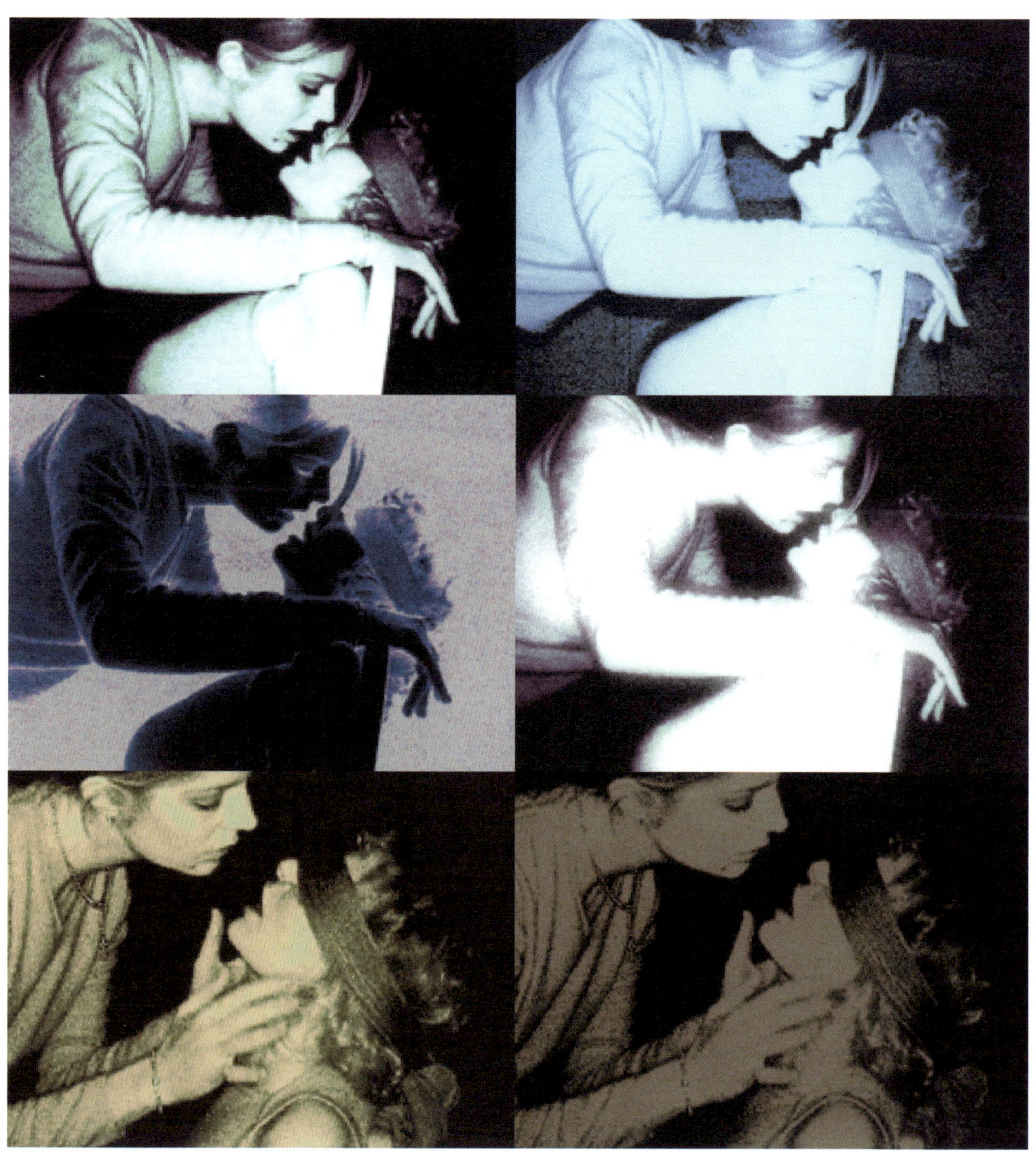

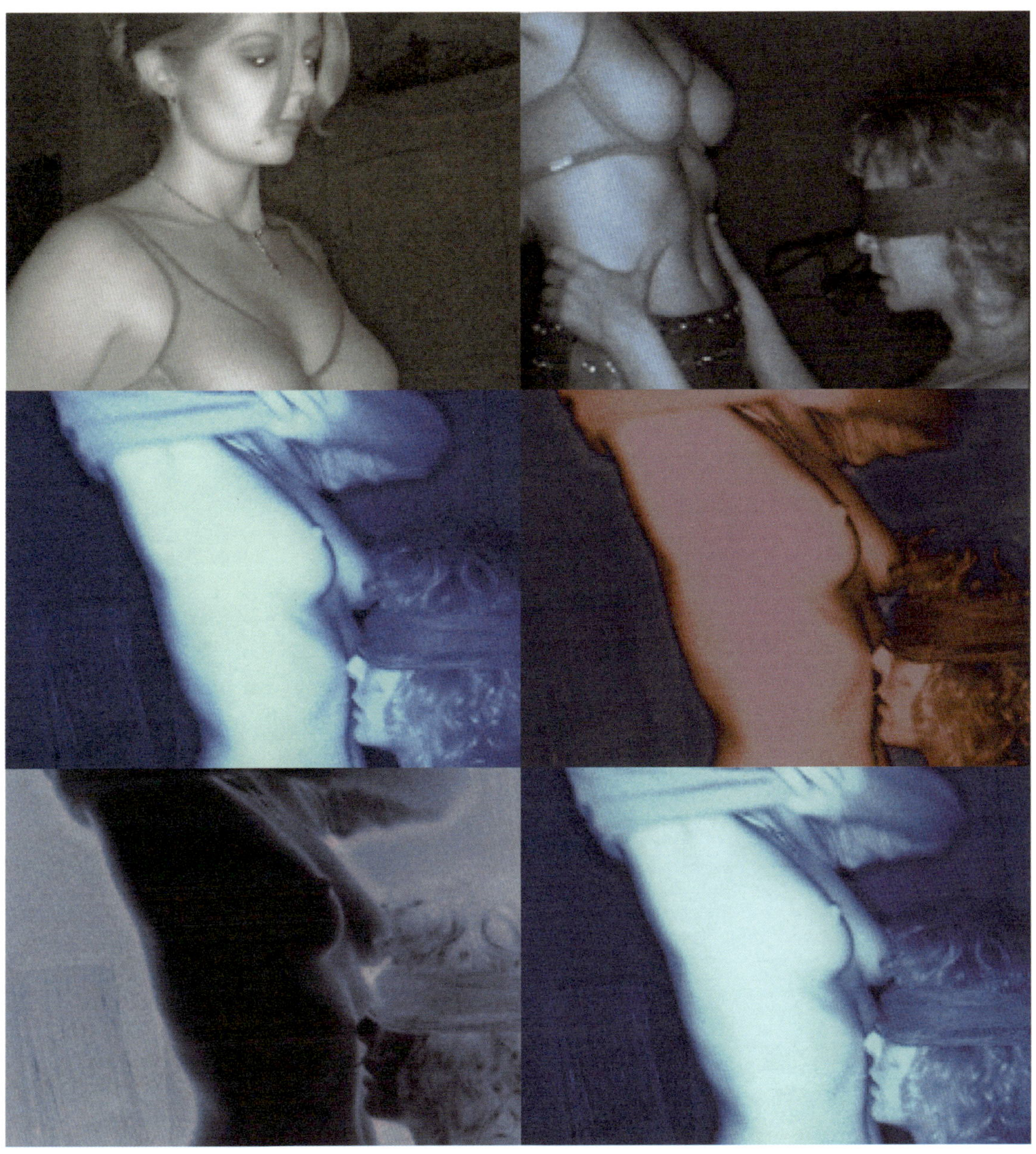

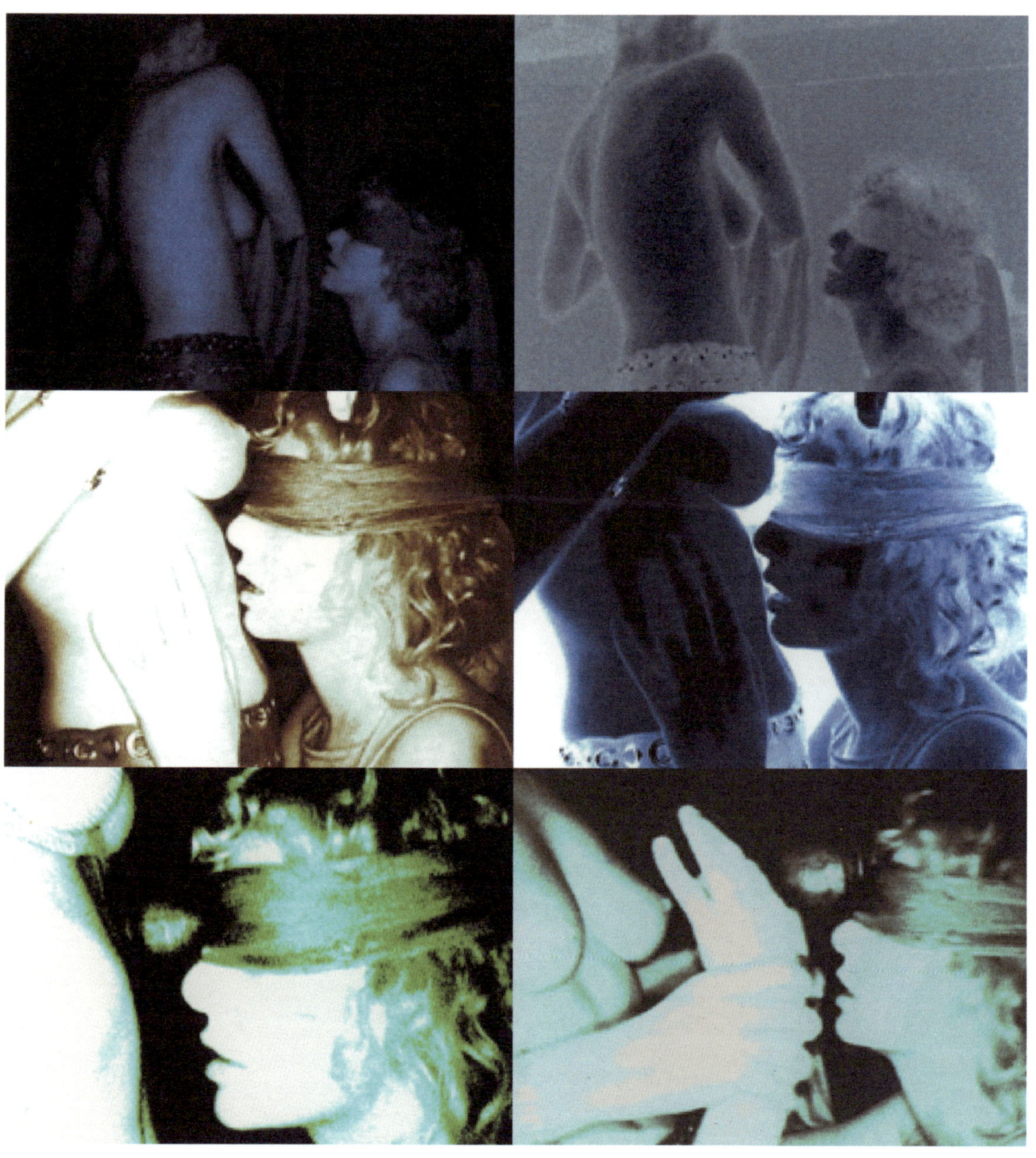

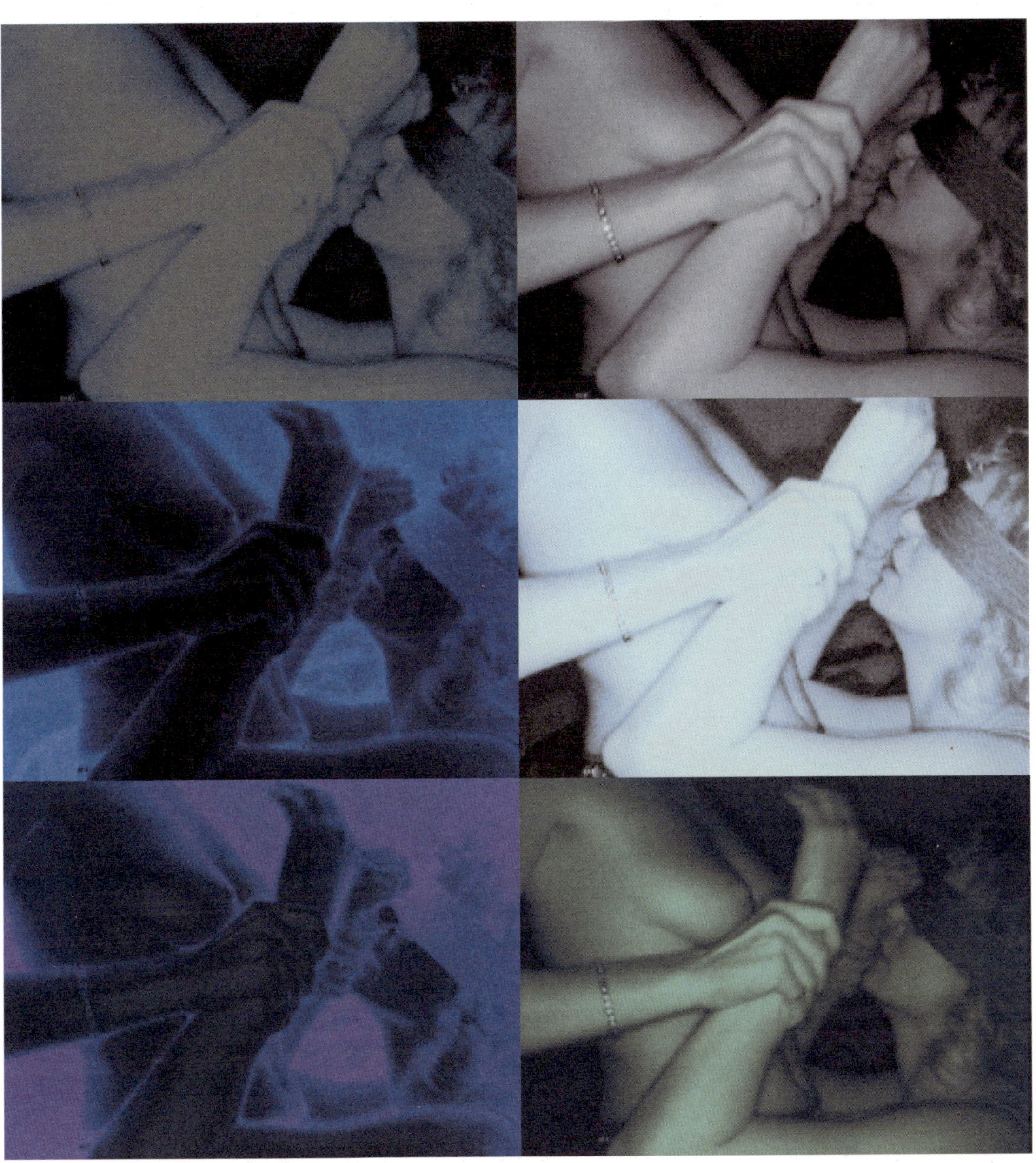

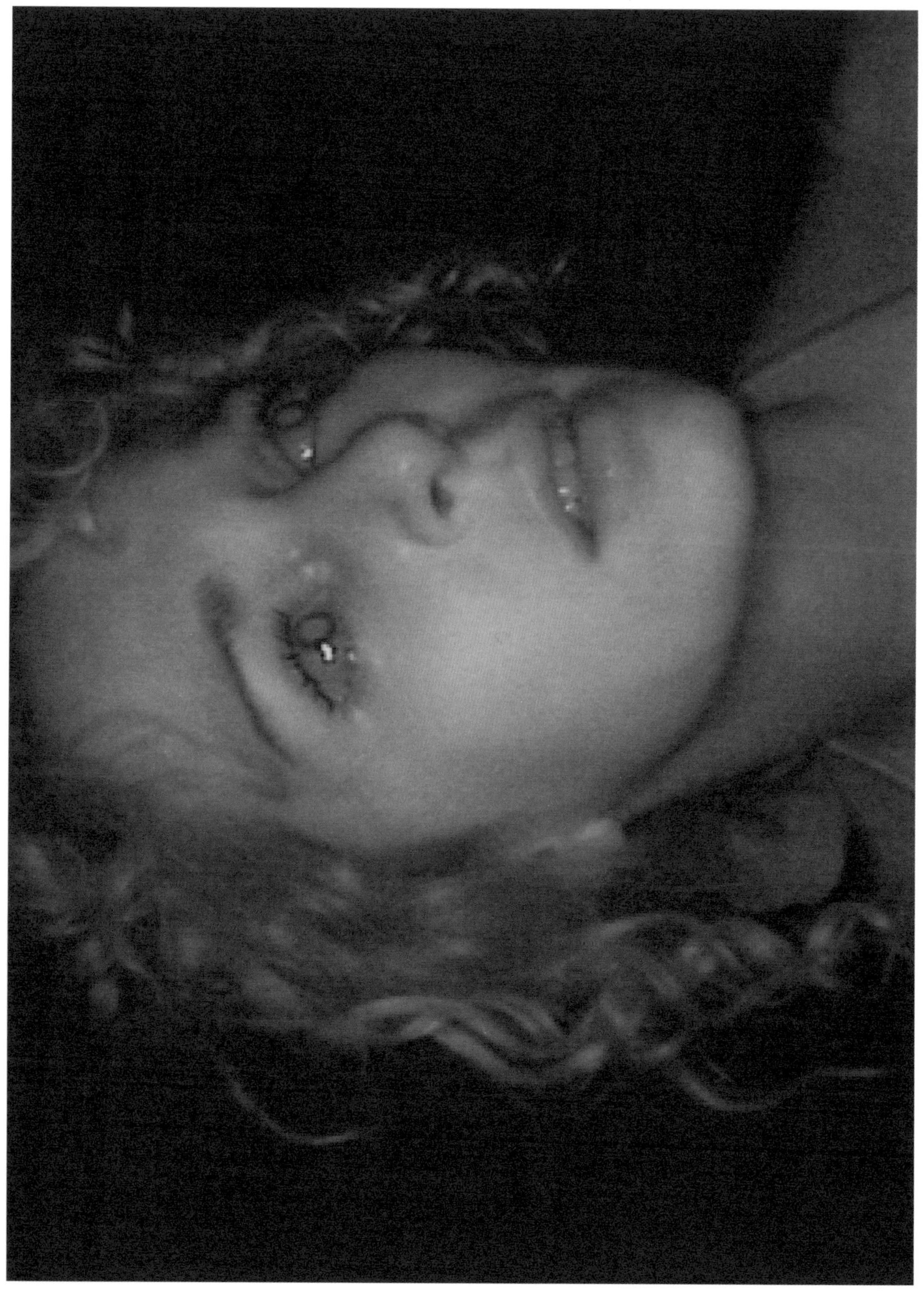

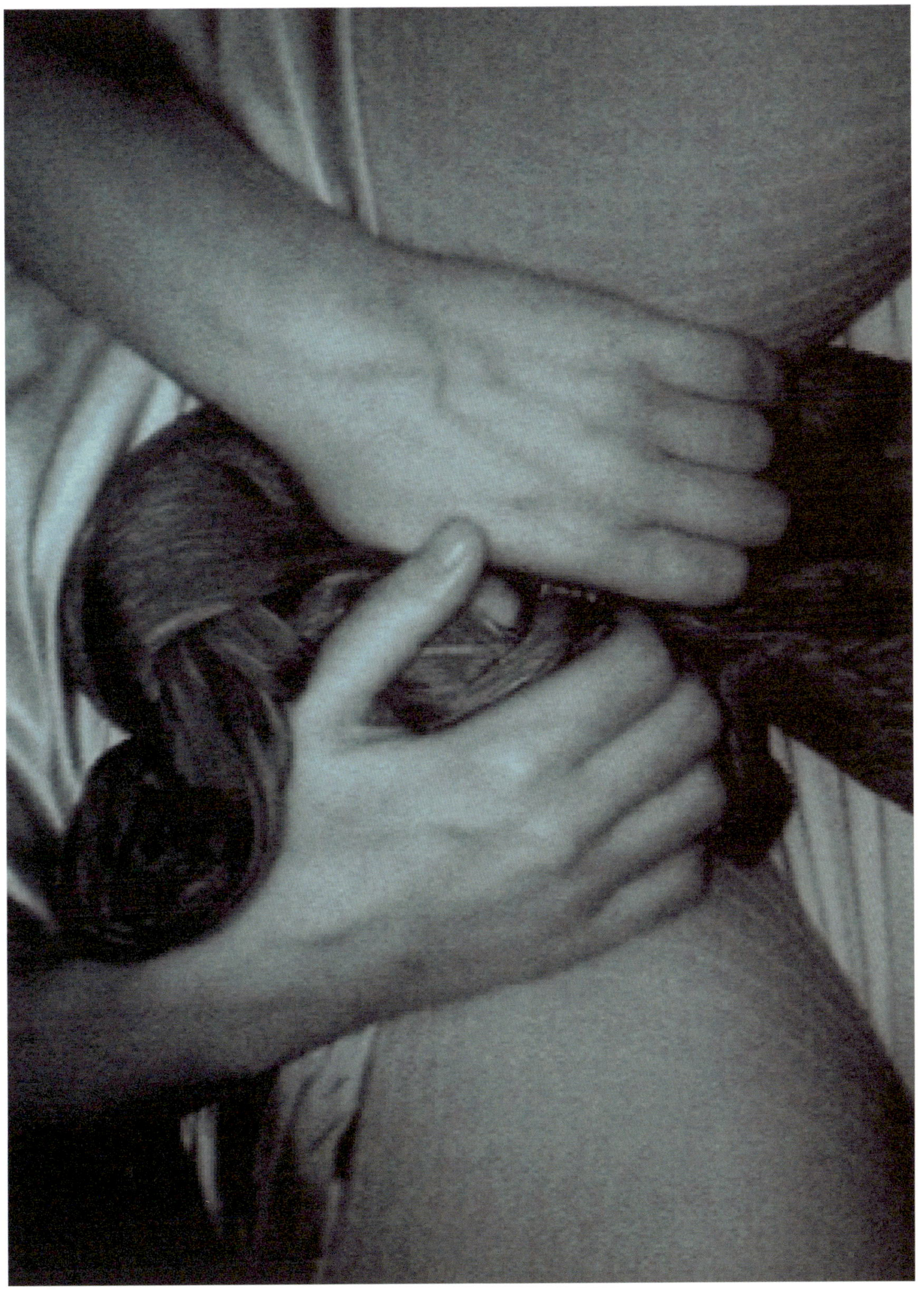

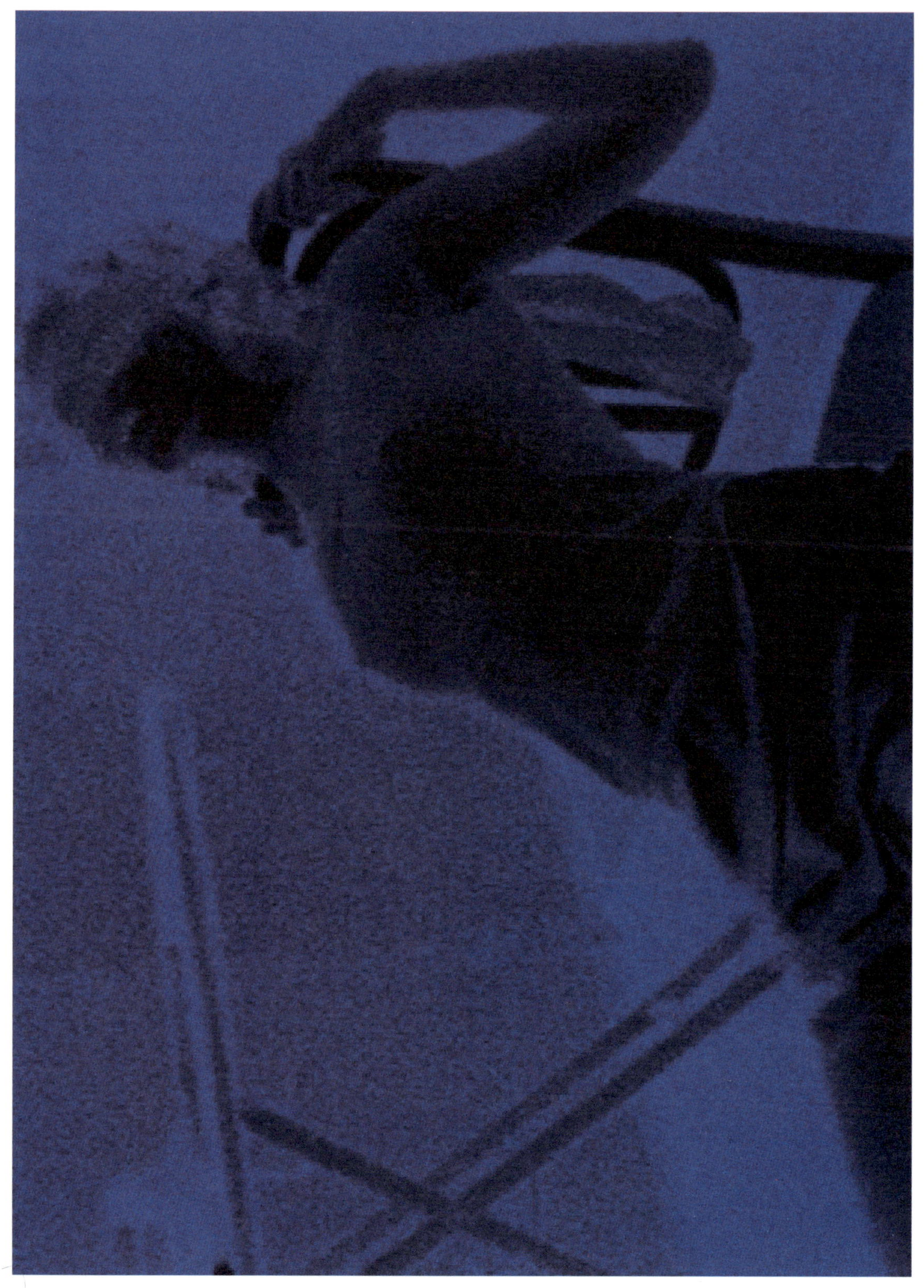

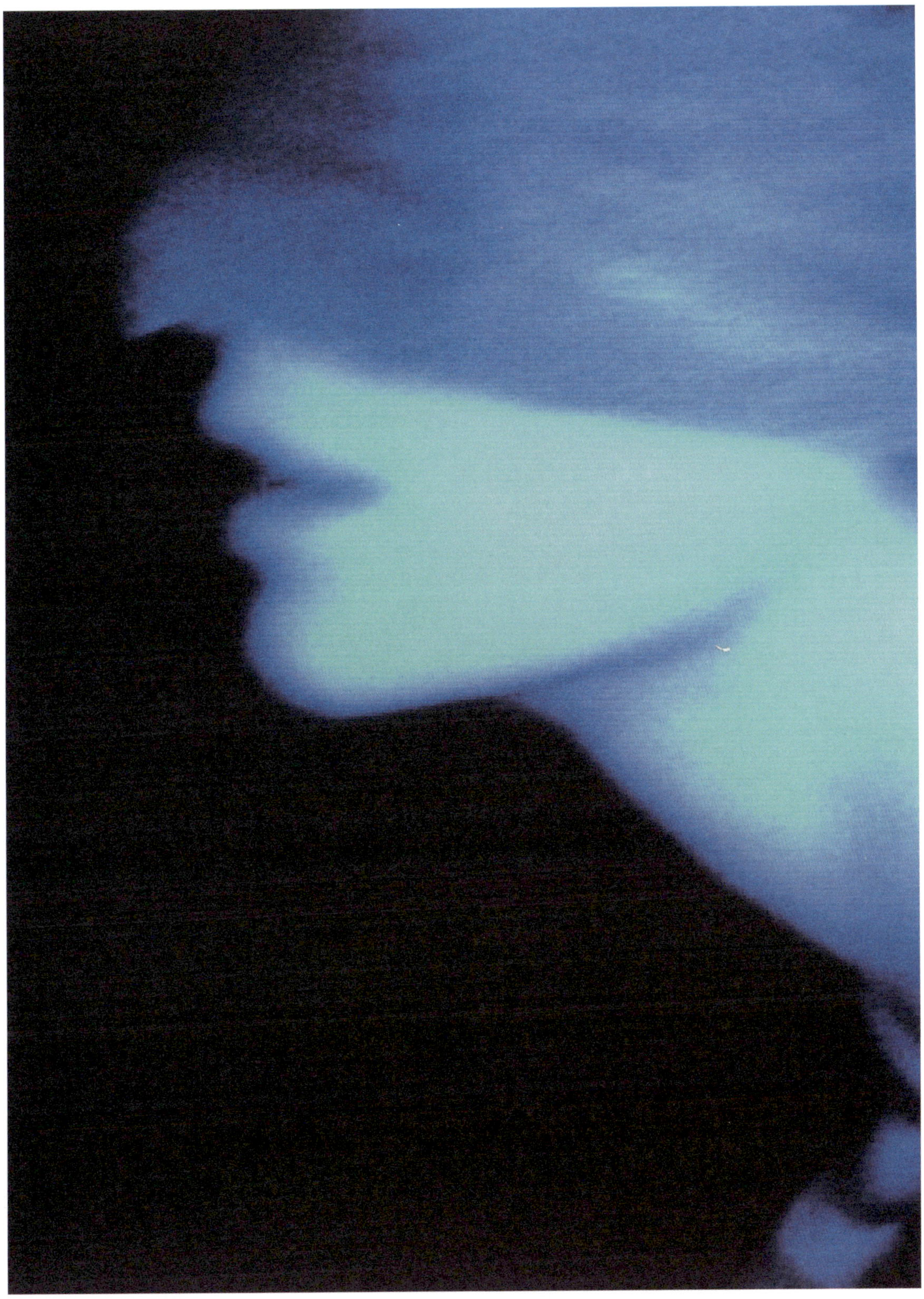

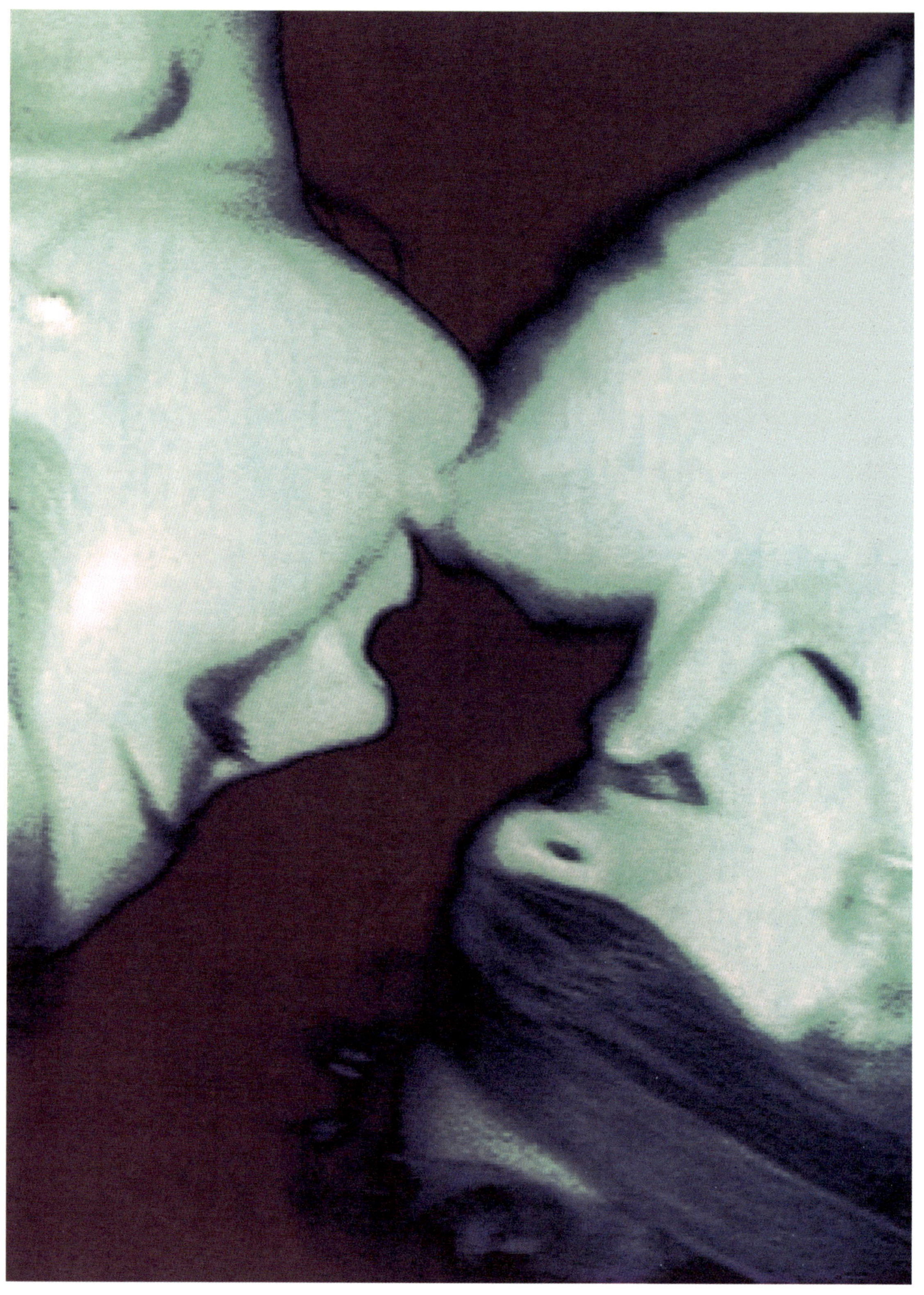

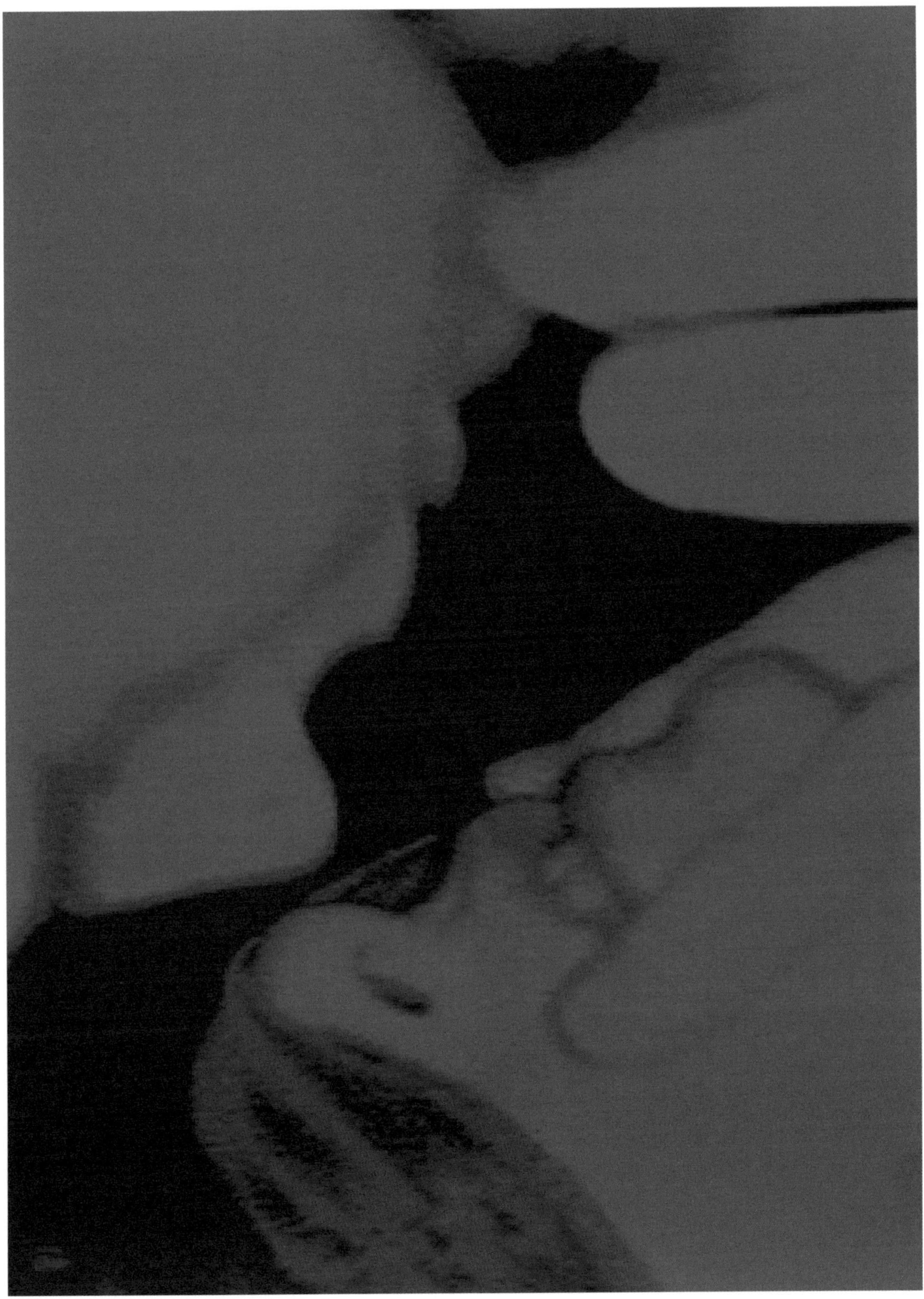

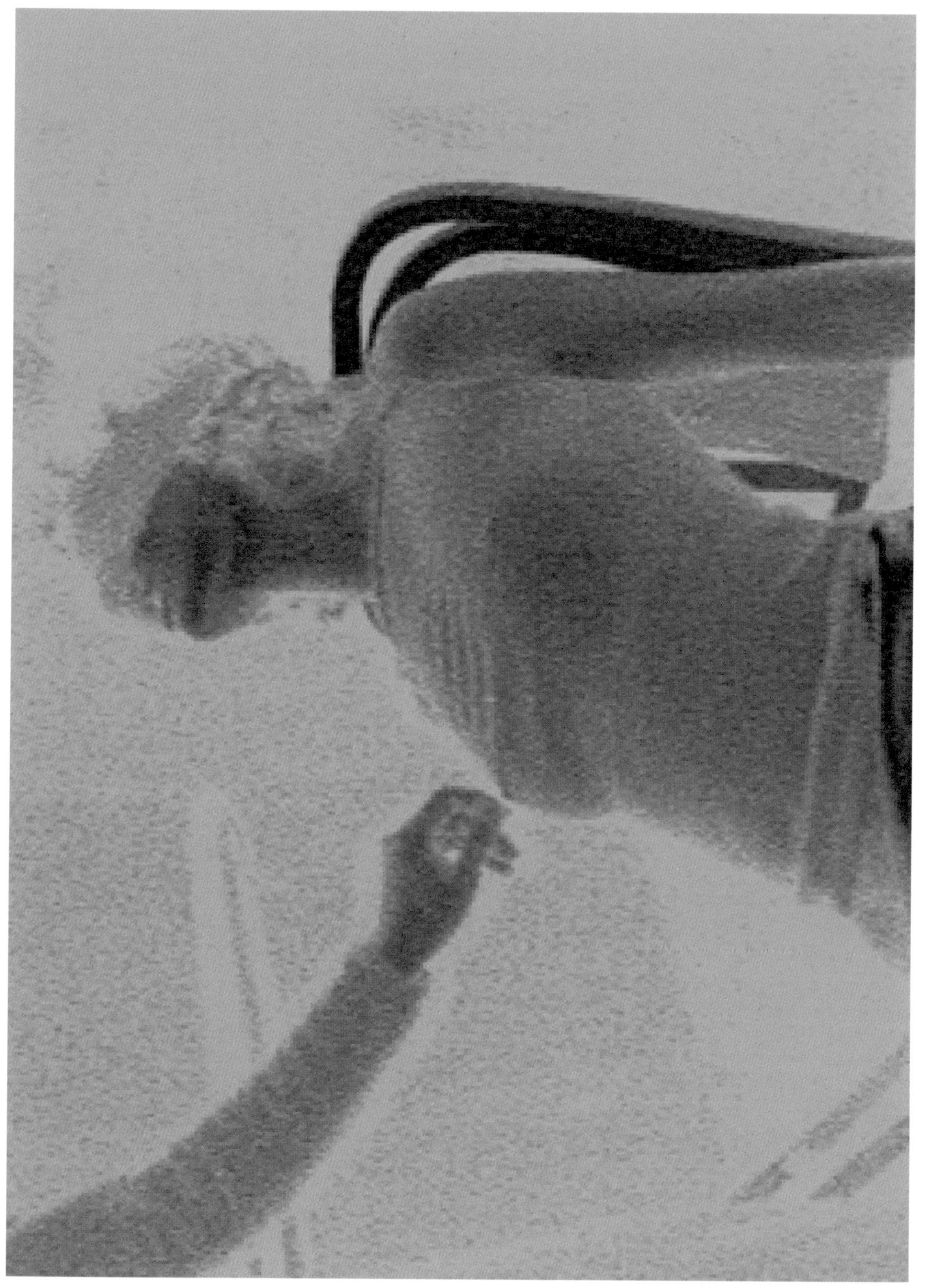

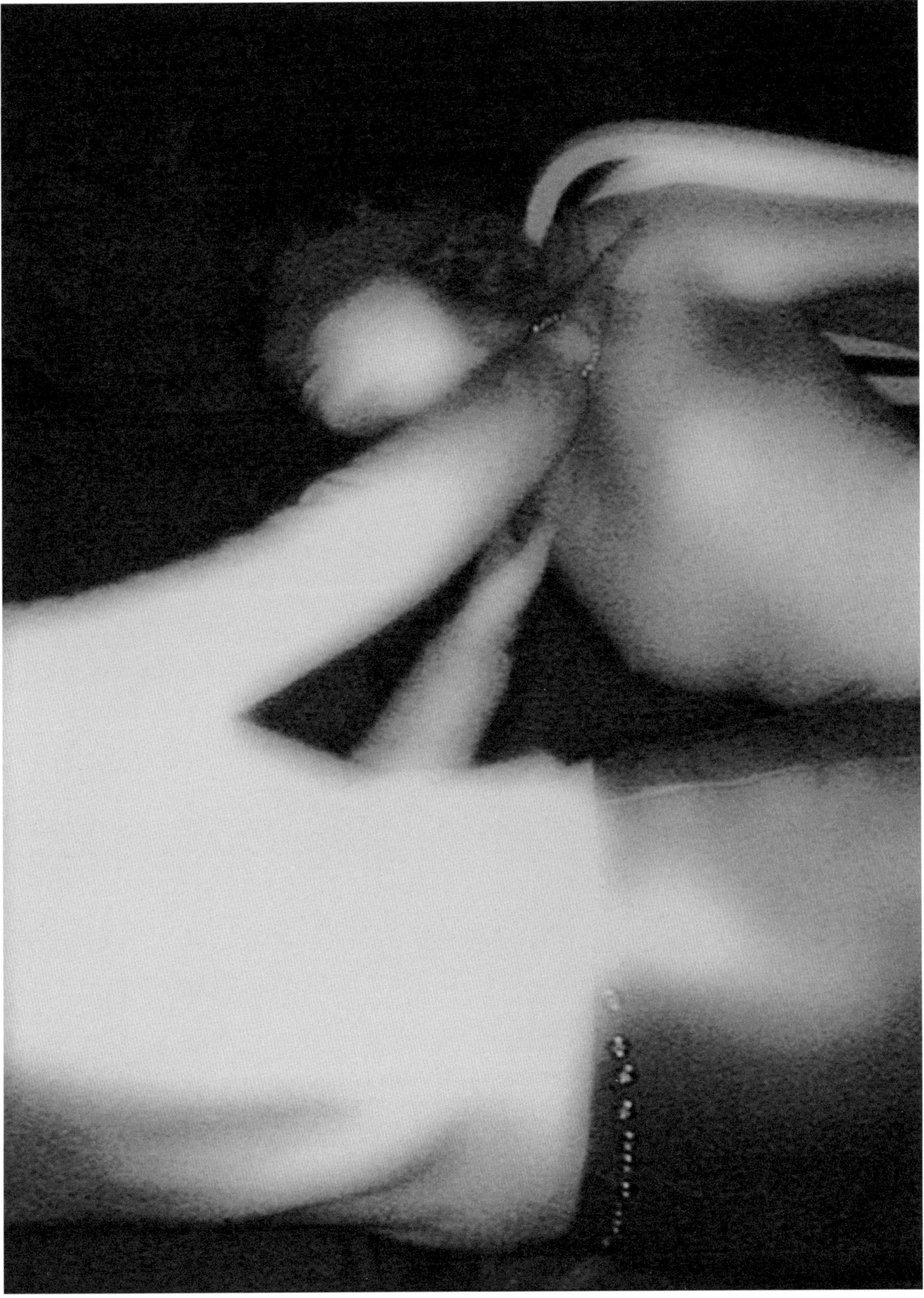

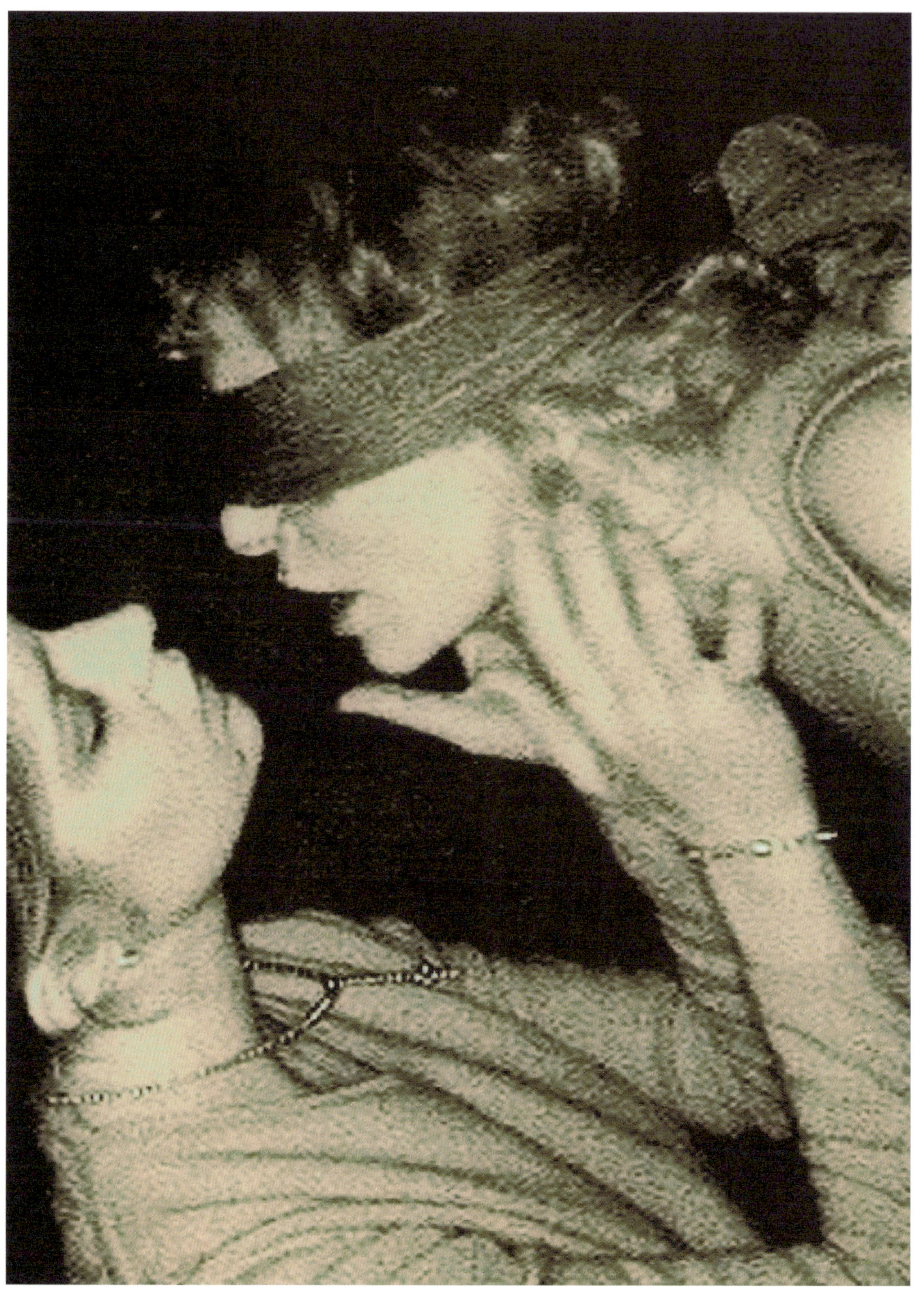

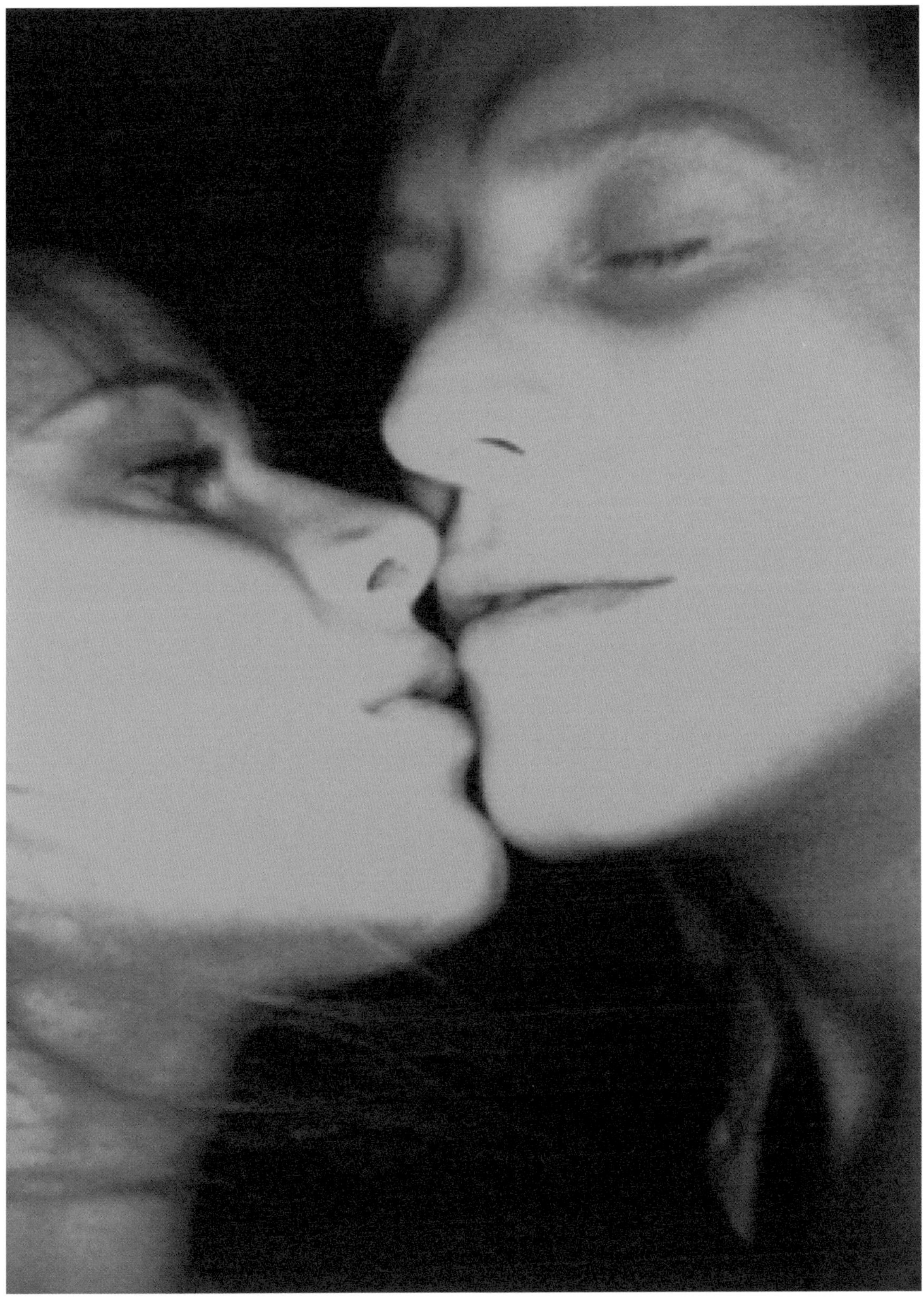

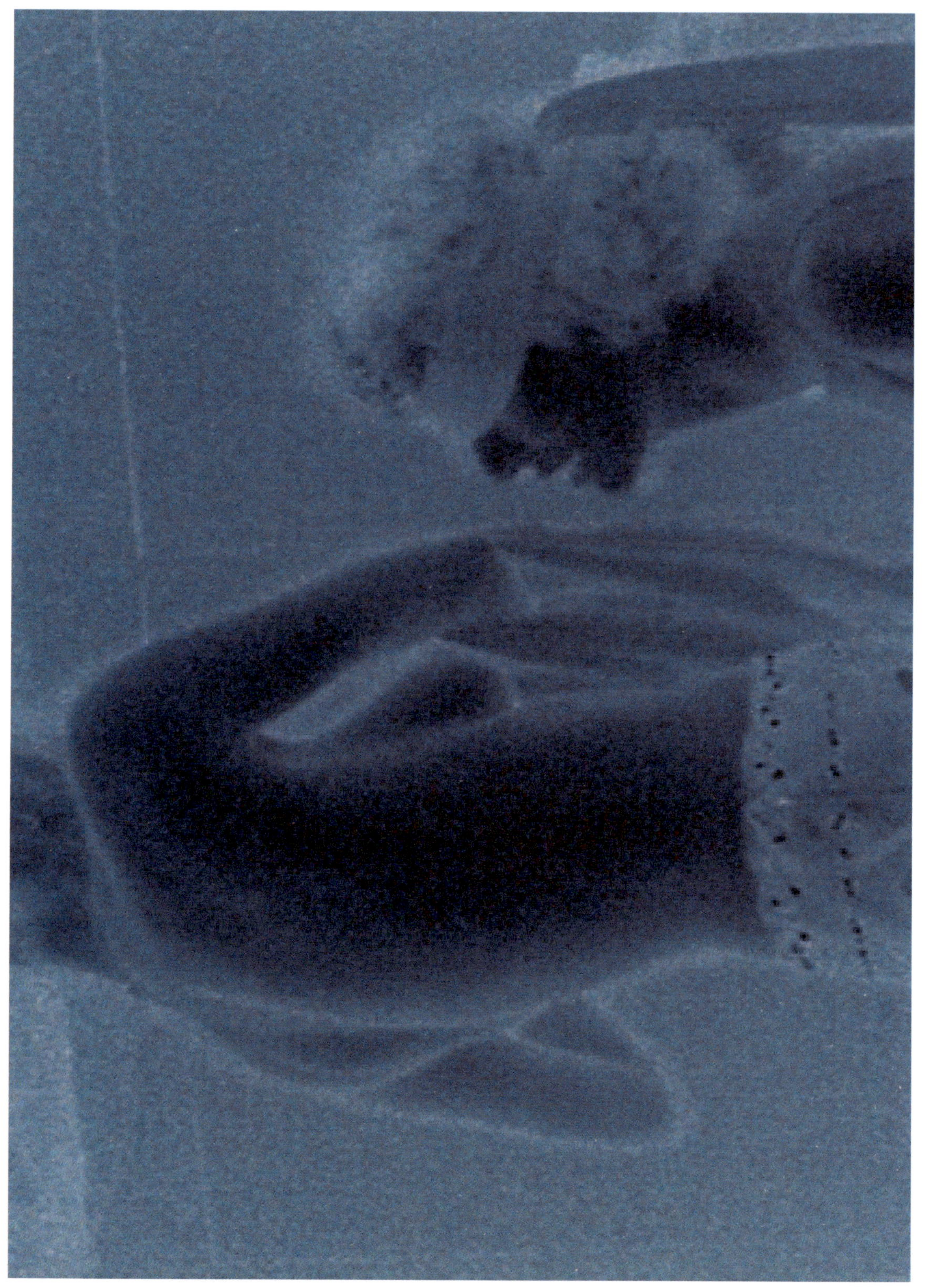

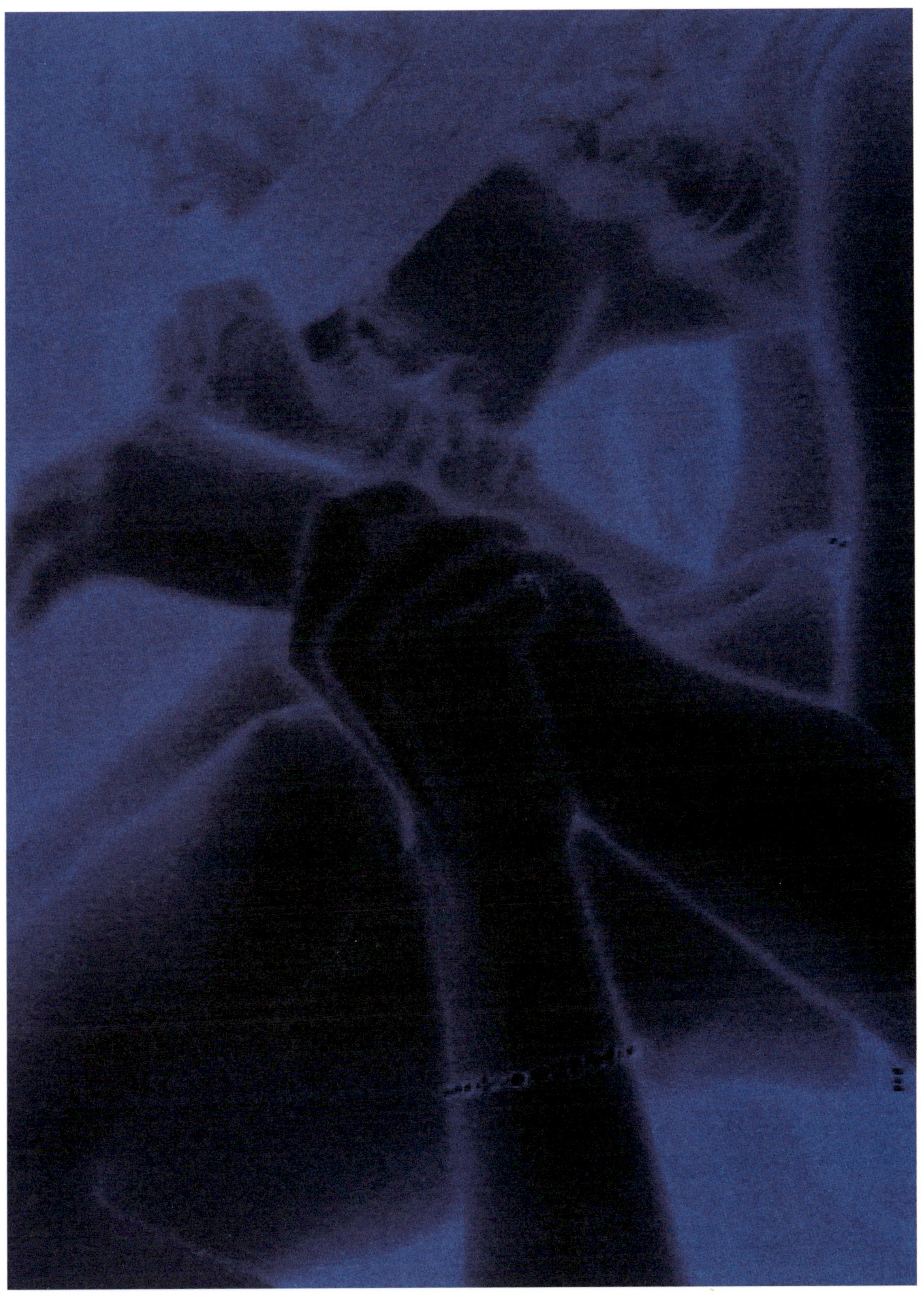

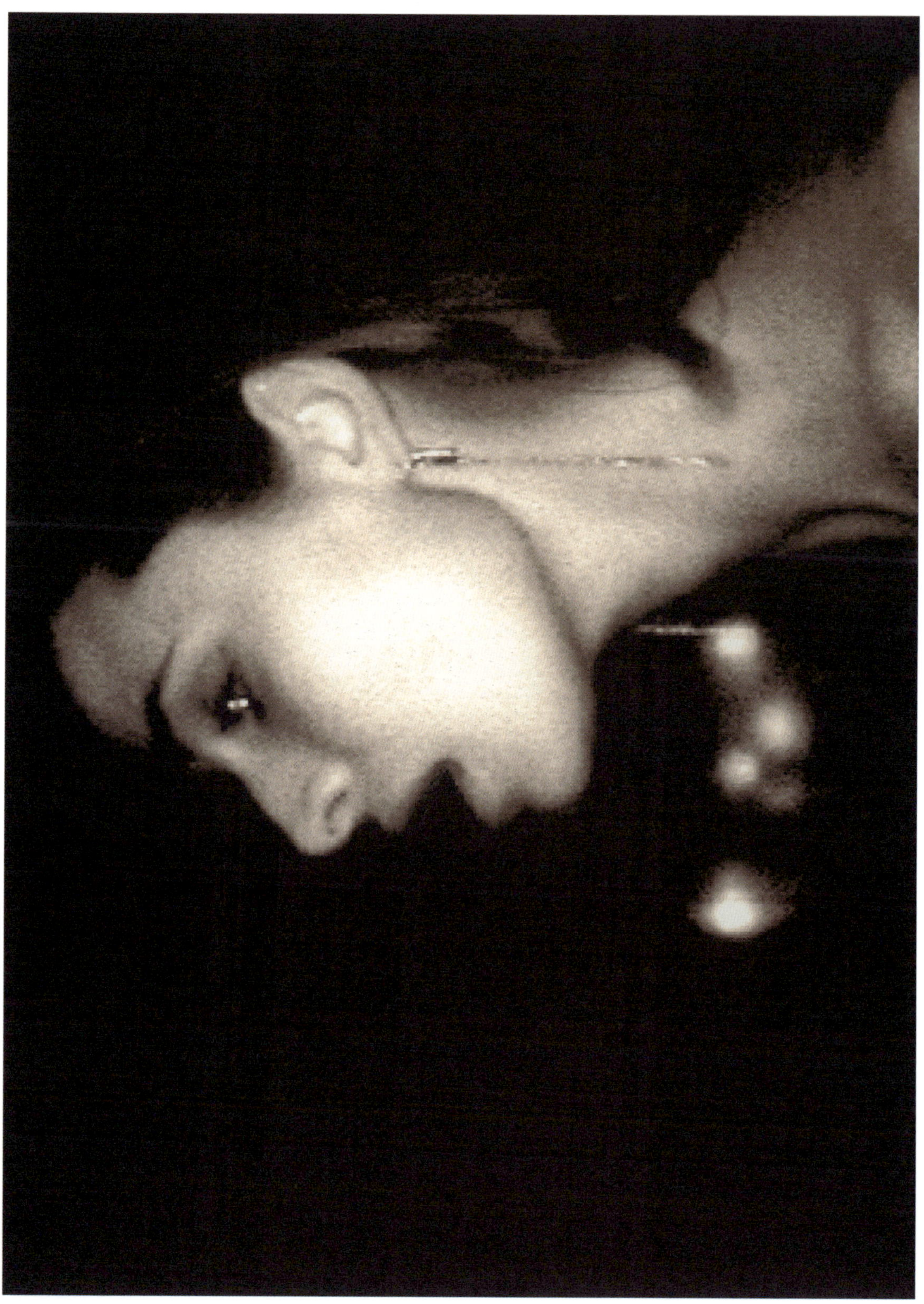

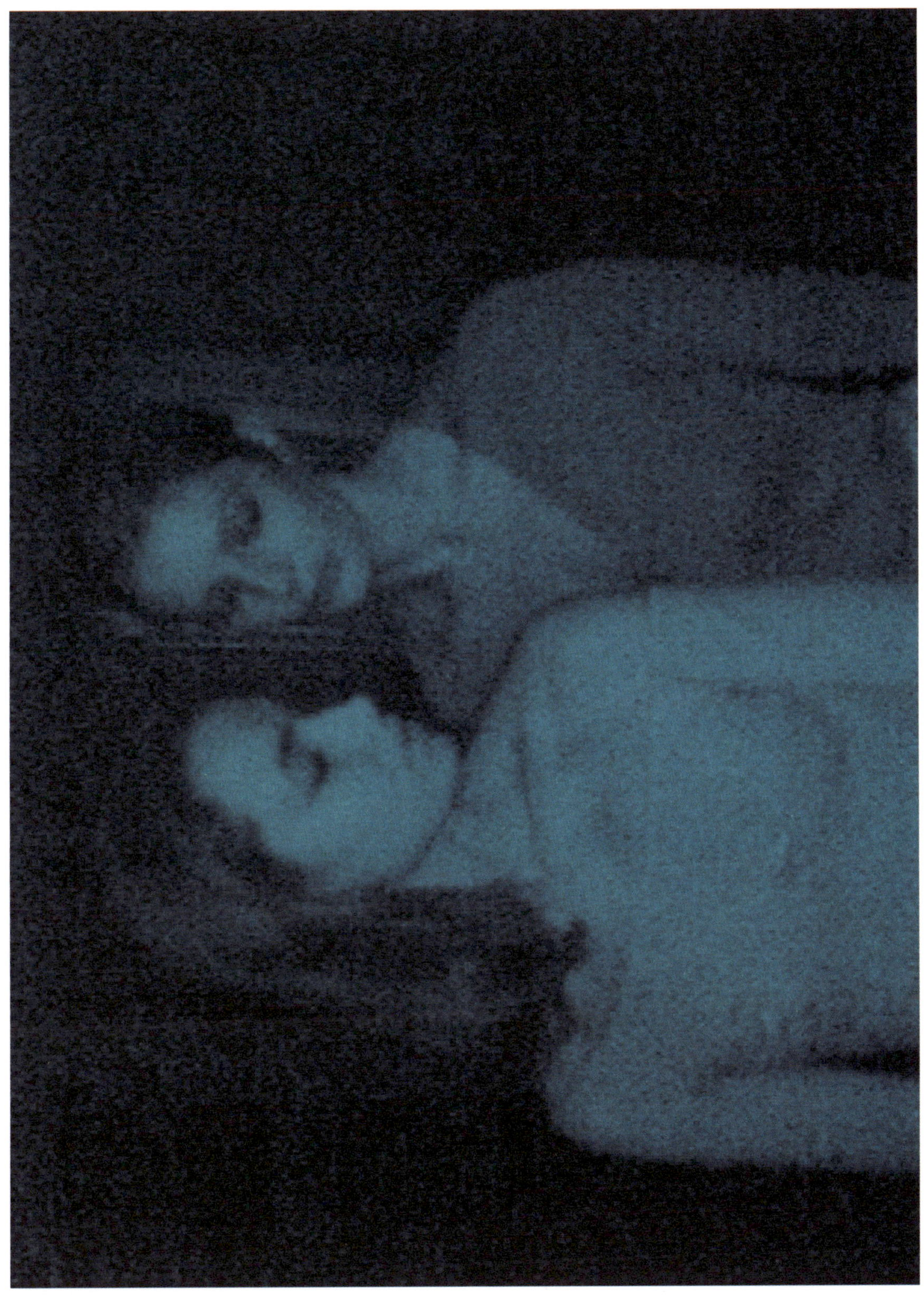

My plan for 'HOTEL' was to use the same music paper system that had worked so well in 'TIMECODE' and 'ABOUT TIME-2". I worked out a new format - Ten 10 min real time scenes, all shot on 4 cameras.

At some point during the first week of the shoot it became clear to me that I was restricting the possibilities by having to stick to a rigid set of rules. I told the actors that we would be abandoning the system from here on in. Which we did. I was then punished by having to spend months and months in the editing room. There is no easy way to make films. With each one you have to start from the beginning again.

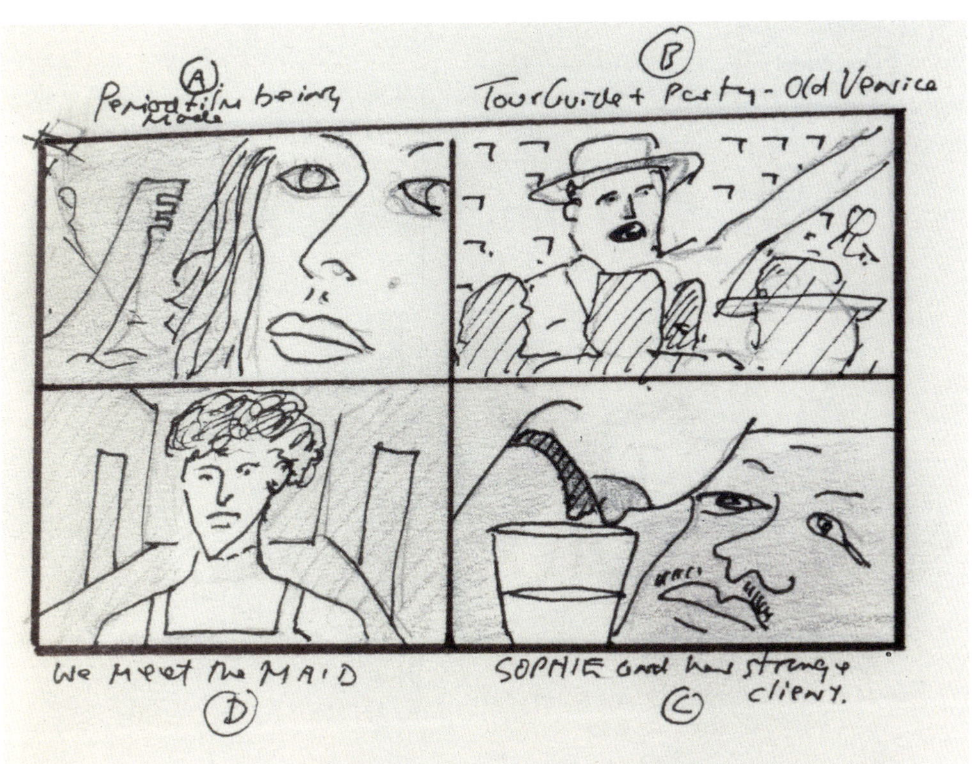
A
Period film being made
B
Tour Guide + Party - Old Venice
We meet the MAID
D
SOPHIE and her strange client.
C

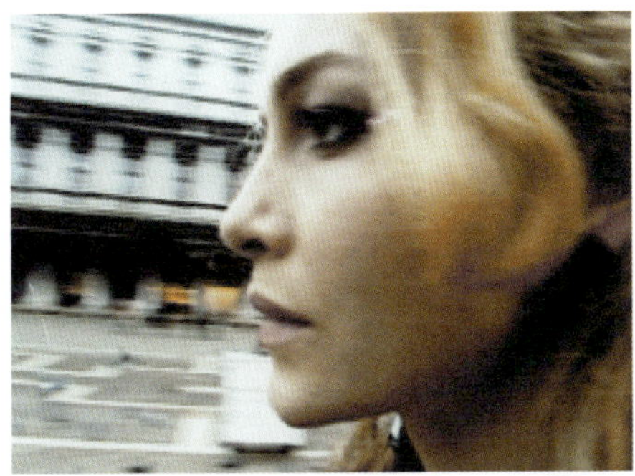

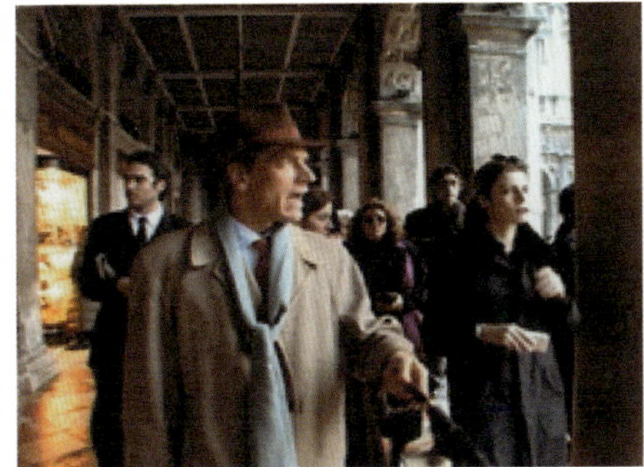

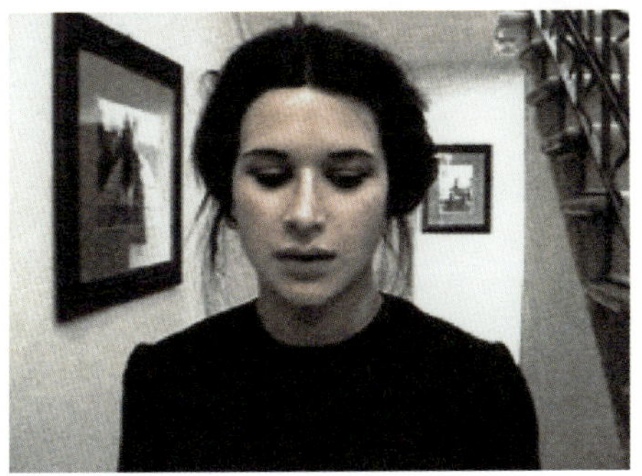

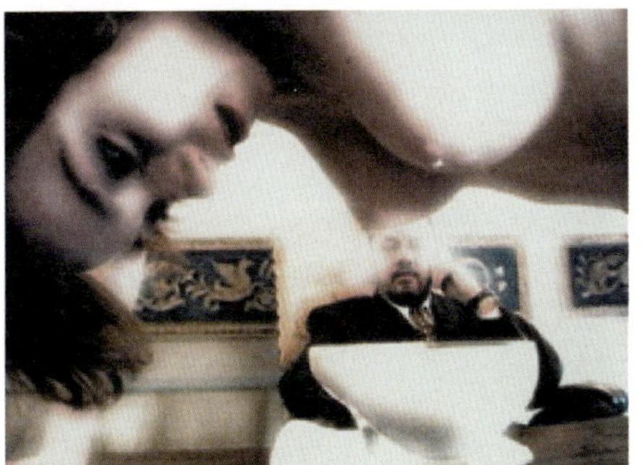

Treatment for the scene when the Director (TRENT) gets shot.

ON CAMERA 2 (top left of screen)

In a stylish apartment we see a HOOKER called **SOPHIE** with a **CLIENT**.

This could be in another room in the hotel or in an apartment near the hotel, (to be decided later).

We join them as at the last moment of truly strange sex. Something that not even in one's wildest dreams has come up as a possibility (suggestions welcome). The **CLIENT** pays her a very large amount of money. Her mobile phone rings and she takes a call from...

ON CAMERA 3 (bottom left of screen)

THE MAGIC GANGSTER. He's handsome, if a little psycho. He's on a speedboat crossing the lagoon.

MAGIC phones **SOPHIE** (*all the actors have mobiles*). (He's got her number from an associate). He wants to meet her soon, he needs to have rough sex and he wants her to be wearing a **RED DRESS.** They agree a price, he doesn't argue a bit...

SOPHIE quickly changes from her black dress to an identical **RED VERSION.** She gives him the name of the hotel and says she will meet him in the lobby in, say, 10 minutes.
She doesn't want him to come straight to the room because the hotel manager is on to her being an expensive hooker.
Meanwhile...

ON CAMERA 4 (bottom right of screen)

A PERIOD FILM is being shot. Very intense Shakespearian dialogue, actors in period costume but with contemporary elements combining with the old beauty of Venice. **TRENT** is directing - he's good, a bastard but good. The producer, **JONATHAN** is watching. He has a huge crush on the actress, **NAOMI.** The scene is intense and seems to be about jealousy and betrayal.

TRENT is very arrogant and each time **JONATHAN** suggests something he dismisses it cruelly. **NAOMI** always sides with **TRENT.** We feel a bit sorry for **JONATHAN;** he is always the underdog, the enabler. Afterwards the film dudes make their way back to the hotel.

OK – that's how the characters introduce themselves. What happens next is, roughly speaking, this...

MAGIC enters the hotel by a back door...

then **MAGIC** appears and shoots **TRENT** several times.

We never really find out why TRENT is shot!

MAGIC then heads for the lobby where he spots **GRETA** waiting for the **BUSINESSMAN.** Another natural mistake ensues as he picks her up (**RED DRESS** again) and suggests they go directly to her room.

SOPHIE waits in the lobby and is spotted by the REAL **BUSINESSMAN** as the woman in the **RED DRESS.** They both make the same mistake and end up in her room where she proceeds to give him the time of his life, as per **MAGIC'S** request...

As the scene is ending:-

MAGIC gives **GRETA** a lot of money.
SOPHIE demands the same amount from the **BUSINESSMAN.**
NAOMI finally discovers **TRENT** on the floor. Unable to speak Italian she goes in search of **JONATHAN,** he comforts her and in their grief there is a moment of tenderness and perhaps even love.
TRENT speaks to us in voice over and we learn that although he appears to be more or less dead, in fact he can hear and see perfectly well – he just can't move any part of his body.

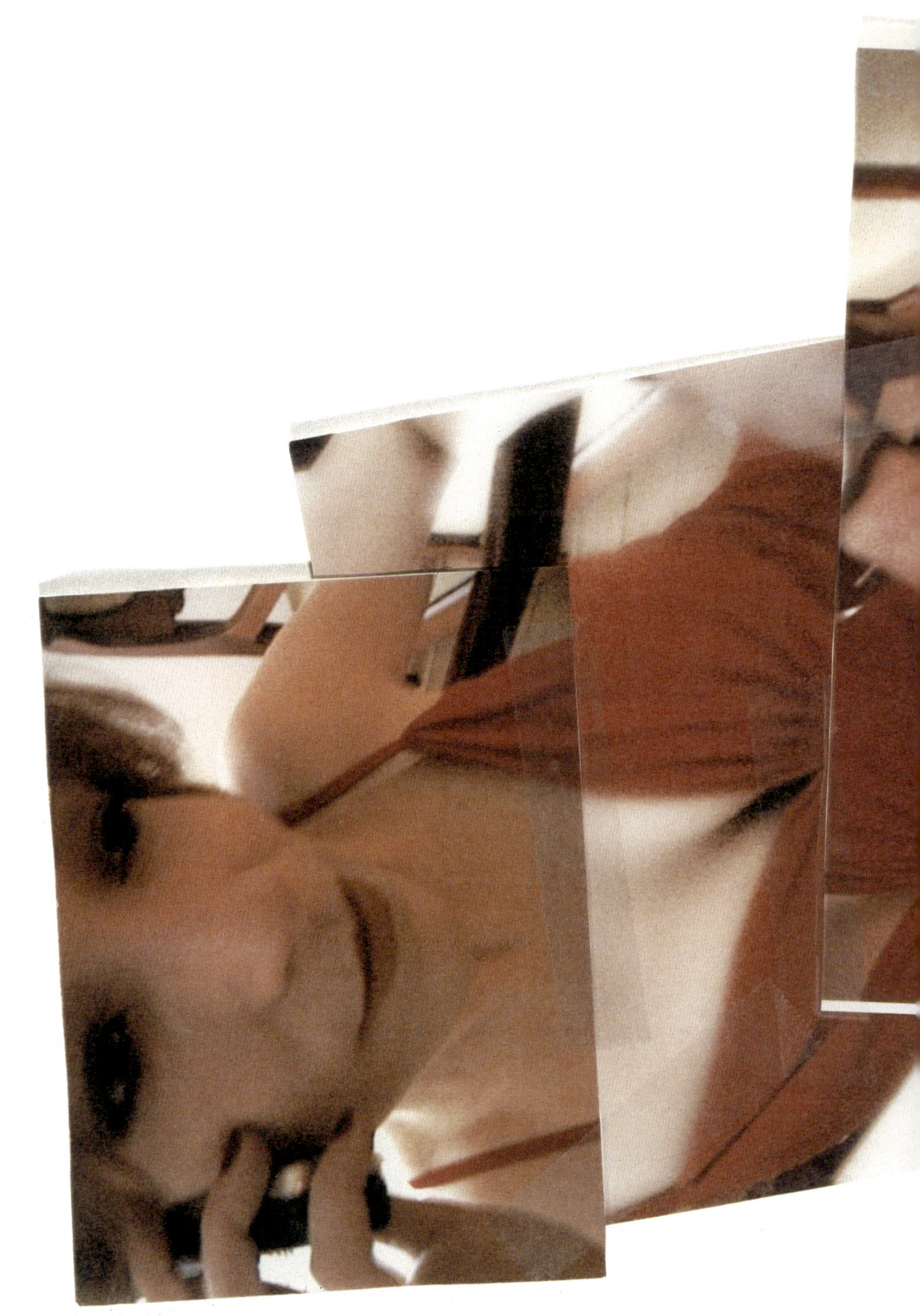

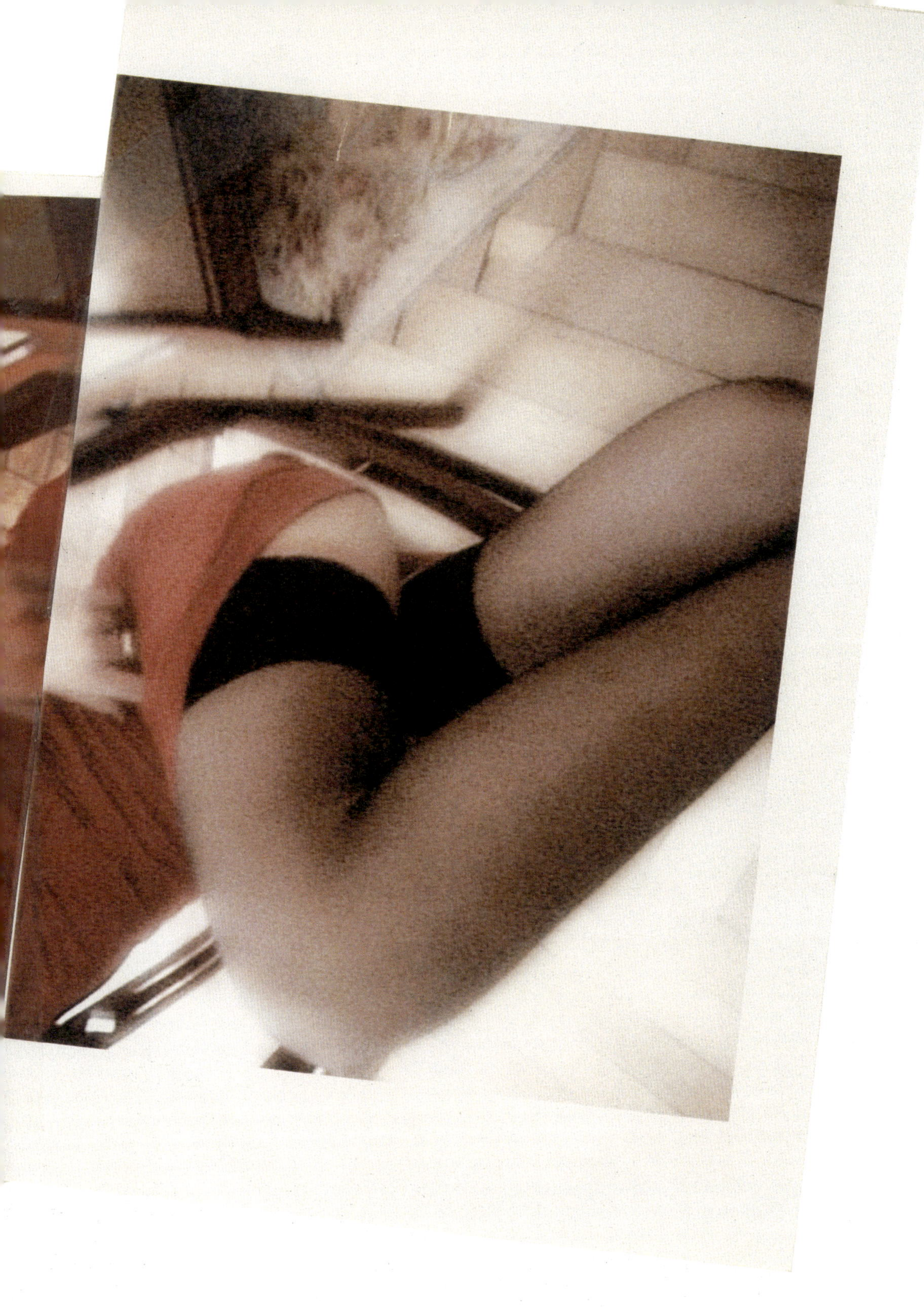

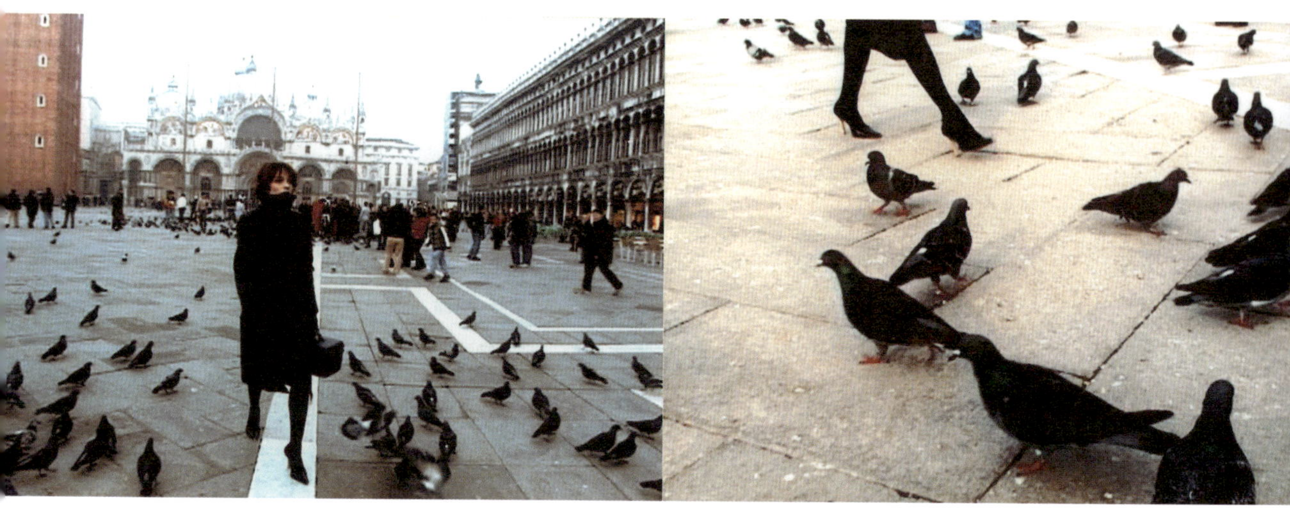

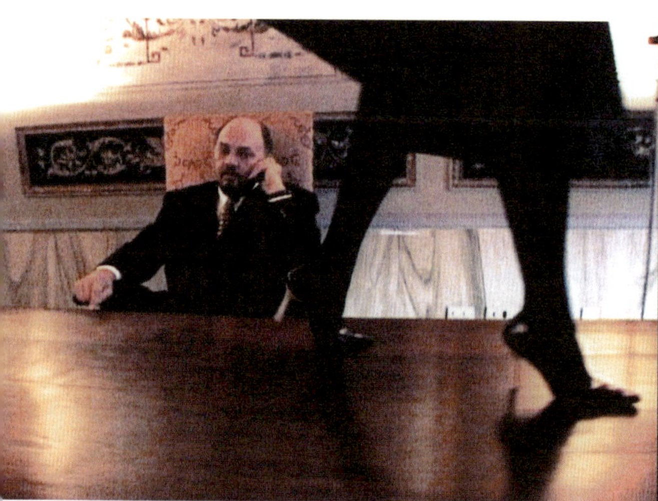

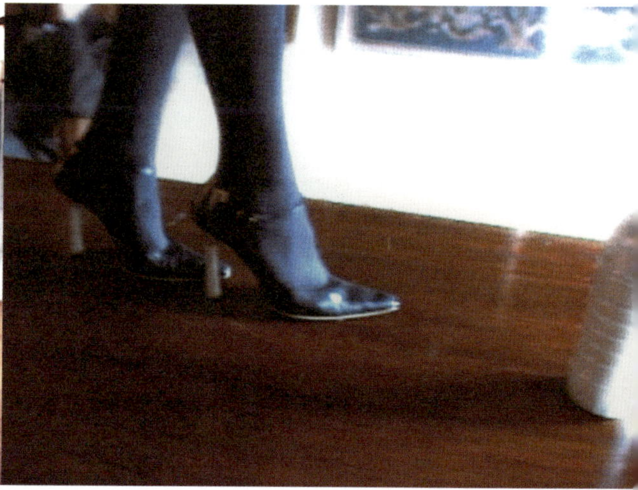

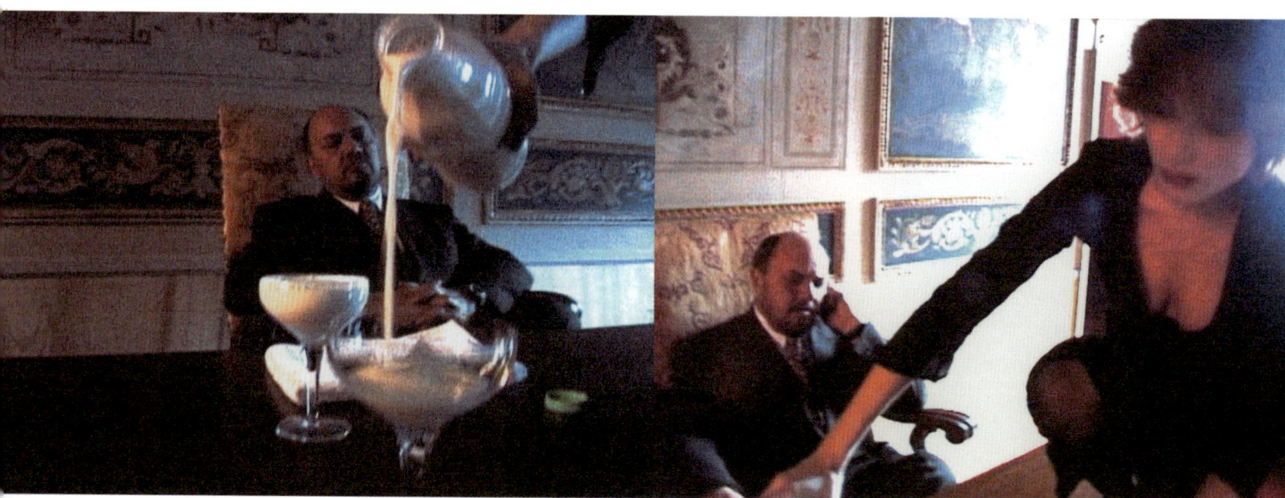

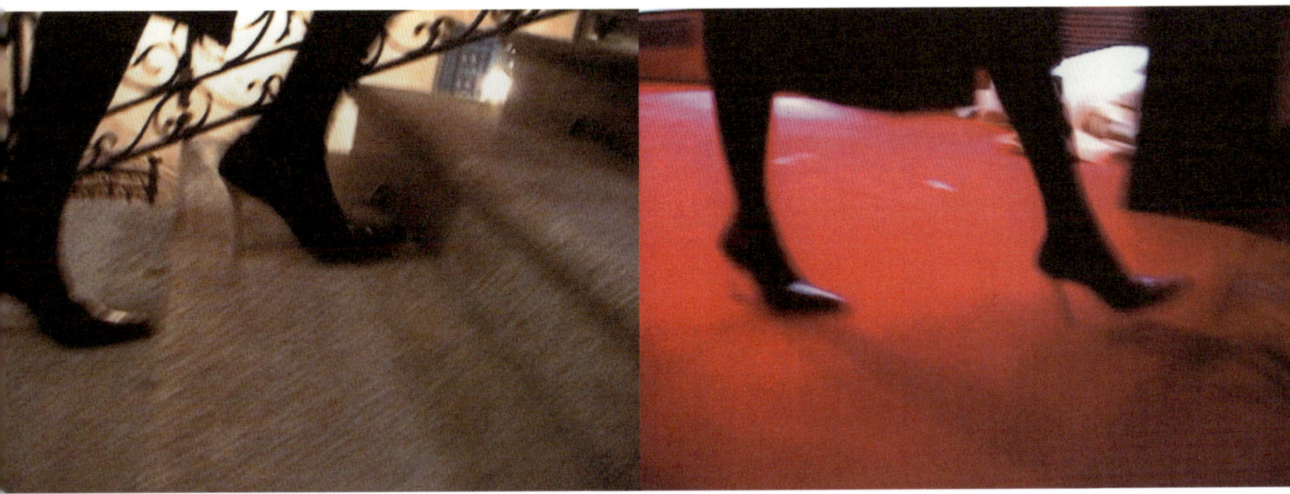

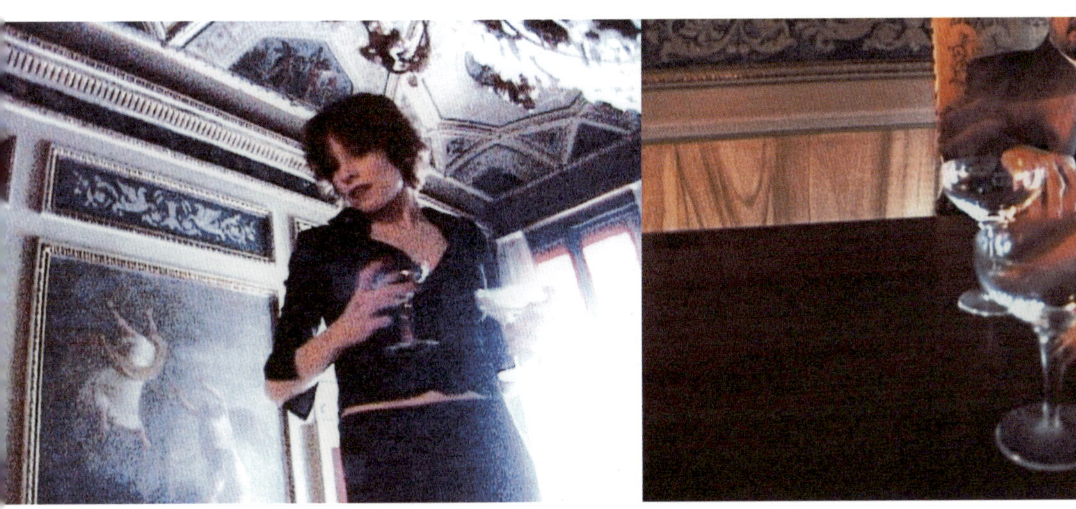

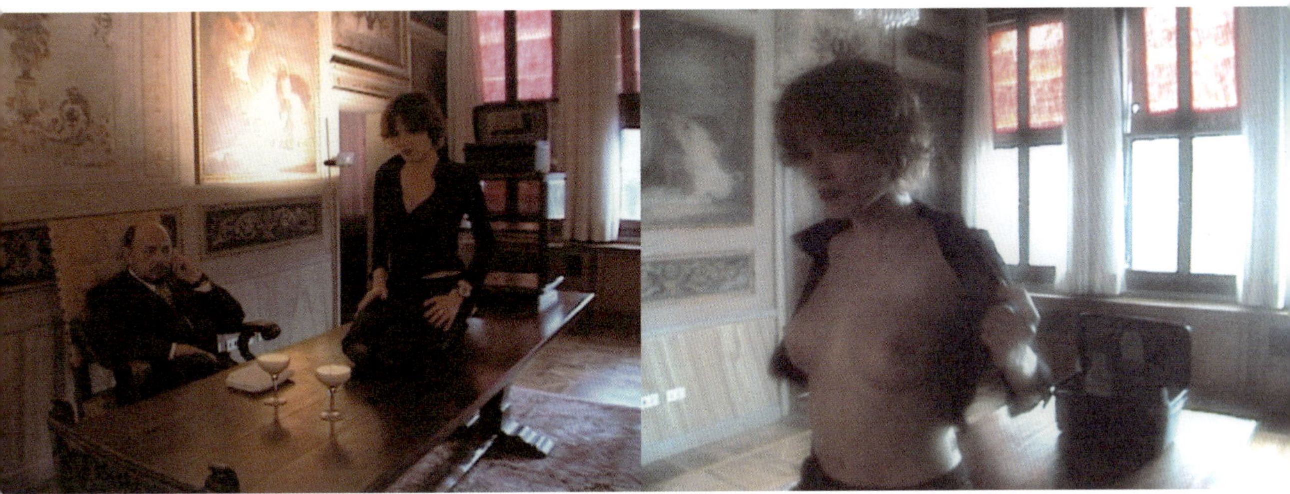

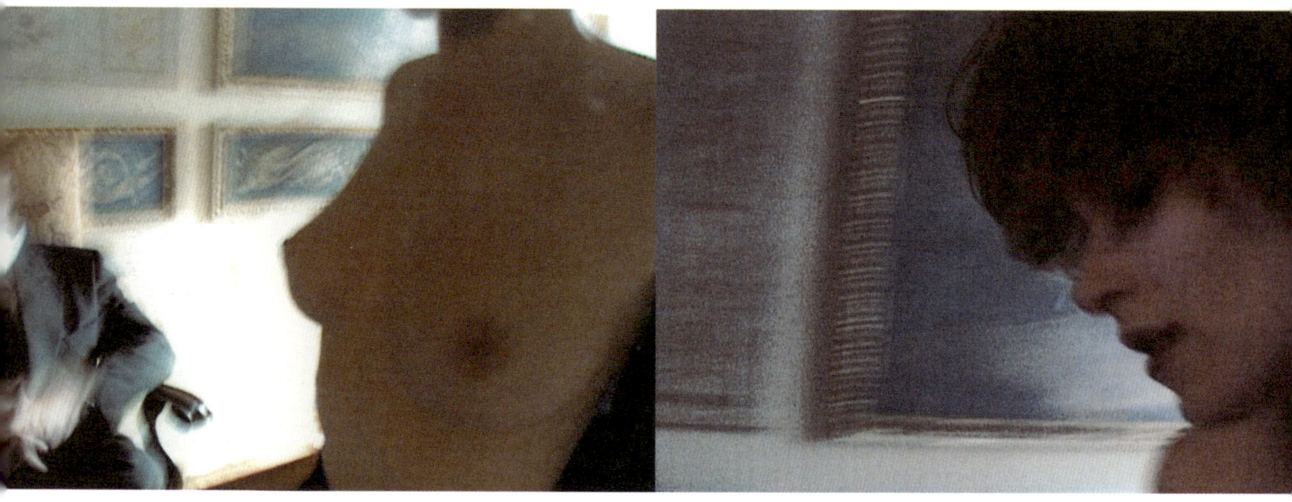

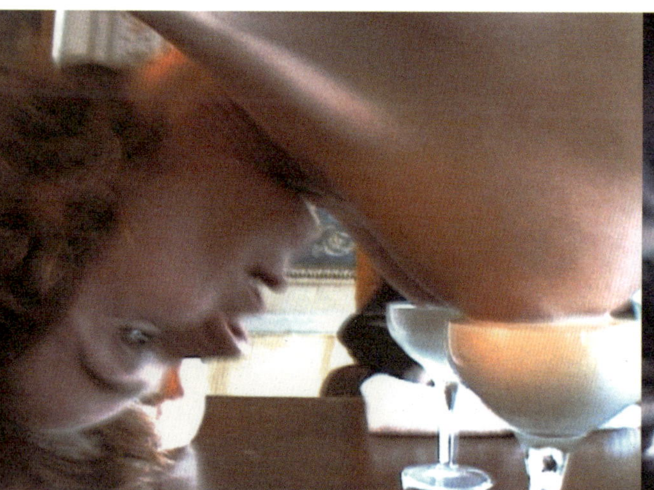

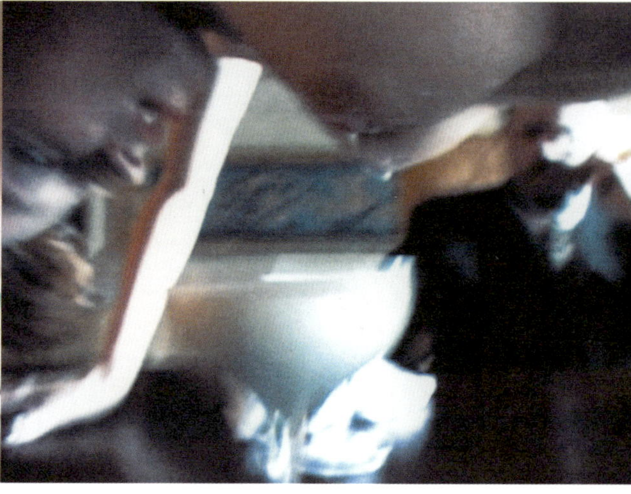

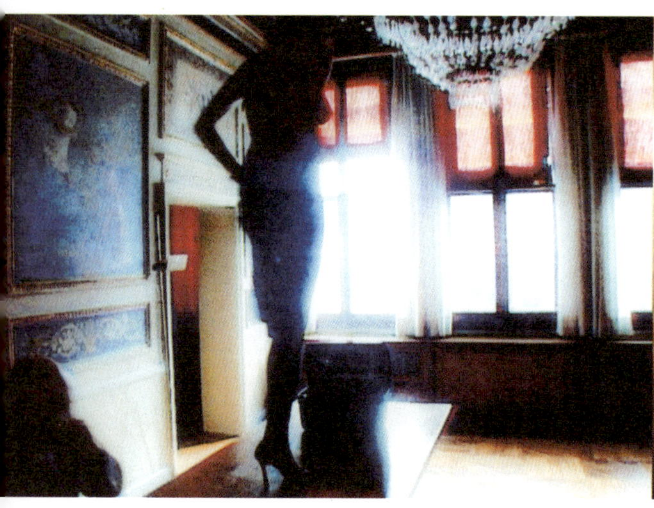

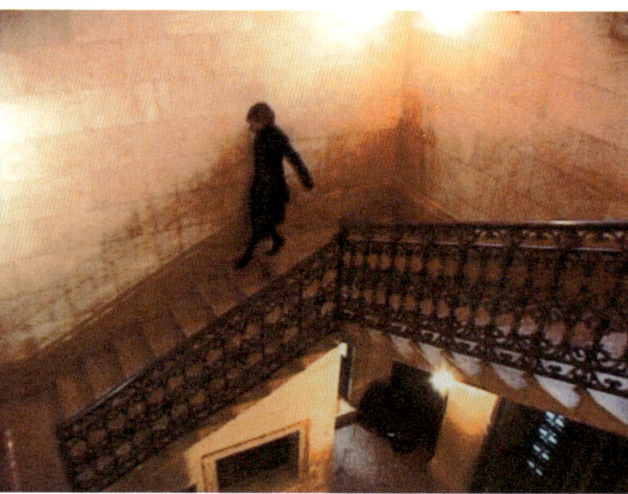

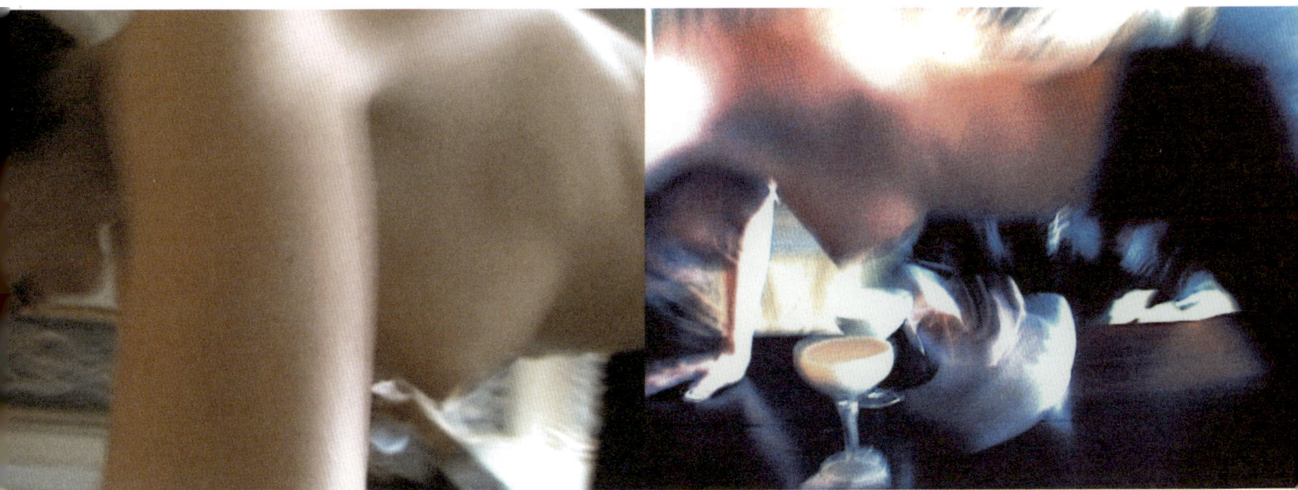

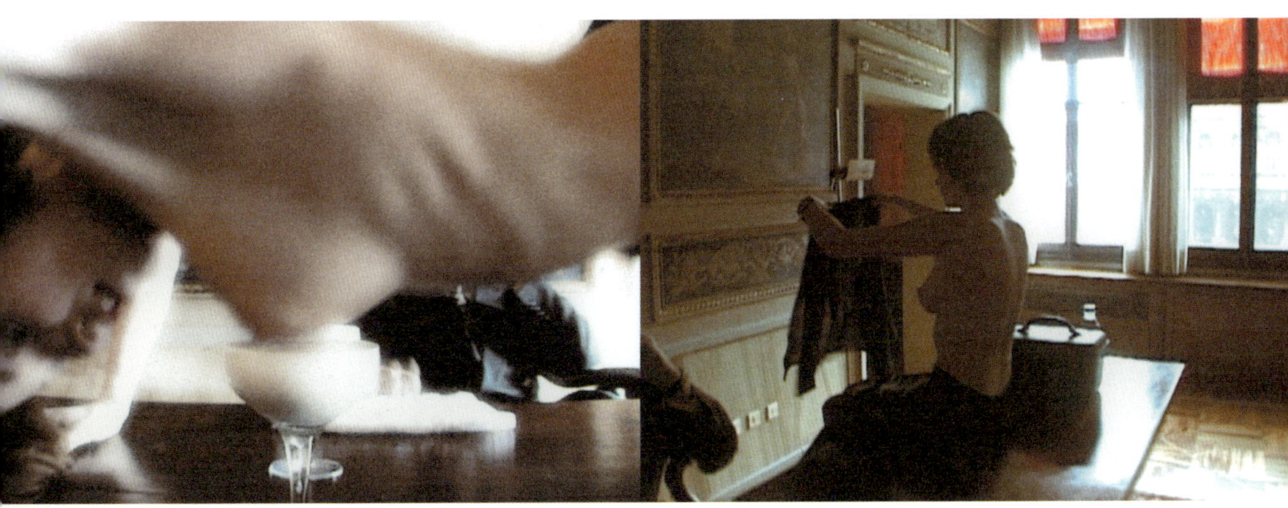

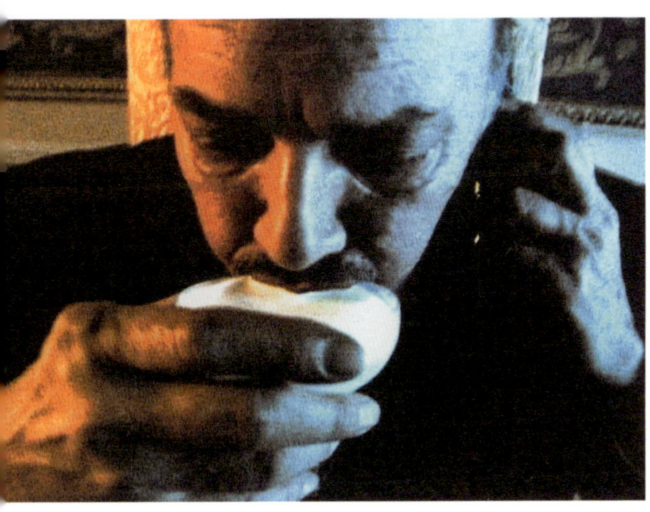

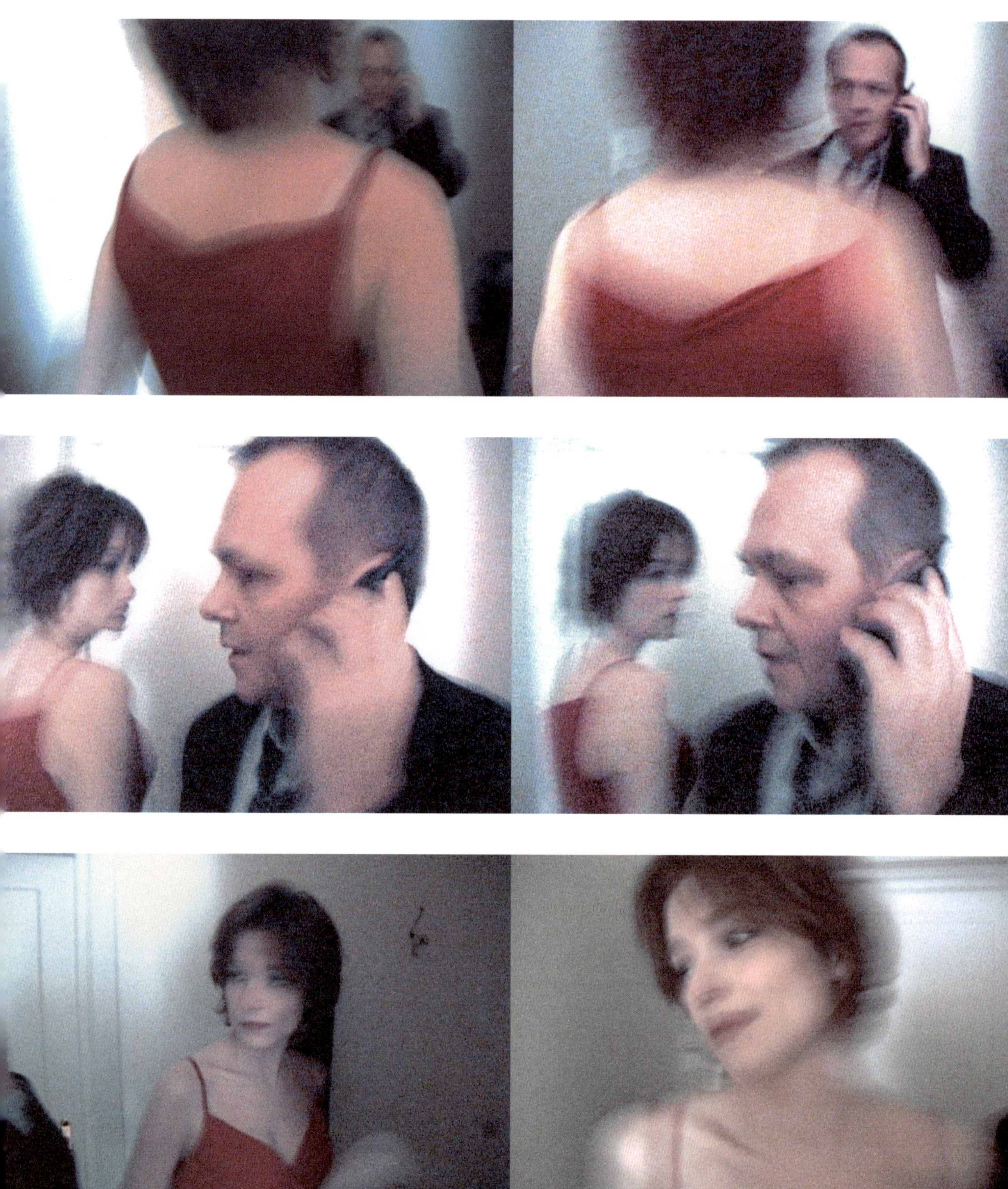

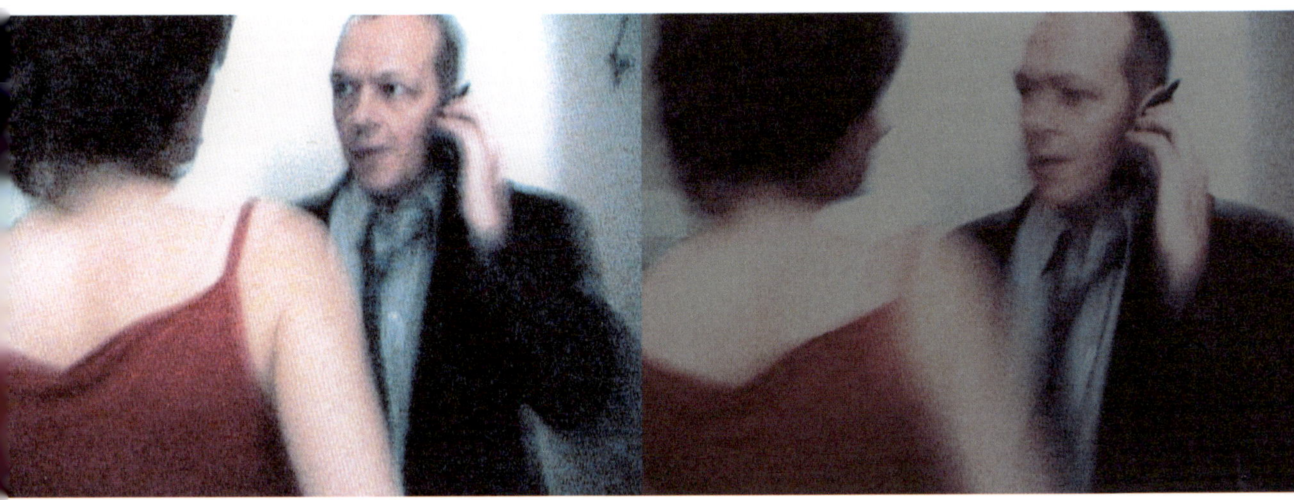

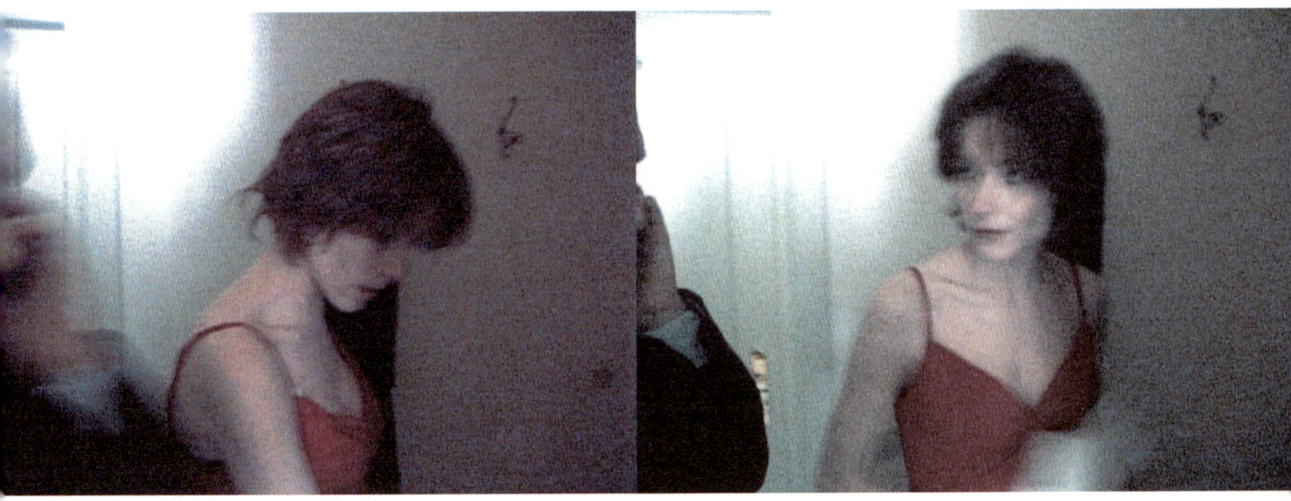

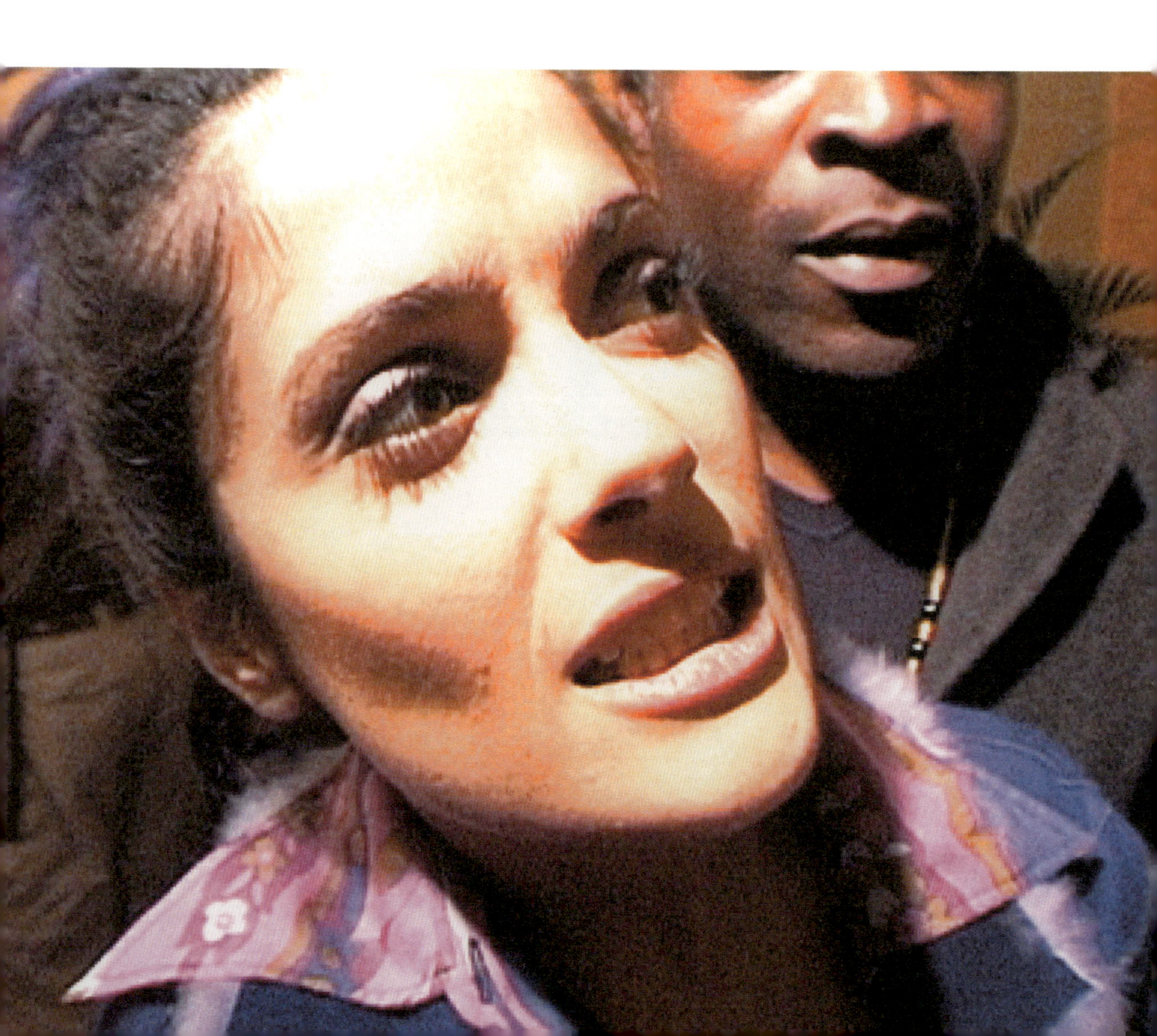

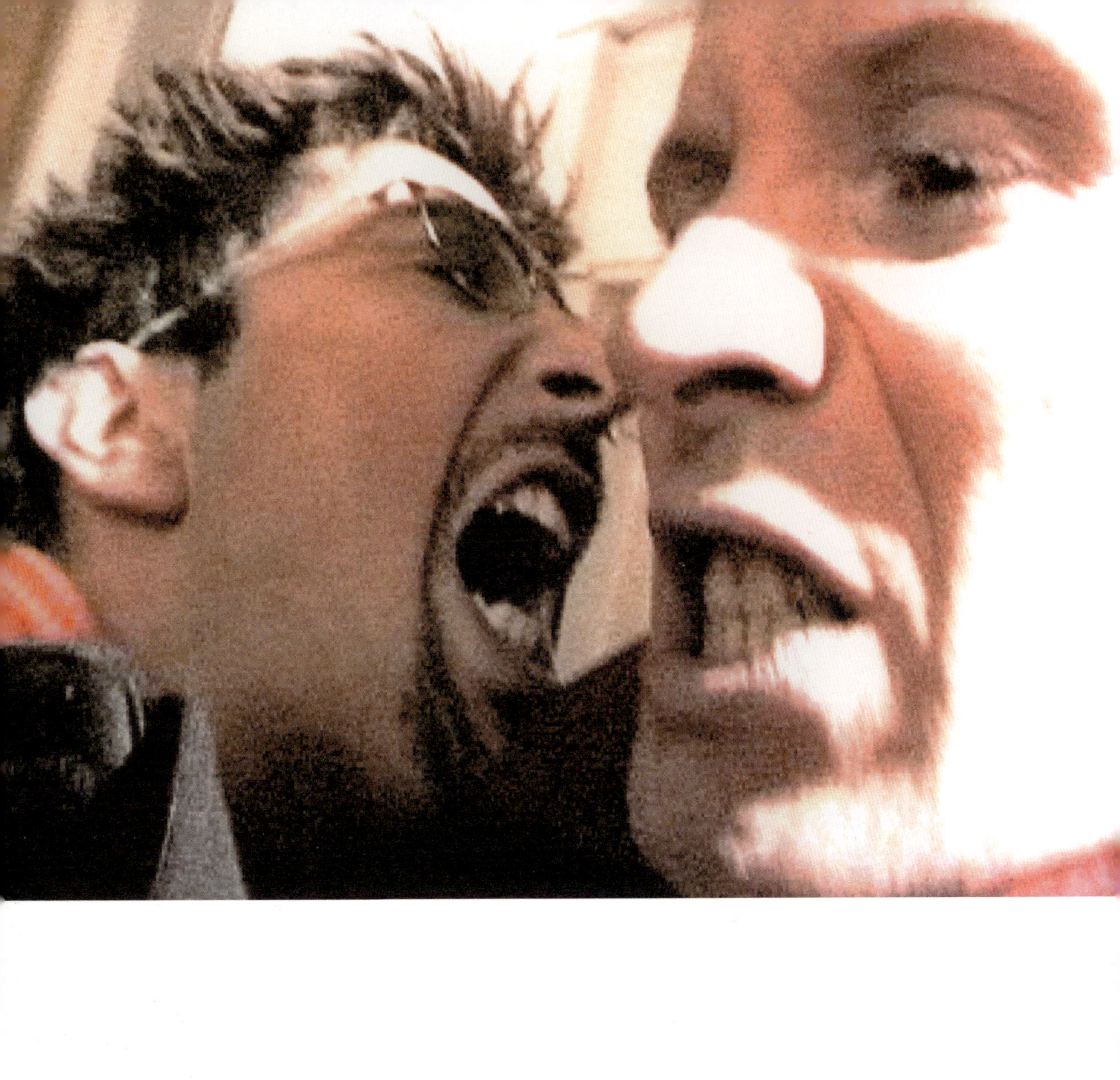

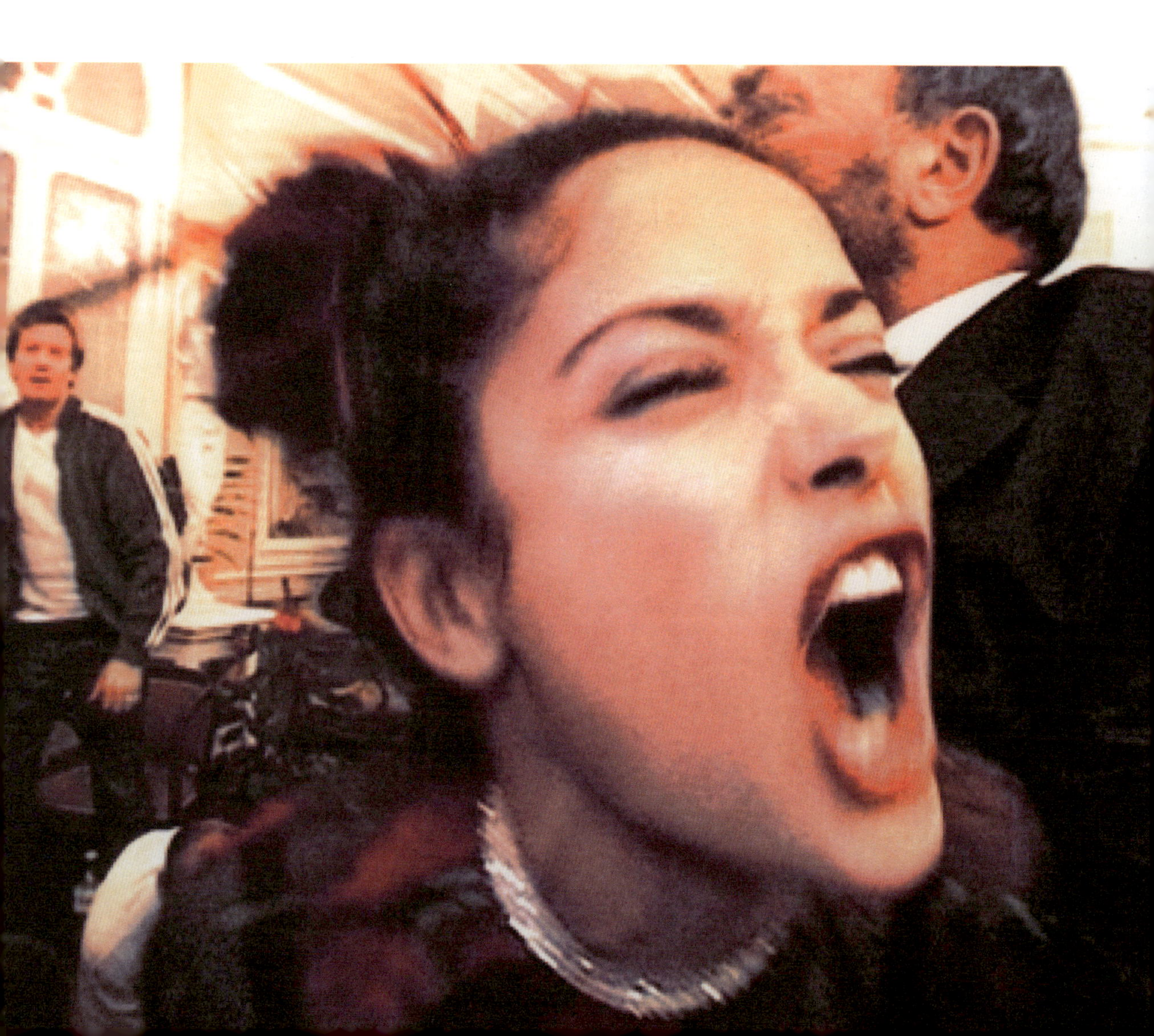

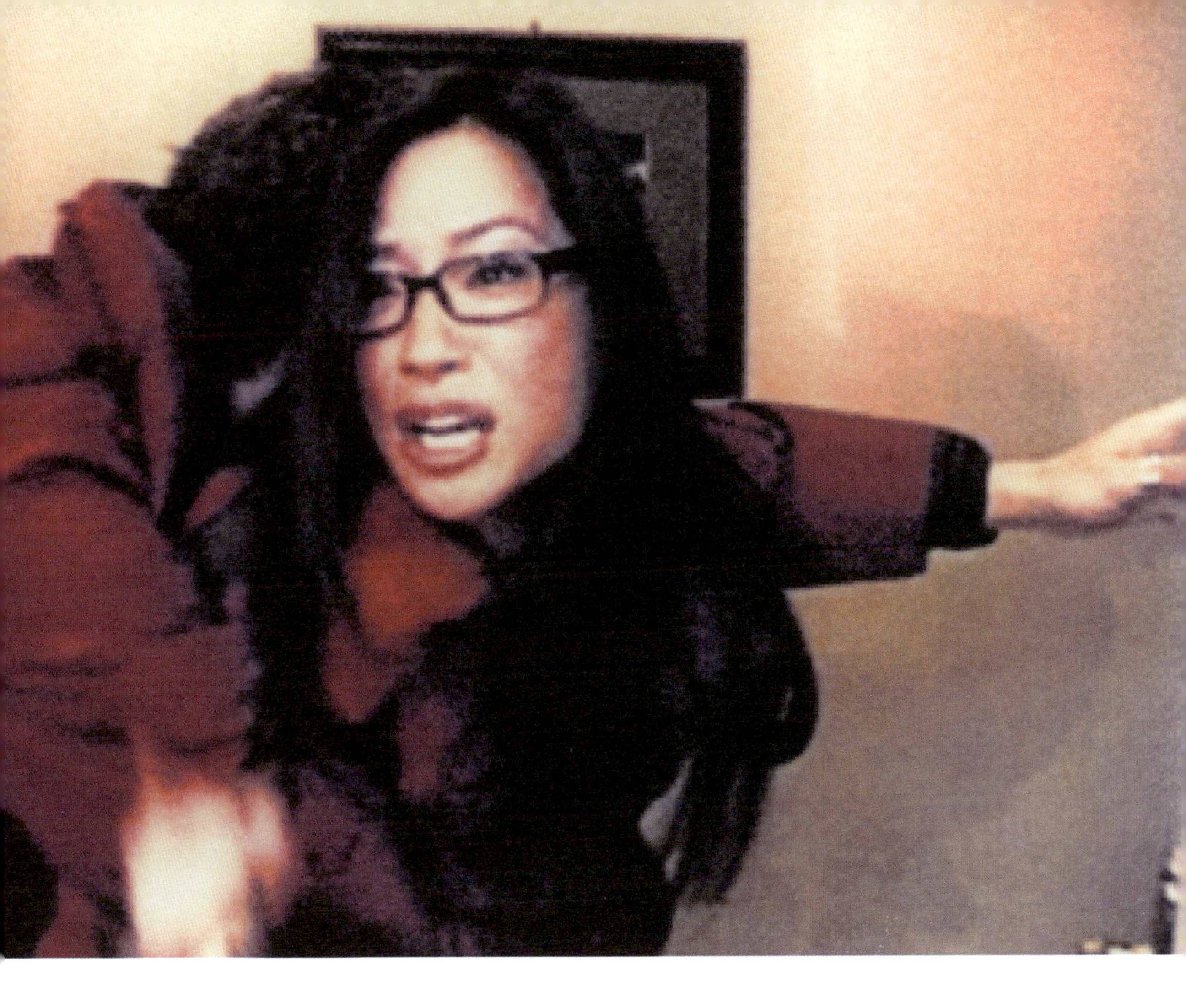

One Killer down

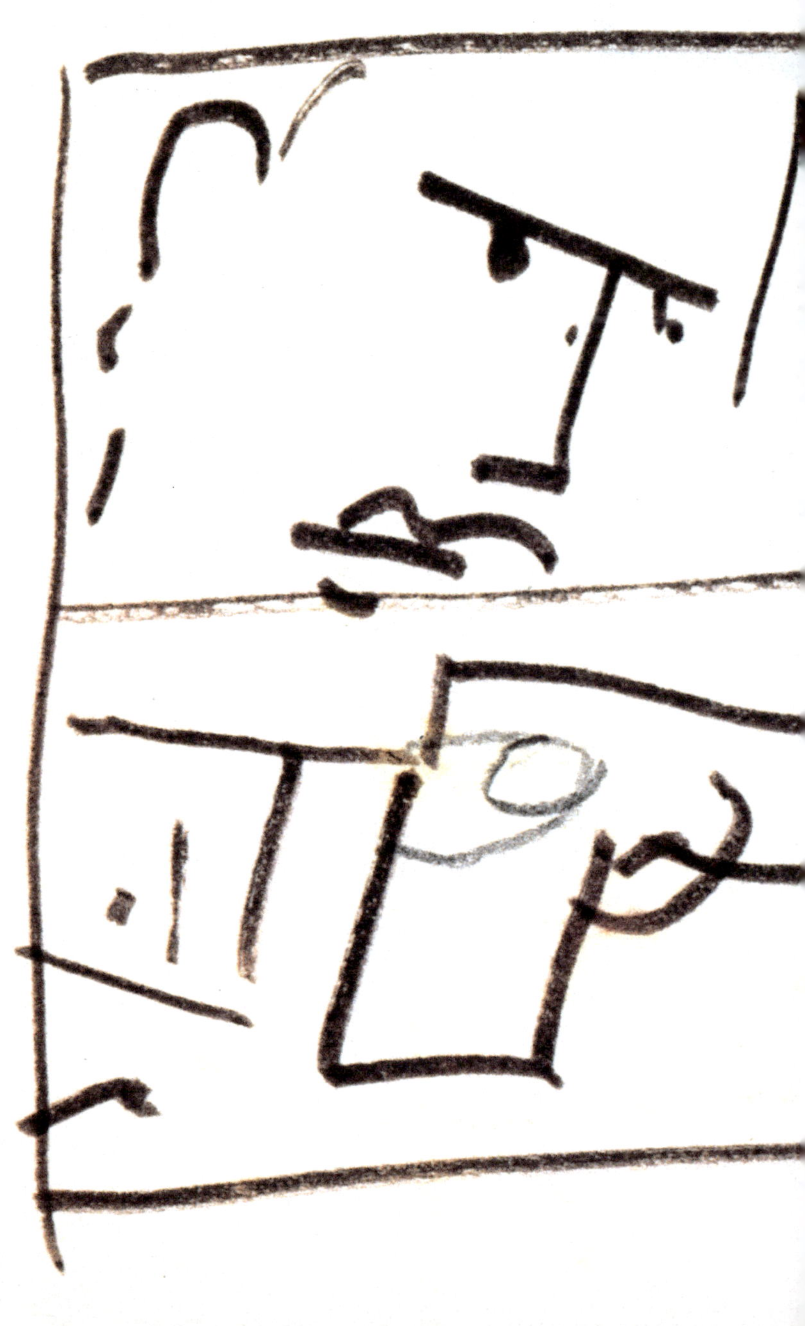

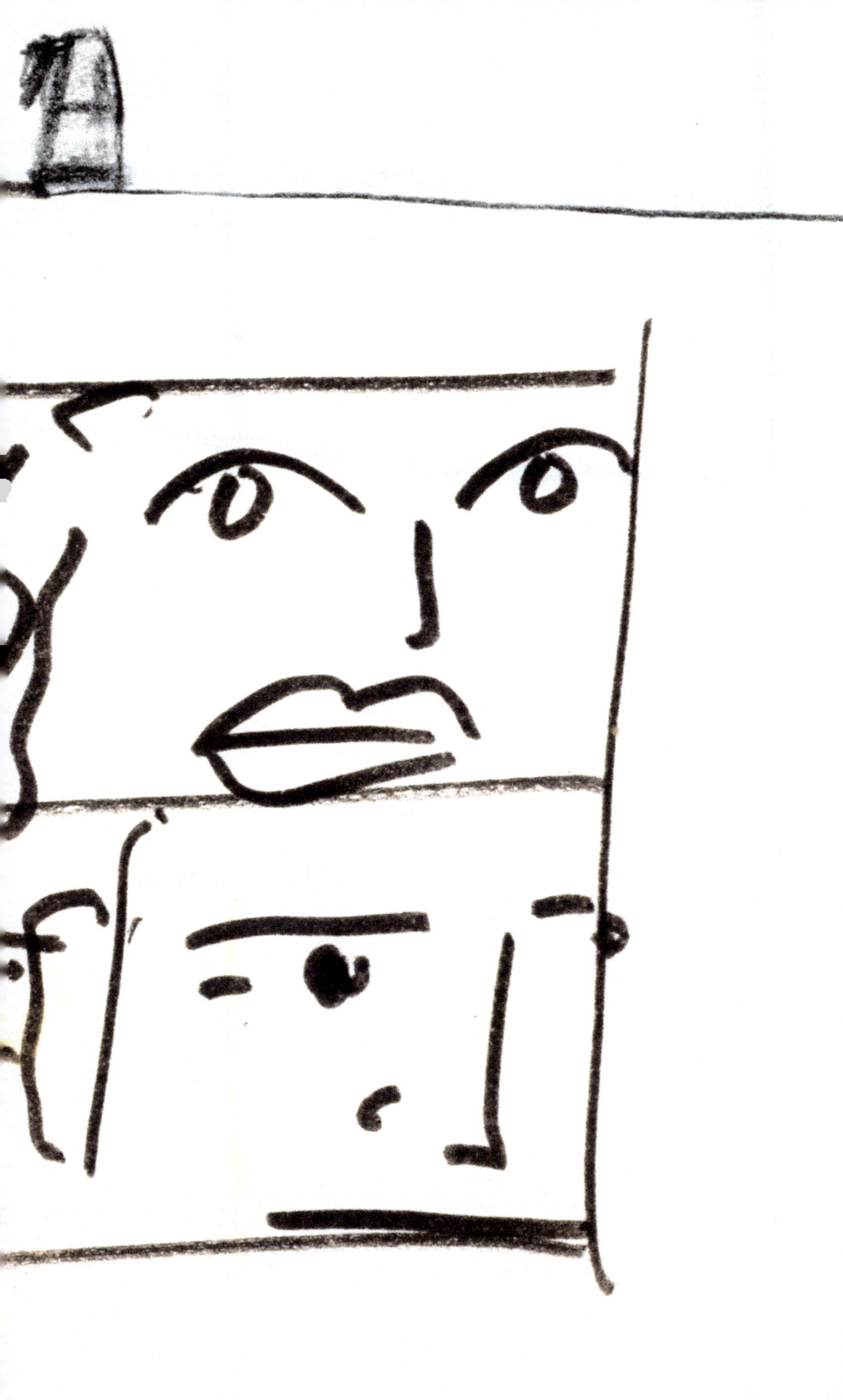

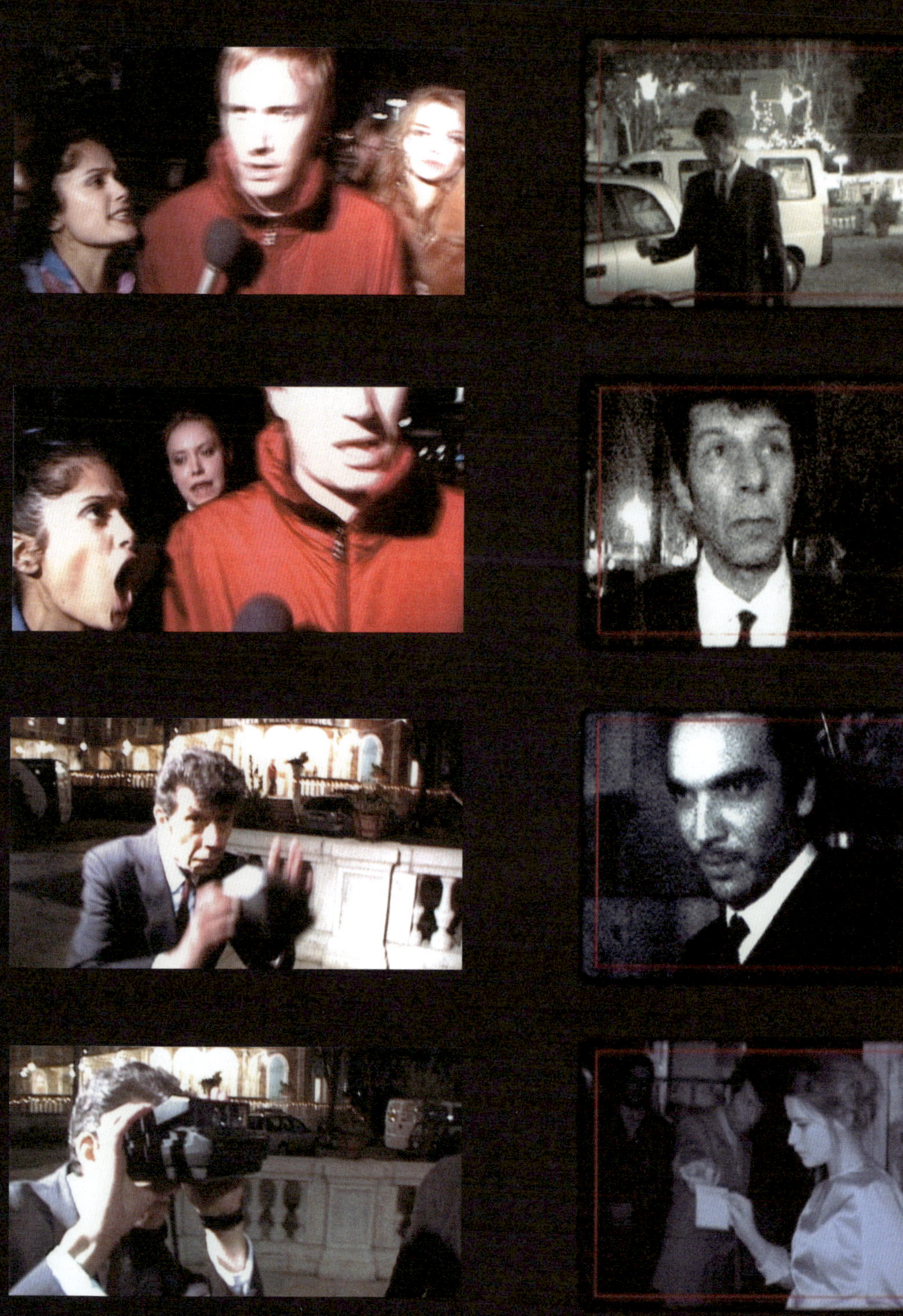

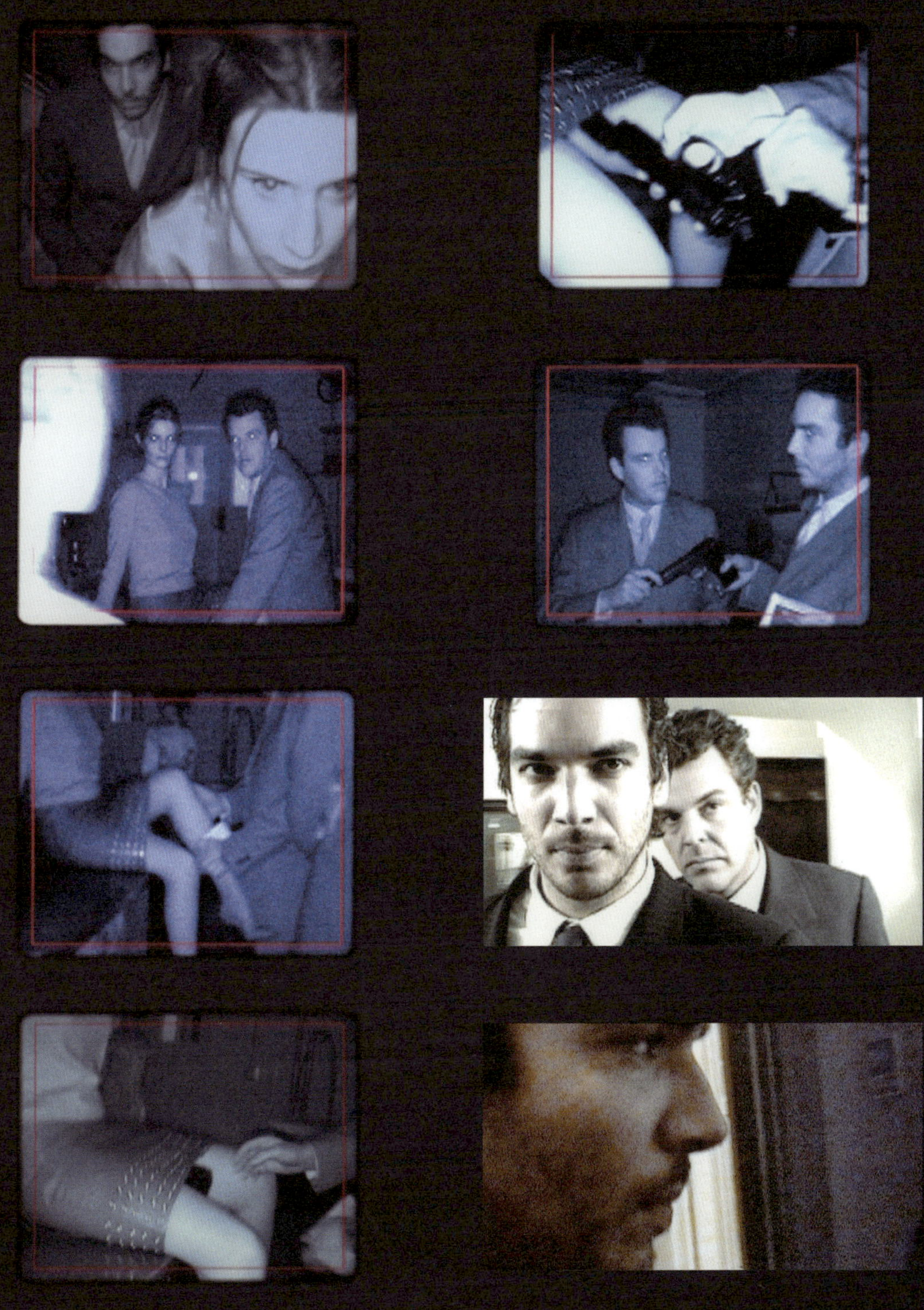

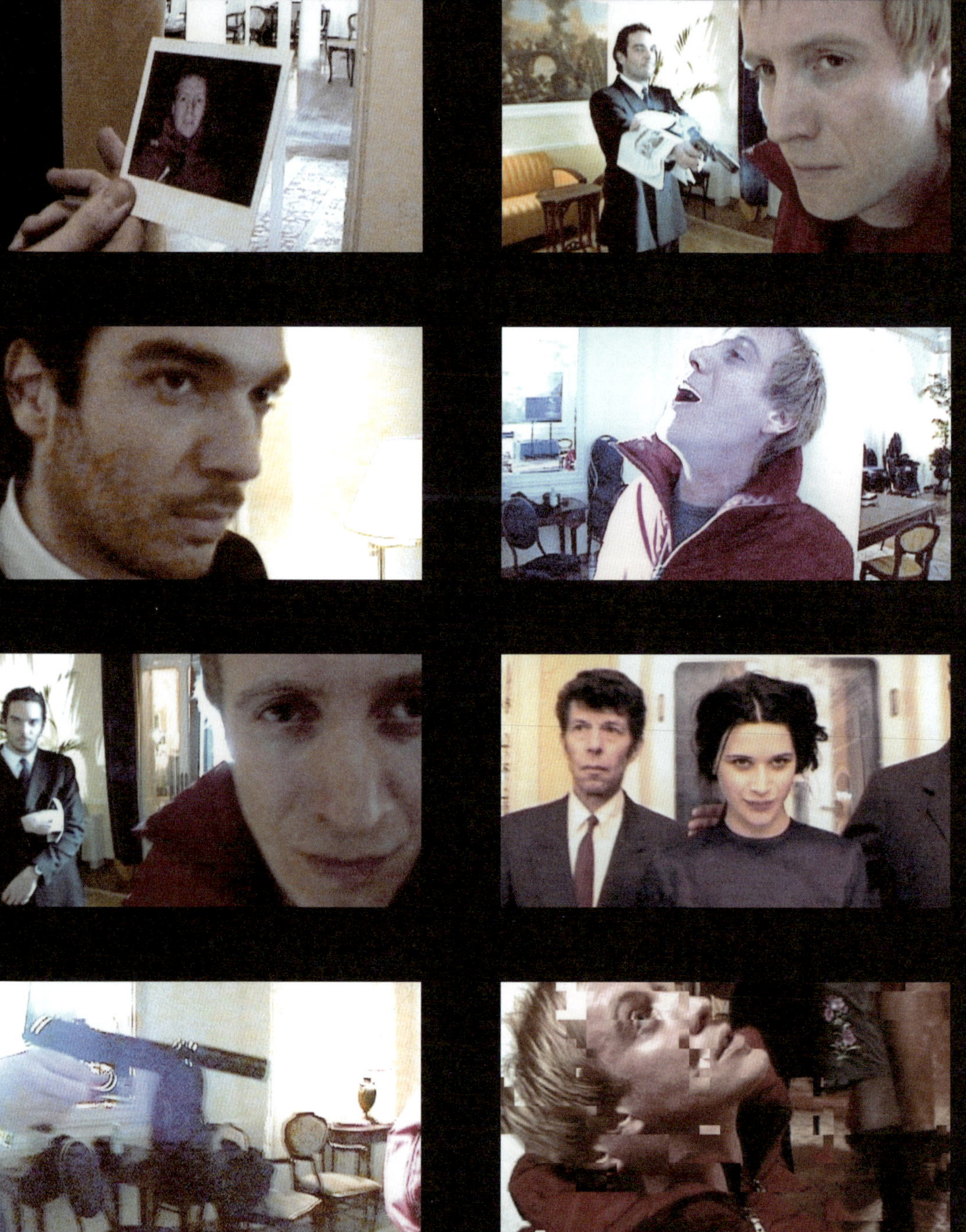

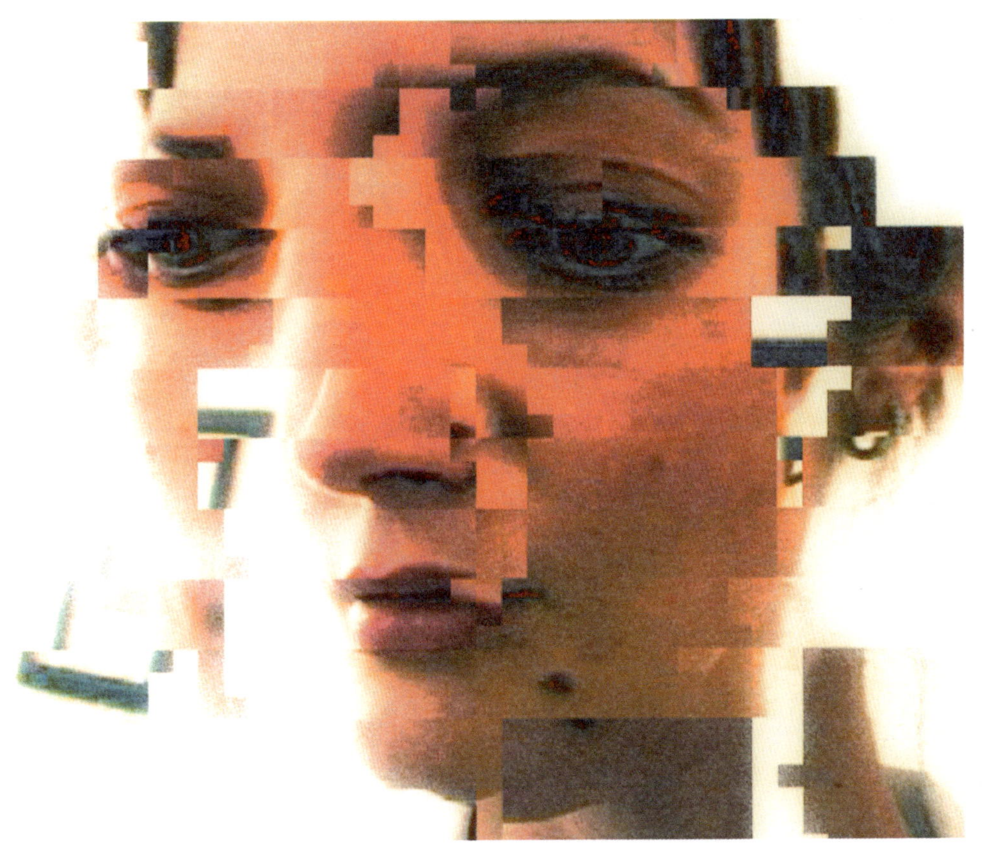

As we began editing the film I realized that there were some beautiful effects being created – just by speeding up the tape – a kind of digital cubism. Images that would have been difficult (and expensive) to fabricate in a post-production facility.

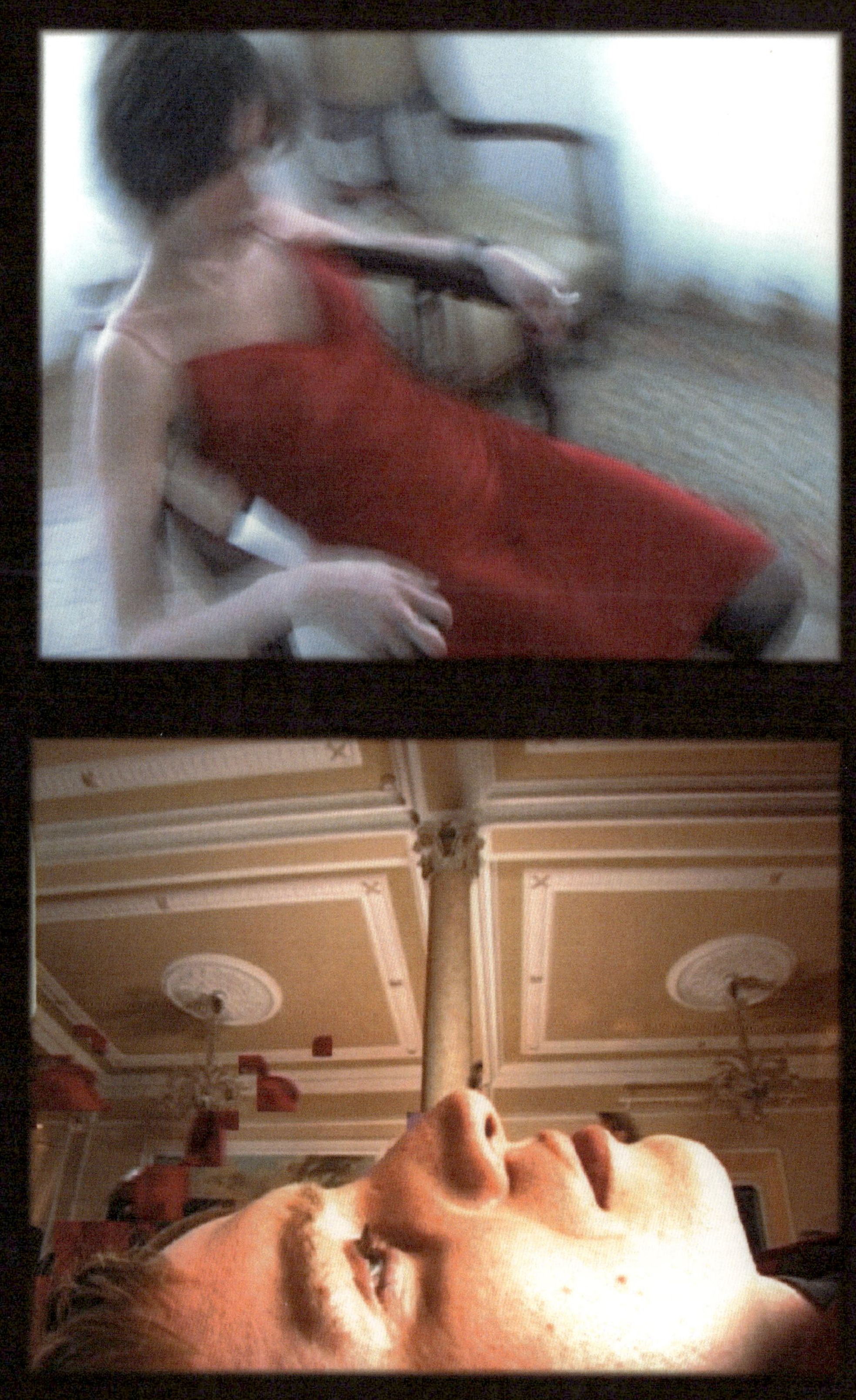

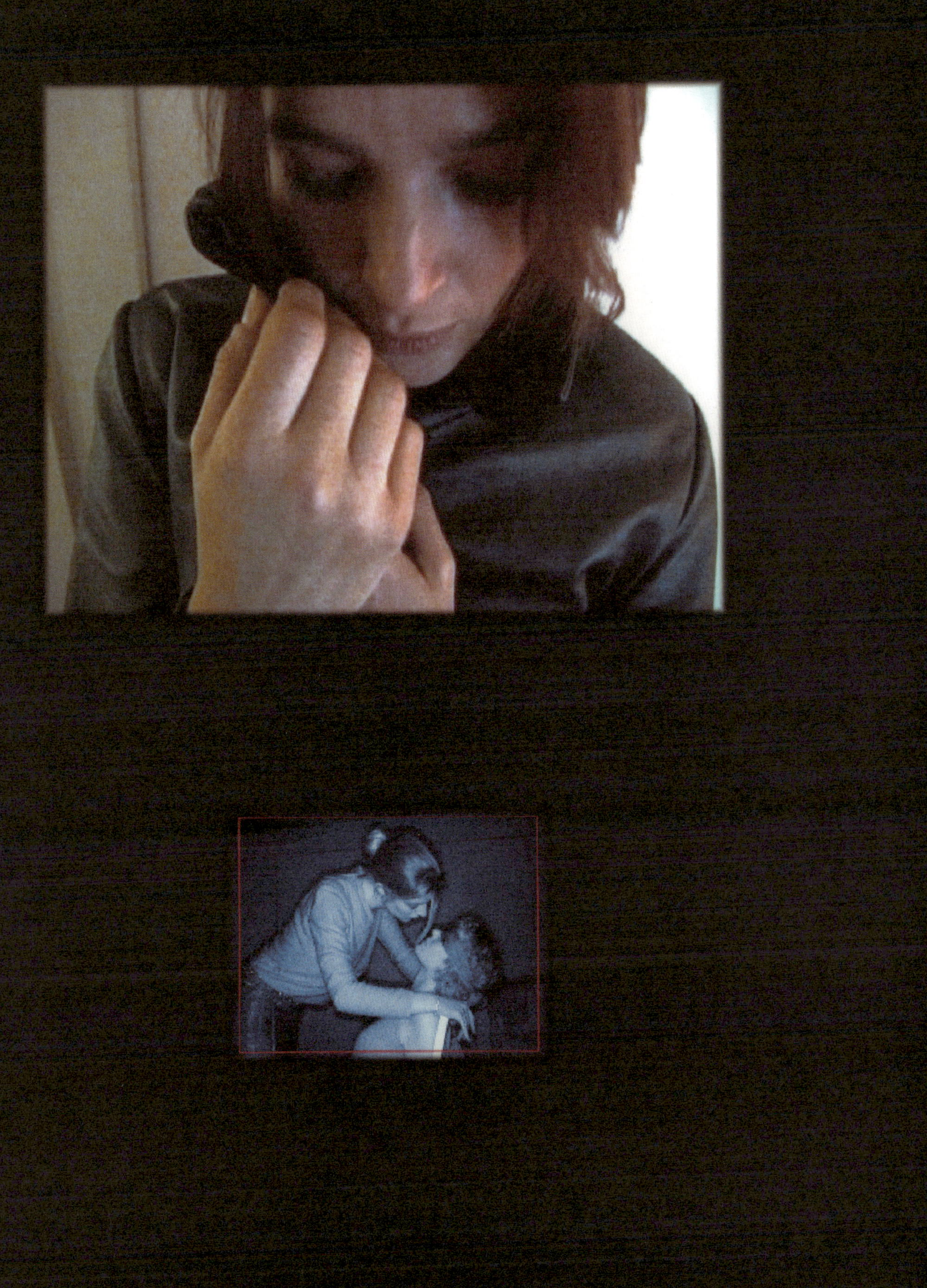

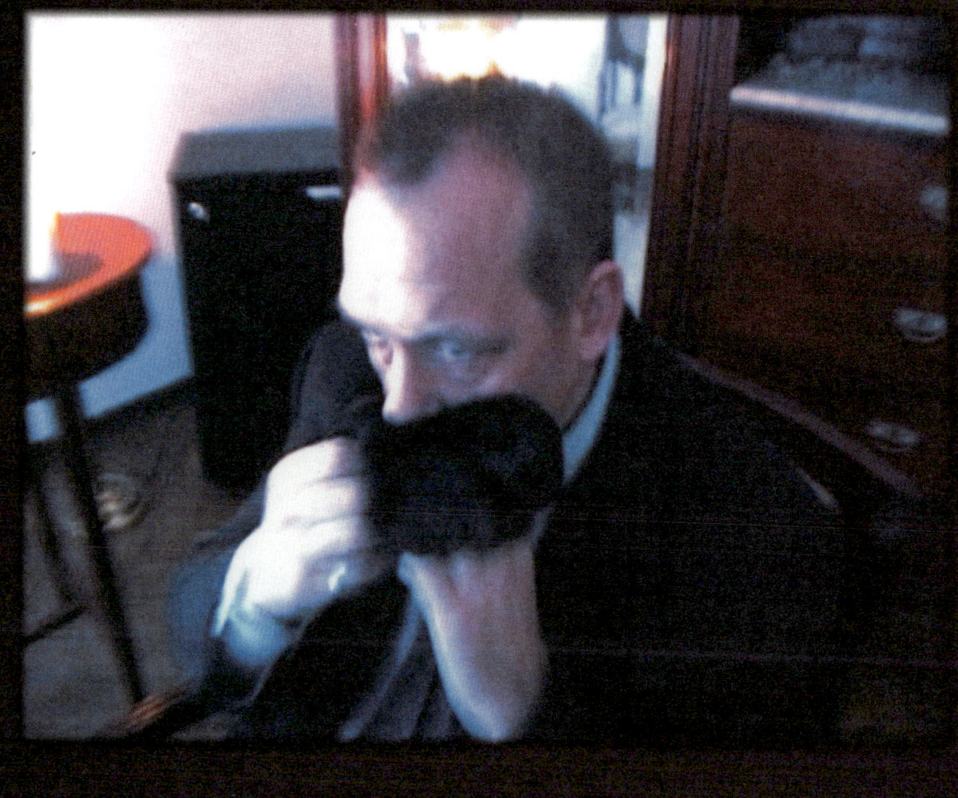

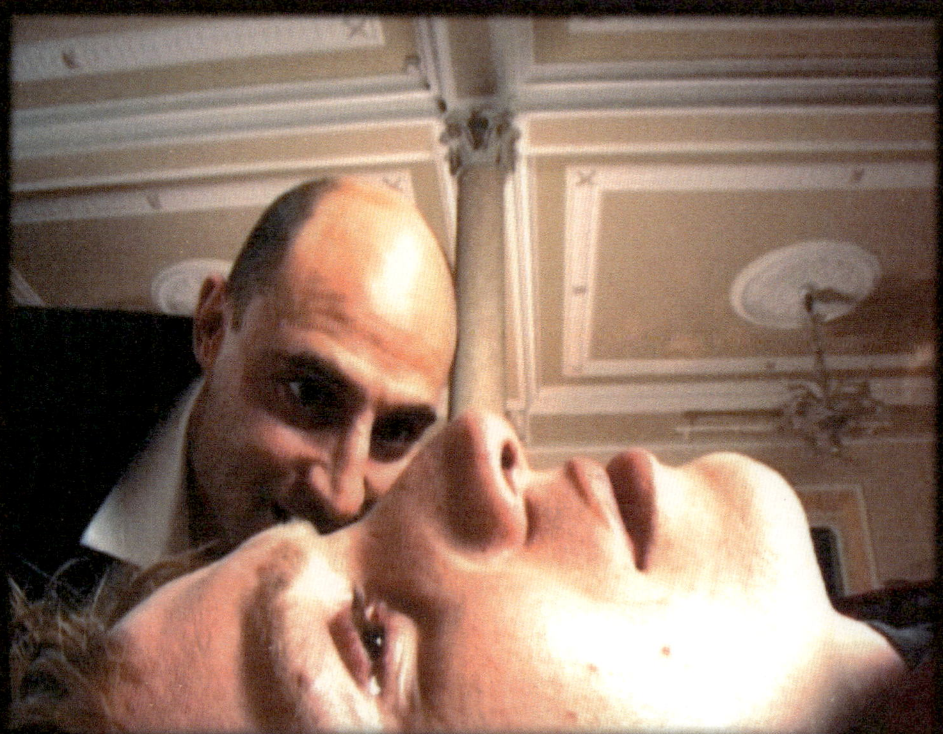

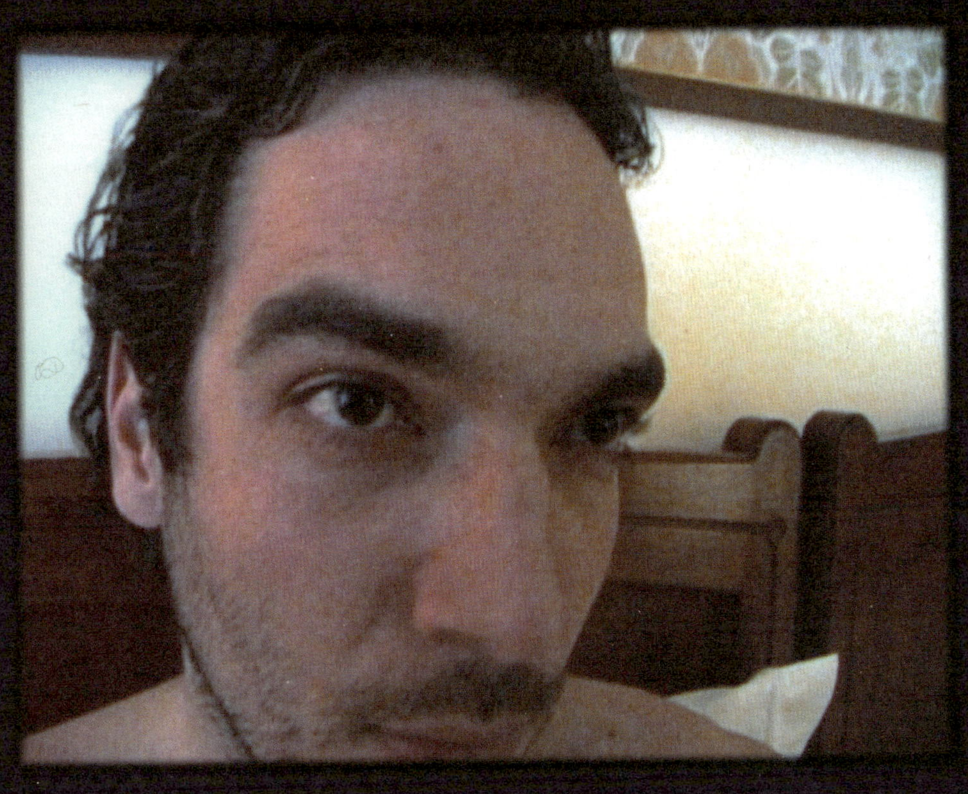

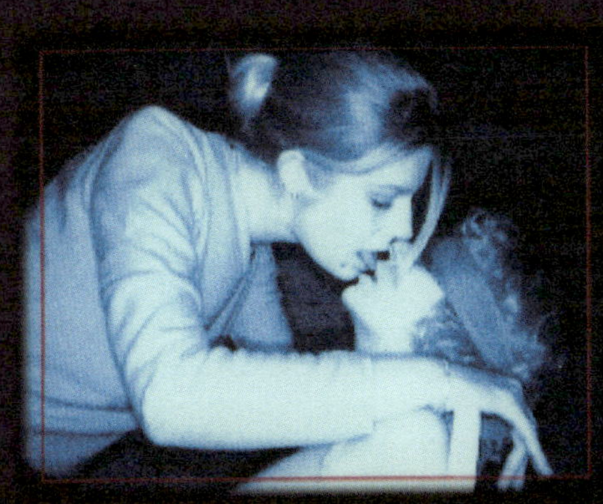

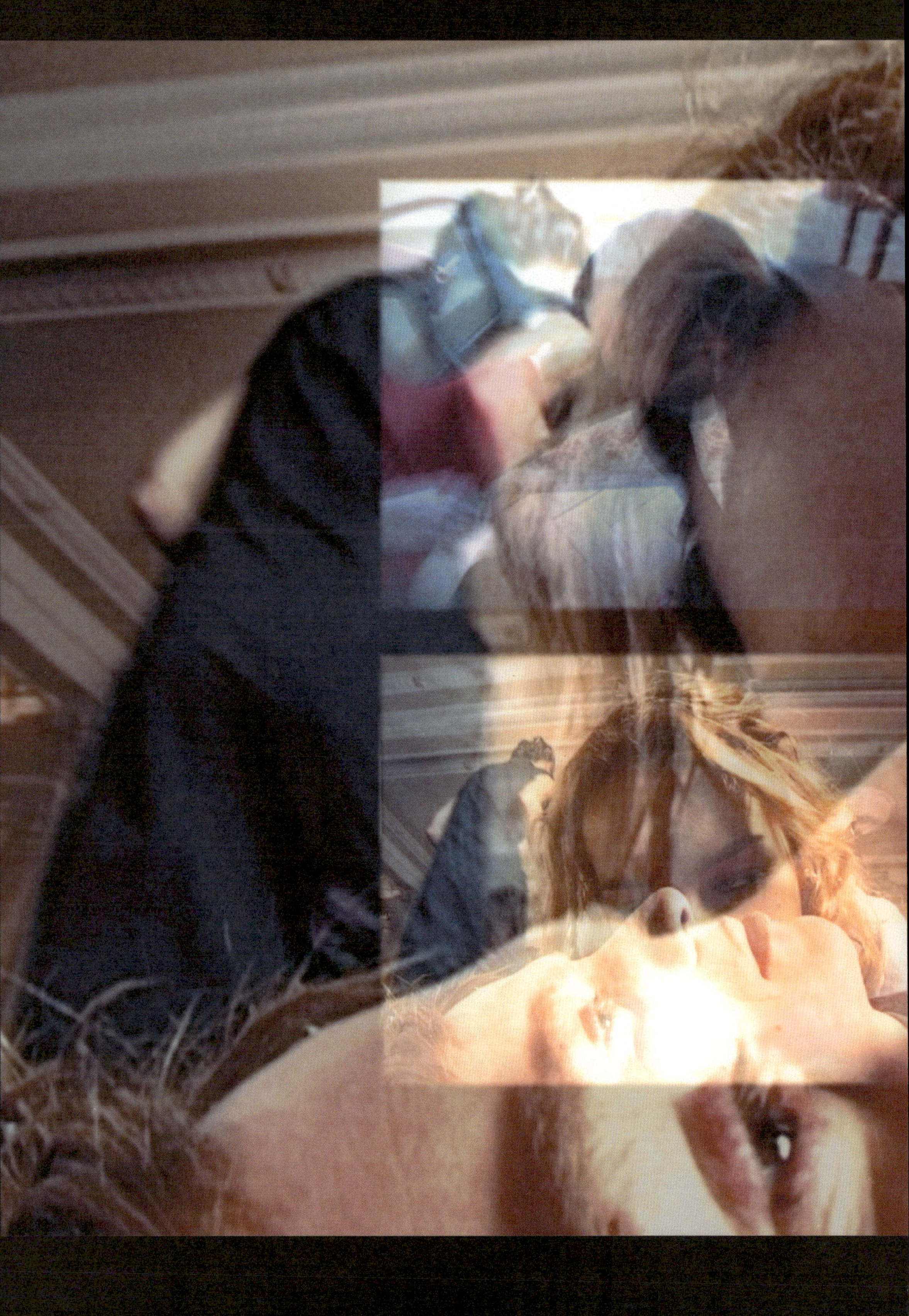

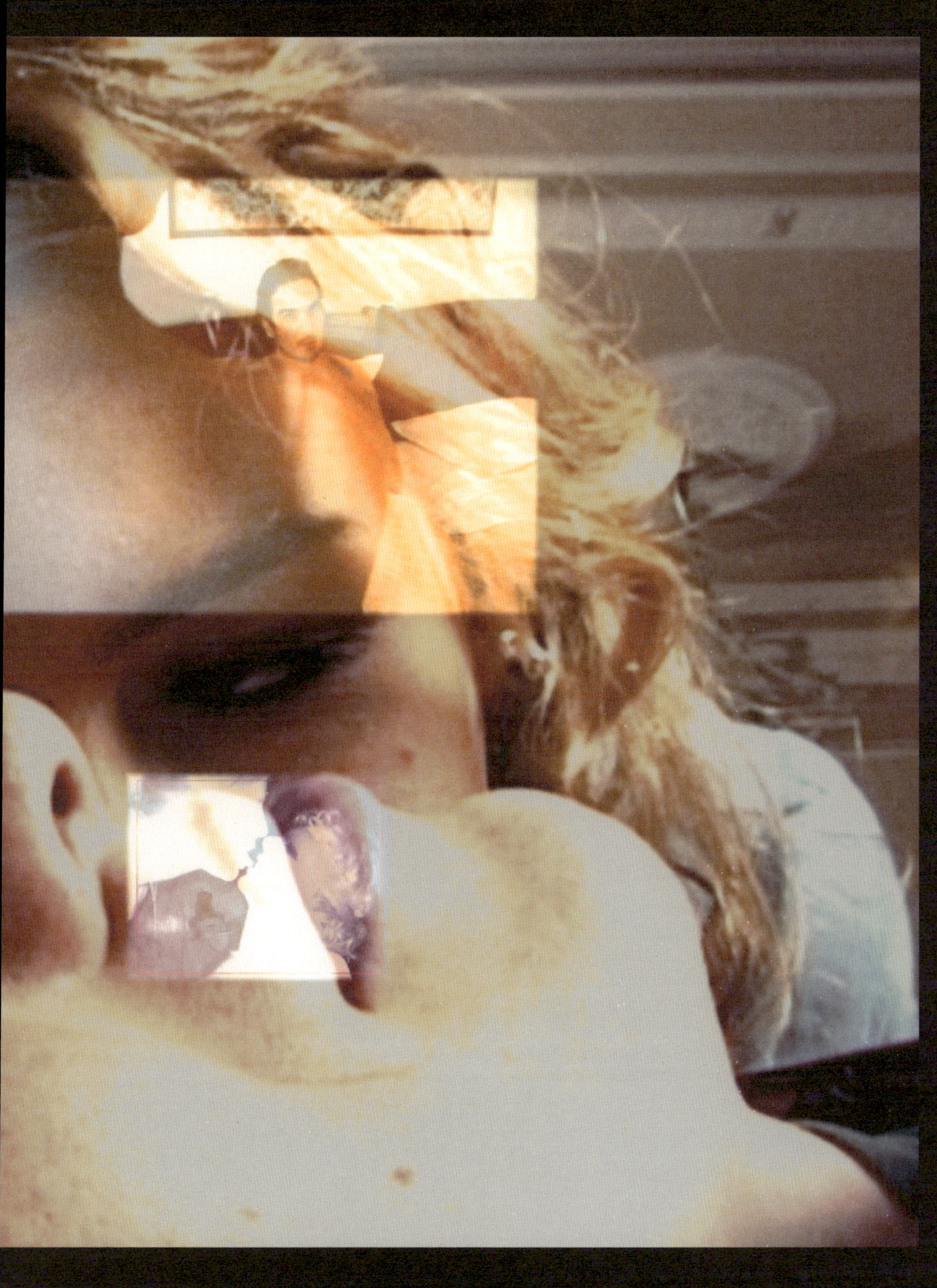

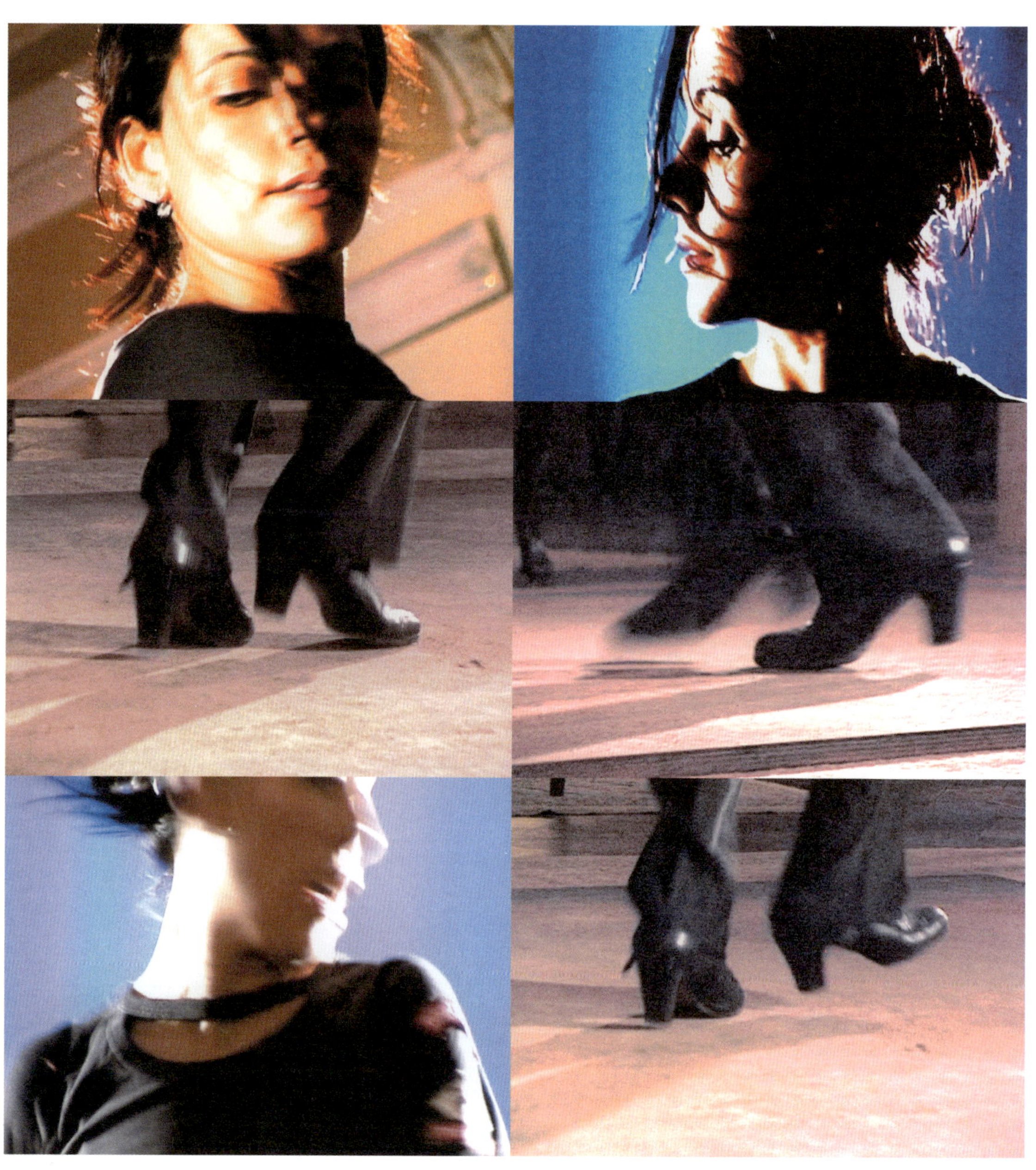

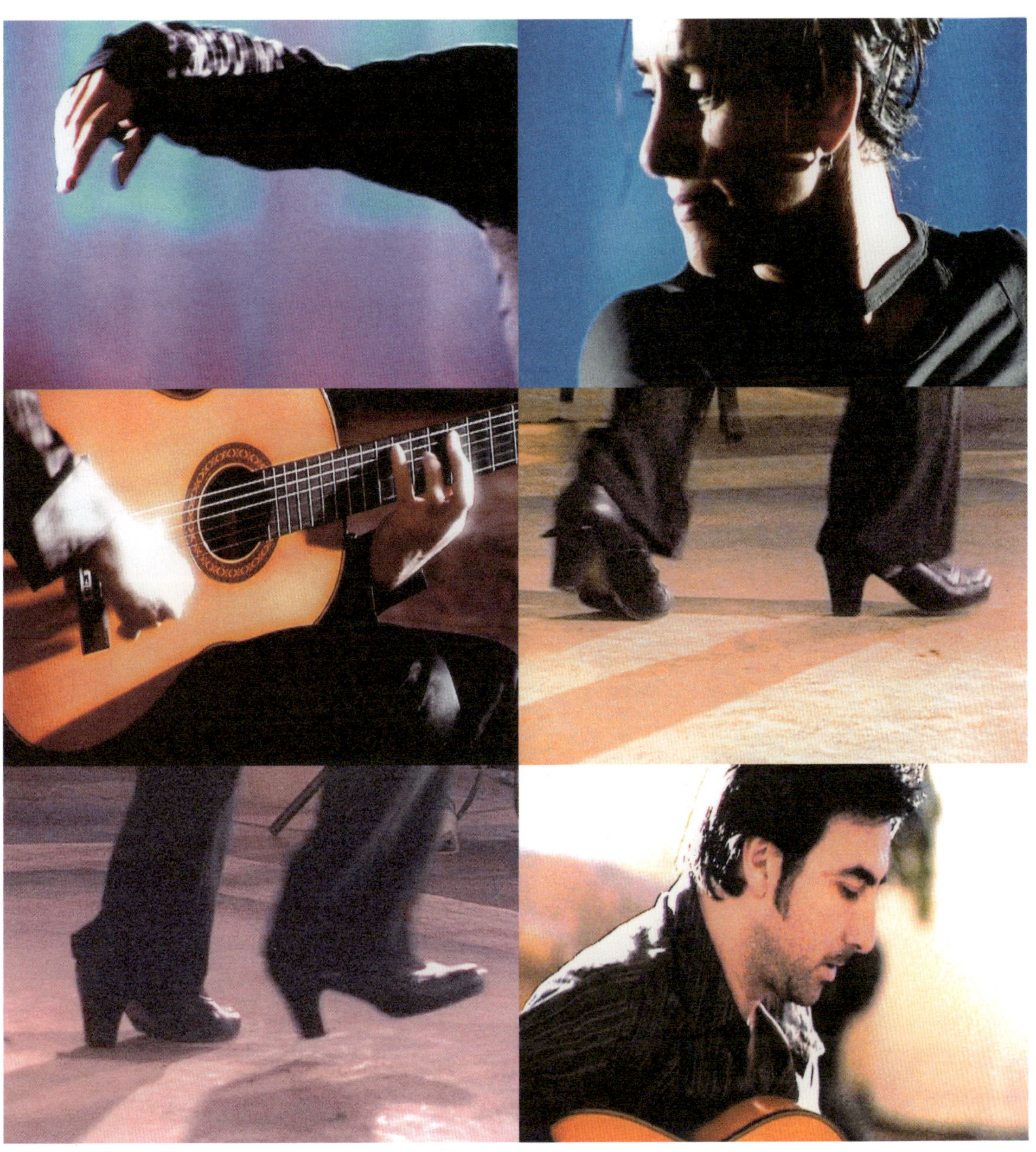

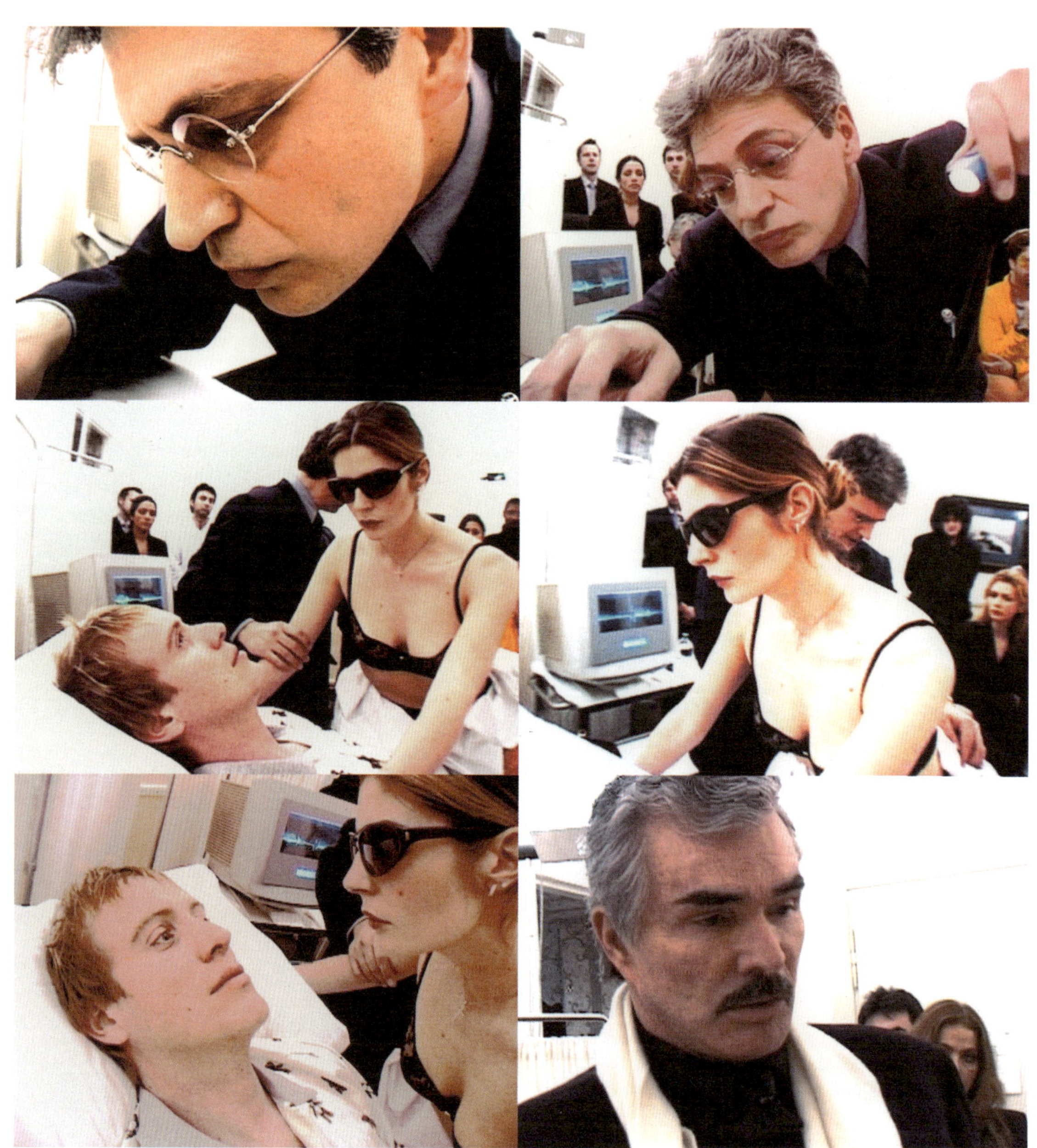

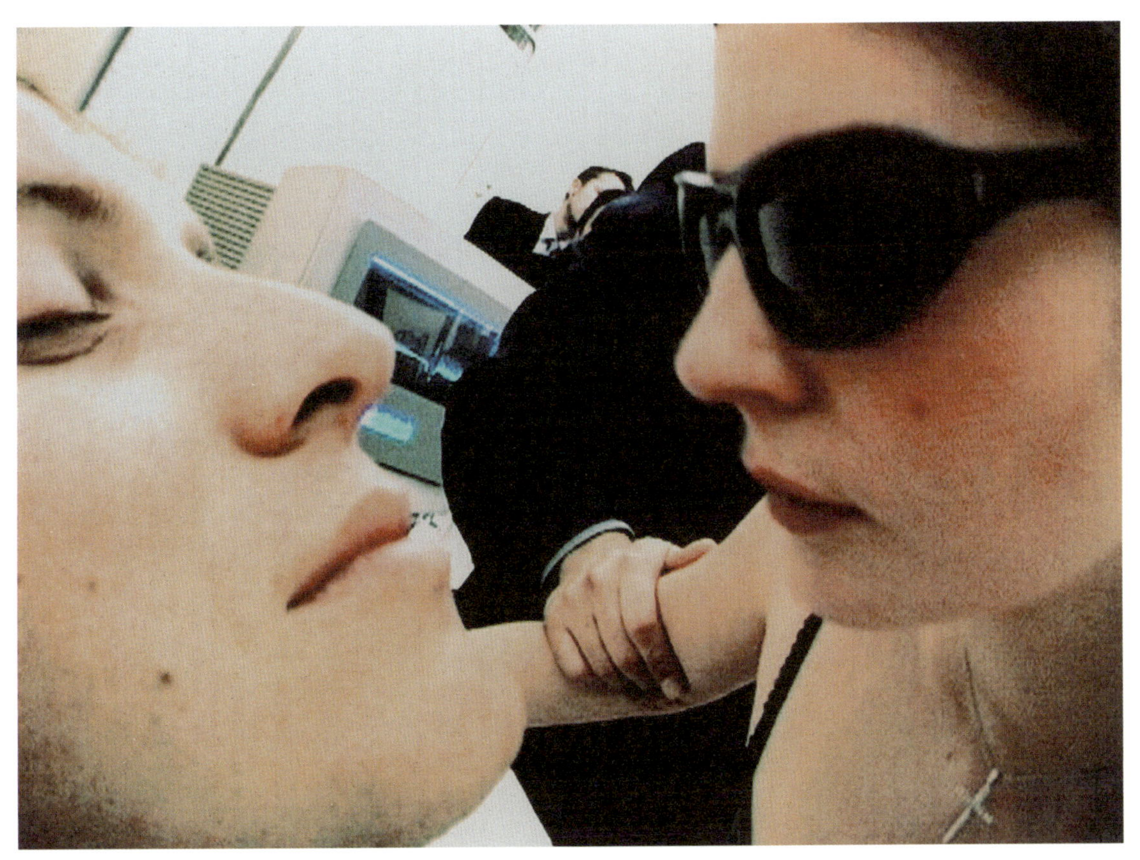

FAMOUS DOCTOR
(heavy Italian accent)
As you would say in America
– the lights are on – but nobody
home.

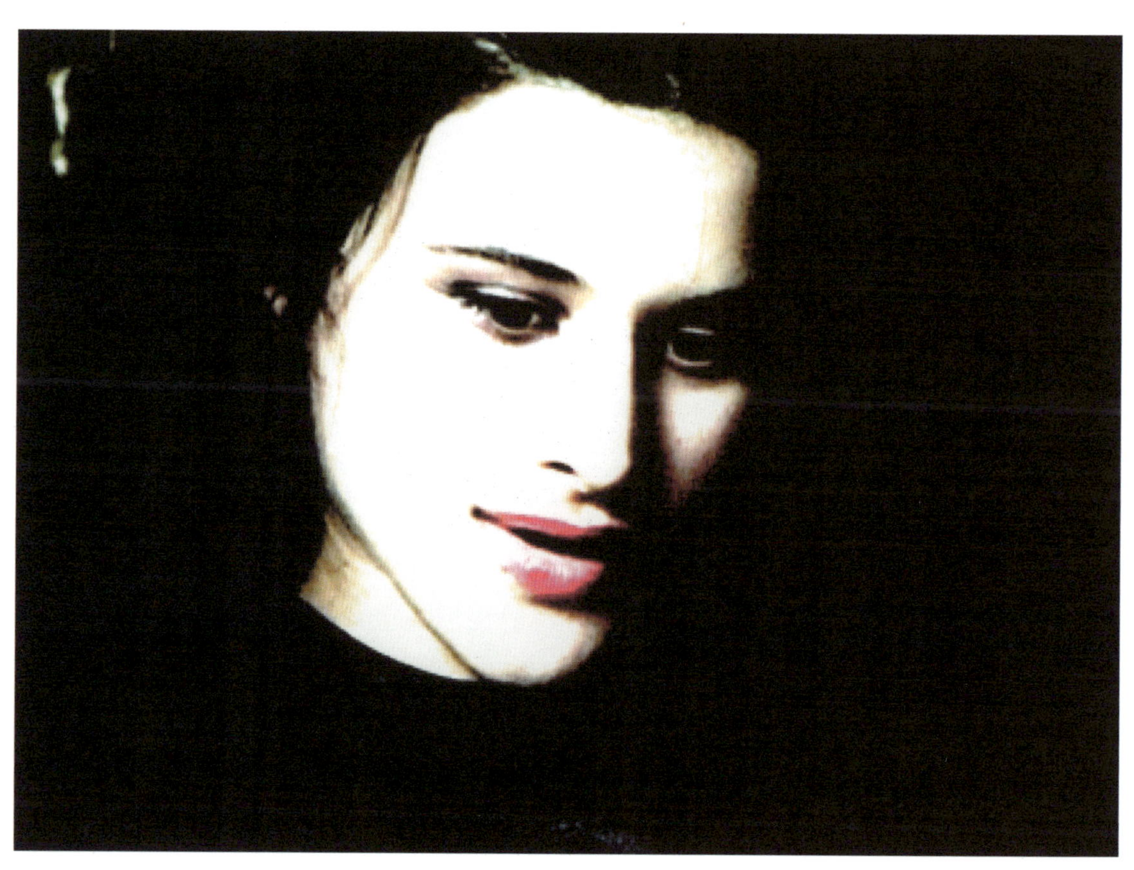

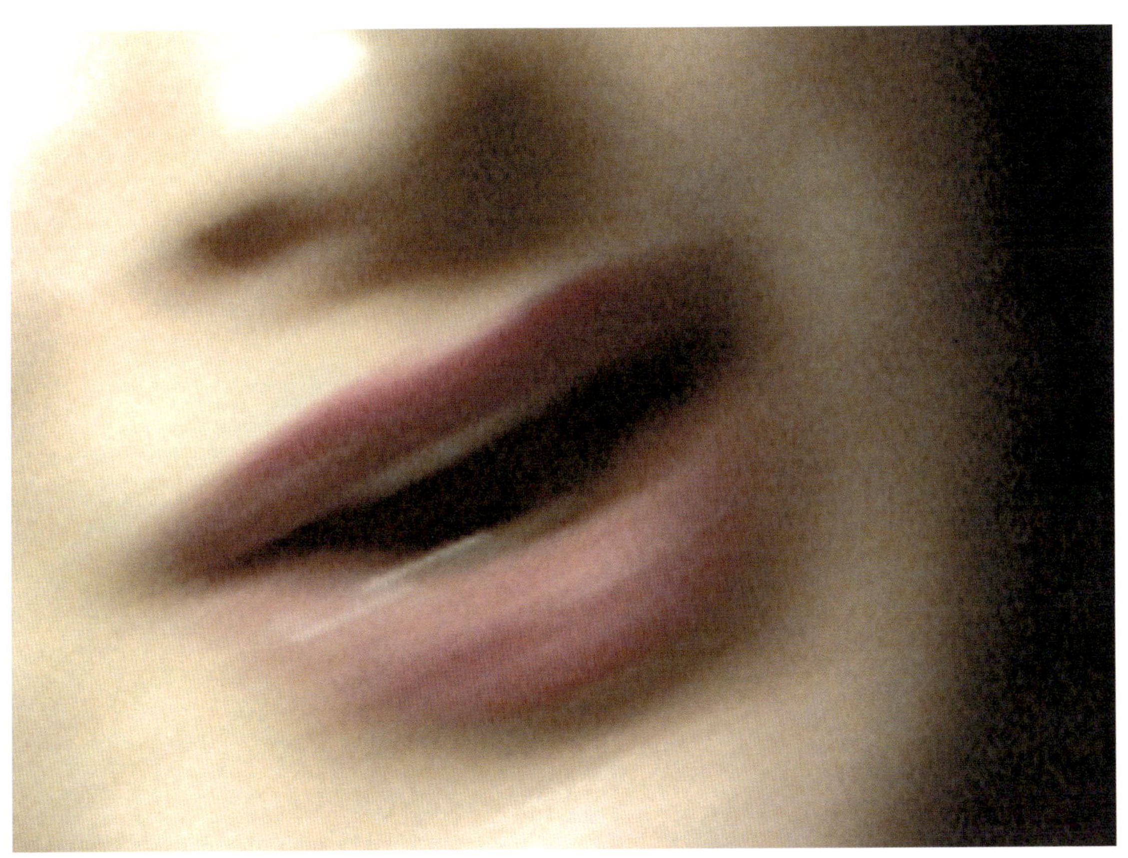

The Maid's Story

1

I was seven when my father died, I mean when my father left us. All photographs of him vanished from the house but I clearly remember him. There were three children and my mother had to work hard to bring us up. I am the eldest. I was my father's favourite, he loved me more than the others, clearly he did not love my mother. I remind my mother of her husband, my father.

When she had her stroke it was me that found her. I was eighteen. She was lying on the kitchen floor. It was midnight. I was supposed to be in by eleven o'clock but I had been out with friends celebrating the end of exams. I had come top in my year, assured of a place at a university. The manager of the hotel where my mother worked agreed to my taking her place as a chambermaid, but at a reduced wage because of my youth and lack of experience.

To the world I am shapeless. I make myself sit badly; it is an effort, many years of ballet rebel against my plan. My clothes are ordinary, nondescript, against fashion. But I know that I am beautiful and it is my secret. Both the men and the women staff are vulgar. The men parade their vulgarity but the women are worse. The men are stupid but the women are calculating. The older men leave me alone because of my mother, the younger men because they think me unattractive. They talk in front of me as if I am not there, as if I am without sex. Some of the prettier girls go with men who stay in the hotel; it's a way of earning more money.

I like the hotel, it suits me fine. The work is not hard and I have all the time in the world to think. In the beginning I was too quick, too good and I was beaten for my sins by three of the women, so now I go at the correct speed. I spend time in the rooms and I never steal if there is a possibility of being caught. And I learn from every room.

People feel safe in their rooms. For a time I considered spying for the government, being an informer like a fifth of the country, but I relished my independence more than the extra money. But I know everything there is to know about the ninth floor. It is my world and everybody on the ninth floor has a secret.

One day I listened to three of the maids talking in front of me as if I were not there. A rich young man, the son of a famous politician was staying in the hotel. One maid was saying that she had reduced him to an idiot by allowing him small glimpses of her breasts when she deliberately bent down in front of him whilst cleaning his room. This strategy had quickly paid off and she seduced him. He thought he'd seduced her and gave her money out of guilt. The other two maids were discussing whether they too should somehow try the same game with him.

My mother had a lover. He was a married man who stayed in the hotel. Every two weeks or so my mother would tell us that she had to work late that night. After the stroke he never came to see her. He still comes to stay in the hotel. I clean his room. He is a very ordinary man with a device for clipping nostril hairs in his toilet bag. A neat man. He always has a packet of contraceptives. There are always three in the packet. One day whilst I was cleaning his room he came in. He watched me the way all men watch young women. For a sign, a clue to their own desire. He found nothing and quickly became bored, waiting for me to finish and be gone.

One of the maids, S...., is fat and ugly but her breasts are large and she is willing to play a role and she excites some men. She blushes and I think this also excites men. Men fantasise about hotel rooms. She is no threat to the men who take her and I think they watch her leave with a sense of philanthropy, of having done her a favour.

Men fascinate me and I study them with the energy that I would have devoted to the subject I could have studied in the university. I neither love them nor hate them but study them as a dying species, their role as sperm carriers already bypassed by science.

I have perfected the art of being invisible as a woman. I can walk into a room full of men without exciting the slightest interest. No molecule is moved by me, I leave no trace behind, I can control my sex.

*

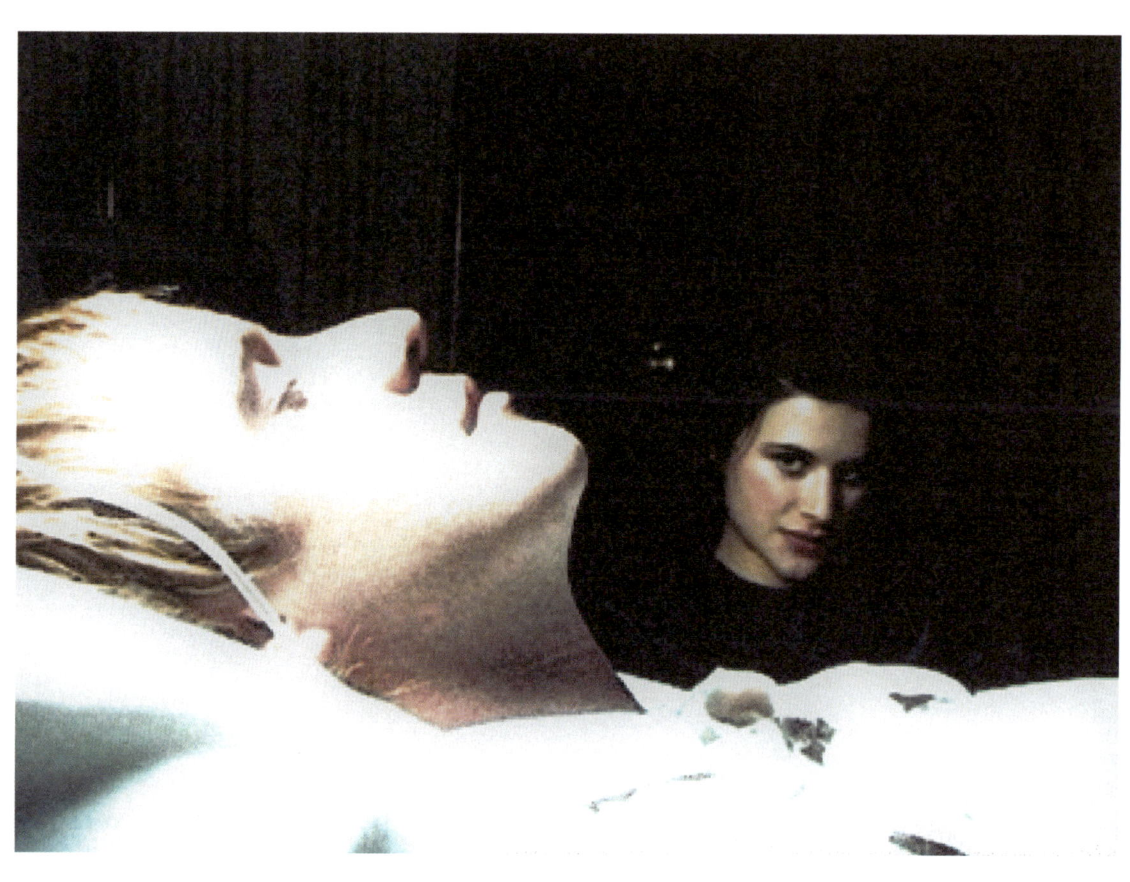

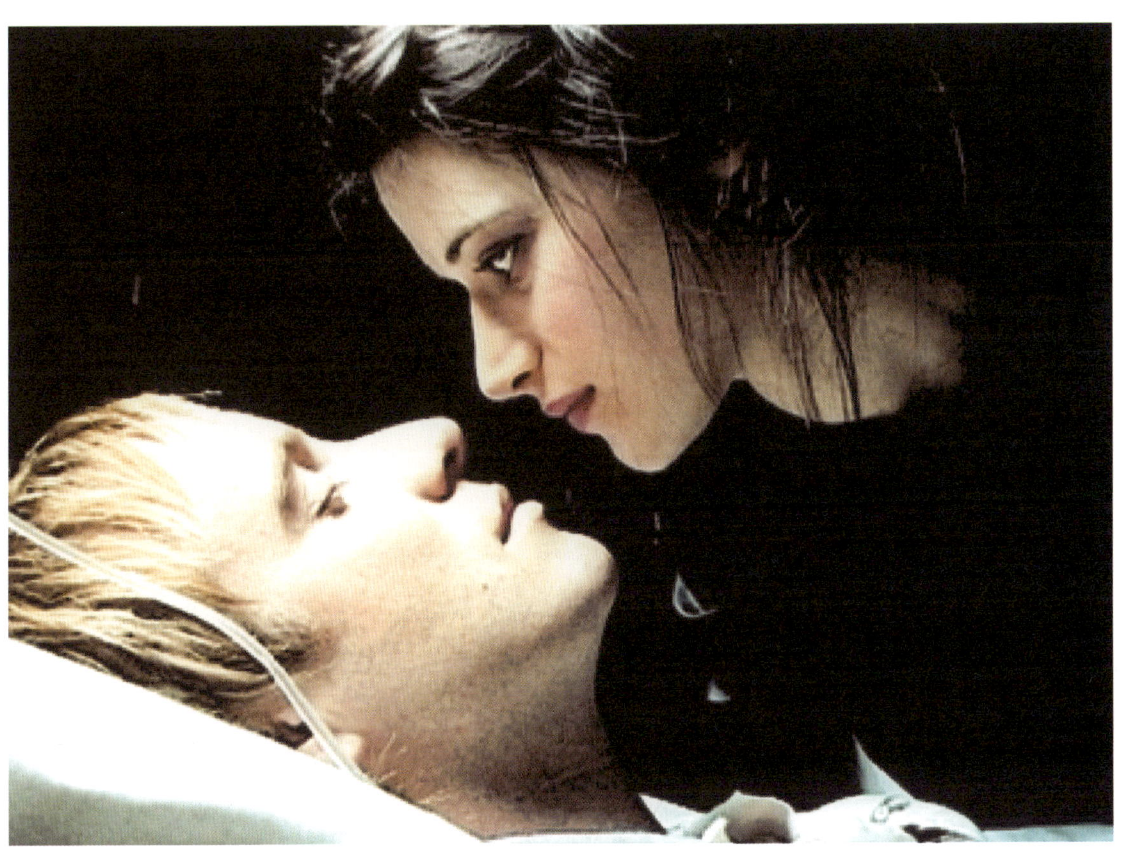

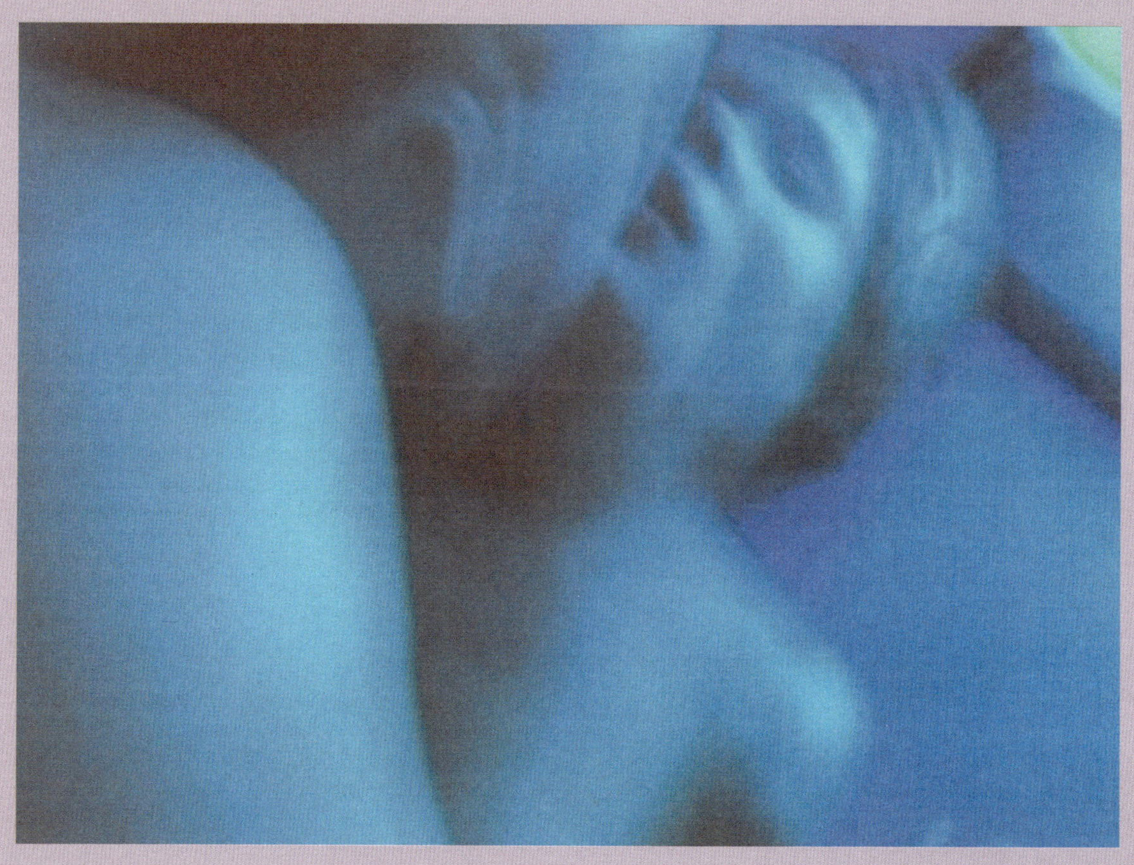

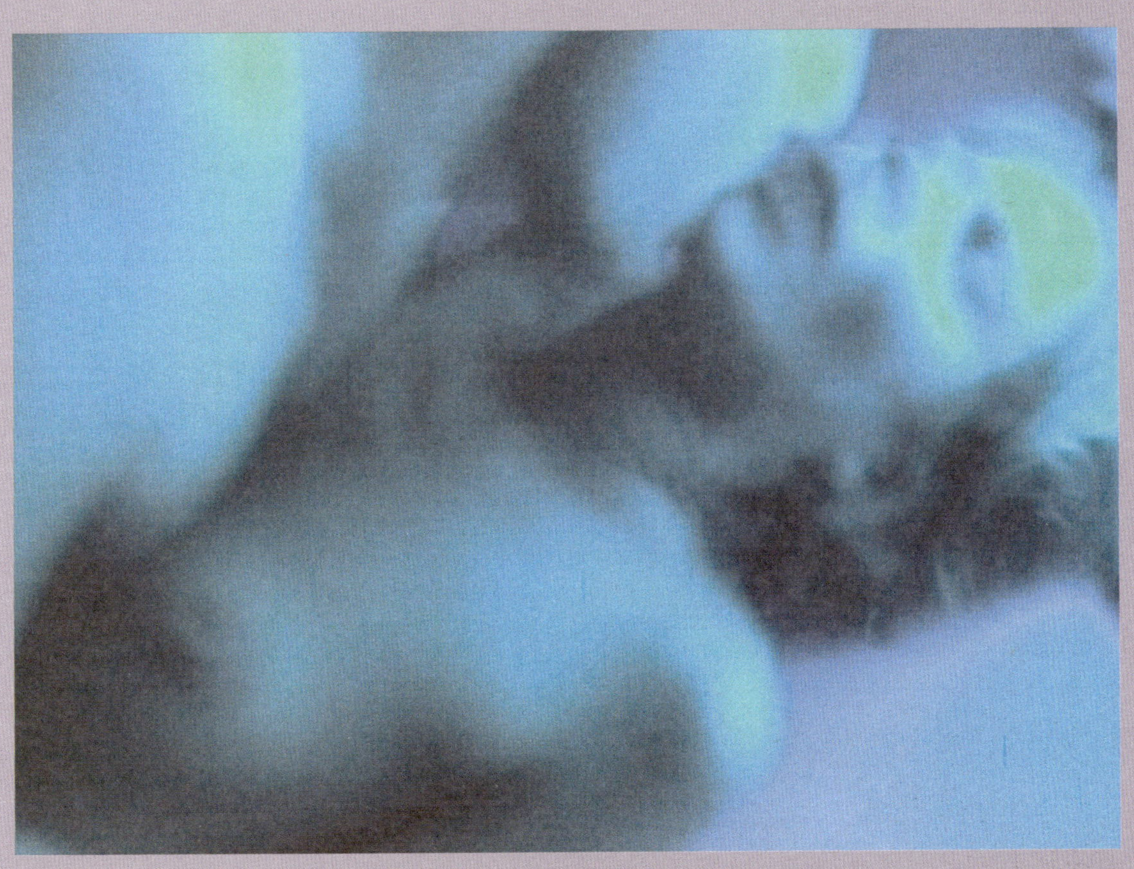

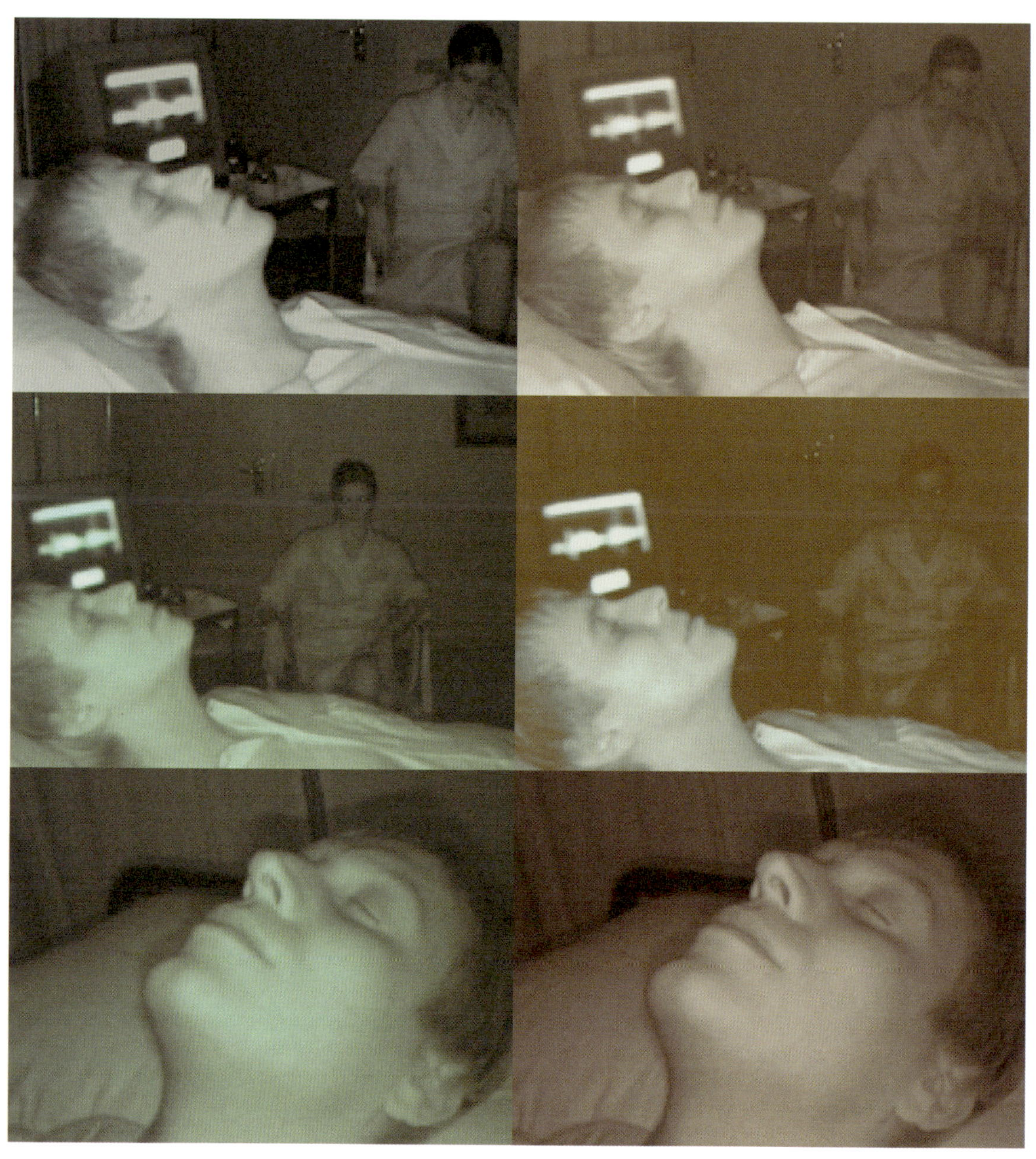

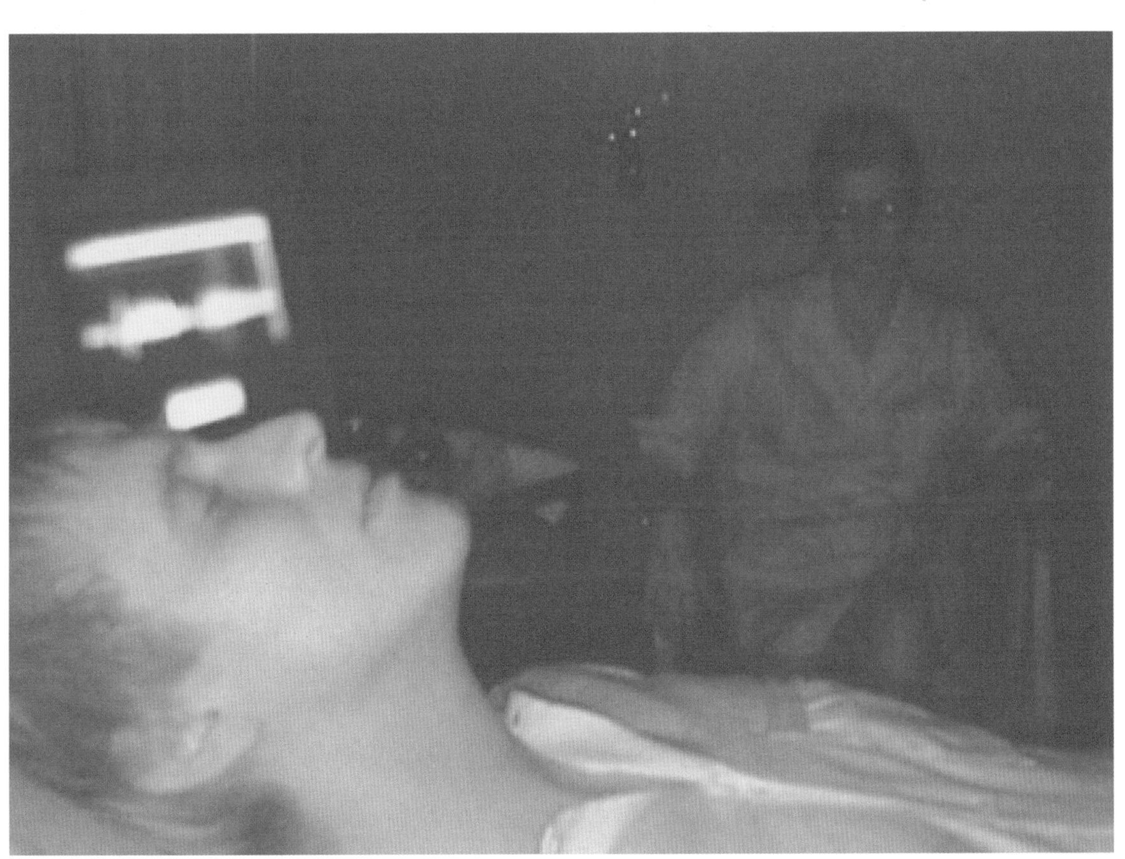

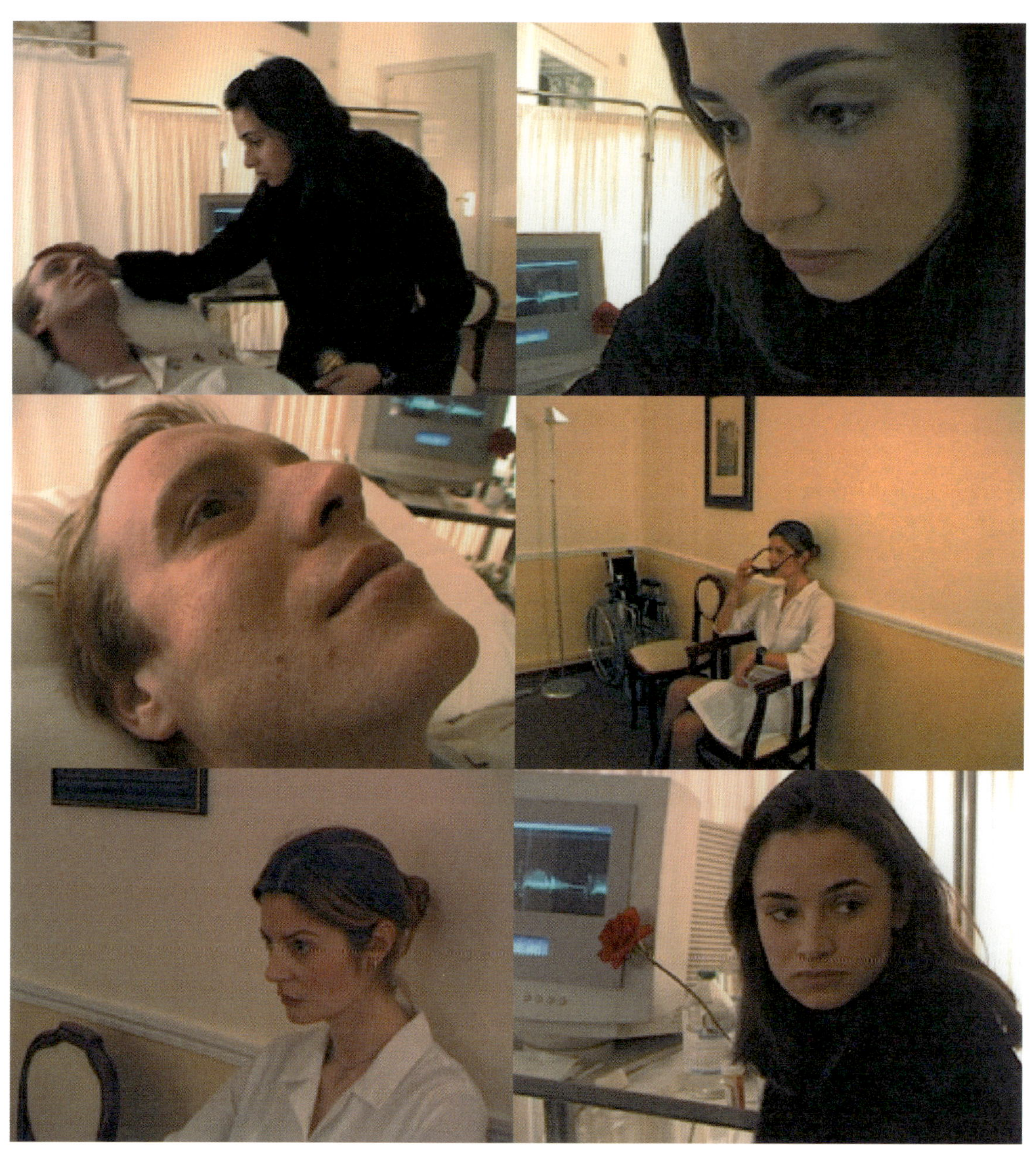

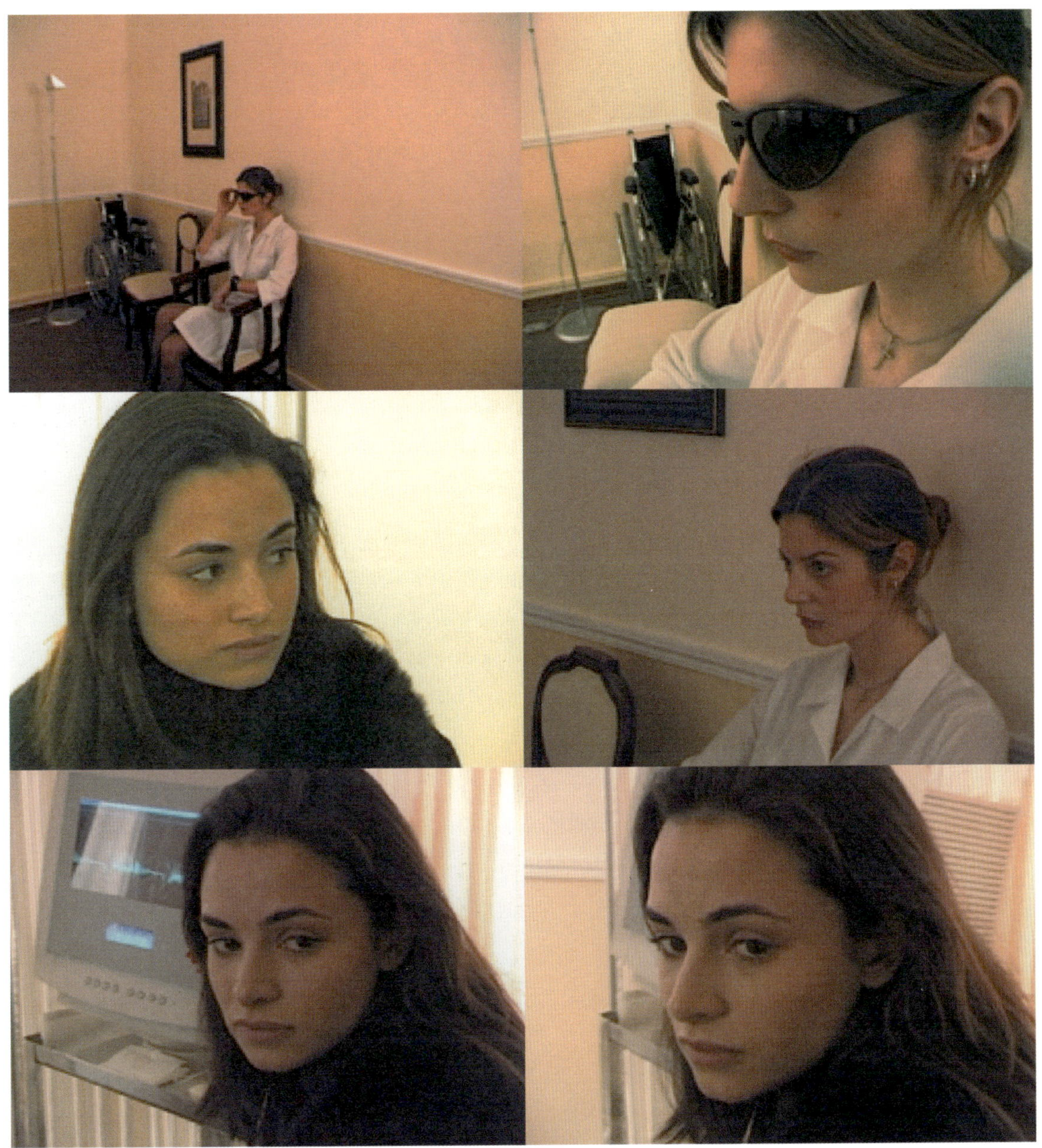

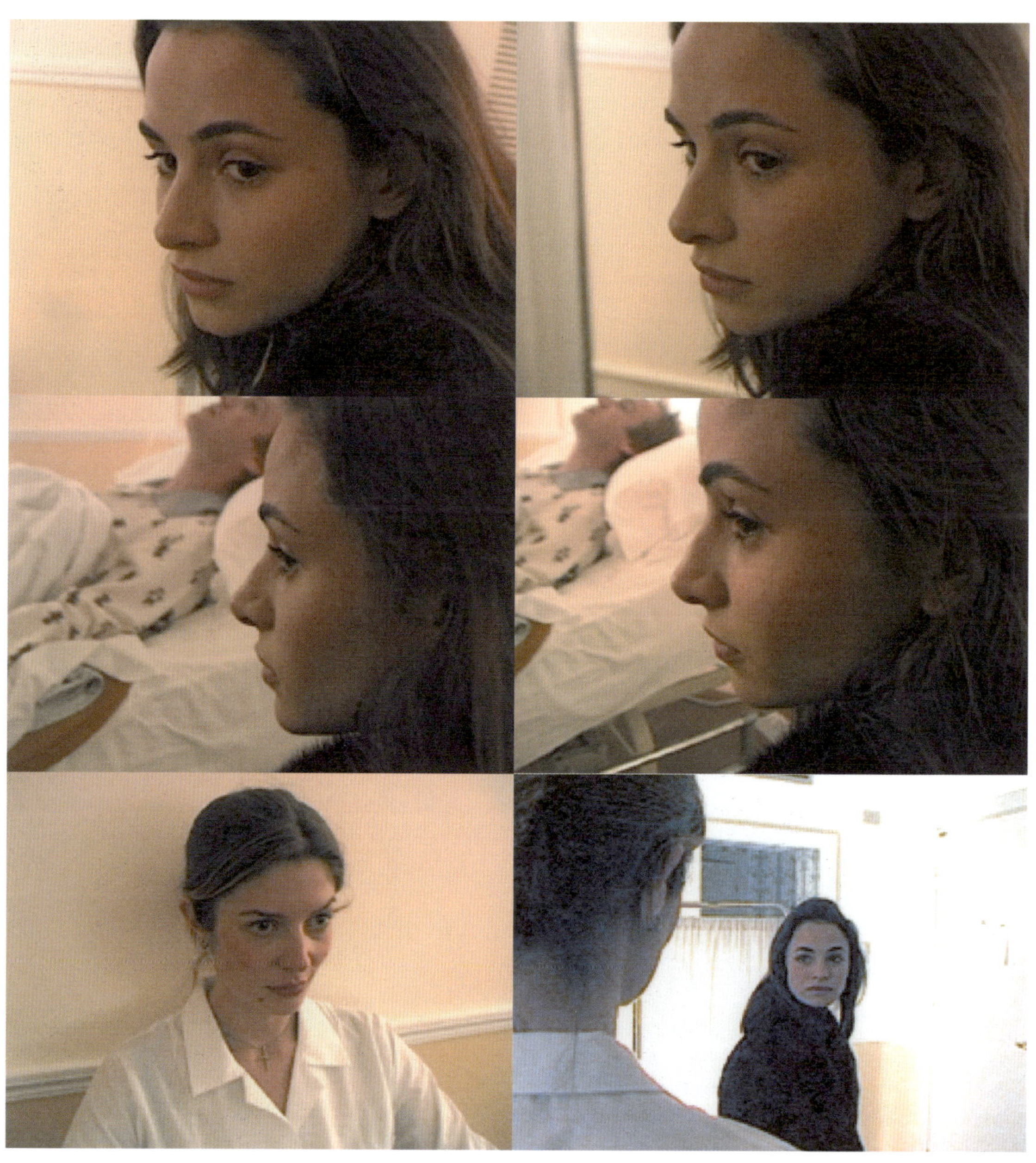

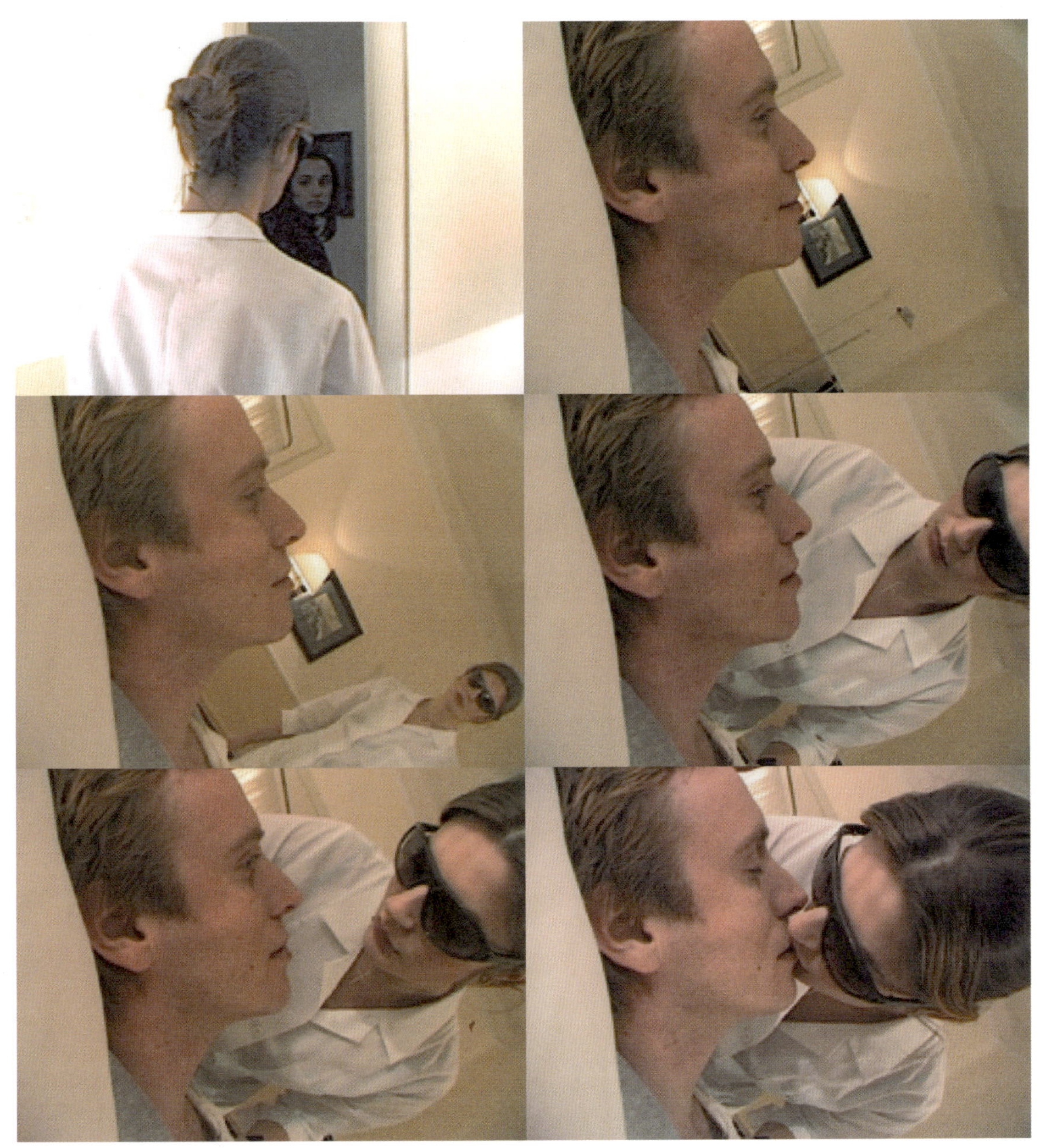

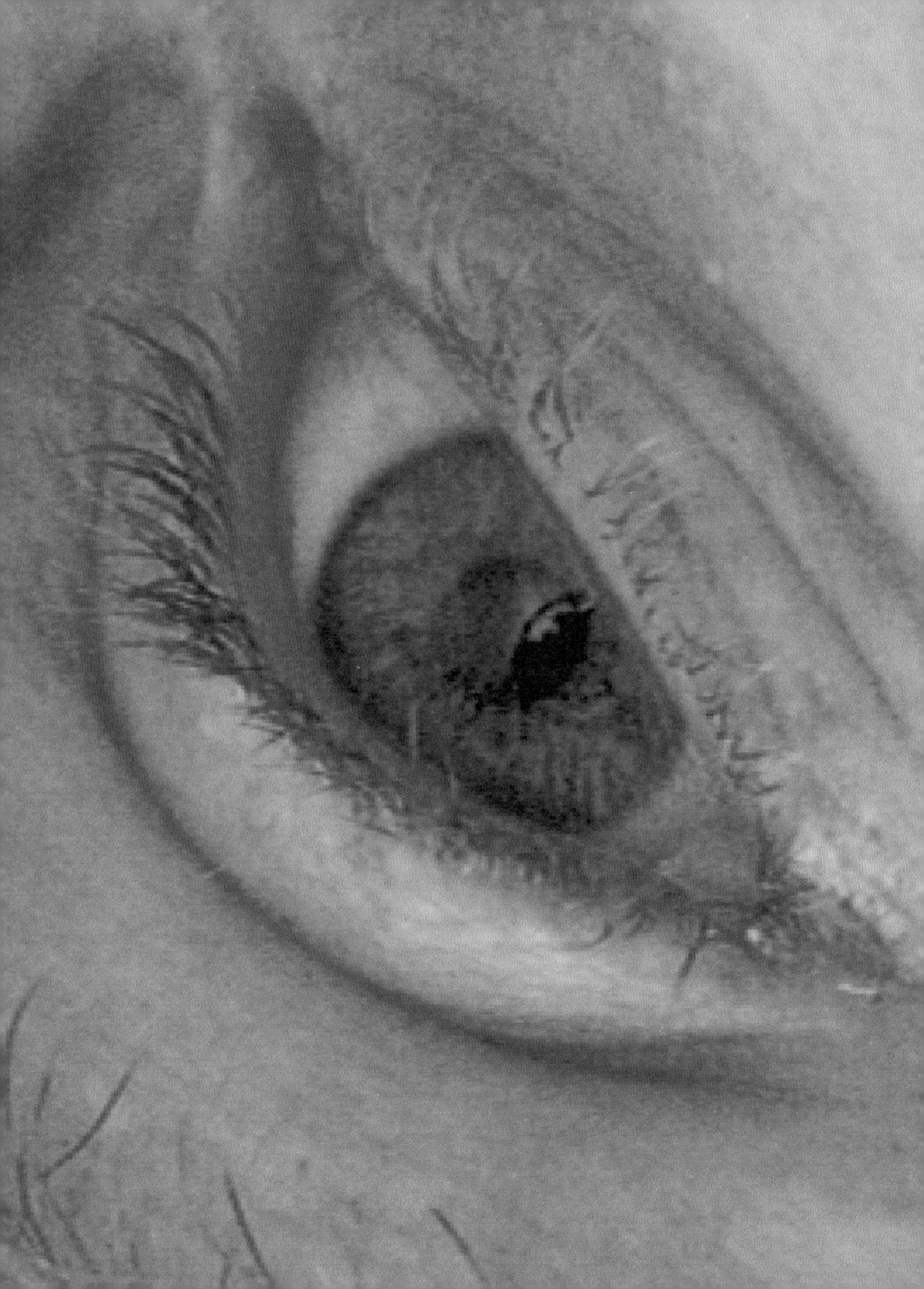

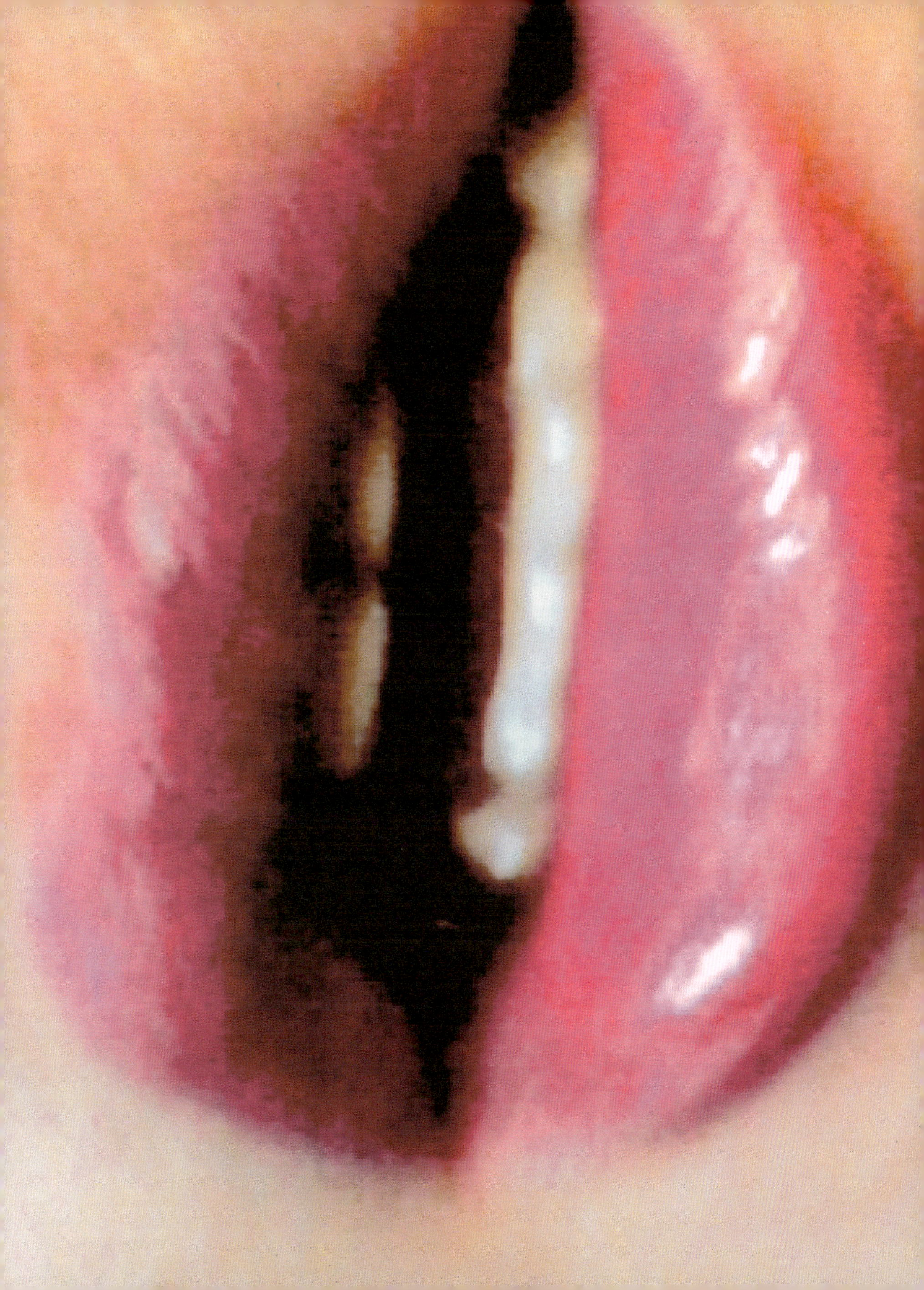

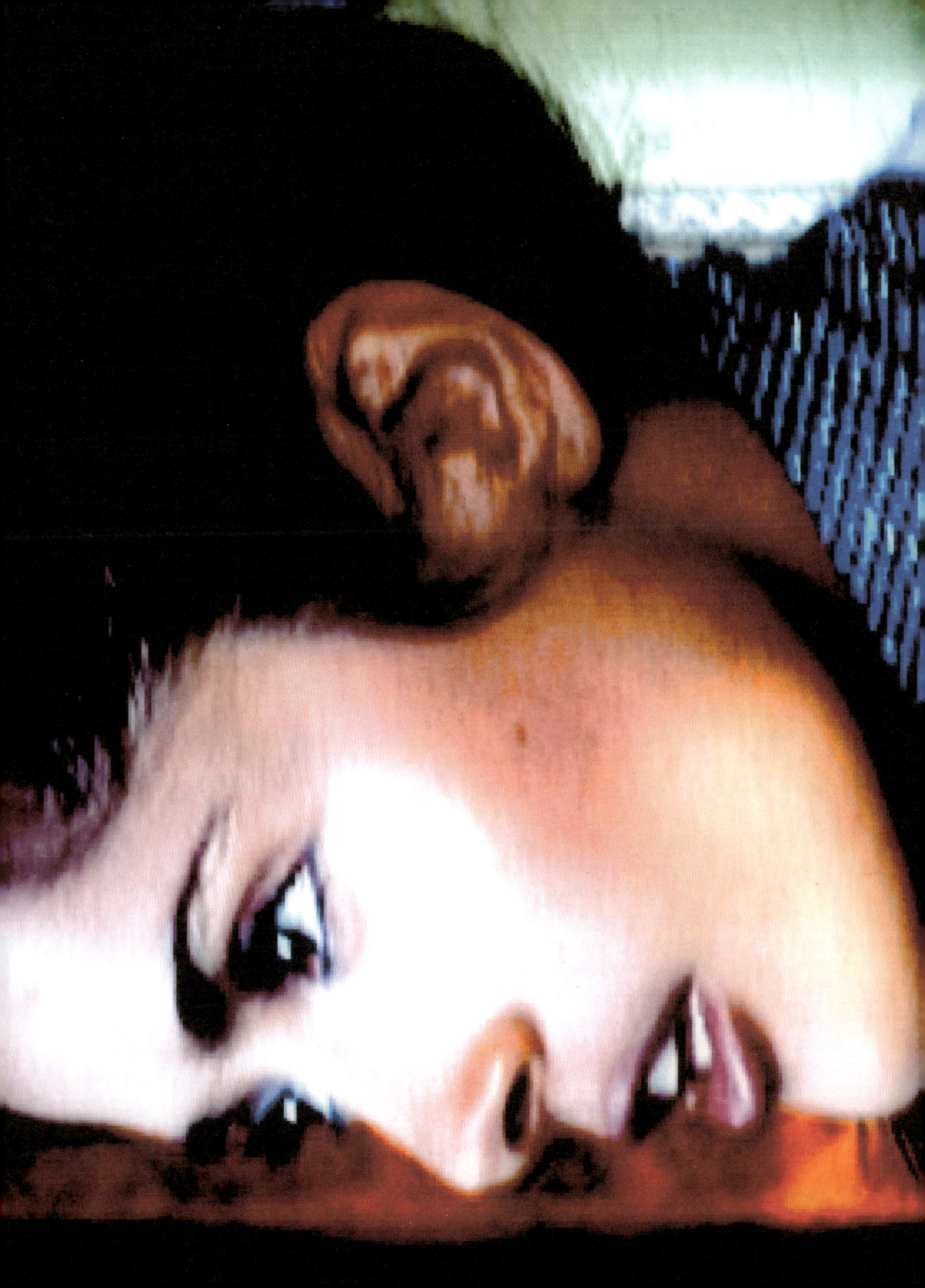

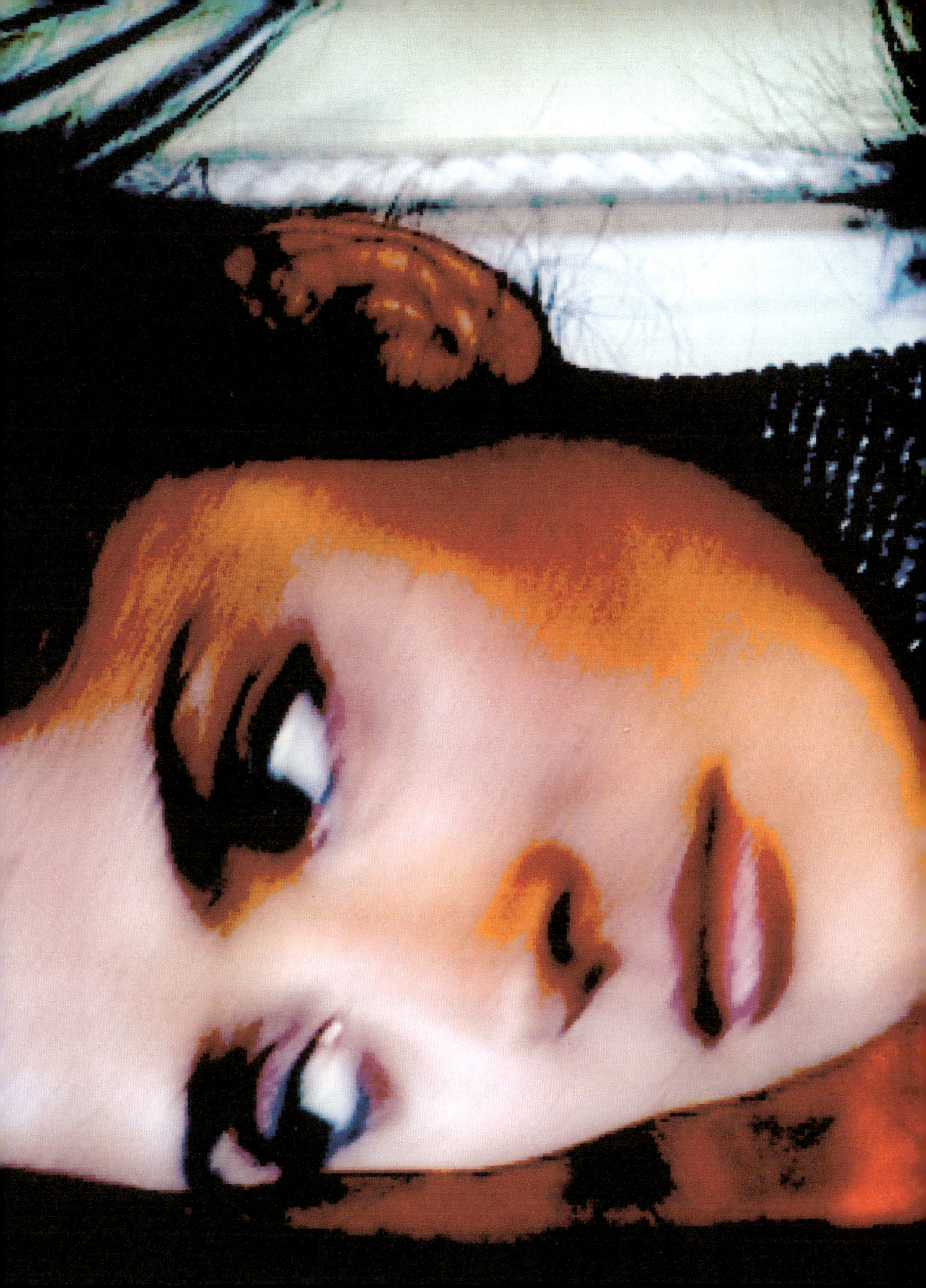

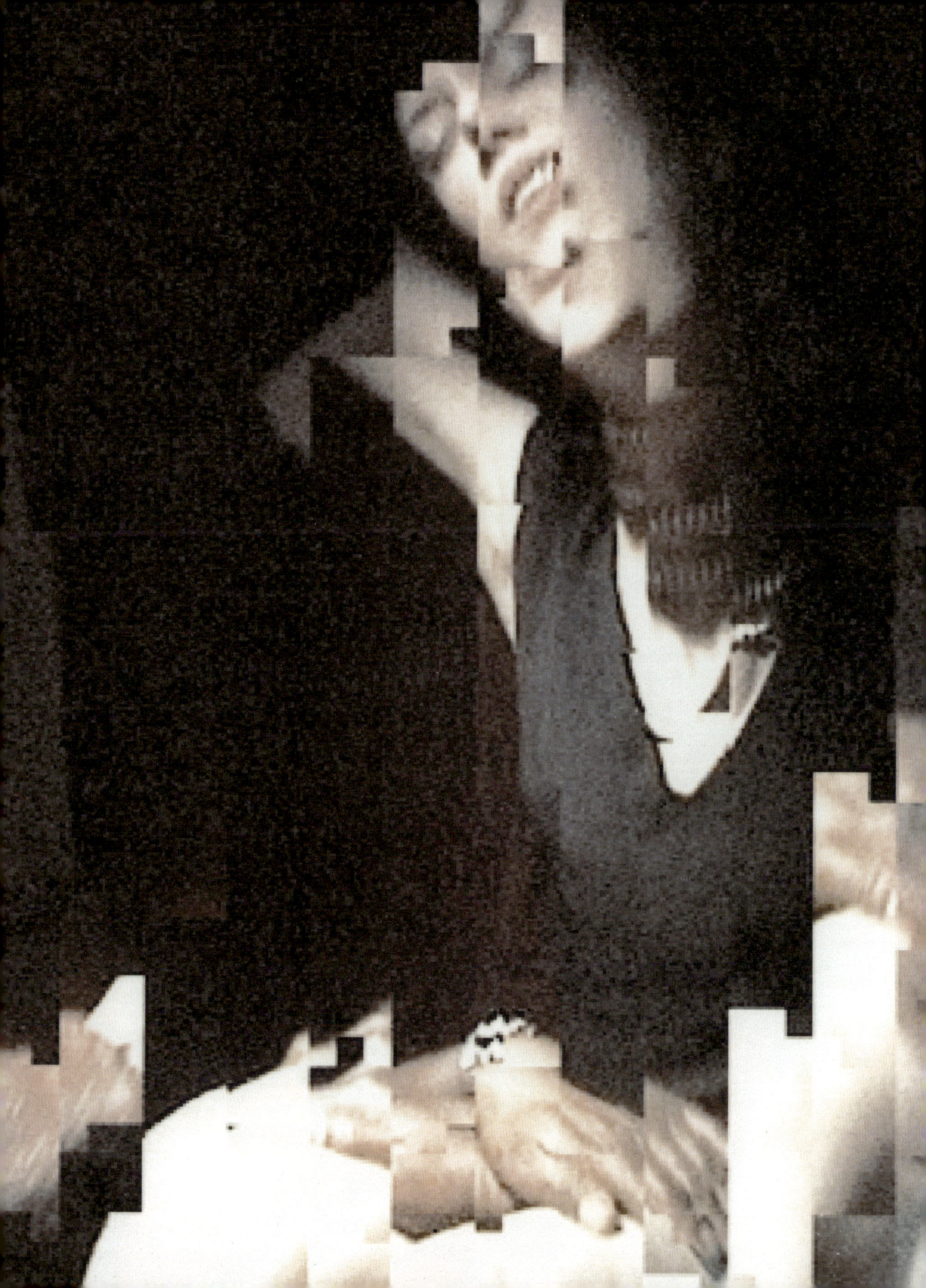

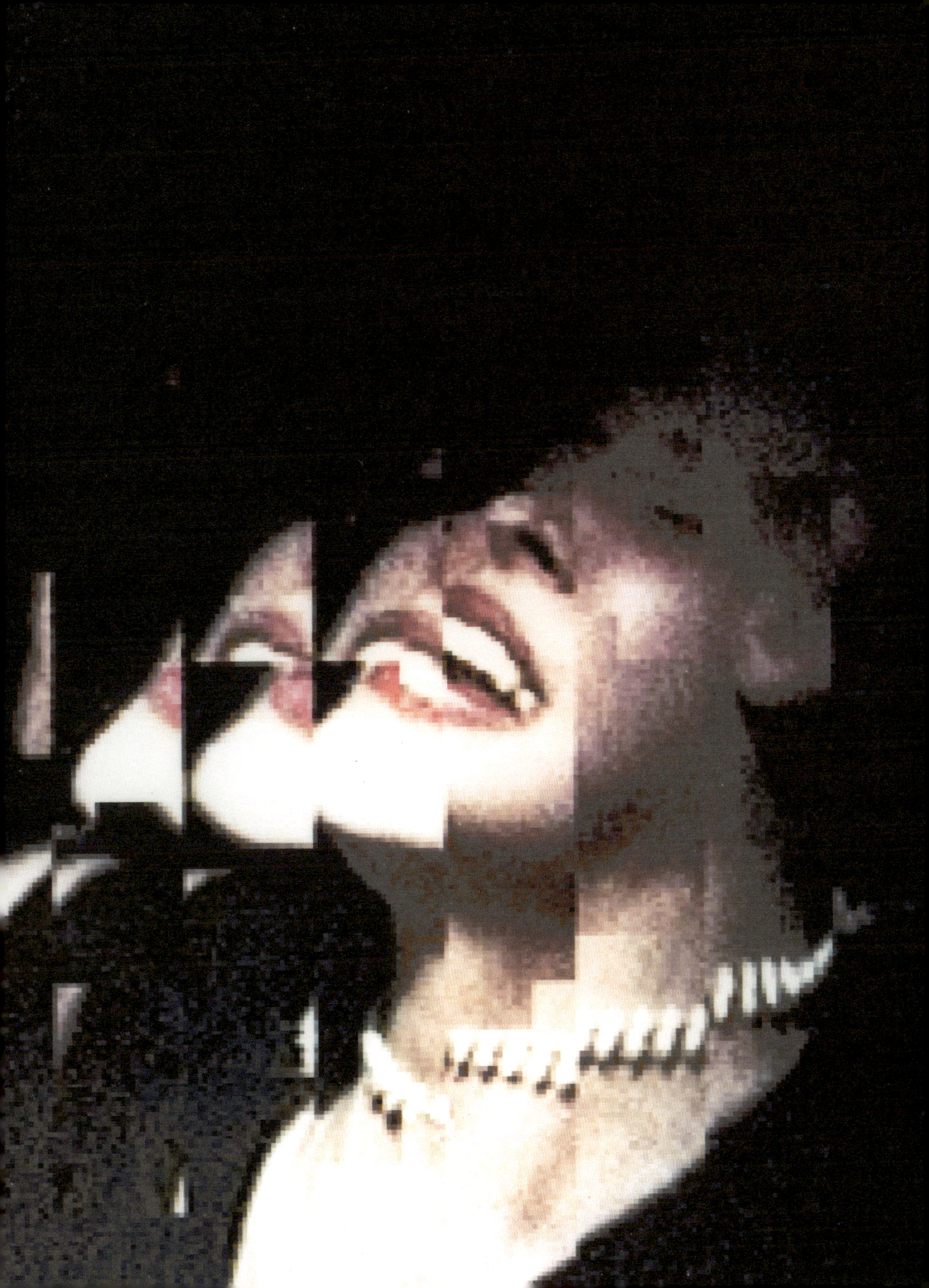

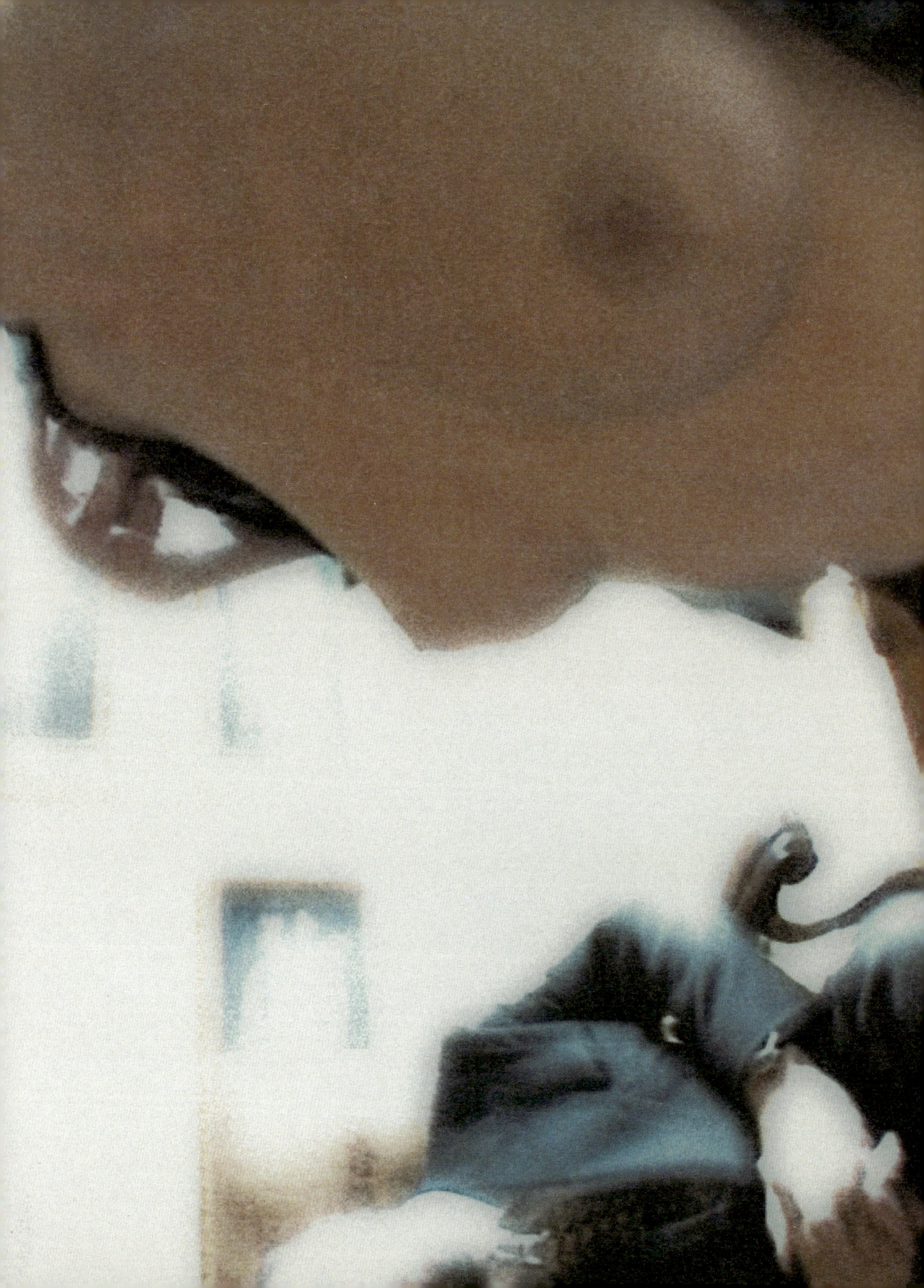

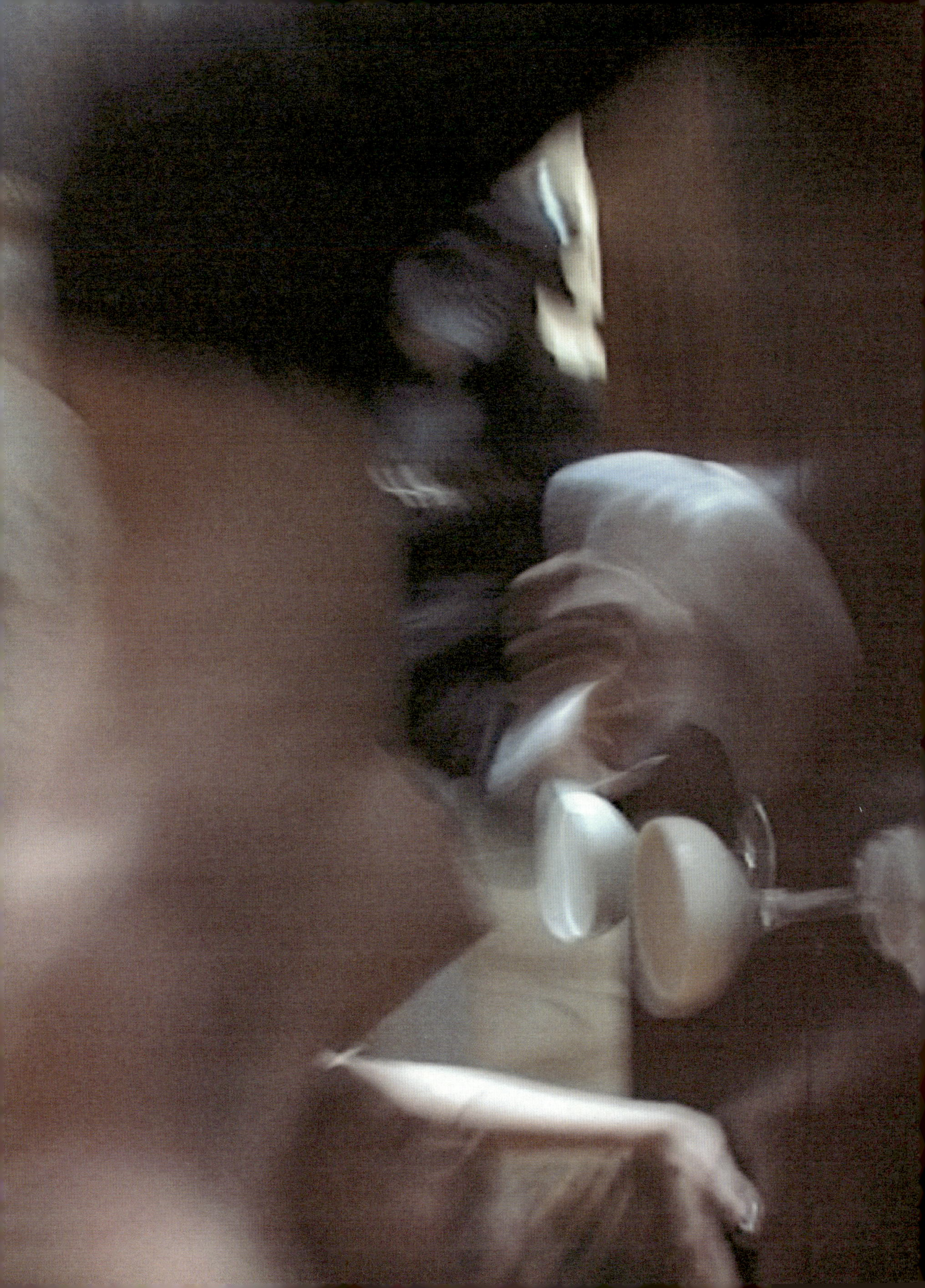

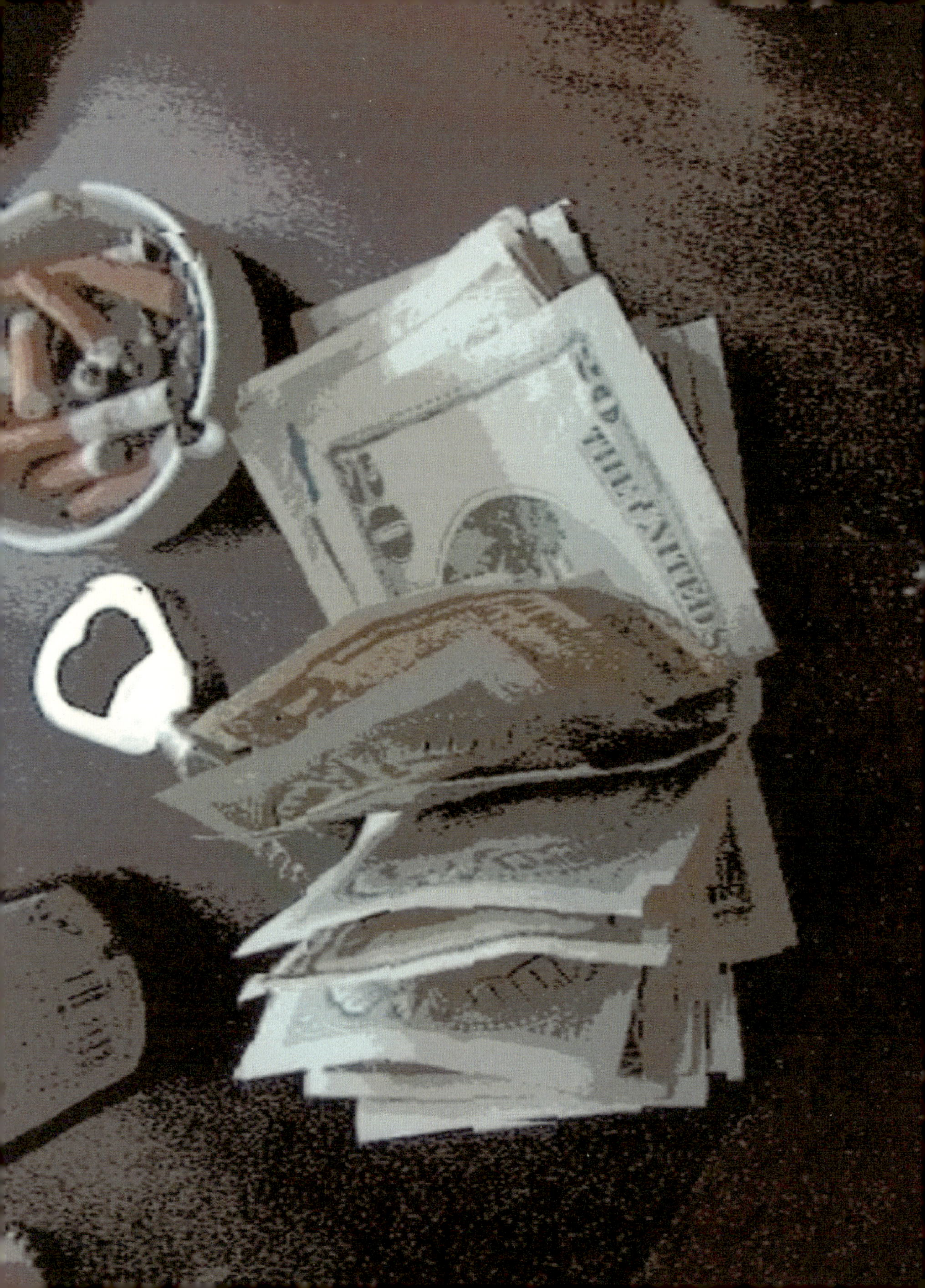
THE UNITED

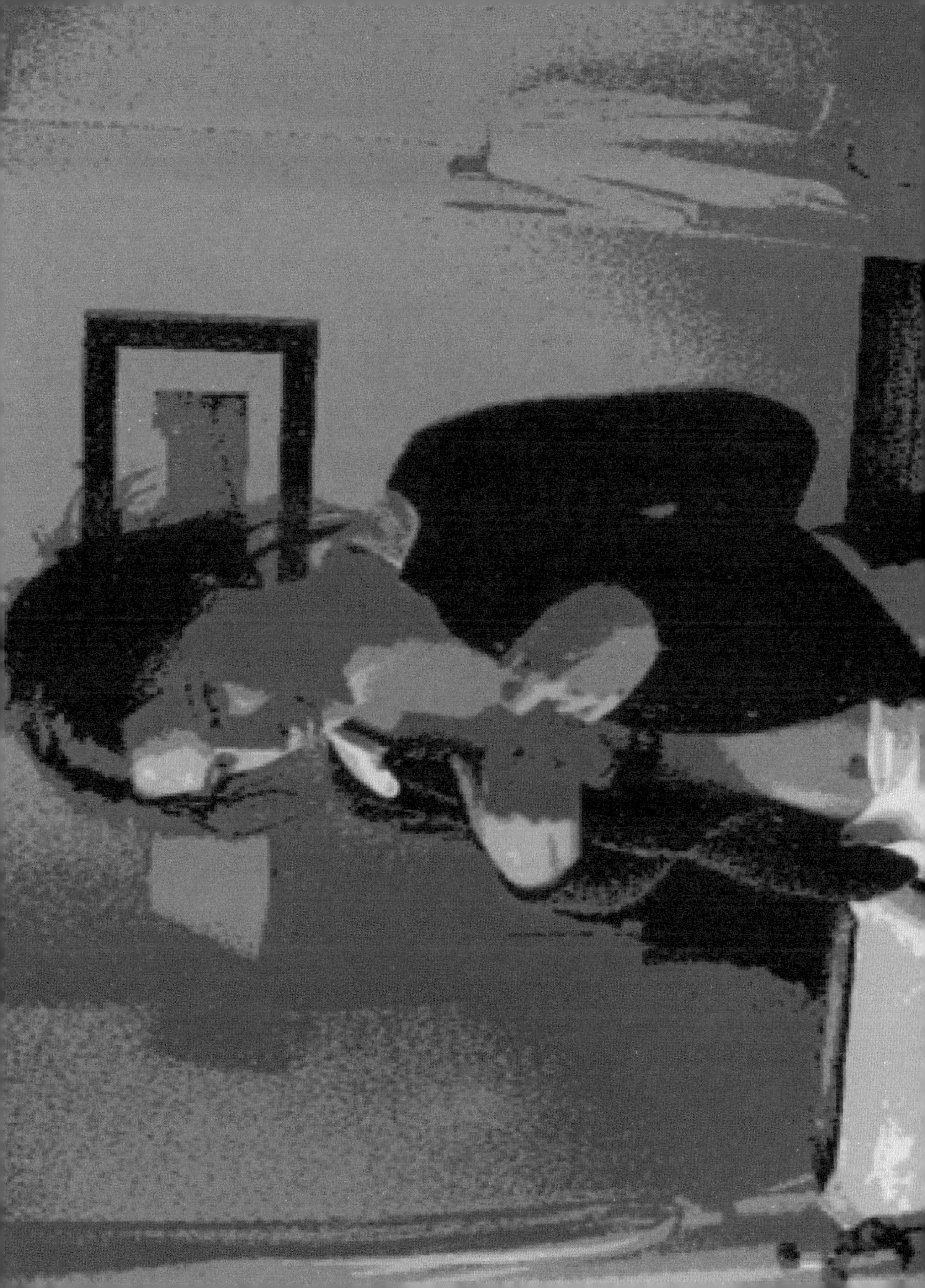

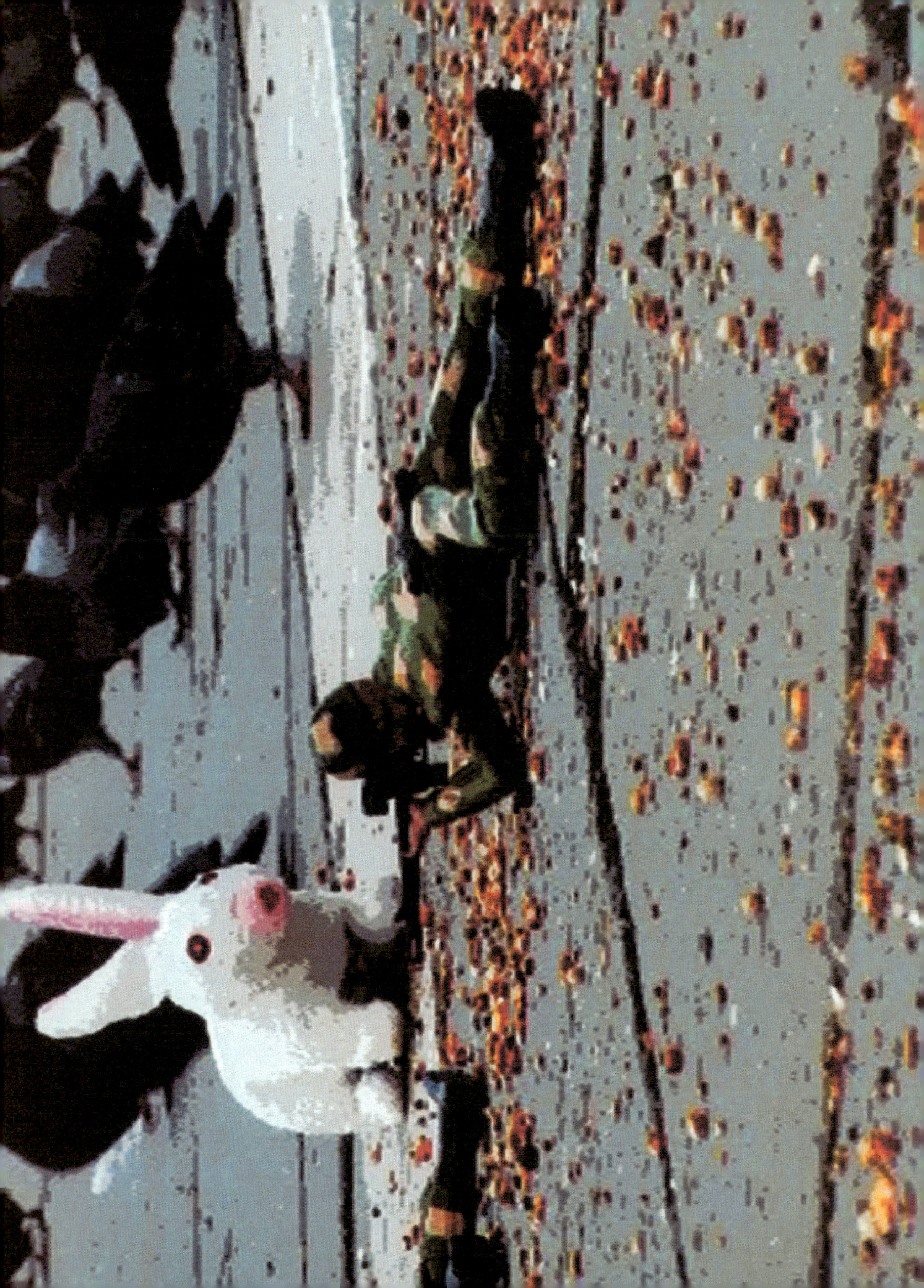

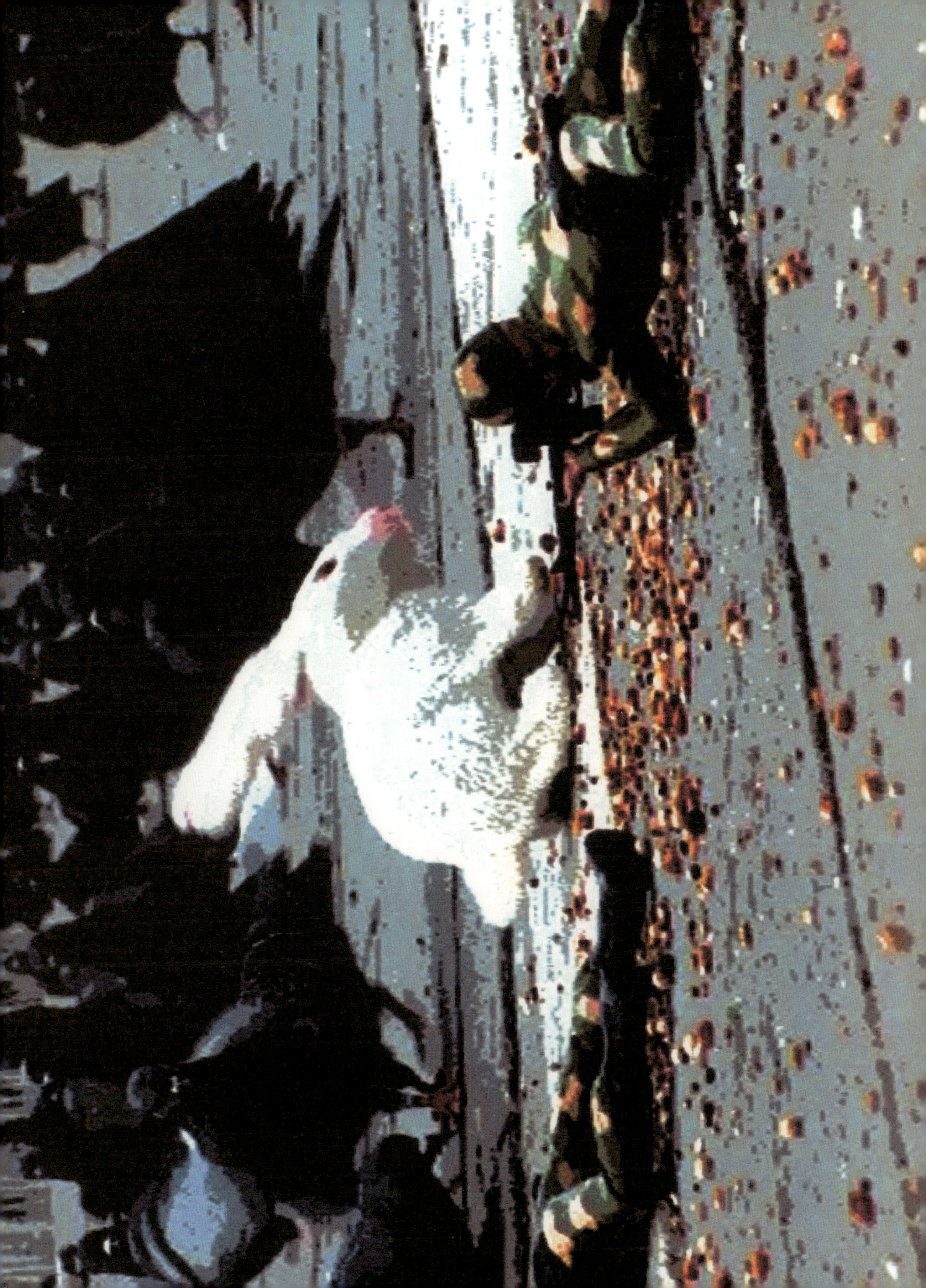

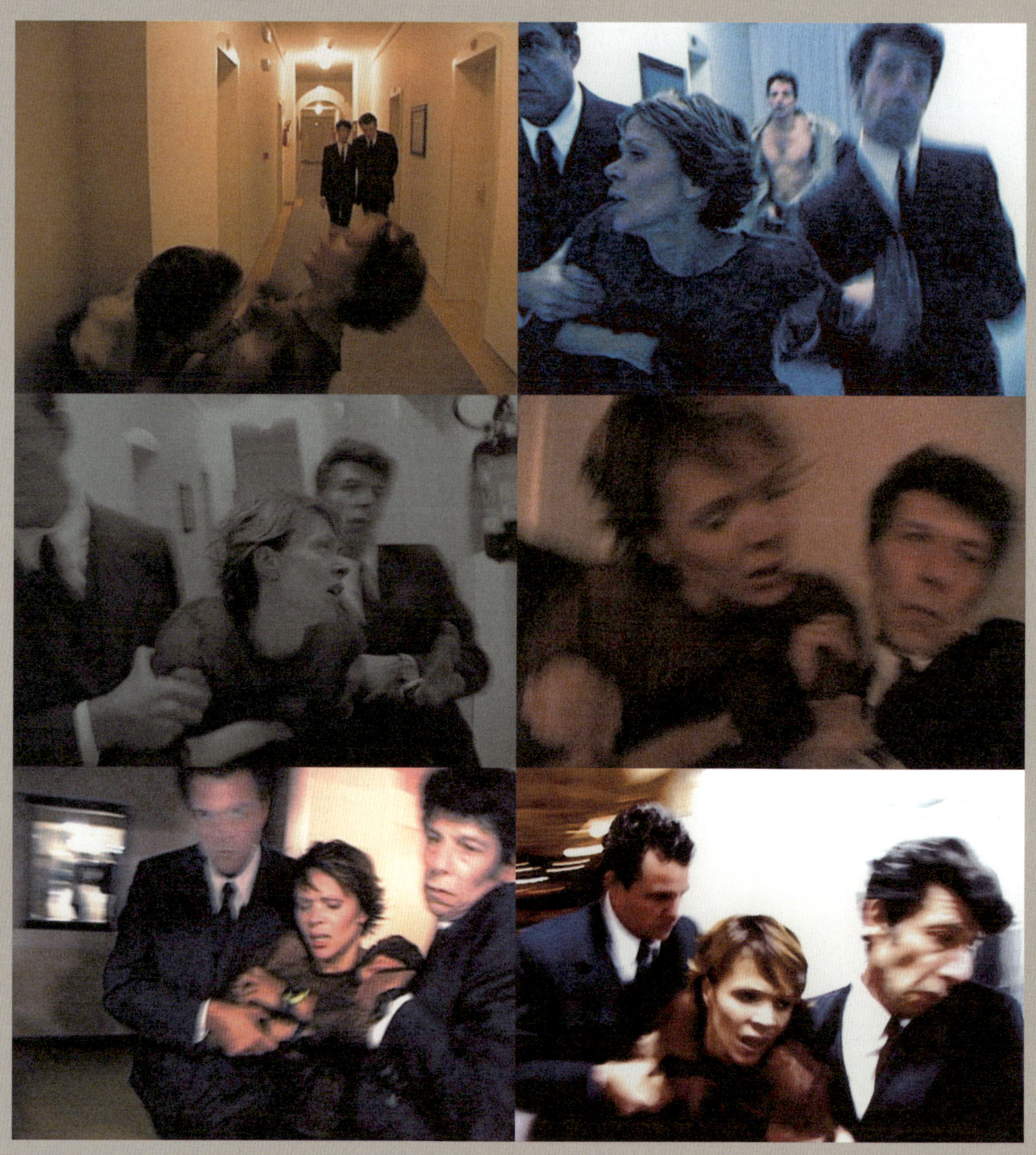

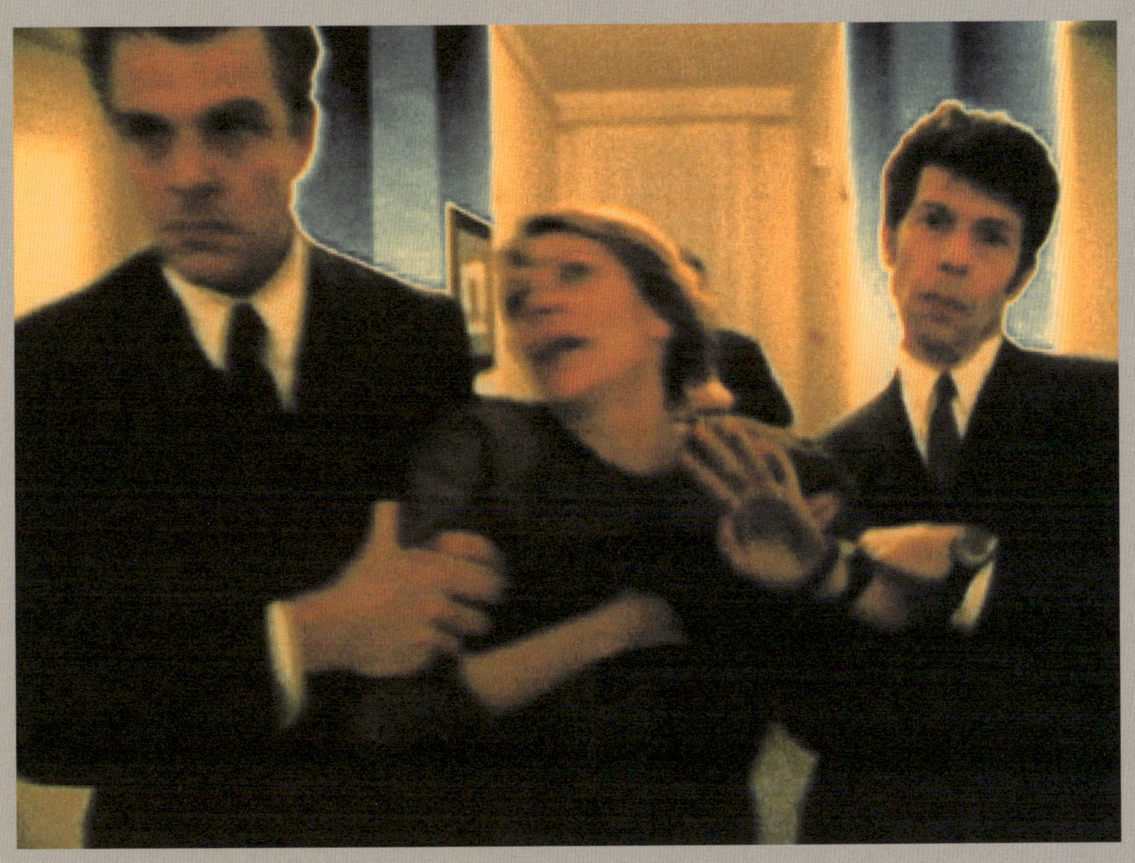

Using the Hotel as a Metaphor - I wanted to create a sense of threat - the idea that at any moment one of the guests could be abducted - taken to the prison in the cellar - to become part of the food chain within the Hotel. We created a romantic couple - 'boy and girl in love' - and abducted the girl. She makes a fleeting appearance as a Vampire in the final sequence of the film.

Heathcote Williams adapted the 'Duchess of Malfi' for me. We chose six scenes – the weirdest, bloodiest, sexiest scenes in John Webster's extraordinary play. We worked on each scene, moving text around, taking liberties – until we arrived at a short 'Fast Food MacMalfi.'

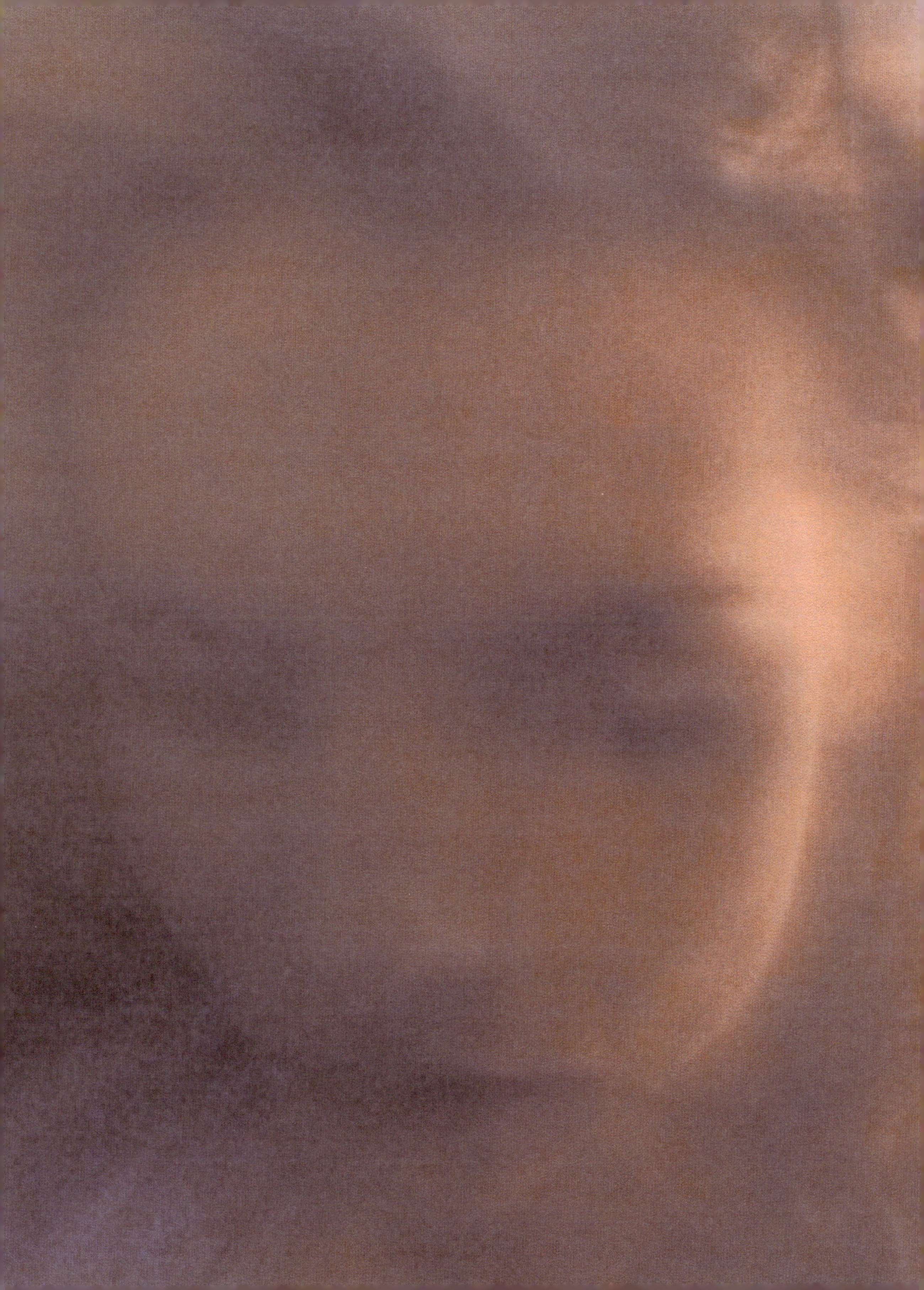

DUCHESS OF MALFI.

SYNOPSIS OF THE PLOT

The DUCHESS OF MALFI is newly widowed, we know very little of the late Duke. Her two brothers, FERDINAND (the Duke of Calabria) and the CARDINAL, drop in to warn her against re-marrying. Ferdinand is by far the madder of the two brothers - he seems to have very incestious feelings about his sister and his language is full of sexual imagery. The play is mostly about their relationship. The Duchess has a child by the late Duke of Malfi but we really don't get to know the kids in this story. The Cardinal has a mistress, JULIA, who is married to some senile court dweller.

Suspecting that the Duchess might not heed their great advice Ferdinand plants a spy, BOSOLA, into her household. Bosola is a great character. He's been around the block, in fact he's been up and down the freeway and he's very complex. Ferdinand obviously feels he has Bosola in the bag but Bosola is his own man and quite peverse to boot.

As soon as the brothers have departed the Duchess and her loyal maid-servant, CARIOLA, summon the handsome ANTONIO. He is the Duchess's steward and seems to manage her housekeeping. She wastes no time in seducing him and marrying him. He puts up no fight and they seem very happy together. However the Duchess makes it clear to Cariola, just before jumping on Antonio's bones that she knows bad things will come of her independence.

Immediately the Duchess is pregnant and shortly after has a child. The father's identity is kept a secret because of the scandal of her marrying beneath her class.

Upon hearing the news of her new child Ferdinand goes into a towering rage, way out of proportion to the situation.

More children appear very quickly (the play jump cuts with surreal ease) and then the crazy Ferdinand turns up at her place and spies on her and discovers that she has re-married (but he still doesn't know who the father is).

He tells her to kill herself, she refuses and now he really starts to lose the plot.

The Duchess tells her hubby to get out of town until the heat dies down - she stays with the kids during which time the crafty Bosola finds out that Antonio is the begetter of her pups.

There's a bit of a war on and armies move around a bit which gets crazy Ferdinand back into the region of the Duchess's house.

With the help of Bosola he contrives to drive her mad. He visits her darkened room and asks her to kiss his hand. Which turns out to be a hand he has cut off a corpse. On the hand is Antonio's ring, so now she thinks he is dead.

Antonio is floating around in Italy somewhere.

Next Ferdinand puts eight lunatics in the room with her - one of them is Bosola in disguise, one is an English tailor driven nuts by the fashion industry - still she doesn't lose it.

Meanwhile Antonio is still alive but she doesn't know this.

Finally Ferdinand has her, the kids and Cariola all strangled by a sinister man. At her dying moment Bosola tells her that her old man is safe and sound. I think he does it out of remorse but it seems a tad cruel, better to have kept quiet about this particular information.

The Cardinal and his Mistress, Julia fall out. She fancies Bosola and lets him know that a shag wouldn't be out of the question. The Cardinal tells her that the Duchess et al have all been topped. She's shocked, of course, and he makes her promise not to tell anyone. He makes her kiss a poisoned bible and she dies immediately.

Ferdinand has now officially gone mad. He accuses Bosola of murdering the Duchess, and then gets a strange disease where he thinks he's a wolf and attacks his own shadow.

Antonio dies (can't quite remember how) and then Bosola has a fit of remorse and kills everyone left (Ferdinand and the Cardinal). He then is killed by accident and the only character left standing is the Duchess's first son, a character we have never seen before. It's a cracking good play.

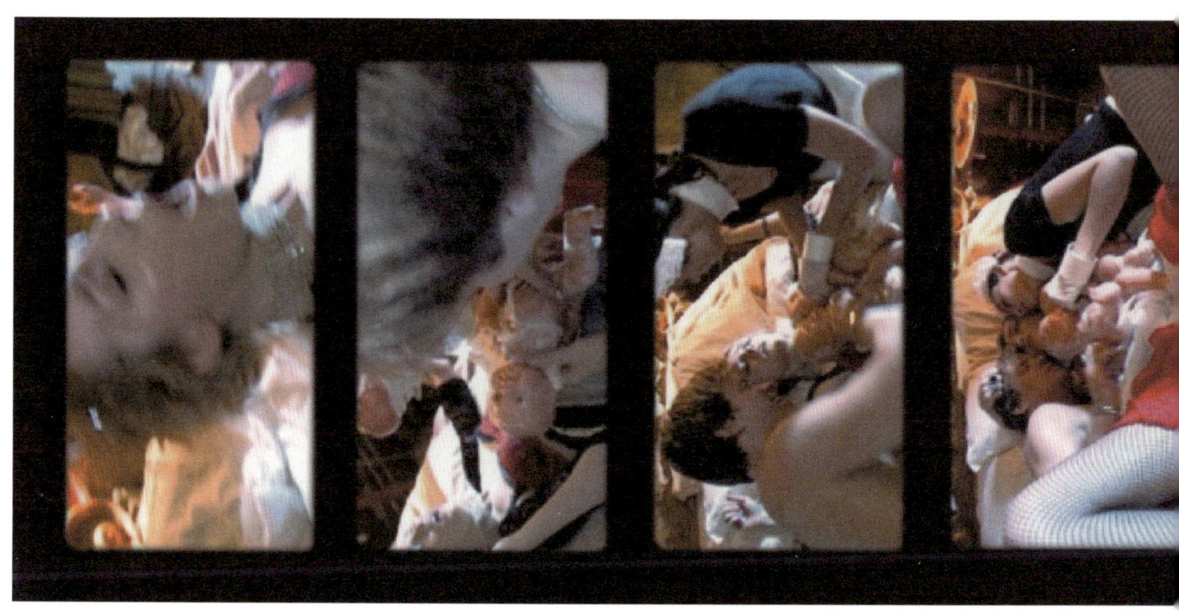

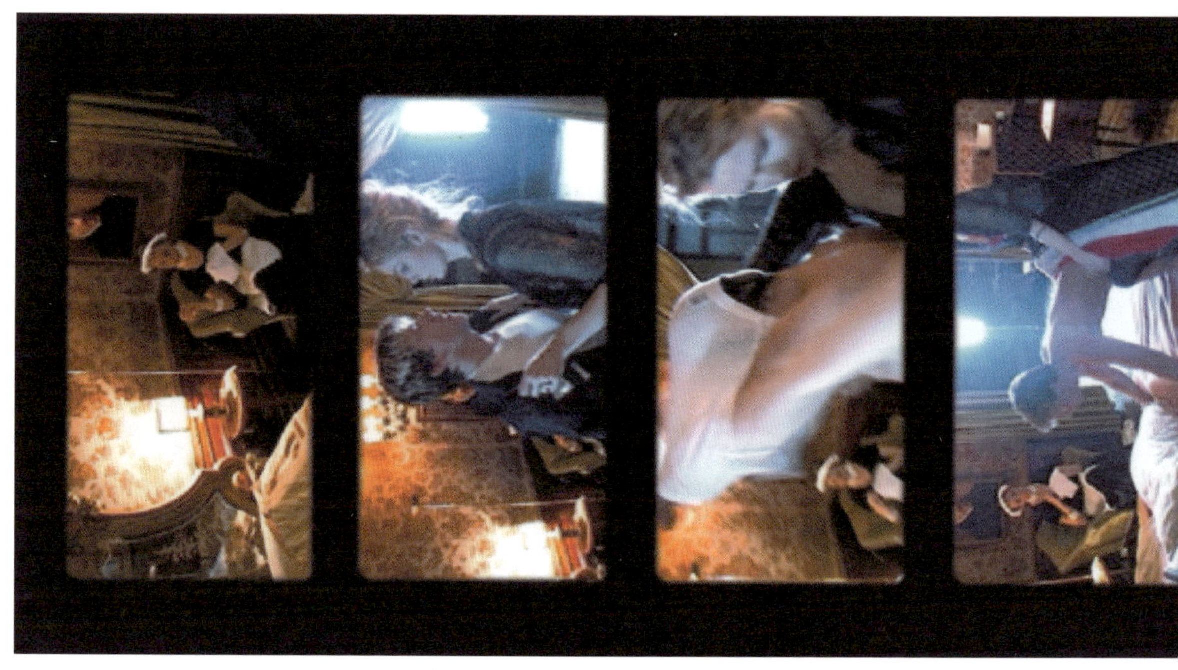

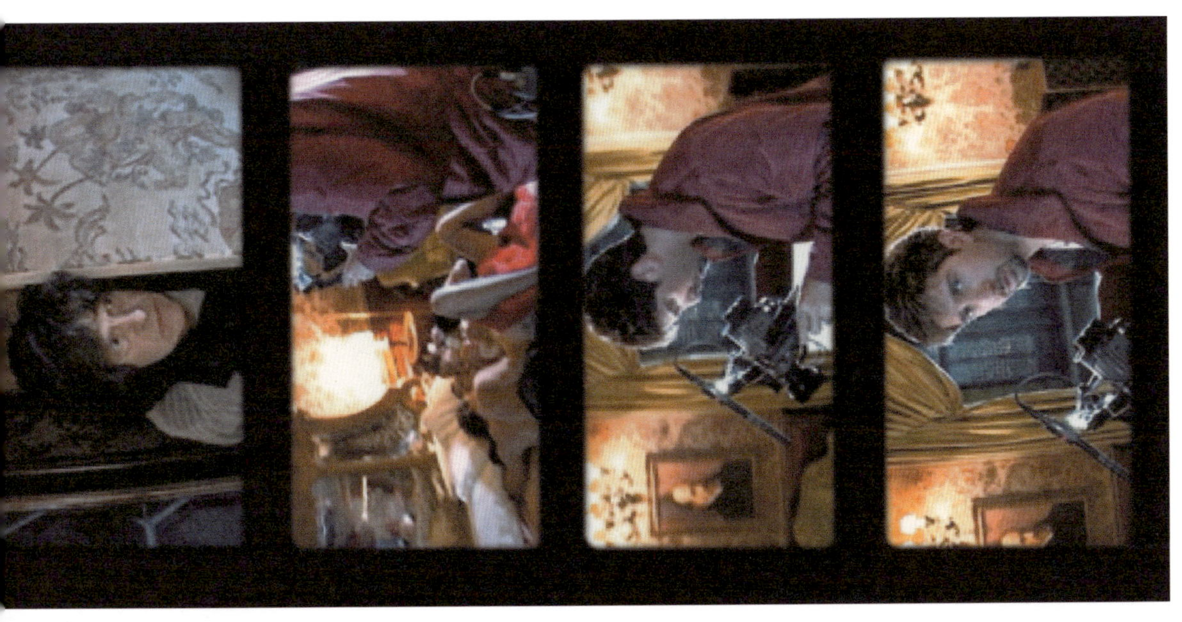

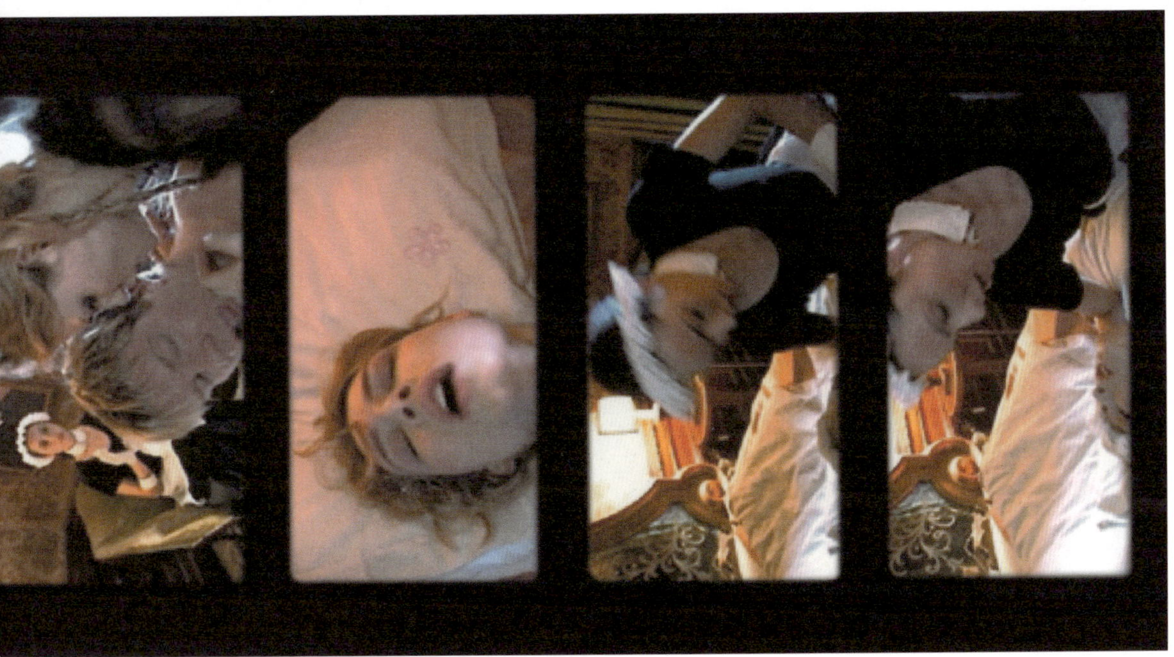

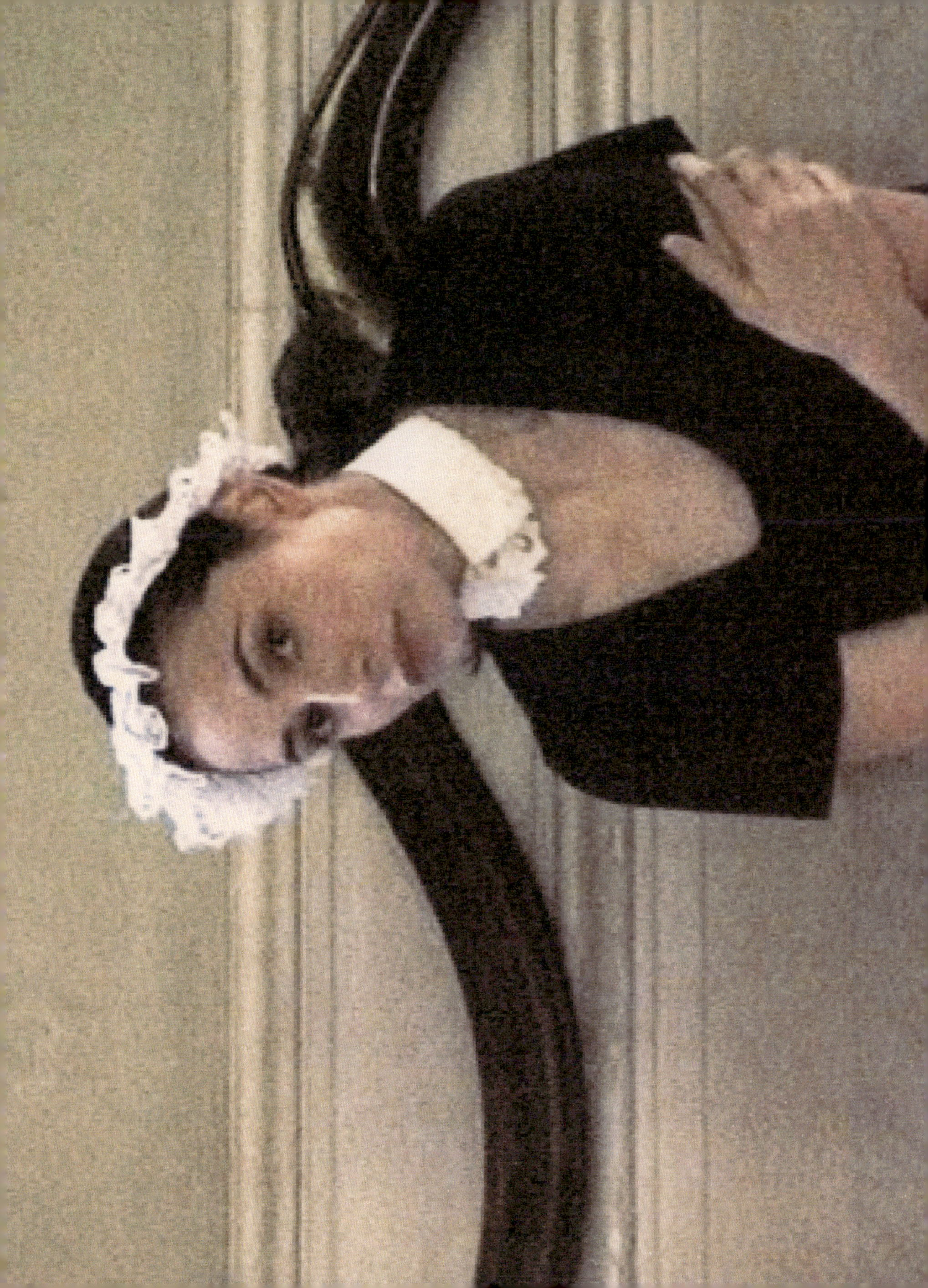

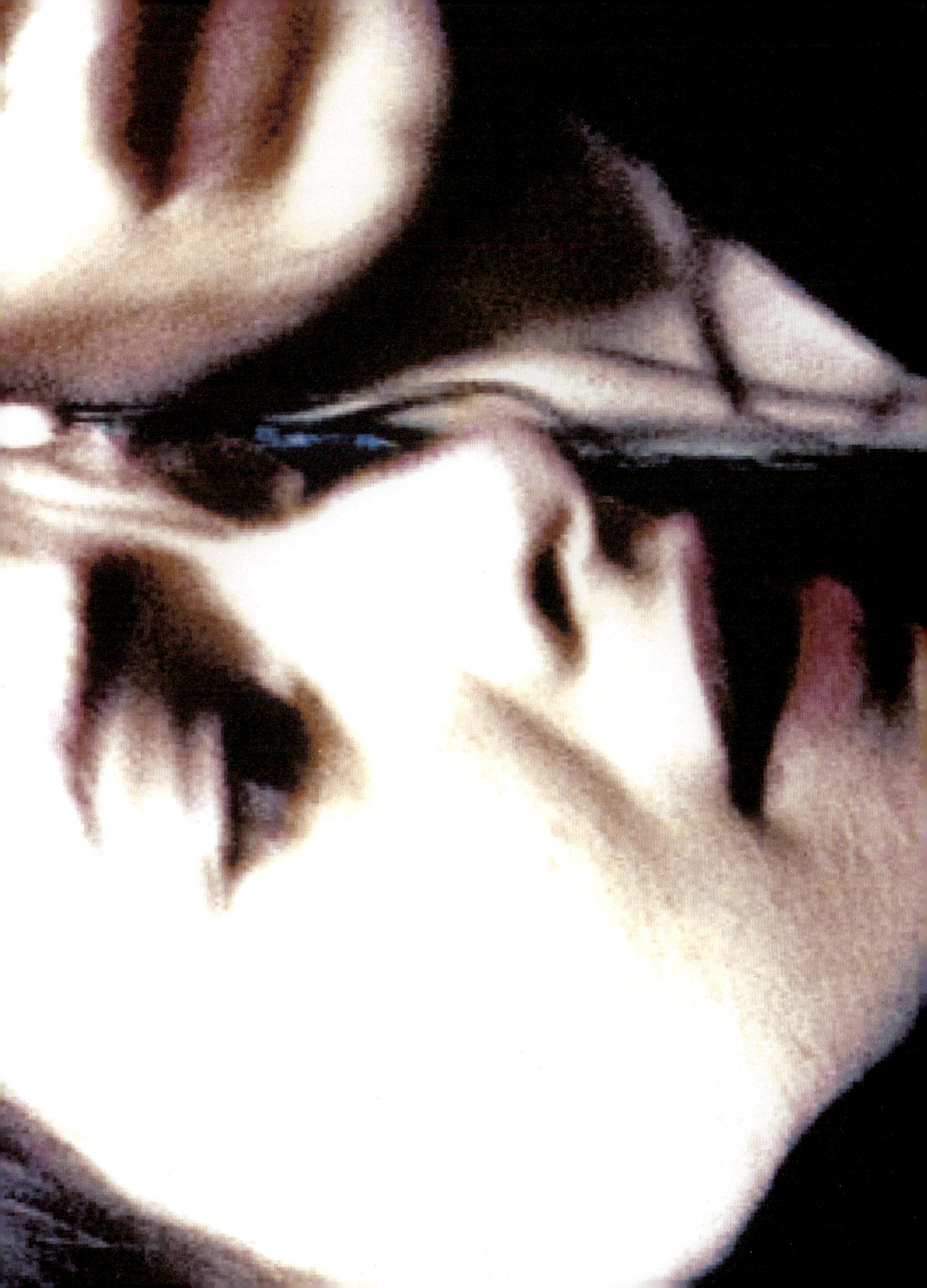

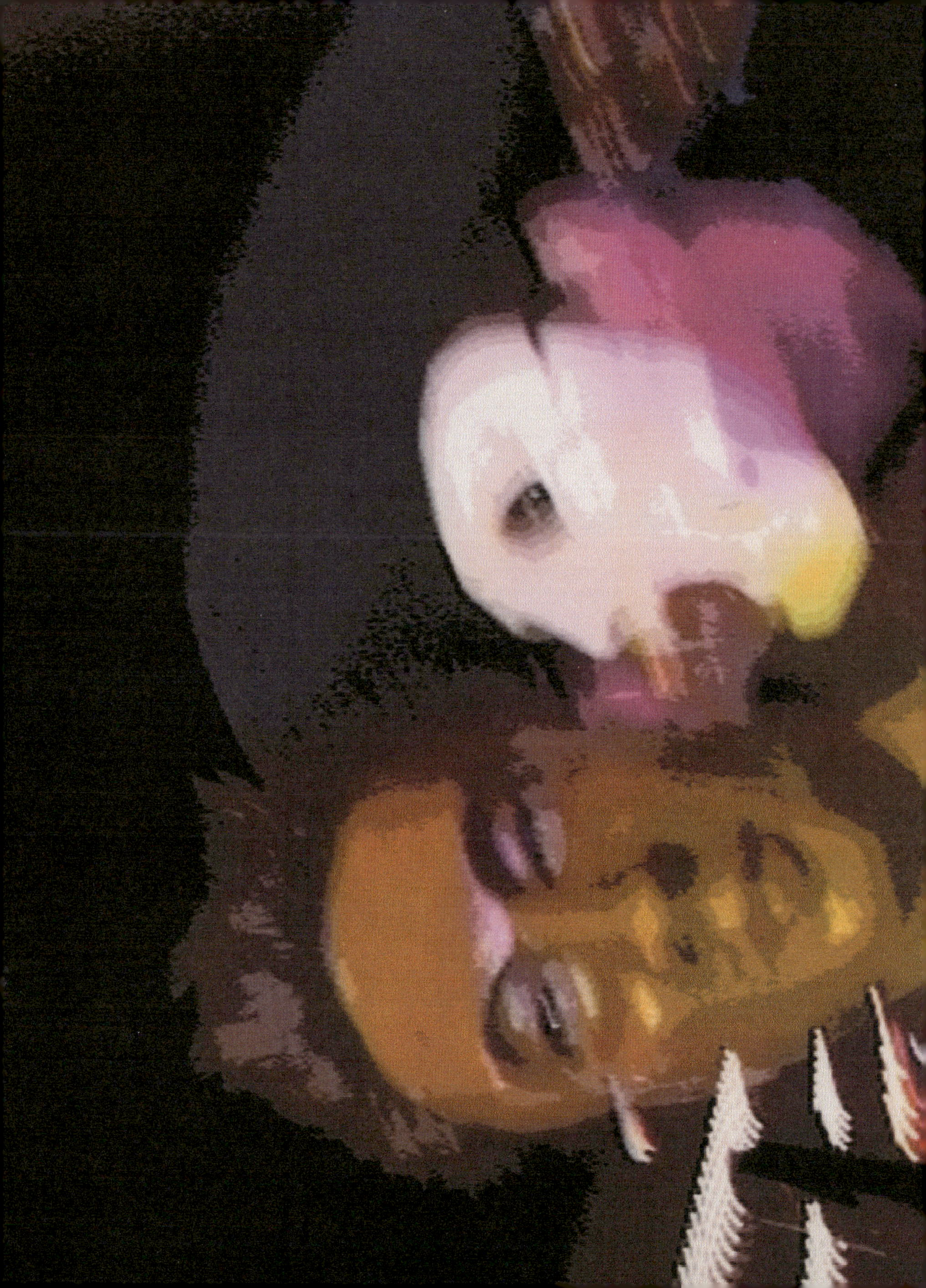

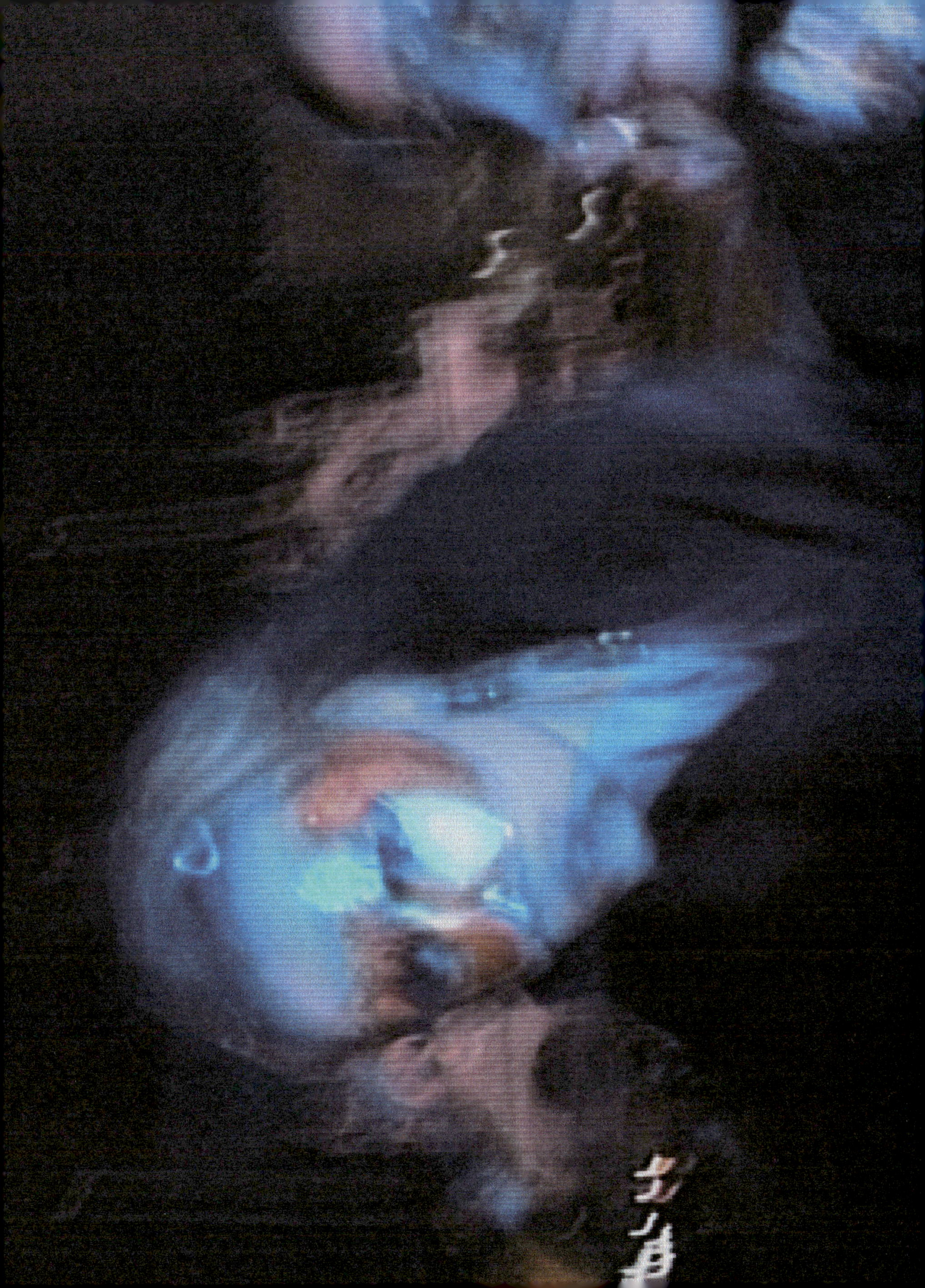

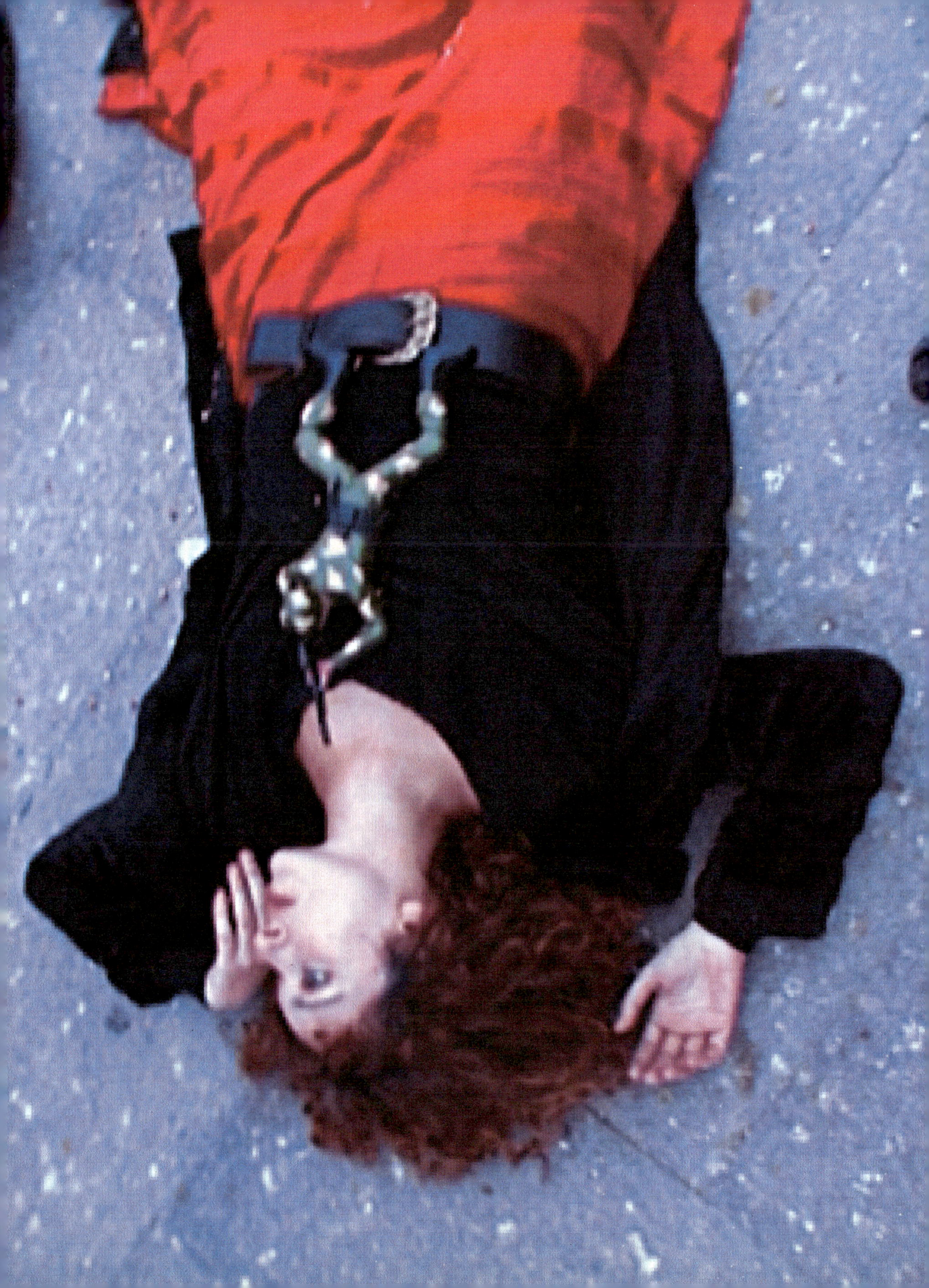

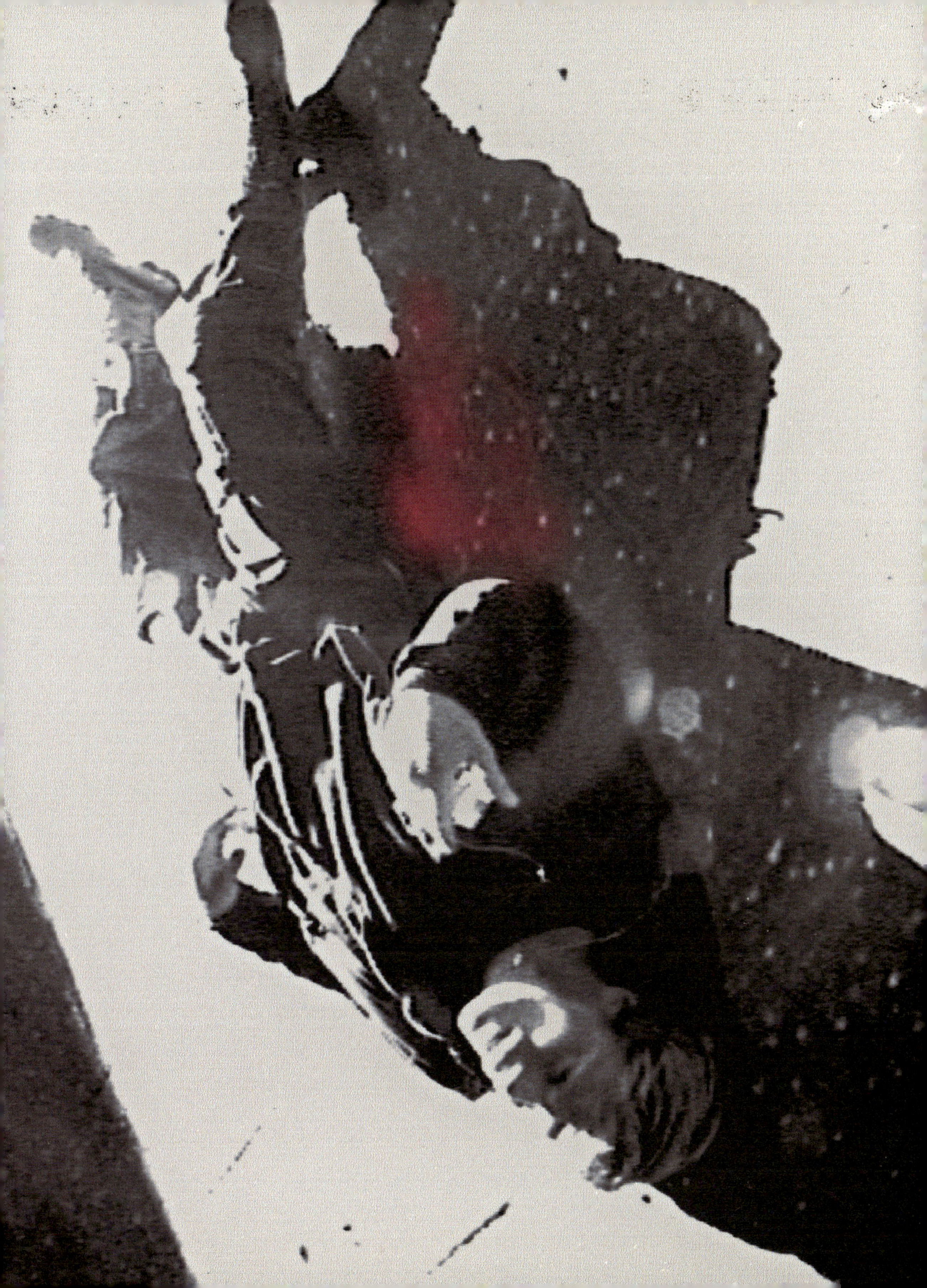

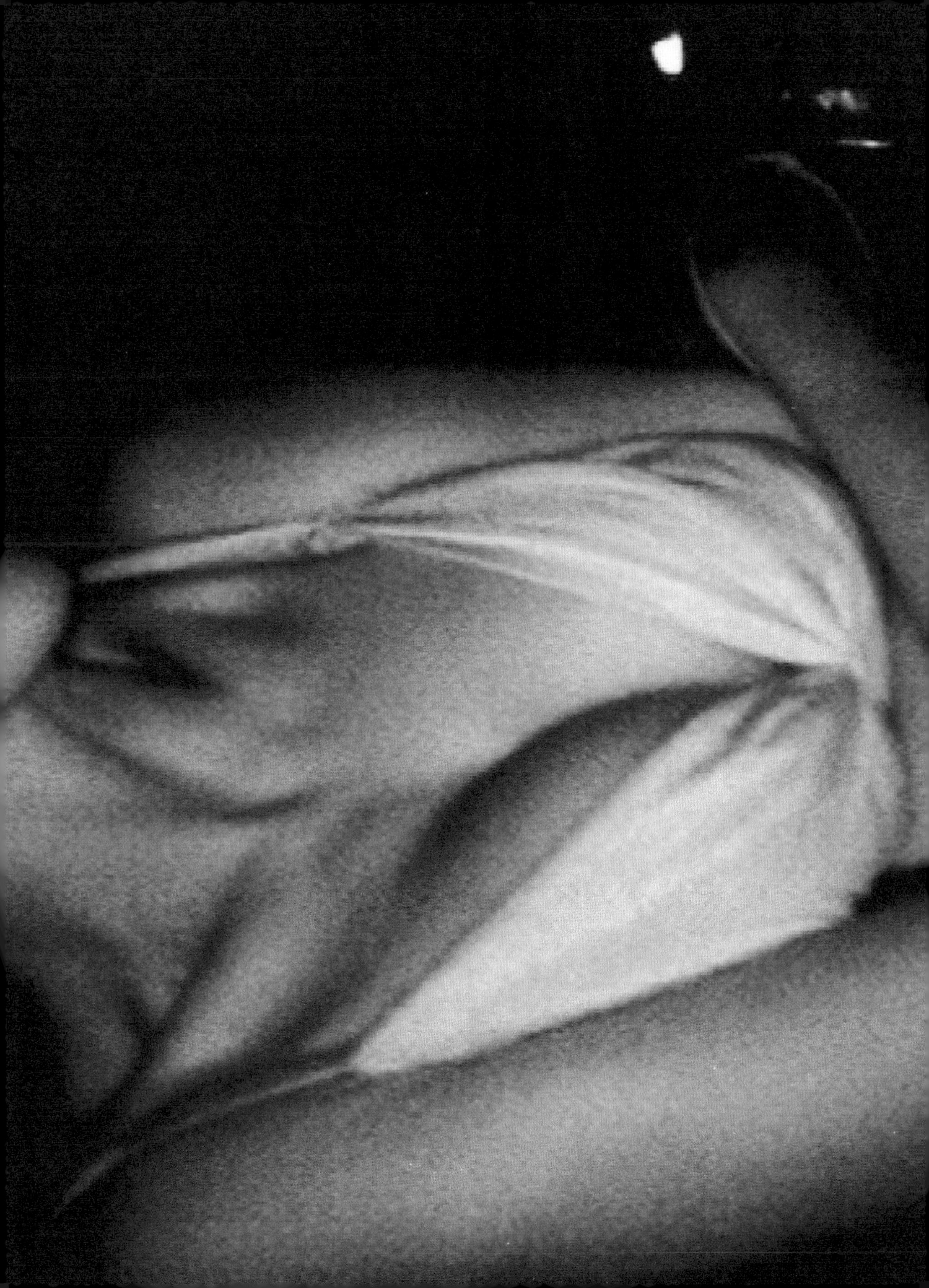

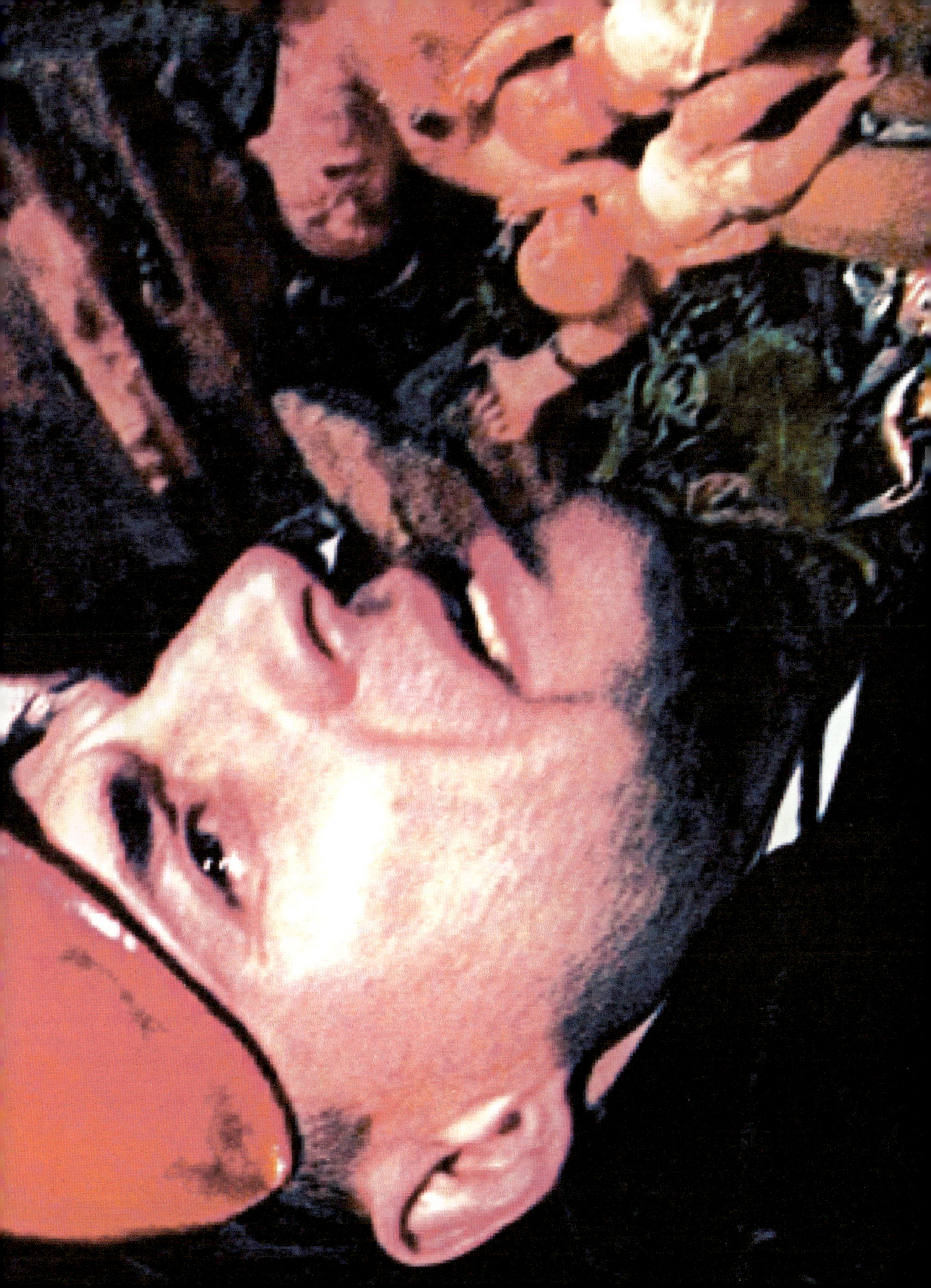

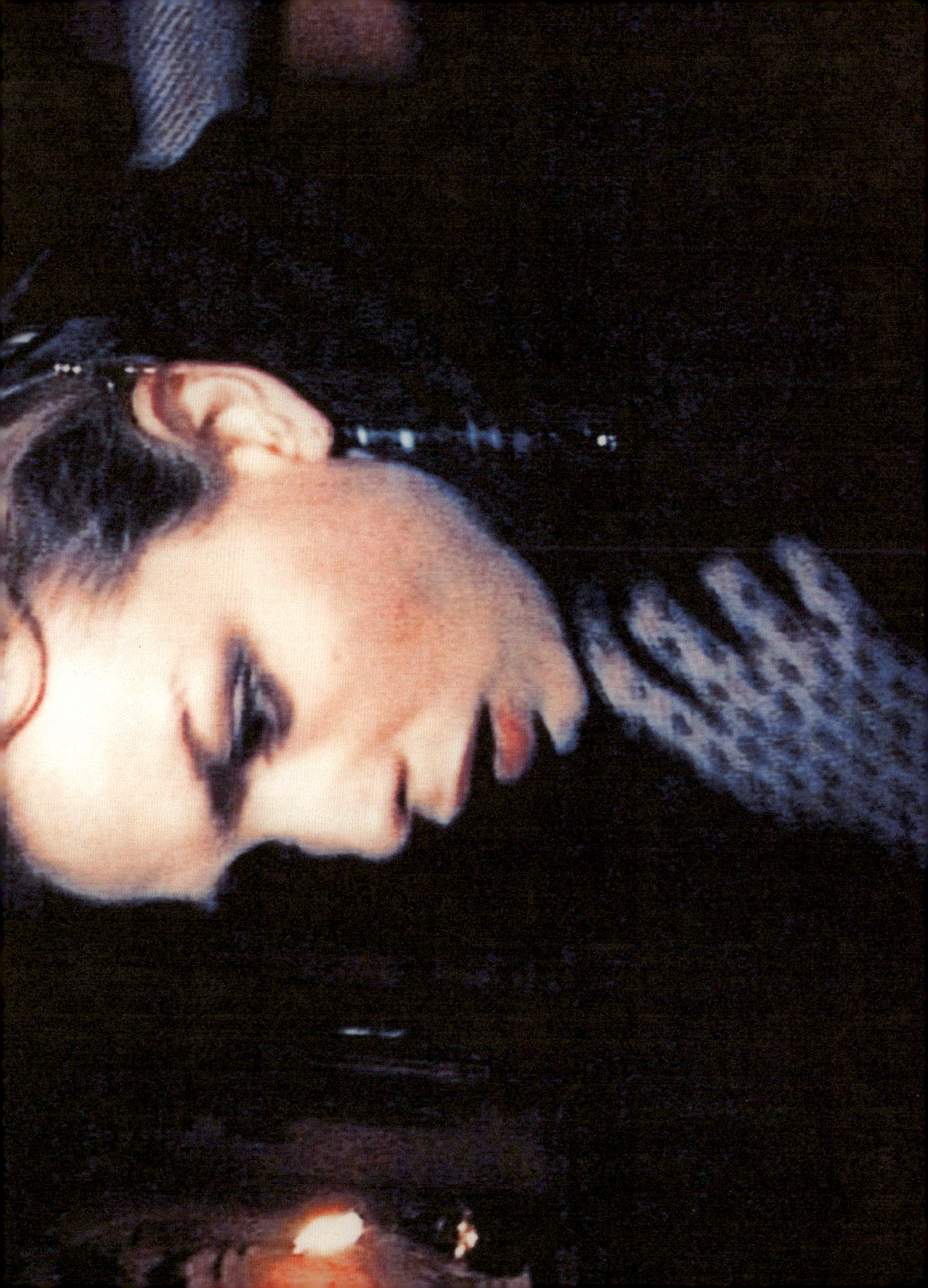

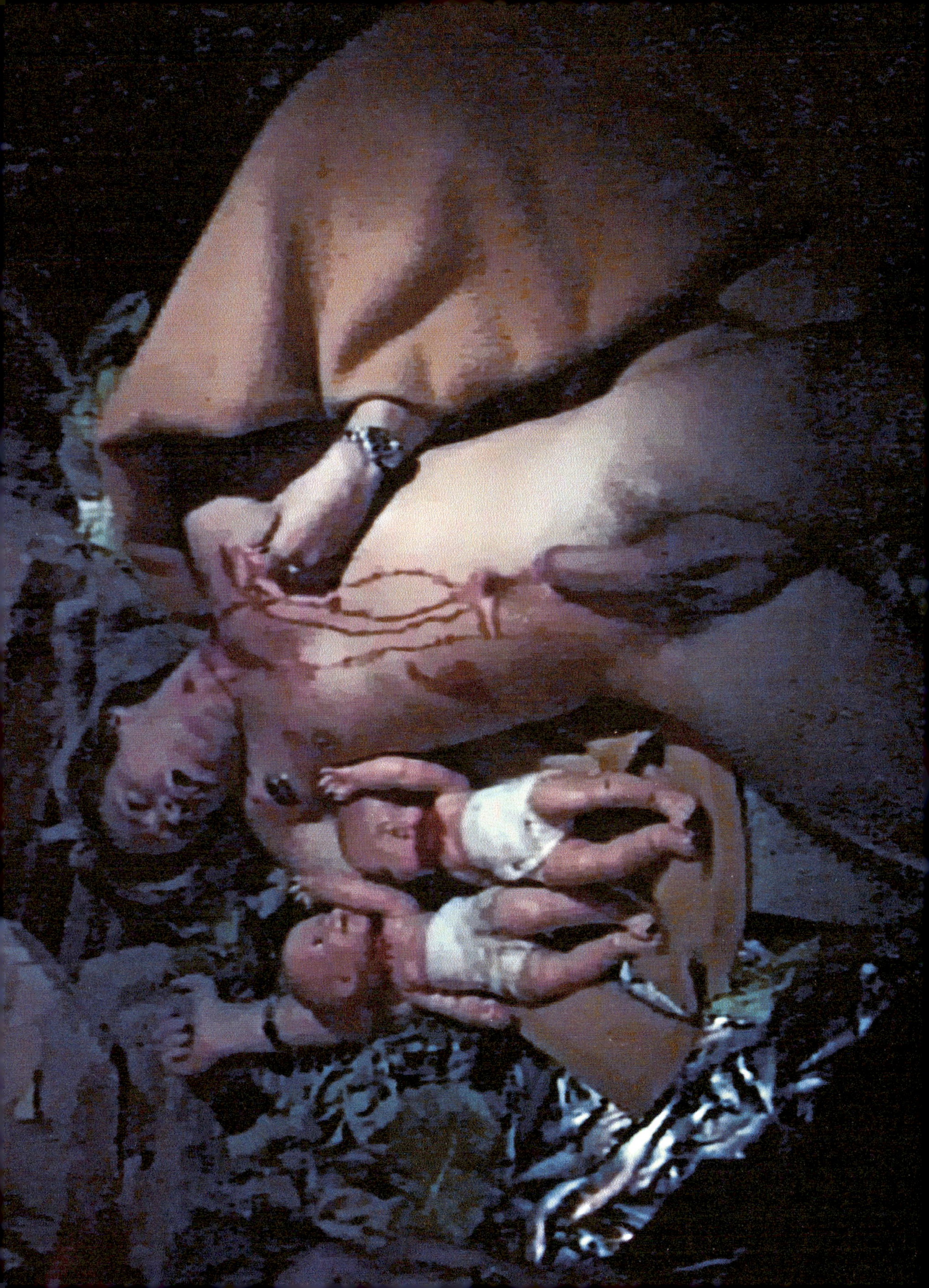

THE DUCHESS OF MALFI - FINAL SCENE.

The DUCHESS and her MAID await the arrival of the DUKE. He strides across the courtyard.

EXT, COURTYARD. VENICE NIGHT

The DUKE, wearing a mask approaches BOSOLA.

DUKE
My revenge still burns and burns and will not slack, until it has spent its fuel. The work is almost done.

BOSOLA is left alone for a moment.

BOSOLA
Hark - how everything is still,
the Screech owl and the Whistler
shrill, do call my dame aloud, to
quickly don her funeral shroud.

The CAMERA reveals the DUCHESS and her MAID who is very agitated.

MAID
Alas, what are you going to do with my sweet lady?

BOSOLA
I've come to make her tomb.

MAID
(to the Duchess)
I'll call for help.

DUCHESS
Please…it affects me not.

The MAID tries to escape but is caught by the KILLER who drags her to a chair and begins winding a long scarf around her neck. The MAID is terrified.

MAID
Leave me, leave me, I must not die,
I'm quick with child.

(cont'd)

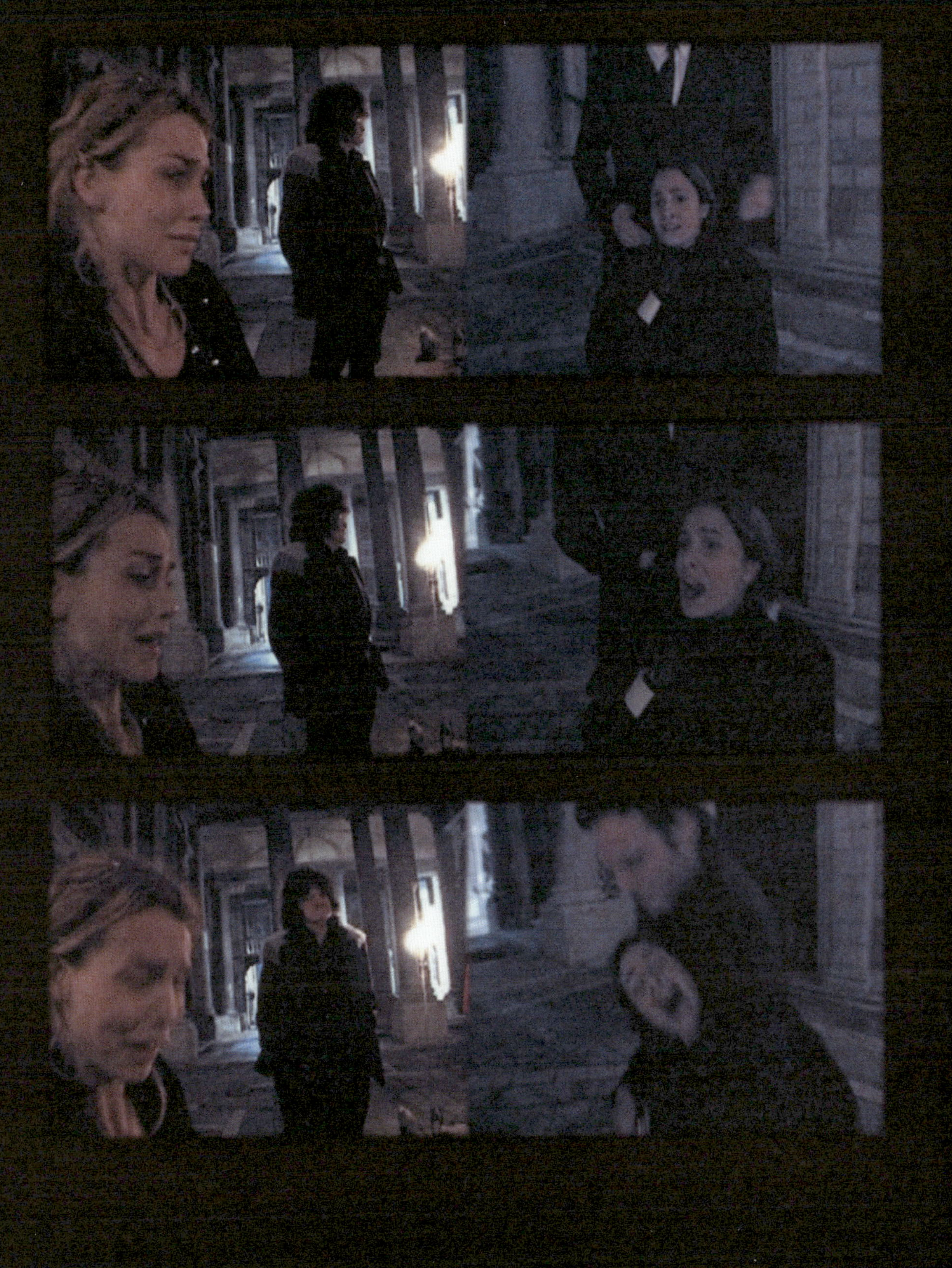

DUCHESS
She is quick with child.

MAID
I'm pregnant.

BOSOLA
Why then your reputation is saved.

The KILLER strangles the MAID and then lowers her to the ground. He makes his way to where the DUCHESS is sitting crying.

DUCHESS
I am Duchess of Malfi, still.

BOSOLA
(mocking)
I am Duchess of Malfi, still. It is that which so breaks thy sleep at night, Duchess!

DUCHESS
Thou art very plain.

BOSOLA
Aye, my trade is to flatter the dead, not the living. I'm a tomb-maker.

DUCHESS
Ah - thou com'st to make my tomb.

BOSOLA
Yes, and this princely gift I bring from your brothers should most welcomingly be received for it brings thy last benefit, thy last sorrow.

DUCHESS
I still have obedience in my blood, so that if this be the only means to make them good, let this be my last presence chamber.

(cont'd)

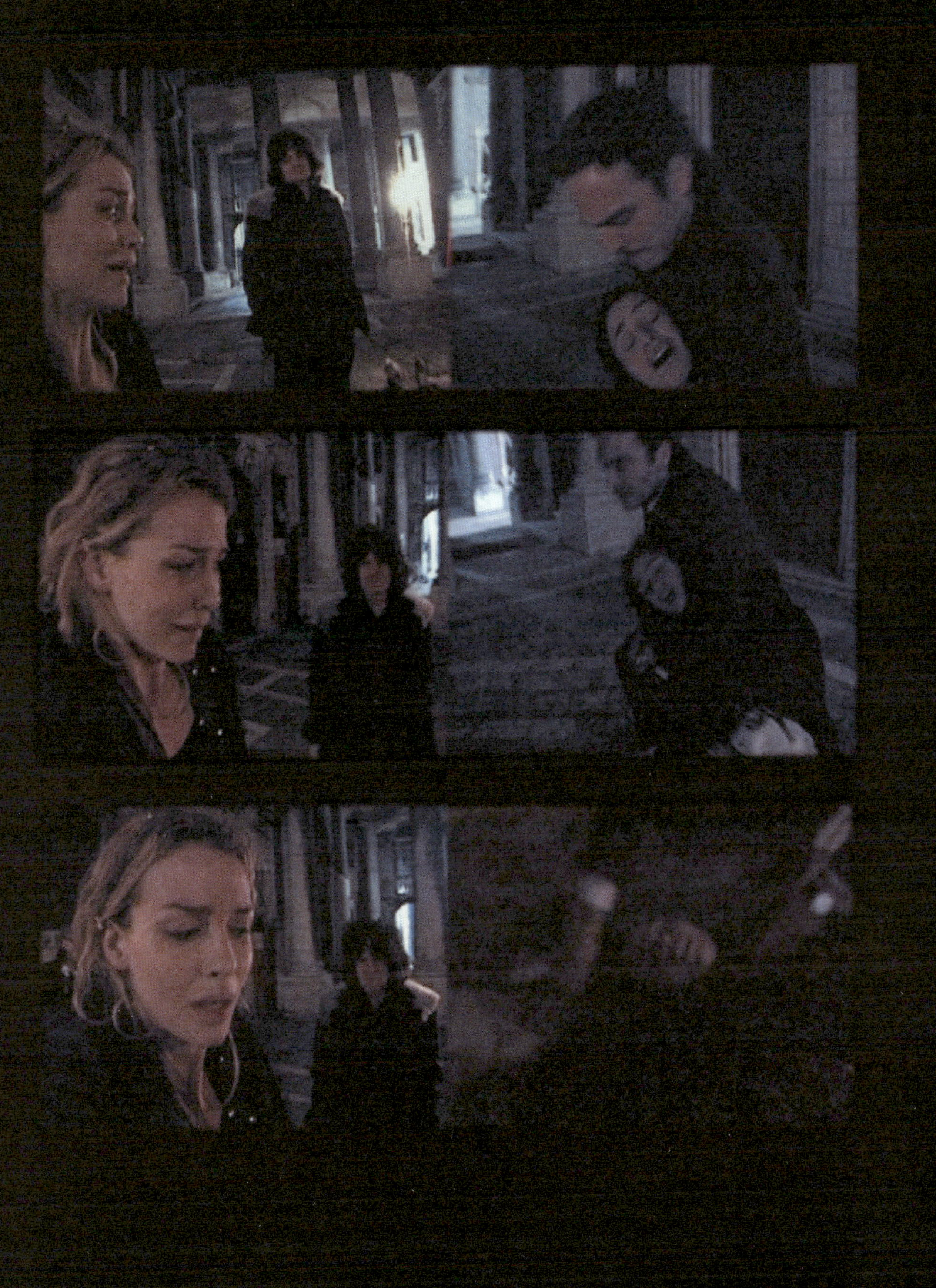

BOSOLA

Art thy not afraid of death? Here is thy executioner!

DUCHESS

I forgive him. The apoplexy, the catarrh or a cough of the lungs will do as much as he.

BOSOLA

Well, it's good to see thou art so well prepared.

(to the Killer)

Strangle her. Art thy not frighted by the cord?

DUCHESS

Not a whit, what would it pleasure me to have my throat cut with diamonds, or to be smothered with the finest perfume, or to be shot with pearls. I know death hath ten thousand several exits and we can open them many ways.

BOSOLA

Strangle her!

DUCHESS

Tell my brothers I perceive death fully and I am full awake. They may say in jest that the last thing to die is a woman's tongue so I shall shortly be silent. Come sweet narcotic of death, help me sleep.

BOSOLA

Finish it!

The KILLER strangles the DUCHESS. The DUKE approaches the camera.

DUKE

From now on - only deeds of darkness.

The cameras move to reveal the DUCHESS and the MAID, dead on the floor.

DISSOLVE TO...

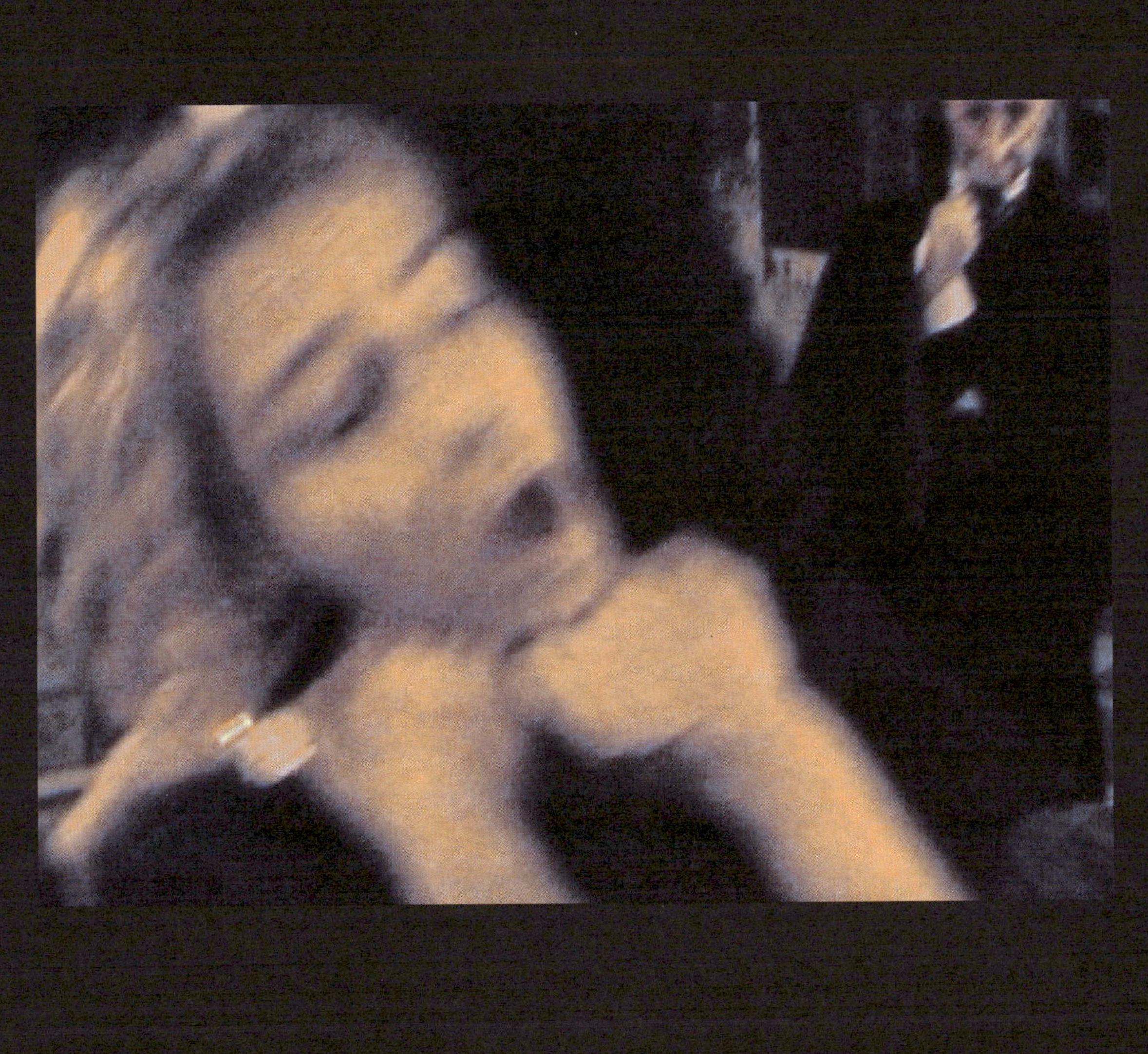

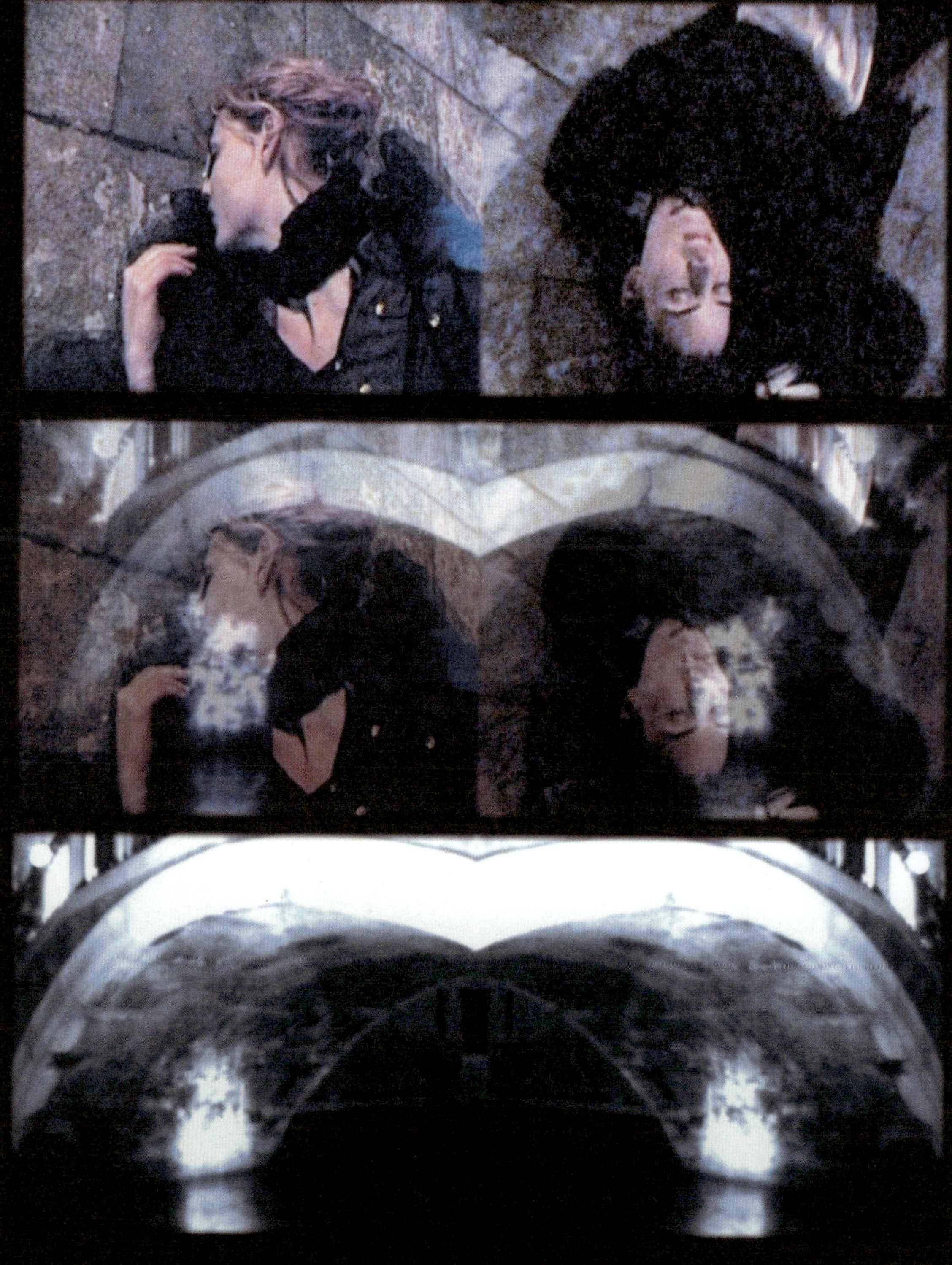

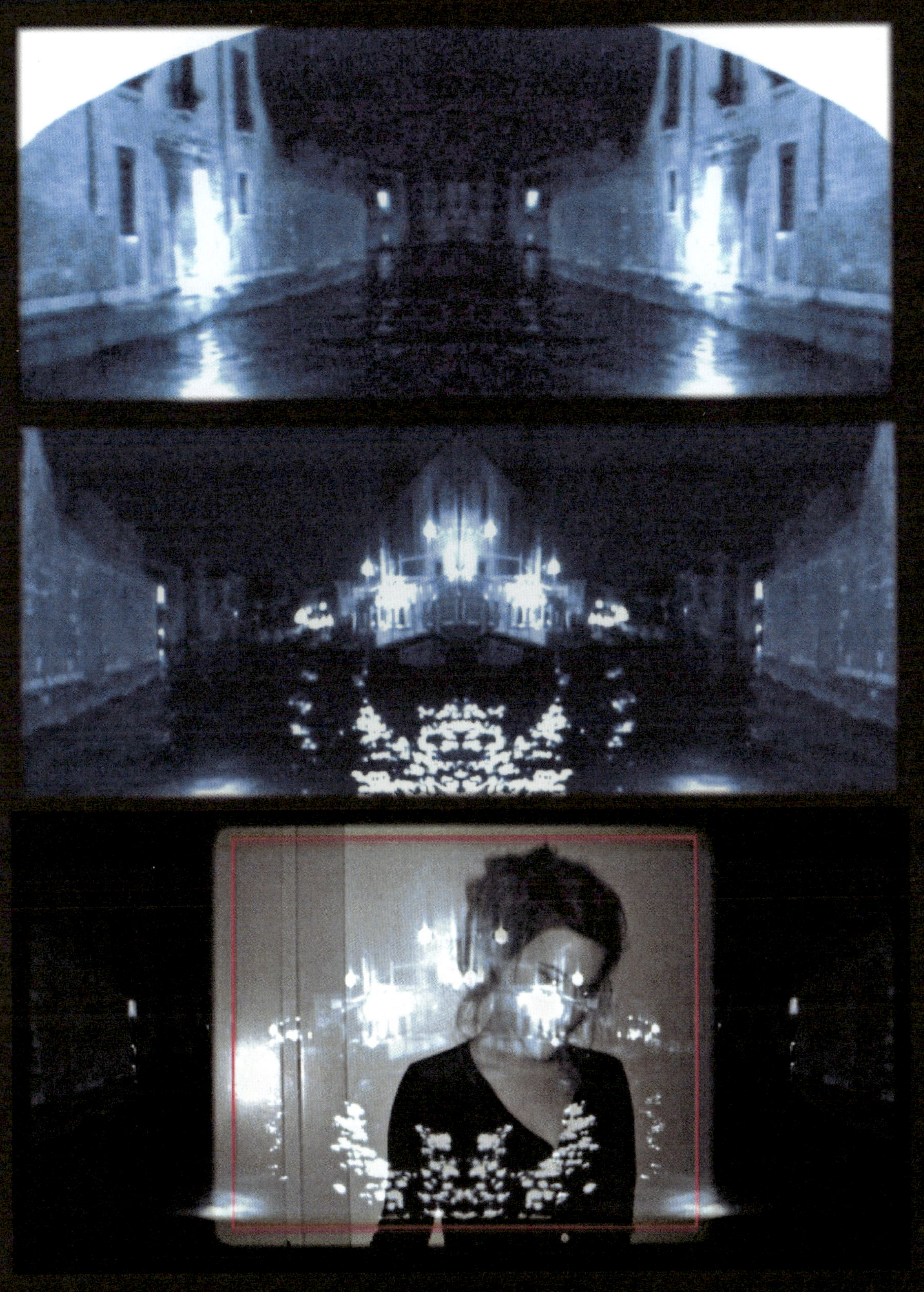

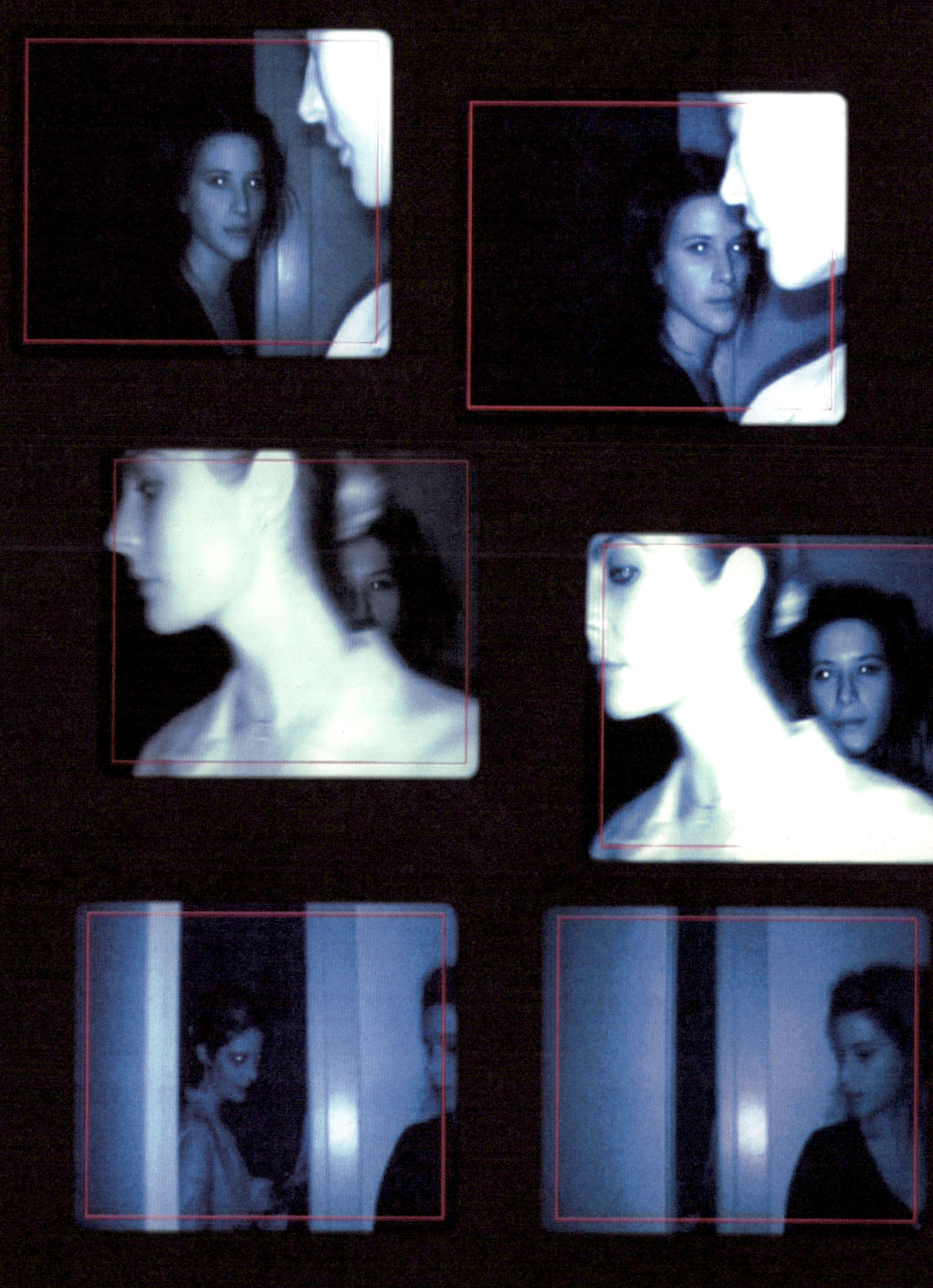

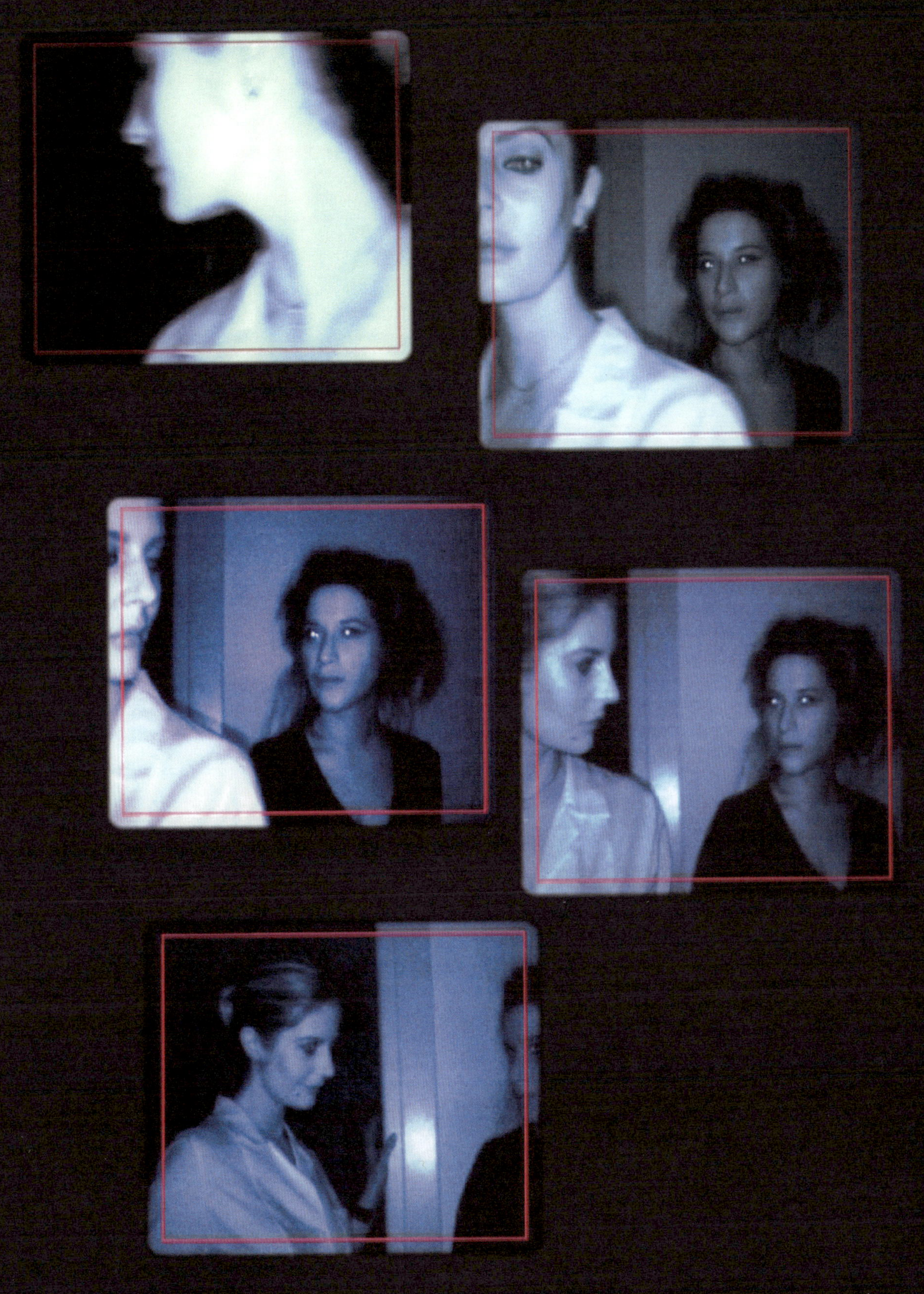

2

As he walked out of the room, the older man, I knew that any danger to me had passed. In leaving he clearly had wanted something to happen between the younger man and myself. This young man had looked at me strangely, had been concerned for me, had desired me. I knew that if I were to cry or ask for his help I could walk out of the room in minutes and all would be well.

In his own way he was already in love with me but despised me for my superiority. He was not unattractive. But he was nothing to me. I let my hands drop to my side, still looking at him. I decided to continue. There were things that I wanted to know about myself and I knew I could use this man.

I undressed for him. Why should this be so interesting? Why should my body be interesting to him? Why should any human body be interesting to anyone else? A puzzle. I decided suddenly that if I was going to do this thing, whatever it was, this experiment, then I wanted also to see him. By now I had taken off my blouse and my skirt and he was staring at me in my underwear.

I walked over to his chair and asked him politely to stand, which he did. Then I asked him to undress. He was embarrassed and nervous but did as I asked. When he was down to his shorts he turned away and I asked him to face me. I heard my voice and it was severe. He turned to face me and I could see that his sex was large and he was almost ashamed of it. So now we both were facing each other. I reached behind to unhook my brassiere and then held it to my breasts. I asked him to look at me as I revealed my breasts to him. The air in the room was cold and I knew my nipples were hard and pointed. I felt nothing for him, no desire. I knew sex, even though no man had been inside me, but I had experienced desire. And I had masturbated from time to time and enjoyed it.

I watched his eyes as I showed my breasts to him. I saw his sex twitching in his pants. I cupped one breast in my hand and used the other fingers to stroke and stretch the nipple and I began to feel something new in my body. It was power. And it went wherever I wanted it to go, to whichever part of my body that I commanded it. I told him to stand against the wall and he did. He was between a light fitting and the window and I thought it would be funny to make a Christ figure so I asked him to stretch out his arms as if he was on the cross. One hand grasped the curtain and the other the wall light.

In fact he looked more or less beautiful for the first time. I wanted to see him naked now, before I was naked. I walked over to him slowly. I knew he wanted to embrace me, to make love to me in a conventional way, in a way that had no interest for me at all. That he wanted love and tenderness and mothering and me to be all of those things and the whore also. I knew he ached to embrace me and so I sharply told him to leave his arms where they already were. He was staring at me hard and for the moment I didn't want that so I put my hand onto his face and closed his eyes as if he had just died, like they do in films. His eyes stayed shut and my hand stayed on his face, my fingers tracing his nose and then his mouth. I wanted to explore more of his mouth so with my other hand I opened his lips and then his teeth.

He was still nervous and his jaw was clenched tight but then it relaxed as he got the idea and with my fingers I touched his tongue and the inside of his cheek which was soft and surprisingly cool. I brought my mouth very close to his and inhaled him, intrigued to see how his smell was. It was suddenly very important to know how he smelled, that if he smelled bad I would not have been able to continue. But it was fine his smell, neither one thing nor the other. A clean smell. And his skin, it too smelled the same. A scent of the hotel soap that I knew so well, having stolen so many for my mother and myself. Different from the soap we could buy in the shops, this soap came from the West.

He was tall, much taller than me and as I stood on my toes to smell him his sex touched me and I was intrigued by how it felt, so stiff and unyielding. But my curiosity was aroused and I knelt in front of him and hooked my fingers into his shorts. There was a small comedy as I pulled down his shorts. His sex pointed up at me and the elastic of his shorts strained against it as I eased them down. I could see that what I was doing must be painful and his stomach muscles tightened and his arms involuntarily came down onto my shoulders as his shorts finally slid to his ankles and his sex twitched angrily in front of my face. I told him to replace his arms where they had been and he obeyed without hesitation.

I examined him for a while, his sex. The colour, the texture, the heat coming off it so close to my face. I took it in my hand and was amazed at the feeling of power that it gave me. The feeling centred in my own sex and up my spine and into my own brain. The smell was not so pure from his sex. It was a dark, somewhat disgusting smell, although not repulsive. I was curious as to how he would taste suddenly and I brought my face closer and then closer and with my tongue I touched the head of his sex. It was incredibly soft, the skin there and I took him in my mouth. I stayed still feeling him enlarging even more.

I crawled away from him until I could feel the cool leather of an armchair on the back of my thigh. I sat in the chair, in my pants. I told him to open his eyes.

At first he looked down at his sex, he would not look at me. I put my right leg over the side of the arm of the chair and then the same with the other leg so now I was open to him. I touched myself, touched my own sex.

He raised his head and looked at me. Looked at my face and then his eyes lowered to where I was touching myself. His sex twitched and moved in spasm as I opened myself, using all my fingers to probe and violate myself the way he would have violated me.

I watched him all the time he watched me.

*

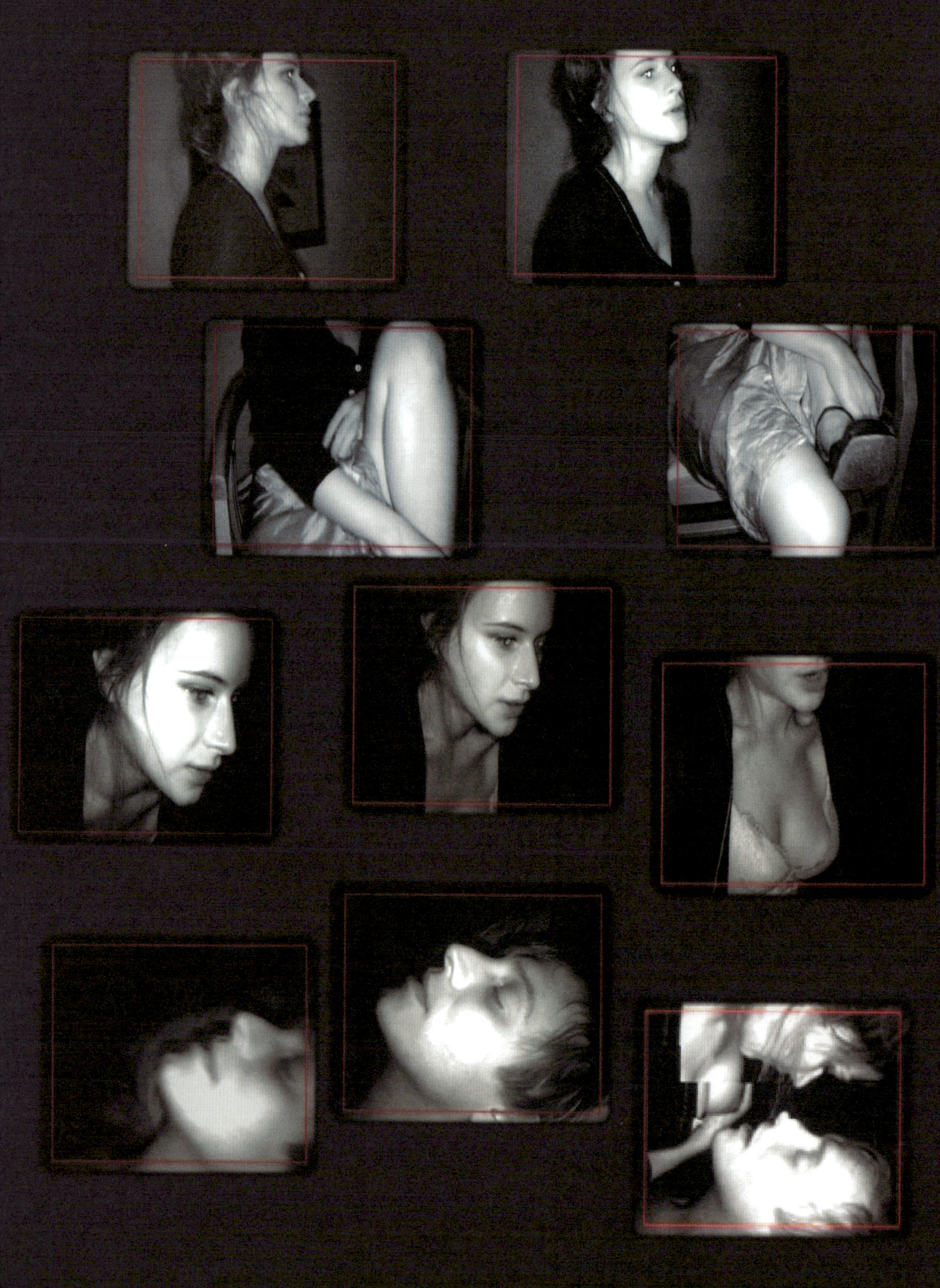

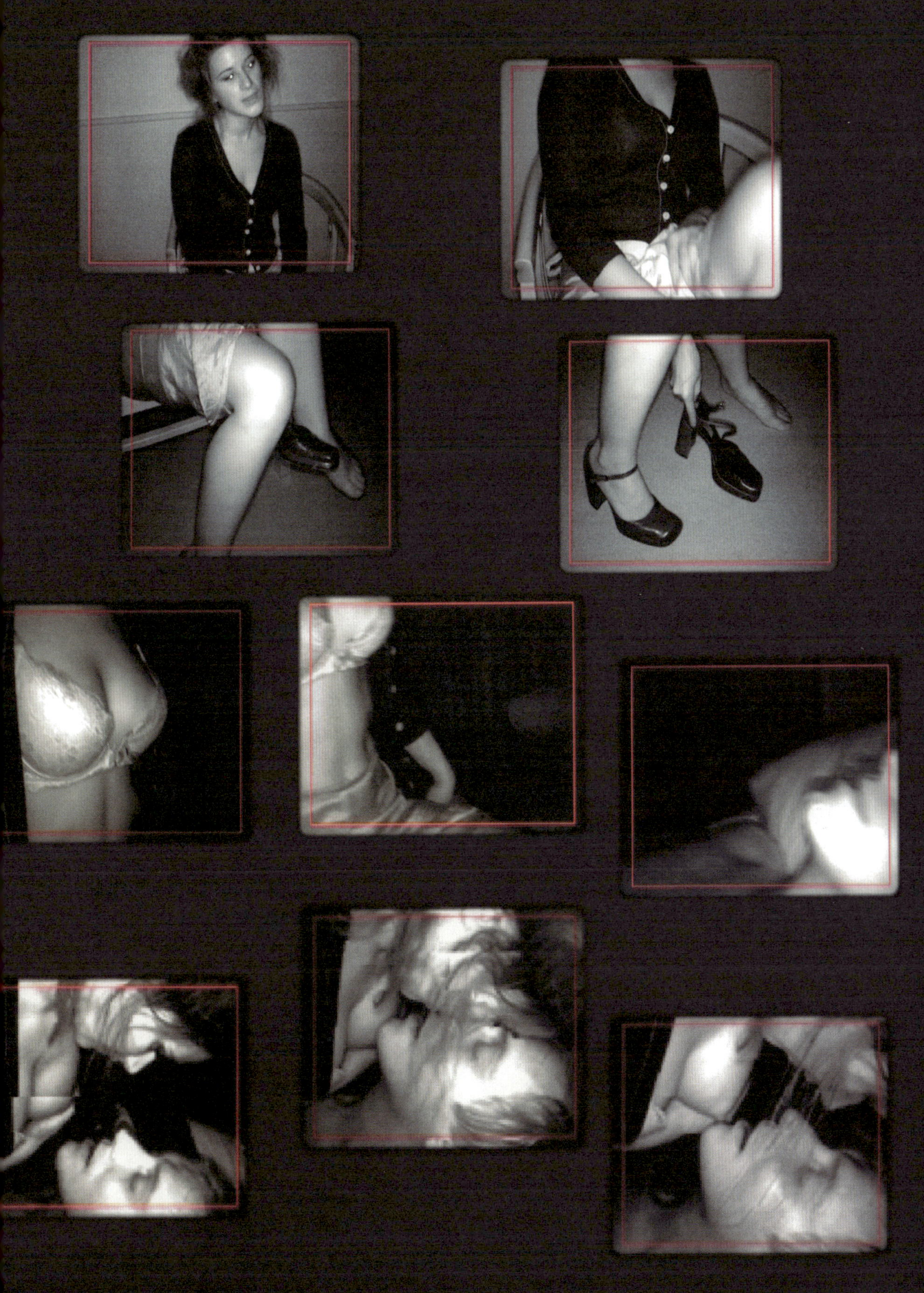

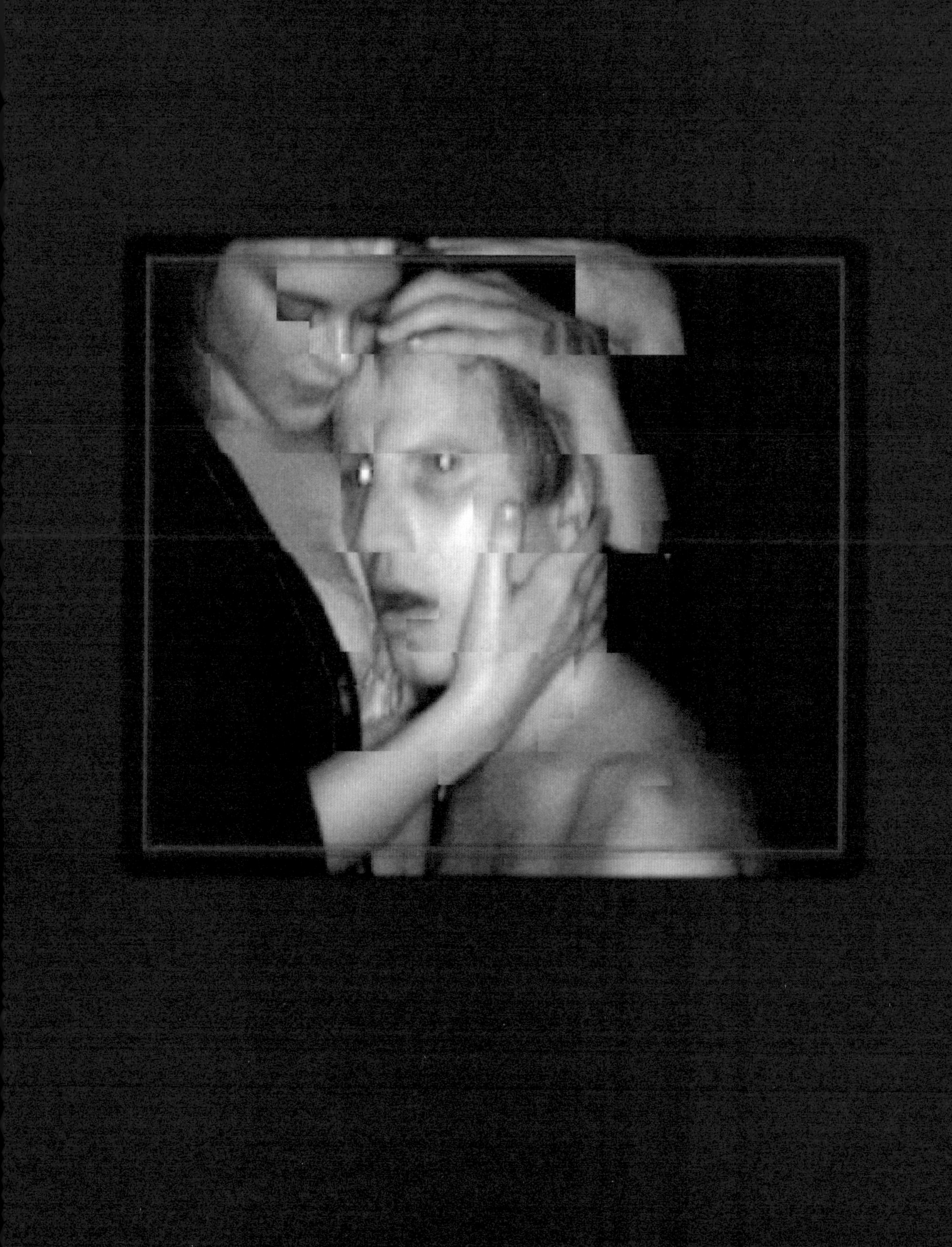

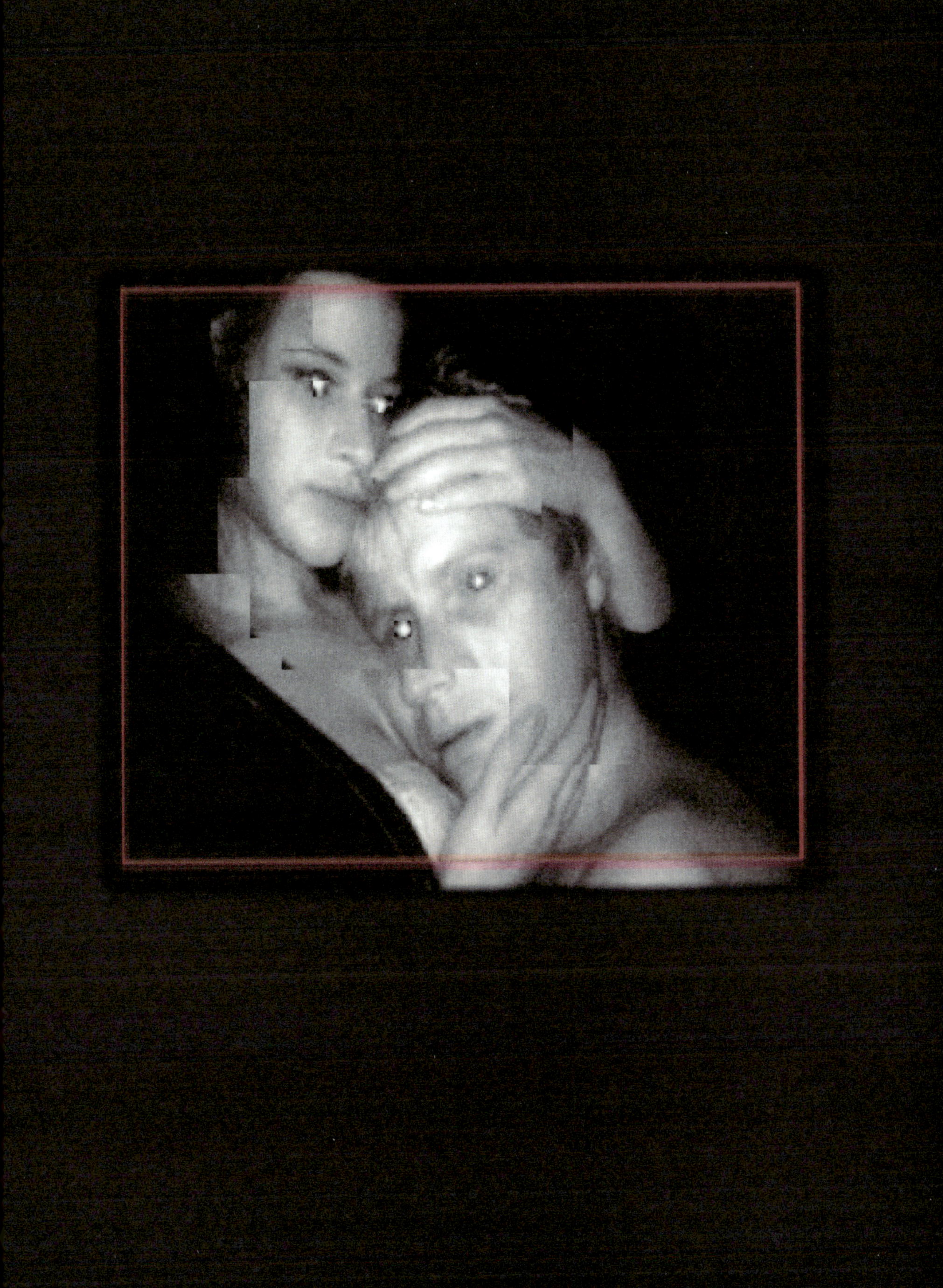

Maud Seduces Trent.

Last two takes are good. Sound is a little borderline because she is whispering.

Start with 11 beginning

In conjunction with "Der Doppelgänger" and the ending of the strangling.

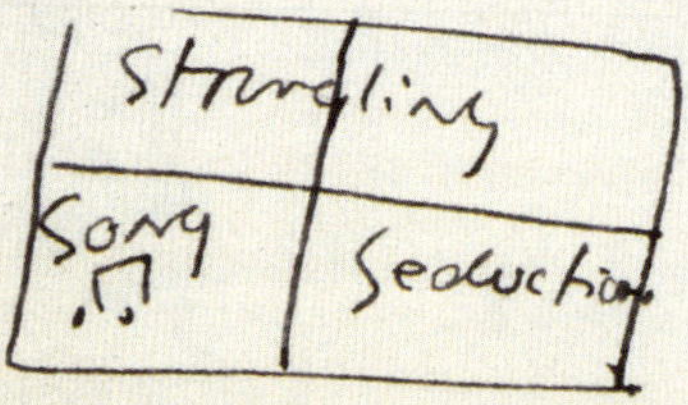

strangling	
song	seduction

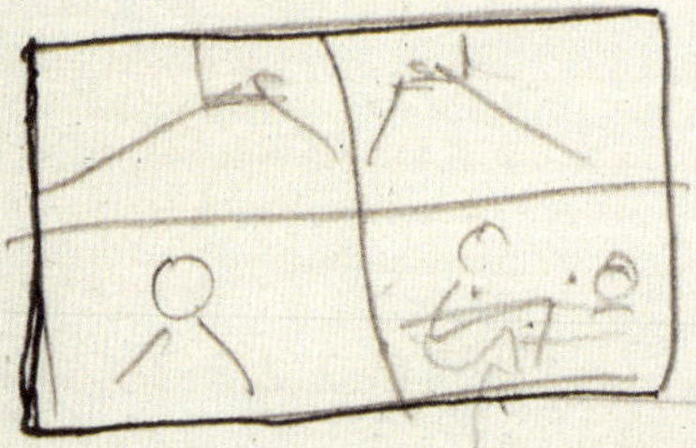

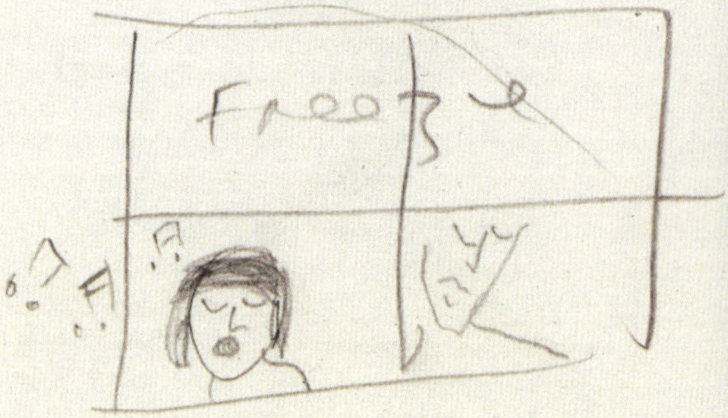

Freeze

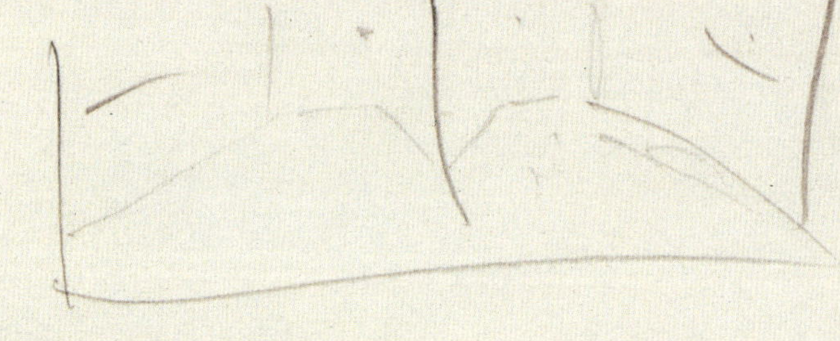

, ,, ,,,

Fade all 4 screens at the same time over then go to full screen.

Last Supper. Moments to come back over the split-screen supper –

← Take 6 →

45° last supper (Split Screen)

Rhys looks down (Single Screen)

Take 5.

15 secs. total
5 secs in
4 secs out.

last supper W.S.

Last Supper M.S.

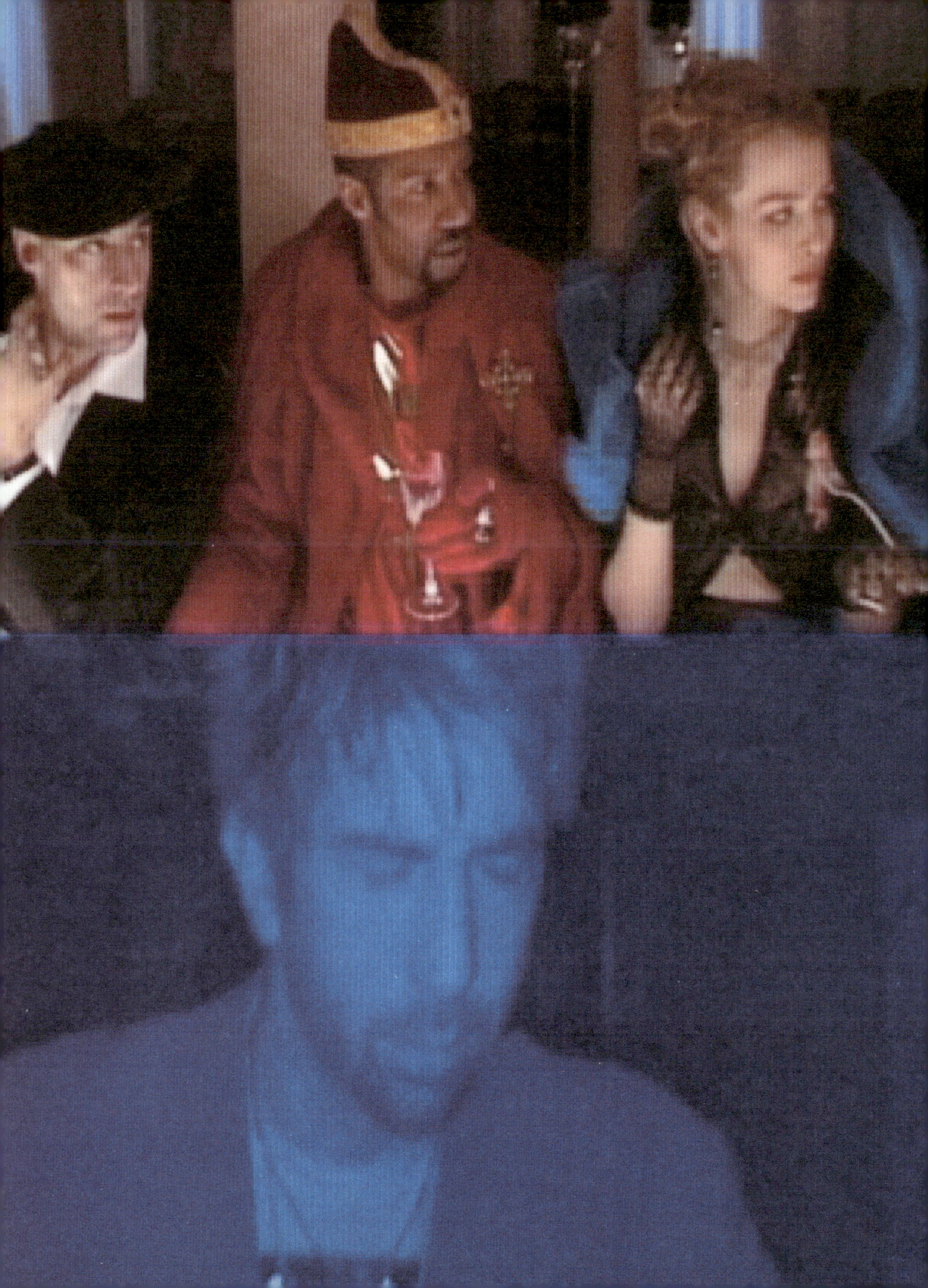

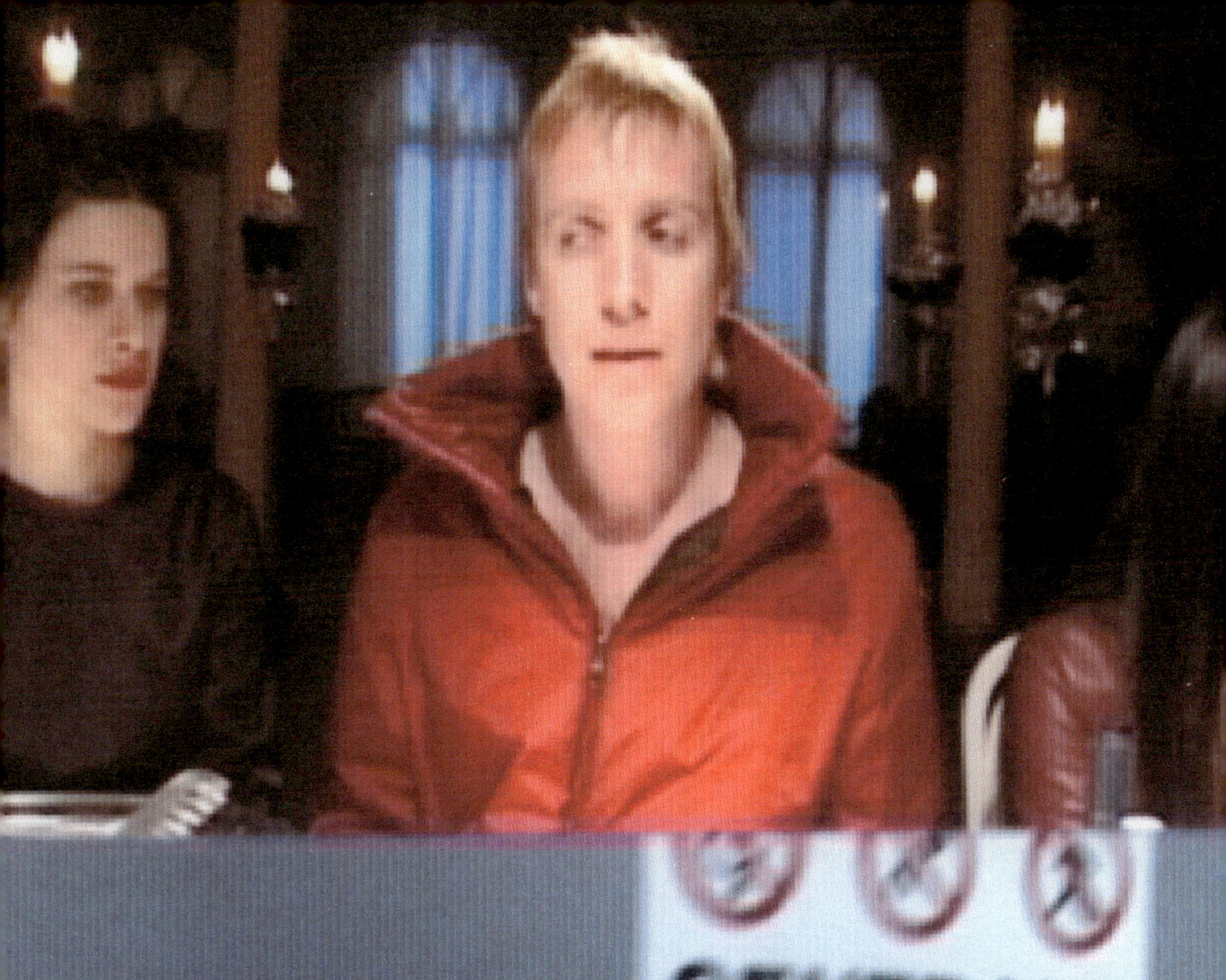

CENTRALE
TERMICA

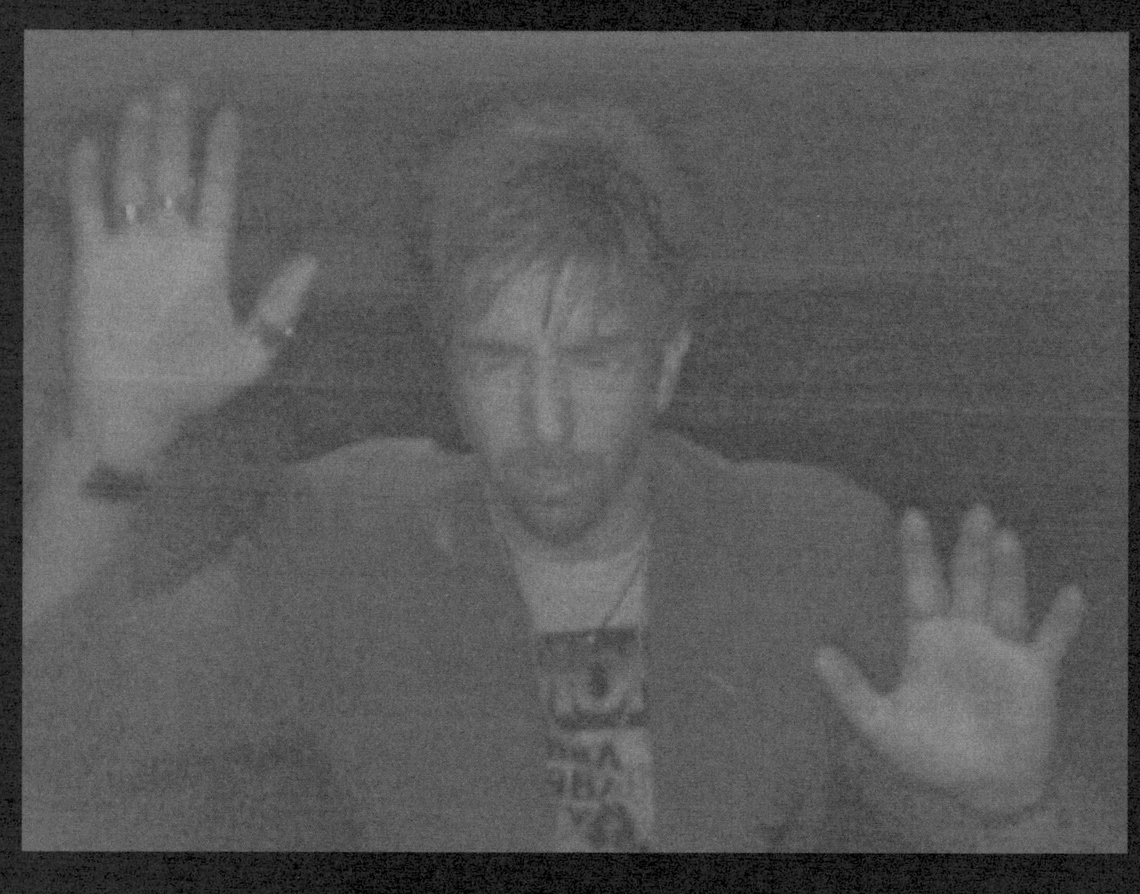

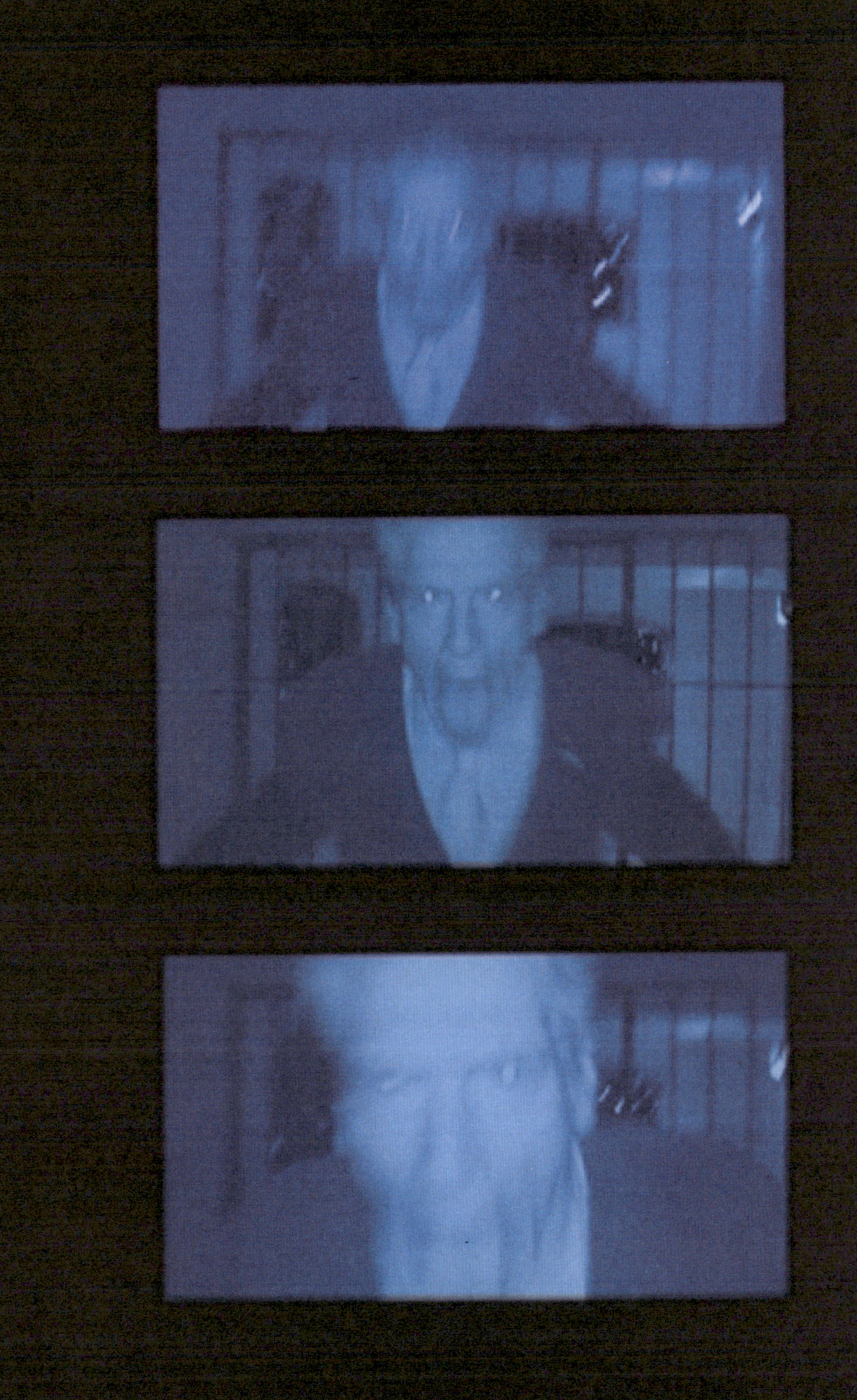

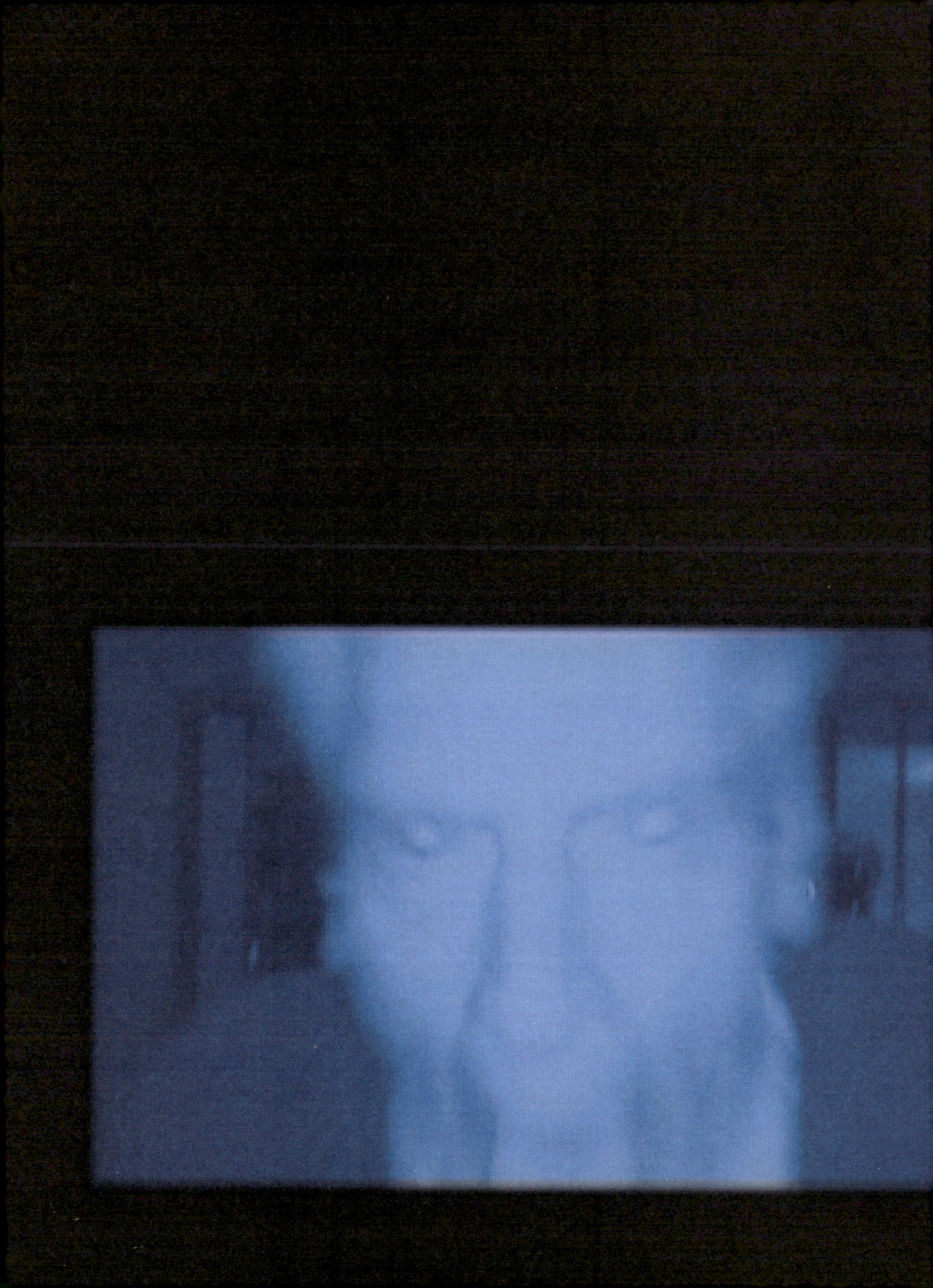

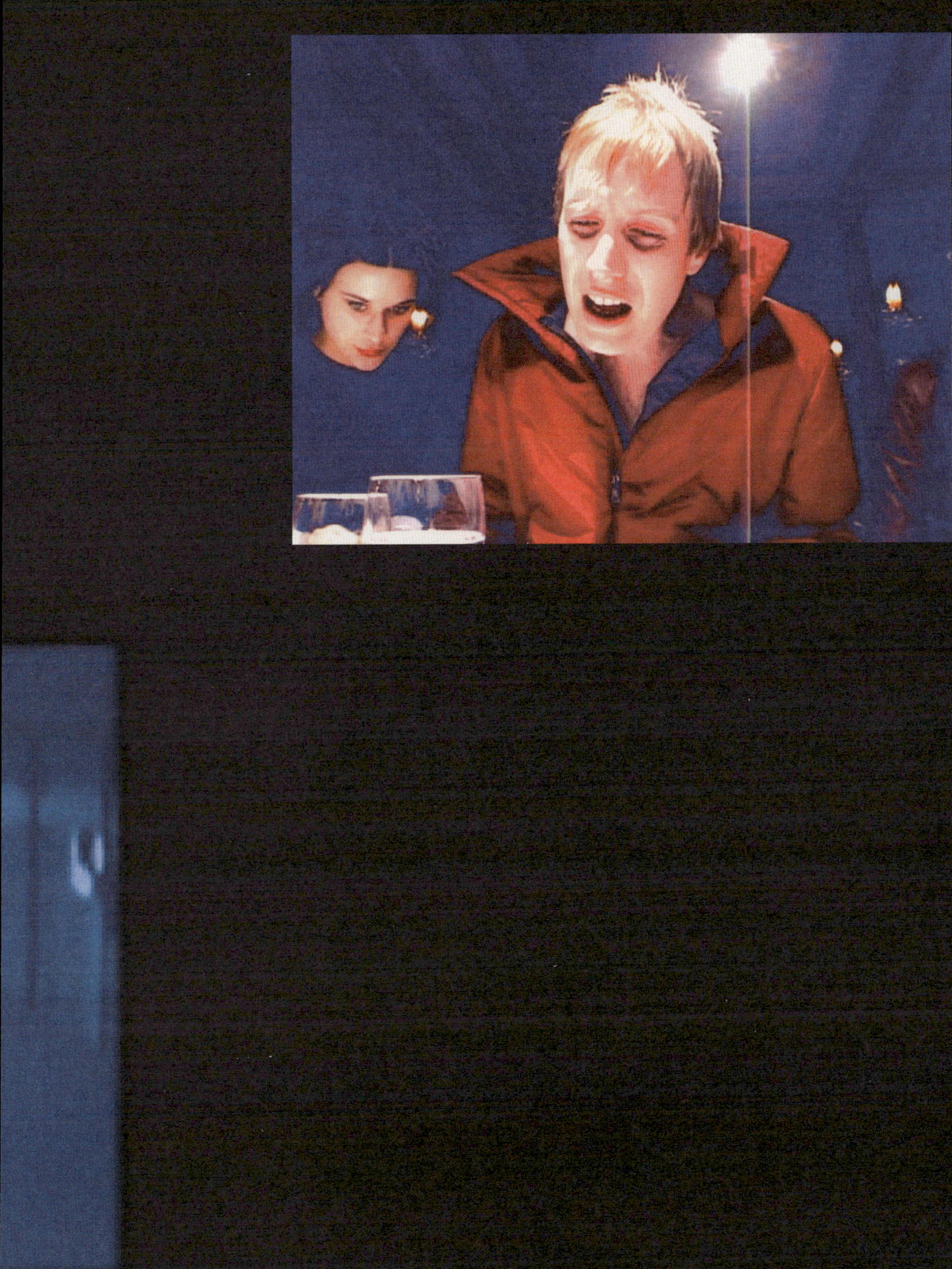

AFTER WORDS, 2001/2002

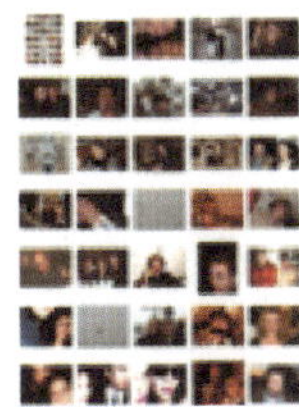 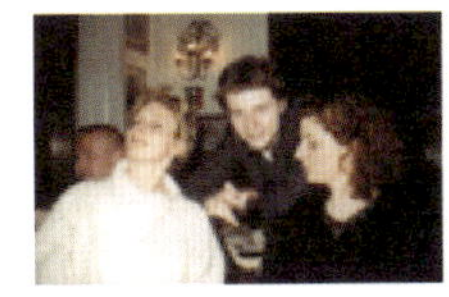 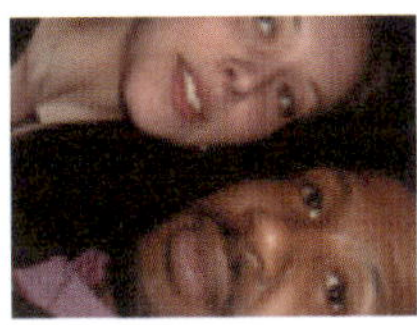 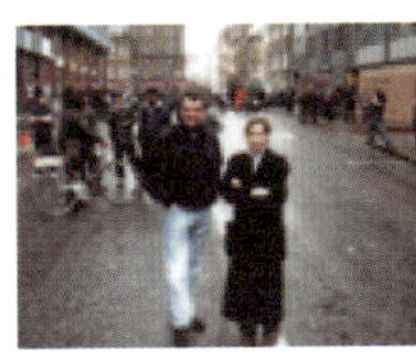 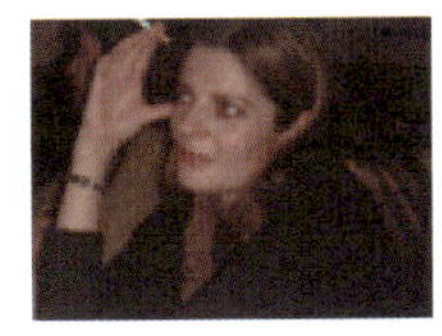

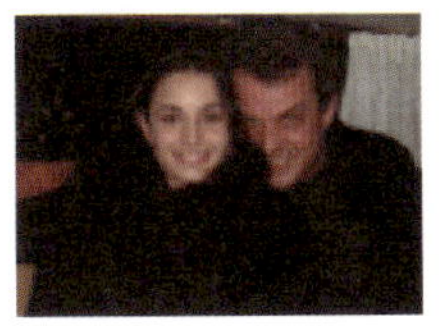 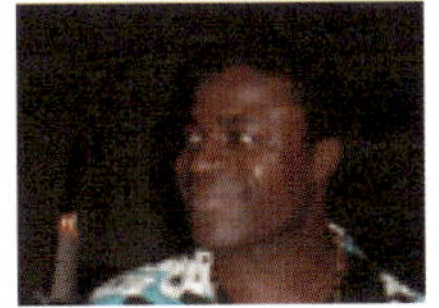 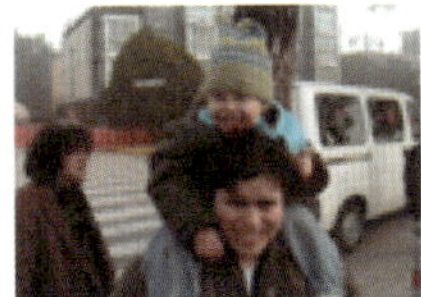 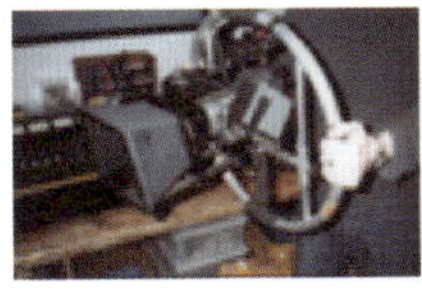 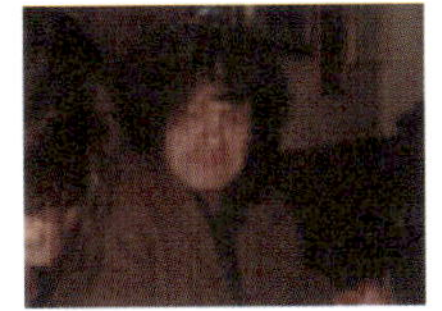

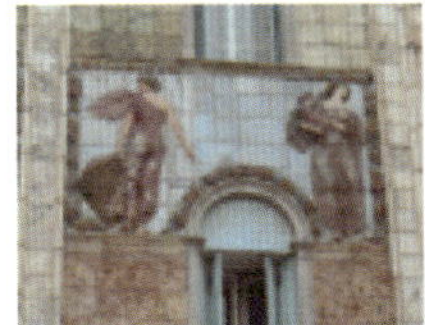 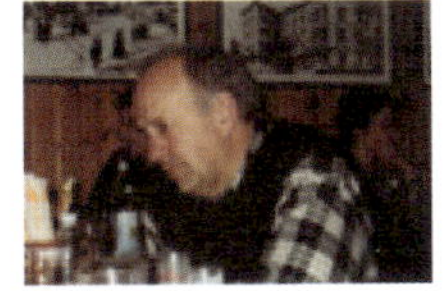 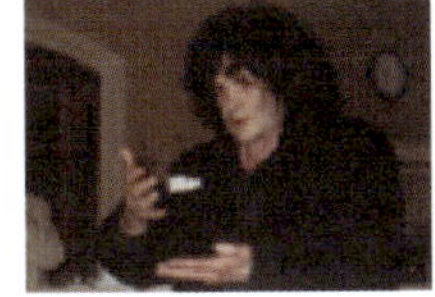 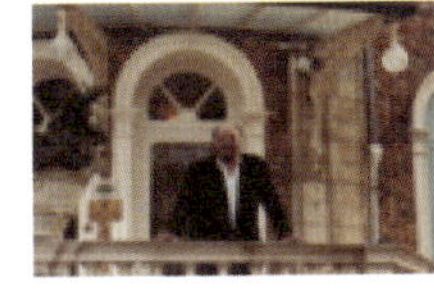 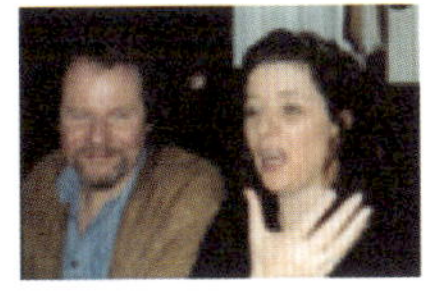

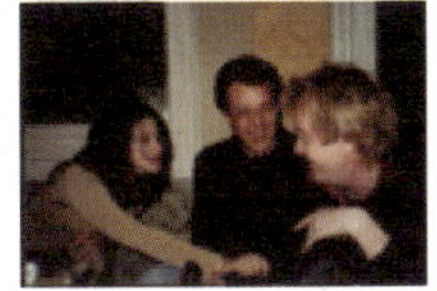 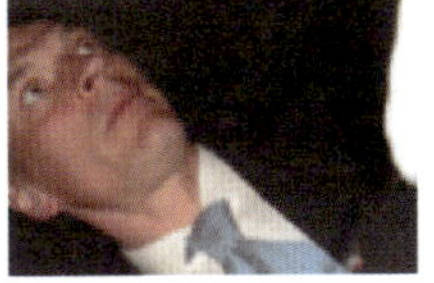 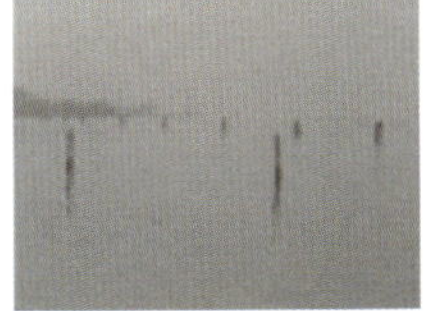 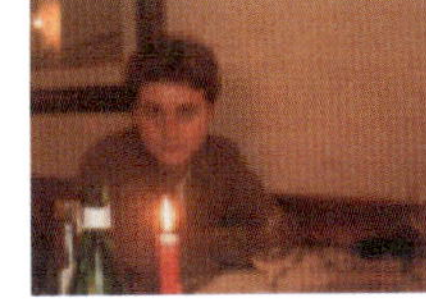 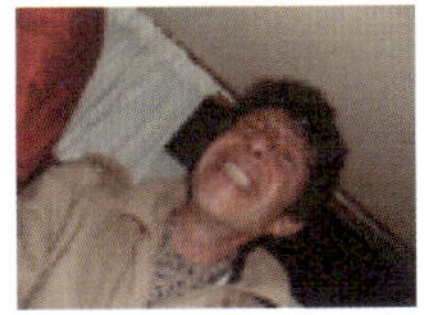

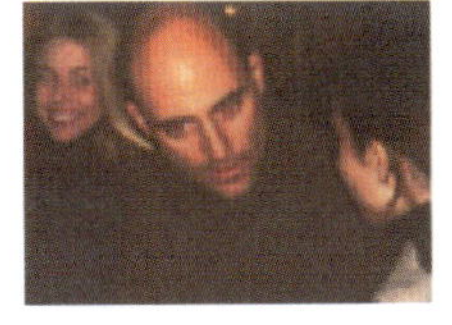 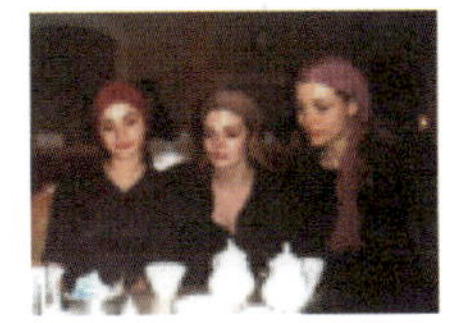 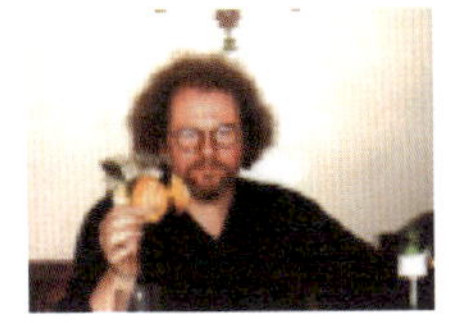 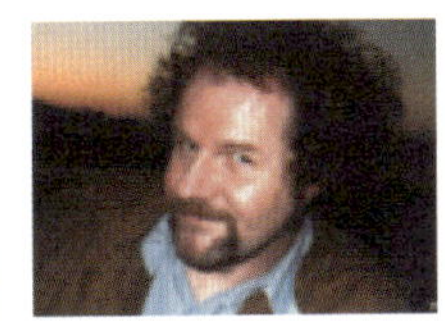 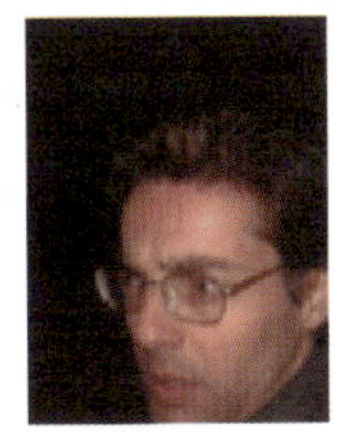

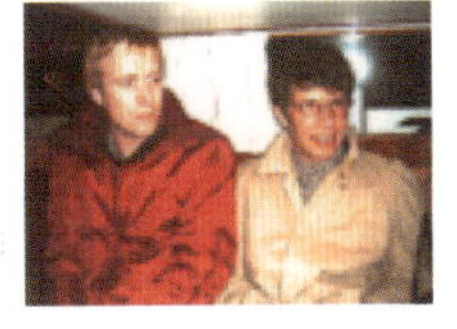 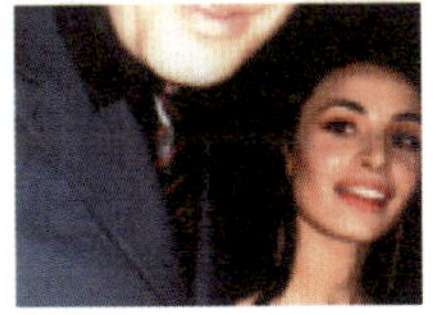  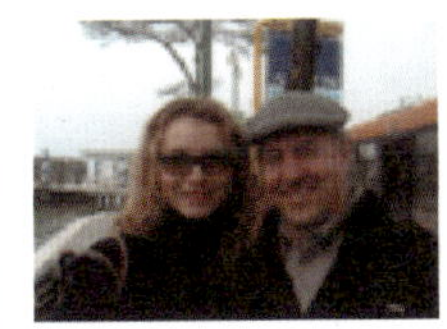 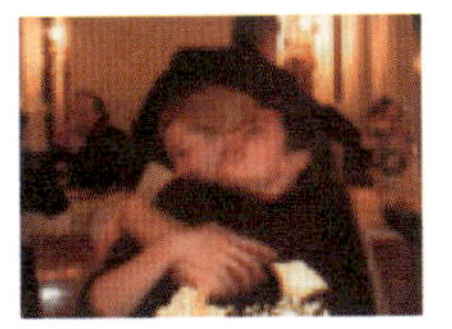

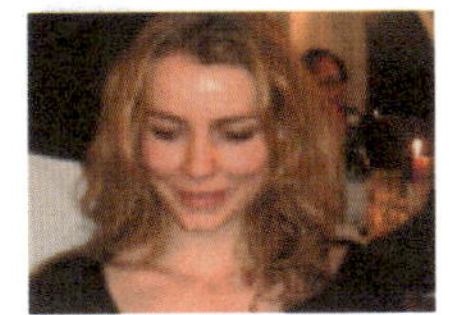 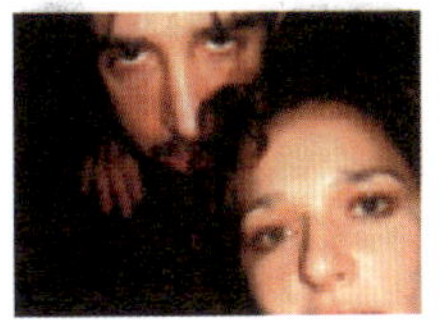 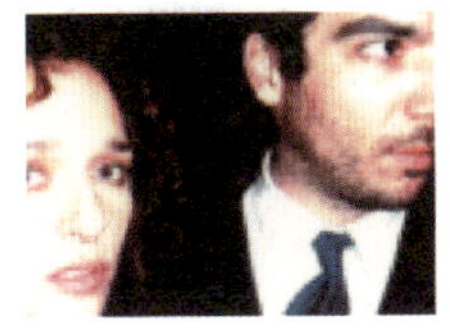 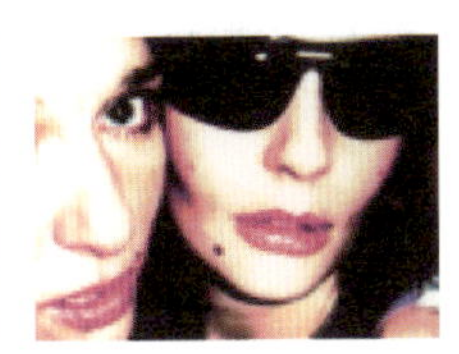 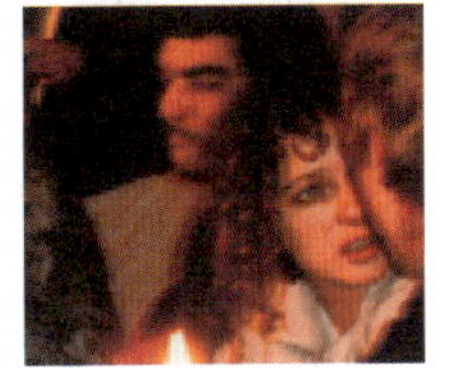

Right now

The reaction to HOTEL, from a lot of distributors and film people, is that if I applied such technically innovative techniques to a mainstream film, I would definitely have a hit. Which poses the question: do you want 1?

To me, what is interesting is that this technology is cheap. Here is an economically sustainable way of working on film, which gives you a laboratory potential. You could do something very avant-garde and make money with it. Sometimes the avant-garde can connect with a vibrant, young part of the culture which is hungry. Right now, I think there is that sort of hunger. I'm thinking about the possibility of dealing with the provocative elements of culture that music and magazines deal with. Think of music lyrics, for example. Film is falling behind in that it does not take on the provocative. HOTEL has really opened up the question of distribution. Hollywood is a job-based industry and it's happy with what it's got. I don't blame it. It will selectively let in the parts of the digital revolution that suit it – in other words, the high-end things which utilise pretty much the same number of people as 35-mm technology.

There is a problem with buying digital projectors because the technology is developing so fast that it is outdated within a year. We who are making experimental use of digital technology are a bit like sucker-fish picking up something that's almost too small for the 2 industries to notice. But I feel this work has only scratched the surface, and my attitude is, fuck distribution. There is a real receptive quality among the community of interesting film makers and other film folk. My ideal plan would be to open a little arts lab and develop the work, screening it almost immediately to give a very fast dialogue with a group of film-makers and actors. You are inviting the actors into something more personal, and some actors would not be comfortable with that. But HOTEL clearly showed that many would be.

I think it is important that cameras themselves have become crucial. We're now looking at the post-Warhol world of multiples and the inability to quantify art in the old way. The camera itself and the way the camera moves has become fundamentally important to the way you perceive an image. When you think of the Rodney King incident, or the Concorde crash, the Twin Towers, the footage is awe inspiring. The concept of the avant-garde and the elite art-core is up for grabs. It is a challenge, and unless we deal with it I think we're going to be hanging on to a useless concept of art. Art has to have a useful concept, a political comment. I think digital technology can help us move a little bit down that road.

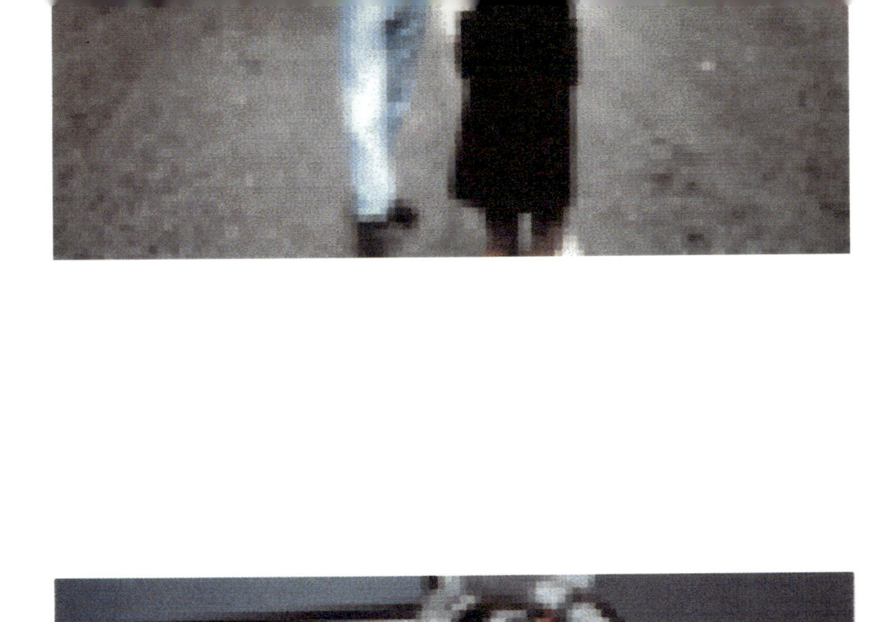
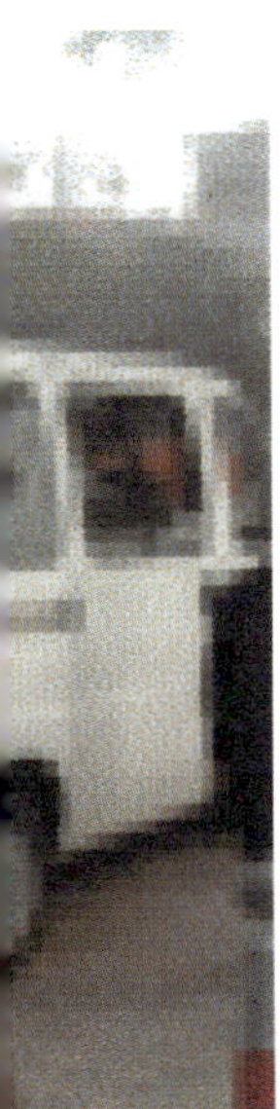
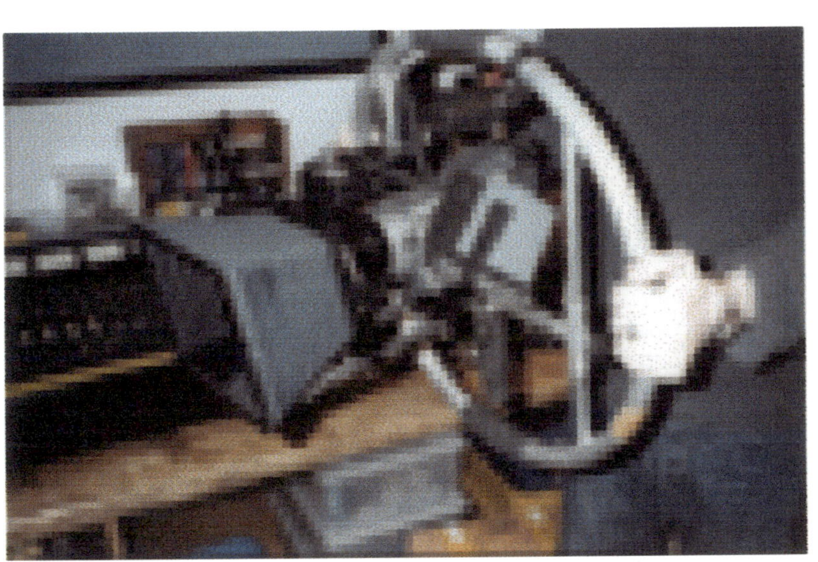

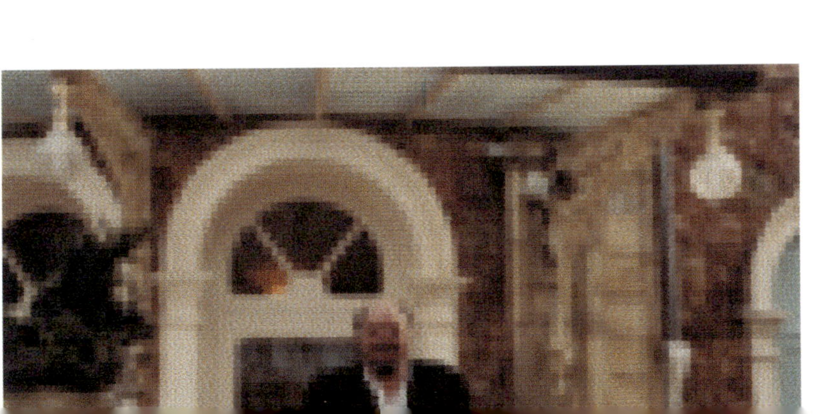

Subj:	Re:Hotel
Date:	Thursday, November 22, 2001 1:01:18 am
From:	(Heathcote Williams)
To:	(Mike Figgis)

Dear Mike,

Thanks for your e-mail. I'd be delighted to help in any way that you think might be useful. After the Wardour Street screening I felt that I could easily have watched another showing of it immediately afterwards, so, yes, I'd love to come to the ICA on Saturday to see it again and have told Louis as much on the phone today. Of course it would be great to conduct another Great Experiment in Digital Consciousness in Tokyo or wherever the fates may blow.

As for a paragraph, I'd be happy to furnish something, but thought that first of all I would send you these (possibly extractable) e-mails to Schwimmer -- written first when the events at the Hungaria Palace were still fresh in my mind and later on when I'd seen the finished film:

"Well hello! Thanks for your e-mail. Yes, you were much missed too. It was great to see you again, after our brief encounter in London, and to hang out -- looning around the 'Shakespeare of cities' -- and to observe your nifty, if not visionary, comedic skills at such close quarters.

The remaining life-forms at the cannibal Hotel Hungaria ground gracefully to a halt in the week or so that followed your departure. This is what you missed: Rhys drank large quantities of grappa and hallucinatory bottles of absinthe which made him feel, he claimed, 'as if I've got 50 people standing right behind me and all of them are friends'. Unfortunately this fantasy army of Celtic Bravehearts didn't impress the air hostess on the journey back, who adamantly refused him any further sustenance, despite being royally addressed in Welsh.

Lucy Liu did a series of interviews with the entire cast, which was a little bit like submitting to laser surgery. We were all fed into the ballroom, one by one, as she sat upon an impromptu throne, under a lighting umbrella, looking for all the world like Genghis Khan. When this imperious figure alleged that she'd seen Mia in an Argentinian porn film -- called 'Breasts as Big as the Andes' -- the hapless Mia burst into floods of tears (it was not clear whether she was in or out of character).

Mark Strong did some more hilarious episodes of 'Clifford Beauchamp -- the actor' (surely a Ridiculous Shite Company archetype) for the website -- which, rumour had it, you were keeping tabs on.

The unspeakable George 'Harvey Weinstein' DiCenzio imported his somewhat surprisingly presentable American girlfriend to the Hungaria, and thereafter began, mercifully, to ration his more blatantly obtuse outbursts and to moderate those remorseless expectorations -- so tiresomely peppered with unvarying expletives. It was noted, however, that whenever Max appeared in the same room as the simpering couple, 'Weinstein' would nervously edge his lissom paramour as far away as possible from Master Beesley and his rampant 'Hickory' -- so unashamedly bubbling over with threatening quantities of testosterone.

Jeremy Hardy, inexplicably, suddenly began to feel marginalised and apoplectically complained to anyone who would lend an ear (both in private and, embarrassingly, at the meetings), about being unloved and under-used; then Valentina diplomatically stepped in and told him that his behaviour, which was now souring into increasingly spiteful tirades against the Management, was perfectly ridiculous as she had just learned from Mike how much he, Mike, loved Jeremy (she had made this up). 'Does he? does he really?' said the gullibly wide-eyed Jeremy. 'Yes, of course', said Valentina. 'He loves and admires you very much'. The normally acerbic and professionally abrasive BBC comedian was then immediately lulled into dormouse mode, and promptly told everyone who would lend an ear, how much he was enjoying himself, what a wonderful time he was having and repeatedly pronounced himself, while getting drunker and drunker, to be 'a very very happy camper'. Valentina's beguiling and transforming fib had worked like a magic spell, leading Rhys and I to conclude that the green-eyed enchantress was one of the Tyllwth Twg, or fairy folk.

We filmed in the fish-market -- inhabited by dark Phoenician-looking Venetians who burst into arias whenever you passed their stalls; we filmed in speeding water-taxis racing across the lagoon, crisscrossing each other's wash and half-throwing you into the water -- with Brian resplendent in his Doge's hat and flapping red garments and Mark in his feathered velvet beret screaming monologues at the four winds in order to launch the carnival of madness that would drive the Duchess to distraction; and then we filmed in a eighth-century flooded crypt that the assiduous Julian had discovered, and finally we went back to the music schools for the discovery of Antonio's body by the Duchess.

After the blow to his masculinity in the palazza love scene (with Max, somewhat humiliatingly, being taken from behind by the Duchess, as you will, of course, recall), Max was at some pains to ensure that -- now that his naked, stabbed body was to be found lying beside a canal covered in rubbish and dead fish -- the Beesley todger should feature as the largest visible object on screen, and that this was the moment when its stalwartly virile dignity could be duly restored and displayed to maximum advantage. Consequently he spent a considerable time fluffing it up in between each and every take -- entirely unselfconsciously and in full view of the crew. To the public at large, observing him (out of the corner of their eyes) implementing this unusual form of 'make-up' so dedicatedly, Max blithely claimed to be doing it, not of course for pleasure, but to correct the unwelcome effects of the penile-shrinking and scrotum-tightening cold. Mia afterwards archly noted that, as far as she knew, few dead bodies were blessed with full-on erections.

Rhys spent hours in the hospital room in his coma, being visited by every member of the cast, for lengthy one-sided chats. These sessions were conducted in private so I've no idea what anyone else revealed, but, according to Mike, the invalid's visitors began to disclose increasingly bizarre characteristics. Andrea, I was given to understand, did something very unsettling with a gun; Stephania apparently delivered a heart-felt tirade against the vagaries of the male sex; but I can only really speak for myself. One day Max had been going out shopping and kindly asked me if there was anything I wanted. I asked him to get a copy of the Guardian. When he came back with it I discovered to my alarm that he'd inveigled a copy of a garishly coloured, heavily laminated and highly disgusting magazine, called 'Over 40s', between the staid pages of the requested newspaper. Once I'd recovered and my heart-rate had settled back to normal, I took it in to Rhys's room in order to show it to him in his coma -- taking him through it page by page. I held it up in front of his impassive face, and the camera, in order to draw his attention to a series of obese women from Abergervenny who were doing interesting things with bananas, and I wondered aloud, perched beside his hospital bed, whether he might perhaps be acquainted with any of them -- since such an unusual number of the gynaecological contortionists I was parading in front of his eyes appeared to come from very his own home-town in Wales. To his enormous credit, he remained miraculously motionless, signally failing to corpse. For a moment I thought he might genuinely be in a coma, in the face of such an hormonal barrage from local lovelies.

Julian took to stripping in the bar on a nightly basis, and then when the novelty of this palled, he took to standing on his head, but unfortunately, one evening, the carpet suddenly slithered away from beneath him, and he crumbled ignominiously to the ground. All those present were vehemently and quite falsely accused of having tampered with the carpet and of wilfully conspiring to show him up, thus doing an irreversible injury to Julian Q's psychotic keep-fit pride.

As the days passed, the horseplay gradually became more pronounced; the bar and the ballroom were nightly trashed, and more and more irate guests threatened to sue the hotel. Remarkably the hotel management seemed to mind less and less. Perhaps they misguidedly believed that the film's graphic implication that their kitchens were full of rotting human flesh would give their establishment some kind of valuable cachet in the future, and ghoulish tourists would henceforth be wending their way to the Hungaria in droves upon the film's release -- in much the same way that Room 100 in the Chelsea Hotel, the scene of Sid Vicious' demise, was booked ahead for years and years after the event.

The cast and crew dwindled. People became very excited to find that they were of the same star sign or shared a birthday, and considered forming astrologically-based gangs. People photographed each other photographing each other. Max obsessively imitated me; I obsessively imitated Danny Huston; Danny Huston imitated Rhys, and Rhys imitated Max. I began to wonder if all our identities were beginning to merge, and, although it was never finally addressed in the digital realisation of Mike's script, it began to look as if Mad Human Disease might, after all, be breaking out in the genteel art-deco surroundings of the Hungaria Palace.

And so it went, amiably petering out amongst tearful farewells as our numbers slowly diminished. It all became rather wistful. I remember sauntering down the main street, the Gran Viale Elisabetta and seeing doppelgangers -- faces in the Venetian crowds of Lido shoppers that momentarily looked just like the people who had left the ensemble. You yourself had an evanescent double, fleeting past me for a few seconds on a pedestrian crossing. 'Wasn't that? ...no'. Other people in the remaining and shrivelling cast reported similar experiences.

What larks we all had! It's a desert axiom that the soul travels at the speed of a camel, so, if you travel faster than camel-speed, you tend to leave your soul behind, needing a few days for it to catch up with your body. As you can tell my soul is still partially resident in Venice and still tingling at the nerve-endings. While all the above trivia were fresh in the mind I thought you might like a brief (or not so brief) resumé of shore-life after you'd sped away across the lagoon.

I had no idea what to expect, 6 weeks ago, when I left Oxford for Venice, but it now feels like one of the high points of my life. Mike mentioned a couple of times that he'd like to do it again, 'next week even', and I must say I've become quite intrigued by the idea of a digital repertory company knocking the germ of a story into shape in some other far-flung region of the world -- if not indeed addicted to the notion. We will see."

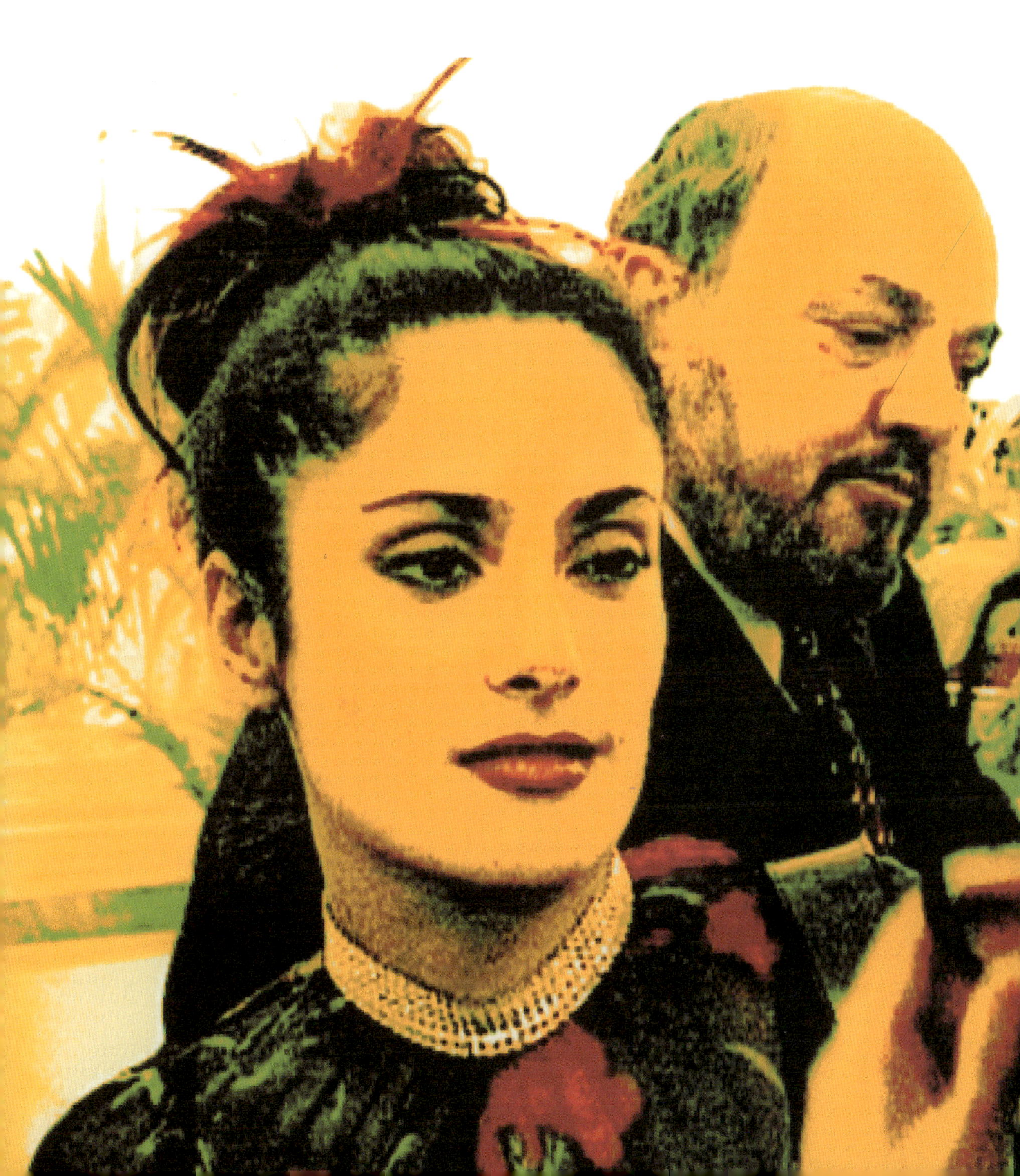

The New York Times

FRIDAY, NOVEMBER 19, 1999

New Digital Cameras Poised To Jolt World of Filmmaking

By RICK LYMAN

HOLLYWOOD, Nov. 18 — A digital video camera was perched like a bazooka on the shoulder of the director Mike Figgis as he carved a path through the oblivious pedestrians on Sunset Strip, following the actor Stellan Skarsgard into a swanky glass-faced office. At the same moment, not far away, three other digital cameras were following other actors as they made their way down the sidewalk, chatted on cell phones or bickered at curbside, the real world swirling all around them.

Whatever this film in progress might add up to artistically, Mr. Figgis, the British director best known for the Oscar-winning "Leaving Las Vegas," is at the very least extraordinarily ambitious, some might say audacious, about exploiting the digital technologies that are beginning to seep into the Hollywood mainstream.

For years digital moviemaking has been a grass-roots movement among aspiring filmmakers who resented the dominance of the Hollywood aesthetic. Mr. Figgis's film, "Time Code 2000," brings the new technology inside the walls of the major studios — in this case those of Sony Pictures, which, not coincidentally, is owned by a company that also manufactures digital equipment. Once inside the walls, many believe, digital moviemaking will have a major impact on the way movies are made and how people view them.

"Time Code 2000" is being shot in real time; that is, as one continuous take, without editing, that lasts a predetermined 93 minutes. The four cameras dance across a half dozen sets and down city streets with a breathtaking seamlessness, following the film's characters in and out of meetings, assignations and confrontations.

Mr. Figgis thought of doing the

Continued on Page C5

NEWS SUMMARY A2

Updated news: www.nytimes.com

"HOLLYWOOD REPORTER" REVIEW OF "HOTEL" at the TORONTO FILM FESTIVAL. 17TH SEPTEMBER 2001.

Having enjoyed success with the experimental "TIMECODE", director Mike Figgis remains in digital mode with "HOTEL", another heavily improvised, stripped down production that constitutes the filmmaking world according to Dogme.
Well, he nails the first three letters, anyway.

An achingly pretentious slab of total nonsense, the picture parades an international cast through their off-the-cuff paces to pointless effect. Given that the Toronto festival audience began checking out a half hour into the screening, **it could be a challenge finding an accommodating distributor**.

Figgis, who penned the mere suggestion of a script, sets the scene at the art deco Hotel Hungaria in Venice, Italy, where missing guests often turn up on the menu.

Convening at the site is a film crew readying a Dogme production of John Webster's Jacobean tragedy "The Duchess of Malfi", but they're not a happy bunch of campers. The despondent producer (David Schwimmer) is engaged in a power struggle with the hotshot director (Rhys Ifans), while the cast, including Saffron Burrows and Valeria Golino, is unhappy about the constantly shrinking script.

Meanwhile, an annoying TV reporter, Charlee Boux (Salma Hayek), has arrived on the set to do a behind-the-scenes report on the production - just before the director ends up in a coma as the result of a bungled assassination attempt.

And did we mention that the hotel was crawling with a growing gang of sexual vampires?

Figgis packages the haphazard material with many of the visual techniques he used in "TIMECODE", including multiple split screens and hand-held digital camerawork, but dispenses with that film's real-time element. **He also throws in a lot of gratuitous nudity.**

Figgis counts on his cast - also including Julian Sands, Burt Reynolds, Lucy Liu, Danny Huston and, in a more-or-less isolated opening sequence, John Malkovich - **to fill in the spoken blanks, but their improvisational skills fall far short of the phenomenal.**

The last scene has a miraculously recovered Ifans relating his coma experience to interviewer Liu, explaining how he'd leave his body and eavesdrop on other people and providing details of a phone conversation Liu had in the privacy of her hotel room.

An initially perplexed Liu asks if it's some kind of parlour trick. "Yes", Ifans responds cryptically. "It's a trick".

And it's a nasty (trick) played on the innocent viewer.

Michael Rechtshaffen

Index of sources

181 Valentina Cervi.
182-3 Valentina Cervi, Chiara Mastroianni.
184-5 Extract from unfinished novel.
186-9 Valentina Cervi, Rhys Ifans.
190-1 Notebook.
192-3 Mark Strong, Brian Bovell, Saffron Burrows, Valentina Cervi, Rhys Ifans, David Schwimmer.
194 David Schwimmer.
195-6 Julian Sands.
197 Rhys Ifans, Valentina Cervi.
199 Composite of cast and crew.
201 The 'Fig Rig'.
202 Email correspondence.
203 Salma Hayek, George DiCenzo.

All documentary texts have been left in their original version.

Mike Figgis – Filmography

THE HOUSE
Directed by Mike Figgis; with Diana Hardcastle, Stephen Rea, Dudley Sutton; UK 1984; 60 mins.

STORMY MONDAY
Directed/Scripted/Scored by MF; with Sean Bean, Melanie Griffith, Tommy Lee Jones, Sting; UK/USA 1987; 93 mins.

INTERNAL AFFAIRS
Dir/Scr MF; with Andy Garcia, Richard Gere; USA 1989; 115 mins.

LIEBESTRAUM
Dir/Scr/Sco MF; with Kevin Anderson, Pamela Gidley, Kim Novak, Bill Pullman; USA 1990; 112 mins.

MARA
Dir/Scr MF; with Juliette Binoche; USA 1991; 30 mins (Short).

MR JONES
Dir MF; with Anne Bancroft, Richard Gere, Lena Olin; USA 1992; 114 mins.

THE BROWNING VERSION
Dir MF; with Albert Finney, Matthew Modine, Greta Scacchi; UK 1993; 97 mins.

VIVIENNE WESTWOOD "ON LIBERTY"
Dir MF; with Vivienne Westwood; France 1994; 30 mins (Documentary; Channel 4).

LEAVING LAS VEGAS
Dir/Scr/Sco MF; with Nicolas Cage, Julian Sands, Elisabeth Shue; France/USA 1994; 111 mins.

"JUST DANCING AROUND"
Dir MF; with William Forsythe; UK 1995; 55 mins (Documentary; Channel 4).

ONE NIGHT STAND
Dir/Scr/Sco MF; with Robert Downey Jr, Nastassja Kinski, Kyle MacLachlan, Wesley Snipes, Ming-Na Wen; USA 1996; 102 mins.

FLAMENCO WOMEN
Dir MF; with Sara Baras, Eva La Yerbabuena; UK 1997; 52 mins (Documentary; Channel 4, VPRO).

THE LOSS OF SEXUAL INNOCENCE
Dir/Scr MF; with Saffron Burrows, Stefano Dionisi, Julian Sands; USA 1997; 106 mins.

MISS JULIE
Dir/Sco MF; with Saffron Burrows, Maria Doyle Kennedy, Peter Mullan; USA 1999; 103 mins.

TIMECODE
Dir/Scr/Sco MF; with Saffron Burrows, Salma Hayek, Stellan Skarsgard, Jeanne Tripplehorn; USA 1999; 97 mins.

ABOUT TIME-2
Dir/Scr MF; UK 2000; 10 mins (Short; part of feature-length film TEN MINUTES OLDER – THE CELLO).

HOTEL
Dir/Scr MF; with Saffron Burrows, Salma Hayek, Rhys Ifans, Mia Maestro, Chiara Mastroianni, David Schwimmer (and others: see pp. 72-73); Italy/UK 2001; 109 mins.

BATTLE OF ORGREAVE
Dir MF; UK 2001; 62 mins (Documentary on the partial re-enactment of the miner's strike at Orgreave in 1984 by the conceptual artist Jeremy Deller; Channel 4).

THE BLUES
Dir MF; with Jeff Beck, Eric Clapton, Tom Jones, Van Morrison; UK/USA 2002; 90 mins (Documentary on the British Blues scene; series produced by Martin Scorsese).

COLD CREEK MANOR
Dir MF; with Dennis Quaid, Sharon Stone, Stephen Dorff, Juliette Lewis, Christopher Plummer; USA 2003; 90 mins.

Images and text by Mike Figgis

Designed by John Morgan

Edited by Liz Farrelly,
Vicky Hayward, Roger Tatley

Printed by Siz Grafiche in Italy

Published in 2003
by Booth-Clibborn Editions
12 Percy Street
London W1T 1DW
www.booth-clibborn.com

ISBN 1-86154-245-3